REFLECTIONS ON
Bonhoeffer

ESSAYS IN HONOR OF
F. BURTON NELSON

REFLECTIONS ON
Bonhoeffer

ESSAYS IN HONOR OF
F. BURTON NELSON

Edited by Geffrey B. Kelly
and C. John Weborg

Covenant Publications
Chicago, Illinois

Reflections on Bonhoeffer:
Essays in Honor of F. Burton Nelson

Covenant Publications
3200 West Foster Avenue, Chicago, Illinois 60625
(773) 478-4676
Printed in the United States of America.
ISBN 910452-85-7 (book edition)
ISSN 036-0934, *The Covenant Quarterly*, Vol. LVII, Nos. 2-4.
                May, August, and November 1999

Contents

Bonhoeffer's Spirituality

Bonhoeffer and Jewish-Christian Relations

Bonhoeffer's Circles

Foreword

It is always gratifying to put one over on a person who likes to surprise others with tongue-in-cheek teasing or pleasant practical jokes. In a public tribute on the first of his several retirements, Burton Nelson was acknowledged as a "trickster par excellence." This is but one of Burton's many endearing qualities.

This *festschrift* is the product of a multi-person conspiracy not unlike the several amusing conspiracies perpetrated by our honoree of Nyvall Hall. Oh, if the walls could speak! Swearing so many to secrecy was not the easiest thing to do, given the independence of all the contributors and the fact that the copy editorial work had to be done by Wayne Weld mostly under the very nose of one who seems to know everything that goes on at North Park Theological Seminary well before the decisions of those involved in running the place. Even this foreword was squeezed out of time that Burton believed was being spent on the spirituality of Karl Rahner, an interest we hold in common. We were helped by Burton's well-known aversion for and ineptitude in computers. Burton still thinks a floppy disk is something one sees a chiropractor for. And digital communication involves knowing how to wave a friendly greeting or how to signal V for victory and other emotions by the creative extending of one's finger(s)!

Occasions like the presentation of a *festschrift* for a distinguished professor of a prestigious seminary need no rationale other than the worthiness of the contributions of the honoree to scholarship and ministry, not to mention joviality, sociality, conviviality, and his perennial conniving. Now that last qualifier should be seen only for what it is worth in the context of Burton's ethical sensitivity and even greater sense of humor.

GEFFREY B. KELLY
Philadelphia, Pennsylvania

C. JOHN WEBORG
Chicago, Illinois

Preface

Frank Burton Nelson was born 22 August 1924 in Mt. Kuling, Hupeh, China. His parents were medical missionaries, commissioned and sent by the Evangelical Covenant Church. Within this ecclesial community, Burton received the sacrament of holy baptism, the rite of confirmation, and in 1949 ordination to the ministry of word and sacrament. A year earlier he was united in marriage to L. Grace Johnson. They enjoy a family life with six children and seven grandchildren, a family embued with abiding fidelity and avid friendships.

He served in pastoral ministry in Chicago and Evanston, Illinois, and Bristol and Plainville, Connecticut. His contribution to catechetics for use in parishes was issued under the title *The Story of the People of God*. From February 1961 to August 1985 he edited a theological journal for use by those in church vocations and interested laity, published by Covenant Publications and North Park Theological Seminary, the seminary of the Evangelical Covenant Church. This journal, *The Covenant Quarterly*, now so capably edited by Professor Wayne Weld, is pleased to publish this *festschrift*.

Professor Nelson has taught primarily in the areas of Christian ethics and theology. He has also taught in the fields of church history and philosophy of religion, areas of concentration while he studied at Brown University (B.A.), Yale Divinity School (B.D.), and the University of Chicago. His ardent commitment to the pursuit of peace was given theoretical and theological impetus during his Ph.D. work at Garrett-Evangelical Theological Seminary and Northwestern University, as he examined the peace documents promulgated by the Ecumenical Movement.

Dr. Nelson was catechized and theologically formed in an ecclesial tradition with deep roots in Lutheran Pietism. Halle and Herrnhut each made its mark on the Lutheran State Church of Sweden, the historical homeland of the Evangelical Covenant Church. Pietism is frequently accused of separating the personal life of devotional disciplines from a life of public discipleship in ways similar to the often presumed separation of the two kingdoms in Lutheran theology. The accusation against Pietism cannot go unchallenged. To be sure, there are pietistic movements in which such a separation does exist. But the Pietism that shaped Professor Nelson cannot be so accused. As demonstrated in the life and ministry of Professor Nelson, there is no final conflict between personal devotion and public discipleship.

Dr. Nelson knew well the story of August Hermann Francke (1663–1727), a story that included the prayer and study done in conventicles and the public work of the redress of social issues in Halle. This included the building of orphanages and schools, resistance to forced military conscription, putting windows in prisons, proposed reform of the judicial system, and skill training for orphans by merchants and townspeople.[1]

Erland Sundström has argued that the conventicle movement was a key development leading to a democratization of Sweden.[2] In the conventicle, cobbler Olsson had as much right to speak as schoolteacher Johnsson. Such persons, often renewed by deep conversion experiences, spoke as equals, whereas in public life only the duly authorized could speak. Theologically, two Lutheran legacies led to this development: the doctrine of the priesthood of all believers and the doctrine of the perspicuity (clarity) of Scripture. Guided by the Holy Spirit, readers did not always understand nuanced meanings, but the main point, the redemptive work of God in Christ, was clear enough. To use jargon language, this mixed group was given voice, acquired agency, and heard each other into speech. A new politics was aborning!

A final example concerns a Lutheran pietistic legacy in the United States. Professor Paul Kuenning has traced the influence of Halle Pietism on the Franckean Synod of upper New York. Almost the entire membership of this synod could trace its roots to Halle Pietism.[3] The debt to Francke is transparent in the name. It was the only synod to take a vigorous stand against slavery and in favor of abolitionism. No final conflict obtained between the two kingdoms or between the life of personal devotion and public discipleship.

For Professor Nelson, the Pietism that shaped him knew no final conflict between the personal life of devotion and the public life of discipleship. On Good Friday he regularly participated in walking the Stations of the Cross, not in a church building, but on the streets of Chicago. The entourage moved from one building to the next, be it the South African Consulate or the headquarters of an aberrant multinational corporation, praying for justice, for victims, all in identification with the mission of God made public in Jesus Christ. Political prayer was as natural for Burton as personal prayer or liturgical prayer.[4] All forms of prayer were the work of the people.

Given the Franckean influence, it is no wonder that Burton should find institutional locations for a portion of his public discipleship. Brought up in a family of medical practitioners (his father and two brothers), Burton nurtured this indigenous medical proclivity into a specialized concern for teaching medical ethics. He serves on the ethics committee of Swedish Covenant Hospital in Chicago and has served on state panels seeking to form workable legislation regarding end of life issues.

Burton served for many years on the Commission on Christian Action for the Evangelical Covenant Church, seeking to shape a theological and ecclesiastical response to various public issues. His commitment to ecumenical endeavors has led to service on the Commission on Interchurch Relations for the Covenant Church. The high level of this commitment has been embodied in his dogged effort to find enough financial support to take a small group of North Park Seminary students to Canberra, Australia, for the assembly of the World Council of Churches. This became a seminar designed for academic credit and afforded a once-in-a-lifetime opportunity to speak with world leaders, experience the ecclesiastical tensions generated by multicultural gatherings, and encounter century-old conflicts between church bodies.

In every way, Burton is self-giving to the core, sharing with God a providential preference for those who have access to almost nothing, and with a passion that Jesus Christ be the center of whatever it is that commands his convictions and commitments. Consistent with Franckean piety, there is no final conflict between personal devotion and public discipleship. They converge at the same place they did for Jesus: in full view of the public.[5]

It is this convergence of exemplary piety and commitment to Christian discipleship in the public sphere that explains Burton's attraction to the theology and spirituality of Dietrich Bonhoeffer. This fascinating German pastor-martyr himself combined a strong personal prayer life with responsible, self-sacrificing action to restore justice and human dignity in a world being shredded by a savage war and barbarous genocide. In many ways Burton and Bonhoeffer are kindred spirits, especially in the struggles for social justice they have embraced.

As one can see from Robert K. Johnston's informative essay and the bibliography of his writings compiled by Norma S. Sutton, a large part of Burton's professional career has been spent in teaching courses related to contemporary moral problems and in research that has produced several significant publications on and lectures about Bonhoeffer's spirituality and the many facets of his resistance to the systemic evils of Nazism and genocide. In the past several years Burton has focused on those illuminating personal reminiscences of Bonhoeffer's family, friends, former students, the Finkenwalde seminarians, and colleagues in the German Resistance Movement. Burton began the "living history" project that in turn has led to documentaries on Bonhoeffer's life and literary legacy and his work in the German resistance. Each year Burton spends several weeks continuing to explore the Bonhoeffer memorabilia, always searching for new insights into the rhythms of Bonhoeffer's spiritual life or exploring the memories of those who knew Bonhoeffer personally or were influenced by Bonhoeffer's life and inspirational writings. Burton's own activism has launched him into a kind of secondary career, namely, post-Holocaust education, for which Bonhoeffer's risky defense of the Jewish people in the Hitler era serves as background and inspiration. In his approach to the scholarship that is shared in the International Bonhoeffer Society, Burton's perspective is always that of the pastor who must lead his congregation to the word of God and who challenges them through the stories of those who exemplify that word. His commentaries on Bonhoeffer's sermons have provided fresh insights into the inner core of Bonhoeffer's spiritual life, his childlike prayer, and his passionate love for Jesus Christ.

Burton was among the first theologians to join the International Bonhoeffer Society–English Language Section, begun in the United States in 1972. In 1976 he was elected to the first Board of Directors and then elected by the board to be vice-president of the society, a position in which he served until his retirement in 1992. He is presently an emeritus member of the Board of Directors. The many essays on Bonhoeffer's life and significant aspects of his theology and spirituality included in this *festschrift* constitute an appreciative expression of the esteem in which he is held by these "Bonhoeffer scholars," his colleagues, whose essays have honored Burton and made this volume possible.

It was, therefore, a gratifying experience to receive so many essays from among these members of the Bonhoeffer Society responding to our invitation to contribute a letter or an article. These essays sent to us are themselves a valuable addition to the growing collection of Bonhoeffer literature. Given the disparate nature of the topics that the authors have addressed, it soon became evident to us that we needed to establish some structure to hold the sections together and to signify just what aspects of Bonhoeffer's theology or spirituality were being explored. Whatever their particular perspectives, the overall intent of all the writers was to show their appreciation for Burton's important work in the Bonhoeffer Society. They acknowledge his contribution to Bonhoeffer studies by offering original texts of their own to honor Burton in the most practical and creative way in this *festschrift*.

To instill an order into this collection, therefore, we devised the following categories:

Burton Nelson: Friend and Theologian. Under this section we placed the touching letters of appreciation of James Gustafson and Sabine

Leibholz-Bonhoeffer with her daughter Marianne, as well as Robert Johnston's testimonial essay on Burton's scholarly achievements in service of his church.

Bonhoeffer and Resistance to Nazism. Here we set the essay by Bonhoeffer's biographer and friend Eberhard Bethge, who offered his talk at the Munich "Church Day" in 1993 on what life was like when lived with all its risks in active resistance to Nazism. This is followed by the essay of Andreas Pangritz, who explores Bonhoeffer's theological motivations for joining the political resistance to Hitler. Ethicist Larry Rasmussen's essay returns to an intriguing subject that he had originally studied in an appendix of his doctoral dissertation, namely, the interrelationship of Bonhoeffer, Gandhi, and the pacifism each practiced. Finally, Robert Bertram offers as a testimonial to his esteem of Burton, whom he calls an "inclusivist," the first part of a longer article on Bonhoeffer's exclusivism when it came to those whom he considered enemies of faith and human dignity.

Bonhoeffer's Spirituality. This section contains the essays by John Godsey, who presents in detail the various facets of Bonhoeffer's spirituality, calling it a spirituality for our time; novelist Mary Glazener, whose essay draws on her vast research into the details of Bonhoeffer's life to offer her analysis of his personal faith; and J. Patrick Kelley, who examines three of Bonhoeffer's sermons to draw some helpful conclusions about Bonhoeffer's christological concretion and sense of the importance of everyday events in preaching. The final essay of this section is John Matthews's original contribution to the understanding of the *disciplina arcani* in Bonhoeffer's life and theology.

Bonhoeffer and Jewish-Christian Relations. In this segment of the *festschrift* Jane Pejsa argues that Bonhoeffer's experience of Kristallnacht served to radicalize him in his sympathies for the persecuted Jews. She calls for memorials to what took place in violent actions against the Jews of Pomerania, lest we forget the victims. Geffrey B. Kelly returns to an important aspect of Bonhoeffer's life as a pastor, theologian, and activist, namely, his attempts to speak up for and eventually rescue Jews, and draws conclusions for the future of Jewish-Christian relations.

Bonhoeffer's Circles. This category allowed us to put into one single section essays covering several areas of connections to Bonhoeffer's life and theology: Bonhoeffer's attitude toward the role of women (Renate Bethge); Bonhoeffer's friendship with Eberhard Bethge's cousin Gerhard Vibrans, who was also one of the early Finkenwalde seminarians, seen through several informative, hitherto unpublished letters that help readers understand Bonhoeffer's friendships and their impact on his life (Barbara Green); an analysis of how the letters exchanged between people in love can affect how they react to a "deadly time," in this case the letters exchanged between Dietrich and Maria, on the one hand, and Vacláv Havel and Olga, on the other (Martin Rumscheidt); a perceptive comparison of Bonhoeffer's *Cost of Discipleship* and Barth's "Gospel and Law" (Jonathan Sorum); and, finally, Karl Barth's treatment of the man-woman relationship, an essay only indirectly connected to Bonhoeffer but of wide interest in studying the deep impact of Karl Barth's dialectical theology on Bonhoeffer in an area that is of great interest today (Clifford Green).

Ecumenical Connections. There are essays by three scholars clustered here: John W. de Gruchy, who has seen the restoration of justice in South Africa and who now, with reference to Bonhoeffer's insights, raises the question of how his society can recover an ecumenical vision and commitment; Richard Bliese, who, while conceding the sparse references to mission in Bonhoeffer's writings, nonetheless develops a Bonhoefferian theology of mission and relates that to the great commission; and Keith Clements, who, like Burton, was born in China of missionary parents, and who writes of "healing the wound" as he takes the reader on an "ecumenical return" to China with Bonhoeffer.

Contemporary Issues. The authors here address several important theological issues related to Bonhoeffer's theology: democracy and the public tasks of theology (Wayne Whitson Floyd Jr.); his appeal for ethical humility (Mark Brocker); liberation theology (G. Clarke Chapman); and the gospel in a secular world (Jay Rochelle).

In a final section set apart from the others we added Charles W. Sensel's "Overview" of Bonhoeffer's theology through one of Burton's favorite metaphors, the "periscope."

Receiving all these essays on disks as different as Macintosh is from Microsoft Word and as Microsoft Word is from WordPerfect created an enormous problem that defied the scanning process. At times Yvonne Macolly, secretary in the Department of Religion at La Salle University, after having seen the hieroglyphics created by La Salle's strange, even bizarre scanner with an attitude, simply tossed the scanned text into a circular file and typed the text anew from a hard copy. That this text reached Covenant Publications in its final form on Microsoft Word disks and in readable hard copy within the deadline is due in no small measure to Yvonne's patience and skills. But that was not the end of the process. All copy went subsequently to Wayne Weld, who had the unenviable task of putting the texts into conformity with the *Chicago Manual of Style* from at least five different styles of annotation and bibliographical data. Even the abbreviations of "standard" Bonhoeffer texts in German and English varied from essay to essay. Wayne also went over the text in his usual meticulous manner to make the corrections that escaped every spell-checker and to make the spellings and some of the quotations more consistent. He had to do all this away from the prying eyes of Burton.

That underway, we entered the penultimate stage of publication, namely, writing a tongue-in-cheek foreword and completing this preface. We thank all those who have contributed of their time and skills to honor Burton. Given Burton's unending admiration of Dietrich Bonhoeffer and his career-long dedication to teaching, lecturing, and preaching on Bonhoeffer, there is no more fitting tribute we could pay to him on this occasion than to offer him this *festschrift* in appreciation of his being for us an admired colleague and beloved friend.

GEFFREY B. KELLY

C. JOHN WEBORG

ENDNOTES

1. Gary Sattler, *God's Glory, Neighbor's Good: A Brief Introduction to the Life and Writings of August Hermann Francke* (Chicago: Covenant Press, 1982). This work contains a historical sketch of Francke's life and work and a collection of texts written by Francke.

2. Erland Sundström, "Structure and Function of Groups in Sweden," *The Covenant Quarterly* 15 (August 1955): 72.

3. Paul Kuenning, "Pietism: A Lutheran Resource for Dialogue with Evangelicalism," *The Covenant Quarterly* 44 (May 1986):37. See also Paul P. Kuenning, *The Rise and Fall of American Lutheran Pietism: The Rejection of an Activist Heritage* (Macon, Ga.: Mercer University Press, 1988), for the more complete history of this issue.

4. Professor Nelson's good friend Dr. Egon Gerdes speaks of three movements in prayer: our crowd (communal), our desert (private), our project (political). Communal prayer is the nurturing ground of prayer, private prayer is the depth dimension, and political prayer is the viability test of prayer. Furthermore, political prayer is the enacted commitment into dying as new patterns of holiness emerge in the polis. (These reflections come from the writer's notes taken down during a course on prayer with Dr. Gerdes in the fall quarter at Garrett–Evangelical Theological Seminary, 1976.)

5. It is of interest that in the field of apologetics some scholars are embracing the notion that the Christian faith is best commended within the context of communal structures which themselves are part of "the reason" the Christian message is plausible. John G. Stackhouse Jr., "From Architecture to Argument: Historic Resources for Christian Apologetics," in *Christian Apologetics in the Postmodern World*, ed. Timothy R. Phillips and Dennis L. Okholm (Downers Grove, Ill.: InterVarsity Press, 1995), 40-55, makes such a case, using the theological and pastoral concerns of Spener and Francke to buttress his argument.

When the life of the community is given such an "evidentiary" role, it bears some resemblance to the model of the church as sacrament. See Avery Dulles, S.J., *Models of the Church*, an Image Book (New York, et al.: Doubleday, 1974; expanded edition, 1987), 63-75.

Tabula Gratulatoria

John and Ann Agurkis
Charles C. Anderson
David and Isolde Anderson
Frances Anderson
Richard and Marilyn Anderson
Phil and Karna Anderson
Bradley and Roxi Bergfalk
Timothy and Kari Bukowski
John and Betty Carlson
Dennis and Mary Lynn Carlson
Richard and Jolene Carlson
David and Carol Dahlberg
Albert and Gladys Damrose
Robert and Dorothy Dvorak
George and Evelyn Elia
Judy and Steven Eng
Luther and Elvira Englund
James Erickson and Cathy Stanley
James H. and Shirley Erickson
Scott Erickson
Steve and Linda Forbes
Sara and Alan R. Forsman
James and Kathleen Fretheim
Gladys Fryhling-Wickman
J. H. and Pamela Gaderlund
Evan and Elvera Goranson
Robert and Eleanor Greenwall
Darryl and Jamie Hales
Timothy and Cindy Hawkinson
Stanley and Mary Henderson
Bob and Marilyn Hjelm

Fredrick and Betty Holmgren
Richard and Linda Holmlund
Chris and Barbara Icenogle
Edward G. Johnson
G. Timothy and Nancy Johnson
Norbert and Elaine Johnson
Jeff and Heather Jones
Paul and Linda Koptak
Janet Lundblad
Carl and Helen Lugn
Ronald and Marlene Magnuson
Aaron and Margaret Markuson
Robert and Carol McNaughton
Richard and Joan Murray
Lars and Florence Nelson
Wesley and Jan Nordstrom
Bruce and Karen Palmatier
Glenn and Sharon Palmberg
Alton and Christie Peterson
John E. Jr. and Dawn Phelan
Jerry and Nancy Reed
George and Maxine Schermer
Lars and Natalie Silverness
David and Susan Sundell
James and Beverly Swanson
Robert and Judith Tenglin
David and Grace Vennberg
C. John and Lois Weborg
Wayne and Mary Anne Weld
Glen and Jane Wiberg

Abbreviations

BOOKS BY DIETRICH BONHOEFFER

AB   *Act and Being*, translated by Bernard Noble (New York: Harper and Row, 1962). Reprint (same pagination; New York: Octagon Books, 1983).

CC   *Christ the Center*, revised translation by Edwin H. Robertson (New York: Harper and Row, 1978).

CD   *The Cost of Discipleship*, translated by R. H. Fuller, revised by Irma Booth (New York: Macmillan, 1963).

CF   *Creation and Fall, Temptation* (New York: Macmillan, 1971).

DBW   *Dietrich Bonhoeffer Works,* edited by Hans-Richard Reuter and Wayne Whitson Floyd Jr., translated by Martin Rumscheidt (Minneapolis: Fortress Press, 1996).

DBW2 *Dietrich Bonhoeffer Werke,* edited by Eberhard Bethge, et al. (Munchen: Kaiser Verlag, 1986-1993).

E   *Ethics*, translated by N. H. Smith. Rearranged edition (New York: Macmillan, 1986).

GS   *Gesammelte Schriften*, edited by Eberhard Bethge (Munchen: Kaiser Verlag, 1958-1974).

LPP   *Letters and Papers from Prison*, the enlarged edition, edited by Eberhard Bethge, translated by R. H. Fuller, John Bowden, et al. (New York: Macmillan, 1972).

LT   *Life Together*, translated by John W. Berstein (New York: Harper and Row, 1954). Paperback edition (same pagination, 1976).

NRS   *No Rusty Swords: Letters, Lectures and Notes*, edited by Edwin H. Robertson, translation revised by John Bowden and Eberhard Bethge (London: William Collins Sons and Co. Ltd., 1970, and Cleveland, Ohio: Collins-World, 1977).

WF   *The Way to Freedom: Letters, Lectures and Notes 1935-1939*, edited by Edwin H. Robertson, translated by Edwin H. Robertson and John Bowden (New York: Harper and Row, 1973).

SECONDARY LITERATURE

BND   John W. de Gruchy, editor, *Bonhoeffer for a New Day: Theology in a Time of Transition* (Grand Rapids: Eerdmans, 1997).

CG   Eberhard Bethge, *Costly Grace* (San Francisco: Harper and Row, 1979).

DB   Eberhard Bethge, *Dietrich Bonhoeffer, Man of Vision, Man of Courage* (New York and Evanston: Harper and Row, 1970).

SCH   Clifford J. Green, *The Sociality of Christ and Humanity: Dietrich Bonhoeffer's Early Theology: 1927-1933* (Missoula, Mont.: Scholar's Press, 1972).

TF   *A Testament to Freedom: The Essential Writings of Dietrich Bonhoeffer*, ed. Geffrey B. Kelly and F. Burton Nelson (San Francisco: Harper and Row, 1990).

Various editions of some of the above books exist. When an edition other than that listed here is used, a complete bibliographical entry will be used in the endnotes in the first occurrence.

Contributors

ROBERT BERTRAM, Ph.D., is Seminex Professor Emeritus of Historical and Systematic Theology at the Lutheran School of Theology, Chicago, Illinois. He is the editor of *The Lively Function of the Gospel* and *Theology in the Life of the Church*.

EBERHARD BETHGE, D.D., is Dietrich Bonhoeffer's biographer and closest friend. Dr. Bethge is also the editor of the collected works of Bonhoeffer and the author of countless articles on Bonhoeffer's theology and spirituality, as well as an international lecturer on Bonhoeffer's legacy. Dr. Bethge is the founding father of the International Bonhoeffer Society.

RENATE BETHGE, D.D., is Dietrich Bonhoeffer's niece and Eberhard Bethge's wife, and an expert on various issues related to Bonhoeffer's life and theology. She has edited, written, and lectured extensively on the spiritual and literary legacy of Bonhoeffer.

RICHARD H. BLIESE, Ph.D., is Augustana Heritage Professor of Global Mission and Evangelism at the Lutheran School of Theology, Chicago. Dr. Bliese is also associate director of the Chicago Center for Global Ministries, and pastor of St. Andrew's Lutheran Church, Glenwood, Illinois. He has published works on Bonhoeffer's theology of ministry and on Christian missiology.

MARK S. BROCKER, Ph.D., is adjunct professor of ethics at Pacific Lutheran Theological Seminary in Berkeley, California. He is currently editor of *Conspiracy and Imprisonment: 1940-1945*, volume 16 of the Dietrich Bonhoeffer Works English Edition. Brocker is also pastor of Trinity Lutheran Church in McMinnville, Oregon.

G. CLARKE CHAPMAN, Ph.D., is professor of religion at Moravian College in Bethlehem, Pennsylvania. He has lectured widely on peace and liberation issues in Bonhoeffer's theology. Dr. Chapman is an activist on peace issues as a member of the Society of Christian Ethics.

KEITH CLEMENTS, Ph.D., is the general secretary of the Conference of European Churches, Geneva. Prior to that appointment, Dr. Clements was tutor at Bristol Baptist College and lecturer in the Department of Theology and Religious Studies, University of Bristol, and Secretary for International Affairs, Council of Churches for Britain and Ireland. He has written two critically acclaimed books on Bonhoeffer: *Bonhoeffer: A Patriotism for Today* and *What Freedom?* and *The Persistent Challenge of Dietrich Bonhoeffer.*

JOHN W. DE GRUCHY, Ph.D., is professor of Christian studies at the University of Cape Town, South Africa, and editor of the *Journal of Theology for Southern Africa.* He is the author of several books on Bonhoeffer's theology with particular reference to the relevance of Bonhoeffer in the struggles of various peoples and societies for liberation from systemic oppression. His Bonhoeffer anthology has been published as a pivotal volume in the Makers of Modern Theology Series, of which he is the general editor.

WAYNE WHITSON FLOYD JR., Ph.D., is director of the Bonhoeffer Center at the Lutheran Theological Seminary in Philadelphia, visiting professor at that seminary, and general editor and project director of the Dietrich Bonhoeffer Works English Edition. He is the canon theologian of the Episcopal Cathedral Church of St. Stephen, Harrisburg, Pennsylvania. He is the author of *Theology and the Dialectics of Otherness,* relating Bonhoeffer's theology to that of Adorno; editor of Bonhoeffer's *Act and Being,* volume 2 of the Dietrich Bonhoeffer Works English Edition; and co-editor of *Theology and the Practice of Responsibility: Essays on Dietrich Bonhoeffer* and the valuable research tool *Bonhoeffer Bibliography: Primary Sources and Secondary Literature.*

JOHN D. GODSEY, D.Theol., is professor emeritus of systematic theology at Wesley Theological Seminary, Washington, D.C., and an emeritus member of the Board of Directors of the International Bonhoeffer Society, English Language Section. He is the author of the first published book on Bonhoeffer, *The Theology of Dietrich Bonhoeffer.* He also wrote the book *Preface to Bonhoeffer.* He is co-editor with Geffrey B. Kelly of *Ethical Responsibility: Bonhoeffer's Legacy to the Churches.* Dr. Godsey is currently working with Kelly on the critical edition of Bonhoeffer's *Discipleship* (formerly *The Cost of Discipleship*), Volume 4 of the Dietrich Bonhoeffer Works English Edition. Dr. Godsey was one of the four founding members of the English Language Section of the International Bonhoeffer Society.

MARY GLAZENER, novelist, is the author of *The Cup of Wrath*, now in its fifth printing, a critically acclaimed biographical novel based on twelve years of meticulous research on the life of Dietrich Bonhoeffer. This book has been translated into both German (*Der Kelch des Zorus*) and Dutch (*De Beker der Gramschap*). The German edition is now in its third printing. Mary Glazener's contribution to the *festschrift* was originally presented as a paper at the Seventh International Bonhoeffer Congress, held in Cape Town, South Africa, in 1996.

BARBARA GREEN, Ph.D., is director of the Churches' Center for Theology and Public Policy, Washington, D.C. She is editor of *Who Is Jesus Christ for Us Today? Dietrich Bonhoeffer after Fifty Years*. She has written and lectured extensively on Bonhoeffer and peace issues and was the Bonhoeffer Lecturer at the University of Berlin in 1995. Dr. Green has also coordinated several national symposia on Bonhoeffer's life and theology at Ghost Ranch Conference Center, New Mexico. She is a member of the editorial board of the Dietrich Bonhoeffer Works English Edition and translator of *Discipleship*, volume 5 in that series.

CLIFFORD J. GREEN, Ph.D., is one of the founders and a former president of the International Bonhoeffer Society, English Language Section, from 1972 to 1992. He is currently the executive director of the Dietrich Bonhoeffer Works English Edition Project. His publications include *The Sociality of Christ and Humanity: Dietrich Bonhoeffer's Early Theology*, hailed as the book that moved studies of Bonhoeffer into the new critical phase in the decade of the 1970s. His latest publication is the critical edition of *Sanctorum Communio*, Bonhoeffer's doctoral dissertation and first published book. He has also edited the Barth anthology for the Makers of Modern Theology Series, published by Fortress Press. Dr. Green is co-editor with Wayne W. Floyd of the valuable research tool *Bonhoeffer Bibliography: Primary Sources and Secondary Literature*.

JAMES M. GUSTAFSON, Ph.D., is a retired professor of Christian ethics at Yale University, the University of Chicago, and Emory University. He is the author of several books and articles on nearly every aspect of Christian ethics. He writes for this *festschrift* from the perspective of a lifelong friend of Burton Nelson.

JAMES PATRICK KELLEY, Ph.D., is living in retirement after many years of teaching at Lynchburg College, Virginia. His dissertation from Yale University is entitled "Revelation and the Secular in the Theology of Dietrich Bonhoeffer." His article for this *festschrift* is a revision of a section of this dissertation. Dr. Kelley has been treasurer and a member of the Board of Directors of the International Bonhoeffer Society, English Language Section, since 1984.

GEFFREY B. KELLY, S.T.D., LL.D., is professor of systematic theology and chairperson of the Department of Religion at La Salle University, Philadelphia. He is also director of the Lasallian Leadership Institute. He was one of the four founding members of the International Bonhoeffer Society, English Language Section, and its president since 1992. Dr. Kelly is the author of *Liberating Faith: Bonhoeffer's Message for Today* and co-editor with F. Burton Nelson of *A Testament to Freedom: The Essential Writings of Dietrich Bonhoeffer.* He also co-edited with John D. Godsey *Ethical Responsibility* and is currently working with Dr. Godsey on the new critical edition of *Discipleship* (formerly *The Cost of Discipleship*), volume 4 of the Dietrich Bonhoeffer Works English Edition.

ROBERT K. JOHNSTON, Ph.D., is professor of theology and culture at Fuller Theological Seminary, Pasadena, California. Formerly provost and dean of the seminary at North Park College and Theological Seminary, Johnston is the author of *The Christian at Play* and co-editor of *The Variety of American Evangelicalism.* He is currently co-editor of the New International Biblical Commentary, Old Testament, eighteen volumes, and is working on a book on theology and film.

MARIANNE LEIBHOLZ is the daughter of Sabine Bonhoeffer and Gerhard Leibholz. She has represented the Leibholz family in several international Bonhoeffer congresses and, most recently, at the special ceremony in Westminster Abbey during which statues honoring ten modern martyrs were unveiled, among whom was her Uncle Dietrich.

SABINE LEIBHOLZ-BONHOEFFER, Dietrich Bonhoeffer's twin sister and the last surviving member of the family of Karl Bonhoeffer and Paula von Hase, died at the age of ninety-three as this book was being sent to press. Her gracious letter of greeting included here will stand as one of the last public words from that generation. Sabine was the author of the widely read *Christmas in the Bonhoeffer Home* and *The Bonhoeffers: Portrait of a Family,* a book that offers a window into the struggles of the Bonhoeffer family in their collective resistance to Adolf Hitler and the Nazi ideology.

JOHN MATTHEWS, M.Div., M.Th., is vice-president of the International Bonhoeffer Society, English Language Section, and editor of the Bonhoeffer Society *Newsletter.* He is a pastor in the Evangelical Lutheran Church in America and a member of the ELCA Consultative Panel for Lutheran-Jewish Relations.

ANDREAS PANGRITZ, Ph.D., is professor of systematic theology at the Rhine-Westphalia Technical University in Aachen. He has lectured both in the United States and in his native Germany on Bonhoeffer's prison theology and the spiritual faith that undergirded Bonhoeffer's participation in the German Resistance Movement. Dr. Pangritz is the author of *Dietrich Bonhoeffers Forderung einer Arkandisziplin—eine unerledigte Anfrage an Kirche und Theologie* (Dietrich Bonhoeffer's demand for a discipline of the secret [*Arcani Disciplina*]: An unfinished question for church and theology).

JANE PEJSA is a researcher and nonfiction author. She has published three books including her prize-winning biography, *Matriarch of Conspiracy, Ruth von Kleist, 1867-1945*, now available in three languages, English, German, and Japanese. Her historical travel book, *To Pomerania in Search of Dietrich Bonhoeffer,* will soon be available in a third edition.

LARRY RASMUSSEN, Ph.D., is the Reinhold Niebuhr Professor of Social Ethics at Union Theological Seminary in New York City. He is the author of critically acclaimed books on Bonhoeffer's social ethics and relevance for today, most notably *Dietrich Bonhoeffer—His Significance for North Americans.* Dr. Rasmussen was honored with the Grawemeyer Award in Religion for his latest book, *Earth Community, Earth Ethics,* published in 1997.

JAY C. ROCHELLE, Ph.D., is pastor of St. Timothy Lutheran Church, Allentown, Pennsylvania. He is active with the Institute for Jewish-Christian Understanding. He previously served in university ministries and as professor and dean of the chapel at the Lutheran School of Theology at Chicago from 1981 to 1995.

MARTIN RUMSCHEIDT, Ph.D., is professor of historical and systematic studies at the Atlantic School of Theology in Halifax, Nova Scotia. He is the author of a number of studies on Karl Barth and Dietrich Bonhoeffer. He is a member of the editorial committee of the Dietrich Bonhoeffer Works English Edition Project and has served as translator of several theological books into English, including *Act and Being*, volume 2 of the new critical English edition of Bonhoeffer's writings.

JONATHAN D. SORUM, Th.D., holds a doctorate from Luther Theological Seminary, St. Paul, Minnesota, where he wrote his dissertation on Bonhoeffer's *Cost of Discipleship.* He is presently pastor of Greenfield Lutheran Church, Harmony, Minnesota.

CHARLES W. SENSEL, B.D., is a retired United Methodist pastor whose ministry was for forty years with the Central Illlinois Conference and the Ecumenical Institute in Chicago. He has published papers on Bonhoeffer and Wesley and on Bonhoeffer's concept of friendship as discipleship. He has served on the Board of Directors of the International Bonhoeffer Society, English Language Section, since 1988.

NORMA S. SUTTON, M.Div., M.A., M.Ln., is seminary librarian and professor of theological bibliography at North Park Theological Seminary, Chicago. In addition to published bibliographical material, she has contributed a study of publisher John Day.

C. JOHN WEBORG, Ph.D., is professor of theology and coordinator of spiritual formation at North Park Theological Seminary, Chicago. With Sister Agnes Cunningham, S.S.C.M., he is the author of the Lilly-funded work *Prayer and Life in the Spirit: A Venture in Academic Excellence and Ecumenical Collaboration.*

BURTON NELSON: FRIEND AND THEOLOGIAN

Memories of a Friend

James Gustafson

T o Jim—My best pal. In moments when contemplation finds education valueless. From Burt—Your roommate." Such is the inscription in a book presented to me by Burton Nelson a few weeks before I left North Park College for the Army in early 1944.

You might think that under those circumstances this inscription would be found in a copy of the New Testament. Or it would be found in a diary of daily readings assembled by a theologian or a pastor. Or it would be found in a copy of Thomas à Kempis's *The Imitation of Christ*, or Meister Eckhart's "Counsels on Discernment," or a book about how to pray, or even *The Thoughts of Marcus Aurelius*. But it is not found in anything so pious or so moral. Rather, it is found in a book the chapters of which were first published as stories in *The New Yorker*, a book of humor (or a humorous book, if you prefer): *The Education of H*Y*M*A*N* K*A*P*L*A*N*, by Leonard Q. Ross.

"In moments when contemplation finds education valueless." What was I to do in such moments? Not devour more academic books; not be spiritually directed to the higher and deeper mysteries of faith; not rage against the pedantic memorization of soon-forgotten information it took to pass an examination in political science or history; not nurse grudges against an institution and its ethos; not sing—but laugh! That inscription in that particular book, given at that transition in my life, is not a bad iconic representation (to use current jargon) of one dimension of Burton Nelson as I have known him since 1942—more as a friend than a professional colleague.

Since I have no special competence in the fields of Bonhoeffer stud-

3

ies and Holocaust studies in which Burton Nelson has made his academic contributions, in another transition in my life, from decades of research and teaching to retirement, I take recourse to reflections on a friendship.

In moments when contemplation finds education valueless—laugh! Fortunately, the inscription does not permit the inference that education is to be denigrated, nor the inference that contemplation is to be prized, nor the inference that either contemplation or education is sufficient itself to get one through a pique or a crisis, not to mention to realize some fullness of human life. But it is good advice. If one is afflicted more than Burton Nelson with the stereotypical Swedish dour or stoic (or combination) outlook on life, it is especially good advice. And, like any advice one receives, it has a special authenticity when it is given by one who, at least as I have known him, tempered seriousness with a variety of unselfconscious injections of humor.

Others have been more persistently and intimately, intellectually and personally, related to Burton Nelson than I have. There is no file of correspondence through the years; there are a few, but not many, occasions on which we heard and responded to each other's academic work; there were decades when we seldom saw each other. And there were, during a period of our most recent residence in Chicago, memorably delightful dinners and conversations as couples. One can hardly say that ours has been a friendship like one about which Montaigne writes: "Our souls mingle and blend with each other so completely that they efface the seam that joined them." Of Aristotle's types of friendship, I have known all three with Burton Nelson, and he has known at least two with me. We had the joy and pleasure of each other's company, as late-adolescent college students attending horror movies in a theater on Randolph Street, subsequently reminiscing about events and persons from our pasts, catching up on current activities, both professional and personal. To some extent we have experienced Aristotle's second type: we have been useful to each other. We did edit a junior college yearbook together, with him finishing what we had jointly begun. I can say, in keeping with Aristotle's third type, that I have come to appreciate my friend's character and characteristics as valuable in an intrinsic way. I dare not say that he reciprocates, though I hope he does. Montaigne cites Cicero as saying, "Only those are to be judged friendship in which the characters have been strengthened and matured by age." It would be presumptuous to claim such a fulfillment, especially given the episodic pace of occasions for the intensity of our youthful companionship. But fidelity over time he has preferred, even when being together in academic conferences has been frustratingly brief due to the clamor and multiplicity of personal meetings in such events.

Self and circumstance both figure in what one becomes from a time of late adolescence to the age when one is presented a *festschrift*. Events and experiences frame choices one makes, and the choices direct us as agents from experience to experience, from event to event. Some commitments are firm and bind us throughout life. Other interests and loyalties are more transient. Capacities develop that have been only nascent; exposure to thought patterns, information, and ideas through teachers and books and articles stimulates curiosity and different depths and paths of professional life. Sometimes themes emerge that, retrospectively more than prospectively, seem to form a red thread of coherence through one's personal and professional choices, through one's teaching, research, and writing. For some that theme is deeply psychological—making sense out of intense relationships or shattering events in life. For some it is spiritual or intellectual elation—having found some clue that bears on through and above the events that trouble others. For some it is a sense of indignation in the face of persistent and recalcitrant injustices and violence to one's community of gender, or to the oppressed of the world with whom one has deep empathy. For some it arises out of personal social circumstances that can be generalized, such as consciousness of bias and partiality that accrues from relative isolation in ethnic, religious, or other social entities. What is interesting intellectually and morally is how persons who share so much in common background of ethnic and religious life, of educational direction, end up differently as their characters have matured by age. A blunt recognition of these differences surely is counter-evidence to the currently popular religious and moral claims that sharing a common story and a common community leads to common character.

Even if it were possible to do, this is not the place to analyze how friends, "best pals," become different, or how their common religious and cultural roots sustain similarities within their differences. No other professional colleague shares as much commonality of background with me as does Burton Nelson. Yet our religious loyalties are quite different; our foci of attention in research and writing are different, even though both come within the scope of the membership criteria for the Society of Christian Ethics. The "audiences" for our scholarly work in teaching and publication overlap, I am sure, but have different centers of attention. To attempt to analyze similarities and differences would require more interpretation of my own experience than interests me, and more knowledge about Burton Nelson's life than I could possibly have.

I can only observe from a distance of time and space that a person whose gift to me as I left for the army was a book of humor has brought his academic life into focus on the life teachings of a martyr of the time, Dietrich Bonhoeffer, and on the history-altering event of inexplicable evil, the Holocaust, that was being enacted. Not much ought to be inferred from this. He was a serious person as well as a humorous one in our late adolescence, and was committed to the ministry of the church as I was not. What became clearer in years following, his voracious appetite for reading widely (I know no other person who subscribes to as many journals as he does), was markedly present. The diligence that led to his higher academic degrees while serving churches and raising a family was noticeable. The turbulence of life with deaths, of family anxieties with family joys, of the inevitable politics of institutions in which we work, has not passed him by any more than the rest of humanity. Perhaps the humor of the book presented to me was intended to lead to equanimity in the face of not only educational frustrations but also life in the army and all that followed in subsequent years. Certainly Burton Nelson's touch of lightness of heart, of smiles and chuckles in the midst of his occupation with the life of a martyr, the martyr's teaching, and the superpersonal powers of evil reveals an enviable equanimity of spirit. It is one that, together with his other gifts to us, gives strength and perspective.

In 1990, forty-six years after reciving *The Education of H*Y*M*A*N K*A*P*L*A*N* on the occasion of a major life transition, came *A Testament to Freedom: The Essential Writings of Dietrich Bonhoeffer* during a transition to interdisciplinary studies from theology and ethics. Its inscription: "To Jim and Lou—'faithful in friendship, making one free . . . ' From Dietrich Bonhoeffer's prison poem, 'The Friend.' In appreciation for nearly half a century of friendship. God Bless—Burton."

"Faithful in friendship, making one free . . . " Our souls have not mingled and blended so completely that they efface the seam that joined them. But we have had the joy and pleasure of each other's company; we have been of some good use to each other; and I have appreciated the intrinsic value of Burton Nelson's character, especially his equanimity of spirit that can be immersed in the life and teachings of a martyr, and in the evil that humans have wrought against their Jewish neighbors, and still smile and chuckle. Maybe both of our characters have been strengthened and matured with age, over now fifty-six years of friendship.

Others in this volume honor Burton Nelson with essays more appropriate than my remarks on the occasion of this tribute. I honor him for the friendship, for the gifts of his spirit, among them equanimity. And the contemplation of the life and writings of a martyr and of horrendous, inexplicable evil, like the reading of a humorous book, can make one feel the limited value of aspects of education we have all perpetrated!

Letter

Sabine Leibholz-Bonhoeffer
Marianne Leibholz

Dear Burton,

We have learned that a *festschrift* is being prepared for you, and we are delighted. We want to send a small tribute to this *festschrift* in the form of a letter of thanks.

Shortly after the death of my father, Gerhard Leibholz, in 1982, you asked me if you could help my mother, Sabine, after the loss of her husband, and me after the loss of my father. You have helped us ever since.

You began by re-editing my mother's book for American readers, *The Bonhoeffers: Portrait of a Family*. We are so very grateful for the time and trouble you took to bring the work to completion. We think it is a very handsome edition. This is a tribute to Gerhard Leibholz as well as to my mother's twin brother, Dietrich Bonhoeffer, to the other members of the family, and to our place of asylum, England.

We are most grateful that during all the years you kept us informed about your work on Dietrich Bonhoeffer. We were fascinated by the various aspects of your activities on his behalf.

We were deeply shocked when we heard of your heart trouble some years ago, and so relieved to hear that your brother Dexter was an eminent cardiologist. We were astounded at how soon you took up your work again. When we opened your envelopes, something new and exciting was bound to be enclosed. You are so very full of ideas! Altogether we found and find your energy miraculous. Often an account of all your activities left us almost gasping with amazement. And how we enjoy your ever-present humor!

Also, we were so very pleased that you kept us informed about the activities of your growing family, with so many lovely photographs of your wife, Grace, and your daughters and son and sons-in-law, as one academic success appeared after the other and the grandchildren were born. We felt, therefore, we could take some part in your life in the United States.

We thank God for giving us such a good friend. We thank God for giving us in you such a good friend. With every good wish for your and your family's future, in 1999 and the new century,

Yours ever,

MARIANNE LEIBHOLZ
SABINE LEIBHOLZ-BONHOEFFER

F. Burton Nelson:
Theologian of the Church

Robert K. Johnston

First as his student, then as a partner in ministry, both in the Evangelical Covenant Church and in the academy, I have valued Burton Nelson's wisdom and friendship for thirty years. In particular, I want on this occasion to thank Burton for his repeated role as a reconciler between individuals and groups. Burton is a friend to all.

B e careful in choosing what you write on in graduate school, for it will influence much of the rest of your career." This adage, often repeated to doctoral students, has proven remarkably true in the life of F. Burton Nelson. Academic trajectories were shaped early for this theologian. In particular, decisions made regarding a paper in a graduate course in contemporary ethics while a doctoral student at Northwestern University, and in selecting a thesis topic for his doctoral work, have continued to open out for him, producing a rich and productive academic career.

In that doctoral seminar, Burton Nelson was asked to select one contemporary ethicist, to read as much as possible of the person's work, and to present a paper in a class session. Nelson chose Dietrich Bonhoeffer and later recounted, "I was hooked."[1] For his dissertation in 1965, Nelson wrote on the topic *The Ecumenical Movement and the Problem of World Peace.*[2] Throughout his educational career, Nelson would continue to focus both on ecumenism and on ethics, and Bonhoeffer would become his ubiquitous theological companion.

Behind Nelson's interest in each of these topics, however, was something more basic, as the title to the introductory section of his dissertation clearly spells out. What Burton Nelson has focused upon his entire career is helping identify and answer "The Challenge to the Church of the Twentieth Century." Page 1 of his thesis quotes W. A. Visser 't Hooft, then General Secretary of the World Council of Churches: "The whole problem of Christian ethics is basically a problem of the Christian Community." And what was thought true of ethics, Nelson has found central to most other theological concerns as well. It is the Christian Church that Burton Nelson has sought to renew and reform, and he has done this as educator, ecumenist, and ethicist.

THEOLOGIAN OF THE CHURCH

Burton Nelson's career has been in the particular service of the Evangelical Covenant Church, his own denomination. But Nelson has always understood his church calling as part of, and one with, his service to the wider Christian Church. Teaching opportunities both at North Park Theological Seminary, where he was called to serve in 1960, and with laity and clergy in a myriad of local churches would extend Nelson's primary interests beyond his student days to include research in Pietism and the Reformation, as well as the Church and the Holocaust, and contemporary third world liberation theologies. But these topics have never been mere academic interests. Instead, they have been viewed as further case studies the Church could learn from as it continues its struggle toward ongoing renewal and meaningful witness. As Nelson concluded after offering a survey of African theology for an article in the *Evangelical Review of Theology* (1990):

> If there is a church struggle being waged in South Africa, and in other parts of the African continent, how would we depict our own Western struggle? In the light of the giant issues we face— racism, sexism, nuclearism, militarism, homelessness, AIDS, violence, affluence, boredom, political corruption, educational impotence, health care costs, sexual promiscuity—is ours not *also* a church struggle with breathtaking consequences? I have no doubt about the answer.[3]

Nelson has written for a wide and varied audience throughout his career. His edited and annotated volume on Bonhoeffer's essential writings (with Geffrey Kelly, his close friend) is considered a standard text in Bonhoeffer studies. His work in Bonhoeffer's oral history has been ground breaking, as for example his interviews with Jean Lasserre, Bonhoeffer's French friend from Union Theological Seminary days. But much of Nelson's writing and editing has been targeted at a lay audience. As his early ecumenical mentor Visser 't Hooft counseled, "only the common thought of the Christian community" can help us move forward. And so

Nelson has written over fifty articles for *The Covenant Companion*, his church's lay magazine, as well as general articles of interest in such magazines as *Radix, Sojourners, Christianity Today, Christian History, Christian Life,* and *Christianity and the Arts.* He also was commissioned by the Evangelical Covenant Church in 1971 to write a confirmation textbook entitled *The Story of the People of God.* This volume provided an overview of Scripture and church history for teenagers as they endeavored to learn about their faith and enter into full participation in the life of the church. Nelson also served on and chaired his denomination's Commission on Christian Citizenship, helping to draft resolutions on such issues as alcoholism, race relations, Christian citizenship, civil disobedience, concern over Vietnam, and abortion.

In particular, however, Burton Nelson accepted in 1961 the editorship of *The Covenant Quarterly,* "a professional journal for the Covenant clergy and theologically-minded laity," a post he would not relinquish for the next twenty-five years.[4] Under his leadership, the *Quarterly* announced that it "nourishes the hope that some fresh dimensions to the horizons of the church will appear." Nelson finished his opening editorial with these words: "Welcome into the society of Searchers for New Horizons—or is it the Society for Seeking New Light on Old Horizons?"[5] Here was Nelson's agenda—to assist that society of searchers in the church who were seeking its renewal and extension, whether through new resources or from new light on previous insights.

Under Nelson's leadership, *The Covenant Quarterly* equipped "churches and church leadership to meet the future with deeper insight and fuller confidence."[6] As one might expect from an ethicist, there were multiple articles on church and society, particularly focusing on urban life and ministry. War and peace, race, and affluence also came under scrutiny. But equally important with regard to the witness of the church, for Nelson, was evangelism. Two entire issues of the *Quarterly* and multiple other articles were given over to helping understand how the church can communicate the gospel more engagingly. When combined with several additional articles on world mission, lay ministry, and issues of church growth, these essays reveal a central passion of Nelson's: the holistic witness of the church.

The worship of the church was not neglected in the pages of the *Quarterly* either. Preaching and the sacraments came under repeated analysis, as did music and church architecture. If one notes as well the articles on counseling and Christian education, one again sees a central theme for the journal under Nelson's editorship: a strengthening of the parish ministry.

The Covenant Quarterly, though edited by Nelson with the assistance of his colleagues at North Park Theological Seminary, was an organ not of the school, but of the Evangelical Covenant Church. Thus, the journal has also included over the years a series of articles within its pages on the historical roots of the Covenant. There have been translations from the Swedish language of significant articles by early Covenant leaders, as well as an issue devoted to the Lutheran-Evangelical dialogue which was held on the five hundredth anniversary of Luther's birth. Equally significant has been the journal's willingness to address theological controversy that has emerged in the Covenant. Under Nelson's editorship, issues of the *Quarterly* were devoted to how the church is to understand baptism, Scripture's authority, the Holy Spirit, and the ministry of women. In each of these cases, the Covenant can be seen through the pages of the *Quarterly* as contributing at an early stage to the growth of what might be labeled "progressive evangelicalism." Here was a theology that was biblically centered, experientially rooted, intellectually compelling, and culturally grounded.

Complementing the journal's focus on the Covenant Church, its theology and history, witness and worship, and consistent with Nelson's own academic work, has been the *Quarterly*'s ongoing interest in the ecumenical church. As early as 1961, Nelson turned his readers' attention to preparation for the Third Assembly of the World Council of Churches in New Delhi. A stream of articles was to follow over the years with such titles as "Significant Landmarks of the Modern Ecumenical Movement" (written by Nelson himself), "Our Lord's Prayer for the Unity of the Church," "The Church of South India" (written by Nelson), "The Church Universal and the Covenant Church," "What Did Uppsala Say to the Churches?" (written by Nelson), "Attitudes of Conservative Evangelicals toward the World Council of Churches," "Ecumenical Spirituality," and "Roman Catholicism since World War II." Such a continuing focus in the *Quarterly* is quite remarkable, given the Evangelical Covenant Church's official stance of nonalignment with any ecumenical organization. And it has proven significant.

In the initial study guide that was prepared in 1993 for members of the World Council of Churches as they sought to formulate a common understanding and vision, a section was set aside for reflection on "Relations with Non-member Churches."[7] This is a growing interest in the council as it faces the challenges of the new millennium. The guide noted, as a practical example of how the WCC's interaction with nonmember churches might proceed in the decade ahead, its long-standing interaction with the Evangelical Covenant Church. It recognized that the Covenant has had both official observers and advisors at the last several assemblies and world gatherings. It even mentioned that a professor from its seminary (i.e., F. Burton Nelson) had brought a group of his seminary students to the Canberra Assembly as part of a course on ecumenism.

Both the WCC and the Covenant have been broadened and enriched by Nelson's ecumenical insights and urgings. His has been a commitment "to the whole task of the whole church to bring the gospel to the whole world" (statement from the WCC's Central Committee, meeting in Rolle in 1951). The Church is in his debt.

In addition to ecumenism, one other topic has repeatedly been included in the pages of the *Quarterly.* This is historic Pietism. If Covenant churches and church leadership could benefit from a greater understanding of the contemporary household of faith, so could they gain deeper insight into their worship and witness by recovering an understanding of their historical roots. Thus, Nelson gave over the pages of *The Covenant Quarterly* at least a dozen times to articles and/or whole issues on Pietism. When it was not in vogue to maintain interest in this area, the *Quarterly* did so for two decades, helping to attract increased scholarly attention for this important renewal movement.

Through academic reflection on Pietism, Nelson sought to correct misconceptions, provide insight, and extend application into the present. For him, one arresting question was this: "Can the format of early Pietism live again today in the context of the world's tragedy? Can we cultivate twentieth-century 'assemblies of piety,' inner circles of sharing and witness, of prayer and praise, of Bible study and spiritual therapy?"[8] Commenting on the continuing caricature that is leveled at Pietism, Nelson quoted from a nineteenth-century novel about the life of Spener by Karl August Wildenhahn: "A Pietist is one who regards it as a mortal sin to wear an embroidered handkerchief and a wig; one who fasts every other day and wears shabby garments; one who talks from morning till night about godliness, and who, on Wednesdays and Saturdays, attends Spener's *examina.* This is a Pietist."[9] He then argued for the need for recovering authenticity in history.

In order to do this, Nelson published papers from a symposium on "The Pietistic Heritage and the Contemporary Church" and from the Pietism section of the American Academy of Religion, where he served as vice president, as well as articles by such scholars as Donald Bloesch, Dale Brown, Winthrop Hudson, James Stein, and John Weborg. His own article "The Pietist Heritage and Social Concerns" also appeared in the *Quarterly.* Nelson's words of introduction to an article by his colleague C. John Weborg express well his passion:

> The central motifs of Pietism are so constitutive of the Evangelical Covenant Church that it is important for us again to be reminded of what they were and what they mean for descendant congregations in our own time. It seems especially appropriate in the one hundredth anniversary year of the Covenant Church to ponder the roots which underlie our corporate existence.[10]

CHURCH EDUCATOR

All that Burton Nelson wrote was unto the educational mission of the church he served. Yet, two particular aspects of his writing deserve special mention as we reflect on Nelson. Serving on the confirmation planning committee for the Evangelical Covenant Church in the early 1970s, Nelson wrote the first-year book for confirmands. Entitled *The Story of the People of God* (1971), the book sought to combine "instruction, pastoral relationship, personal decision on the part of the students, and participation in the life of the church." Nelson's emphasis was "on God's selection of a set aside people whose task it has been to channel his message, his blessing, and his word to the whole world."[11] He therefore surveyed both Old and New Testaments, as well as the history of the church, seeking to highlight leaders, movements, and events that are central to our life in the church today. Nelson stated his goal clearly in an introductory article in *The Covenant Companion:* "There is a pointed effort to keep the 'mission' of God's people in front and center, challenging each young person to a life-lasting commitment to Jesus Christ and his church."[12]

Nelson's writing would highlight his service to the educational mission of the Evangelical Covenant Church in other ways as well. His article on lay academies introduced the idea of seminary faculty teaching weekend schools in local Covenant churches; his article on "The Theological Seminary and the City" introduced models of theological education for ministry in an urban context (an interest that Nelson has continued throughout his career at North Park Theological Seminary); and his report on "The Summer at Covenant Harbor" summarized his ministry as camp director, a position he held for a number of summers at Lake Geneva, Wisconsin.[13] Nelson was (and is) an educator for the church.

When Nelson began his teaching at North Park Theological Seminary, he was assigned a class in church history, among other courses. Wanting to broaden the impact of his study, he wrote in the *Quarterly* to pastors on "Church History in the Church." After discussing the goals of studies in church history ("to discern the impact of Jesus Christ upon his first followers"; to "dialogue with the past"; to discern the "inner history" as well as the "outer history" in the unfolding story of the Christian Church; "to discover the common history which we share with all those who have named Christ as Lord"; "to provide preparation for the tomorrows in the church"), Nelson turned, in what would prove characteristic of much of his scholarship, to a discussion of the relevant materials and aids that a pastor might use in a congregational program of teaching church history.[14]

Nelson continues to be a voracious reader and something of a bibliophile. (Anyone who has entered his office knows of his love for books. They are everywhere!) Thus, it has been natural for him to provide "bookshelves" for pastors on such topics as Christian citizenship, a theology of the laity, ecumenics, and Christian worship[15]; to write reviews on nearly one hundred books for *The Covenant Quarterly*; and to write articles introducing new theological movements or personages by providing an overview of major books and writers in the field. Three of these latter articles have, for example, introduced those in the church to studies on Dietrich Bonhoeffer, to theologies "from below," and to the works of African theologians.[16]

CHURCH ECUMENIST

After looking in his dissertation at a welter of ecumenical data, Burton Nelson concluded by asking if there was an "ecumenical mind" concerning the problem of world peace. Has there been a consensus of basic conviction, a consolidation of disagreement into coherent form, and thus a stimulation in ecumenical study?[17] And his answer was yes. With regard to war, churches believe it to be the enemy of humankind, an insanity that is contrary to the will of God and a consequence of the disregard of God. Given such mass murder of human life, the Church has believed it must condemn war, rise above all divisions and boundaries, work for reconciliation, promote justice and peaceful cooperation both by reminding governments of their duty and by working to remove the causes of war, and offer a vision of unity that transcends race, nationality, and class.

As a world Christian, Nelson has consistently sought the "ecumenical mind." Perhaps nowhere was this more forcefully presented than in his article "A Call to Church Unity," which was part of the volume of essays enlarging upon the Chicago Call statement (1978), of which he was a co-signer. Nelson reminded his evangelical readers that unity is a given in Christ; the New Testament makes clear that "it is a gift to be received and then cultivated." The Reformers and those involved in later movements of evangelical renewal saw the unity of the body as integral to the Church and sought to embody it. Such unity should not be spiritualized, but made visible and concrete, as in the 1973 Chicago Declaration of Evangelical Social Concern and the Lausanne Congress on World Evangelization in 1974. But evangelical expressions of unity are insufficient in and of themselves. "Evangelicals should now be encouraged to cultivate increased awareness, increased discussion, and increased cooperation both within and without their respective traditions, earnestly seeking common areas of agreement and understanding."[18] We must be evangelical and ecumenical.

To help his own Evangelical Covenant Church better understand the ecumenical mind, Nelson published two series of articles early in his career. Both appeared in *The Covenant Companion*. Wanting to help the church move beyond destructive labels in its dialogue together, he wrote four essays on the meaning of "fundamentalist," "evangelical," "liberal," and "neo-orthodox." While critical of liberal and fundamentalist extremes, the tenor of the articles is conciliatory as common ground is sought in the need for a contemporary re-interpretation of the biblical theology of the Reformers.[19] A second series, which ran in the *Companion* during the Covenant Church's "Year on Interchurch Relations" (1961), explored the diversity of denominations within the Christian Church. After a historical introduction, individual articles described the origins and present shape of Lutherans, Presbyterians, Episcopalians, Methodists, the United Church of Christ, Baptists, and the Disciples of Christ. Characteristically, Nelson ended the series with a description of mergers and negotiation between denominations. Finding inspiration in the mergers that produced the Church of South India, Nelson cautiously hinted that new frontiers in unity should be explored.[20]

CHURCH ETHICIST

In his dissertation, F. Burton Nelson wondered whether pronouncements of the World Council of Churches should be "primarily reflective of the constituency or are they to be prophetic utterances?"[21] Such a question has continued to be at the center of Nelson's ethical reflections throughout his career and perhaps is best answered for Nelson by his ecumenical mentor, W. A. Visser 't Hooft: "And so the voice of the Council [one could substitute Burton Nelson] is at the same time a voice *of* the churches and a voice *to* the churches. It is both institution and movement, instrument and leaven; its calling is both to serve and to challenge."[22] Nelson has sought, as the church ethicist at his denomination's seminary, to be both a guide to direct his church's thinking and a spokesperson to speak to the world on its behalf.

As a guide for his church's ethical reflection and action, Nelson has written a nine-part series on "The Gospel and the Ten Commandments."[23] He has also written articles for laity within the church on such contemporary ethical issues as the population explosion (1960), Christianity's encounter with Communism (1961), race relations (1963), Christian citizenship (1964), the church and peace concerns (1981), and the health-care crisis (1990).

As an alternative approach to church ethics, Nelson has also introduced to church laity pivotal, prophetic figures in the life of the Church. Three examples bear mentioning, in addition to Dietrich Bonhoeffer and his associates, who will be dealt with below. In 1966 Nelson wrote a lengthy review of Joseph Fletcher's *Situation Ethics: The New Morality.* Nelson spoke *for* his denomination in being straightforwardly critical of Fletcher's reduction of the Ten Commandments to guiding principles, his individualism in moral decision making, his rejection of prescriptive morality, and his unhappy caricature of Pietism. But Nelson also spoke *to* his own church as he found in Fletcher's ethic a "reminder of the central-ity of love in New Testament ethics," a "caution against a negative, prohi-bitionist perspective on the Christian life," and a recognition that the complexity of some ethical issues demands that a high premium be placed "on responsible decision in Christ."[24]

A second article from this early period in Nelson's career introduced readers to three of William Stringfellow's books.[25] Nelson challenged his church through Stringfellow's writing to become involved in the world as a necessary part of its existence. We must come to know the frustrations and tragedies of our world, confess our own shortcomings in light of these, and look again at the gospel's call to obedience. A similar theme of Christian faithfulness is taken up by Nelson, later in his academic career, in his article commemorating the fiftieth anniversary of the Barmen Dec-laration ("Barmen 1934: A Lesson in Christian Faithfulness").[26] Rather than simply speak of the declaration, however, Nelson chose to frame the discussion within a tribute to Lutheran pastor Martin Niemoeller, one of its signers. Niemoeller became an early, outspoken critic of Hitler and of those "German Christians" who affirmed him, and he was jailed for it. To allow the state to "muzzle" the church was unthinkable to him. The church must instead be called back to its Reformation foundations, back to God as sovereign Lord. Those at Barmen, wrote Nelson, should have uttered a prophetic word about the situation of the Jews, but both what they said and what they didn't can find meaning for us in our own time.

A BONHOEFFER SCHOLAR

F. Burton Nelson learned from those such as William Stringfellow and Martin Niemoeller. But it is to Dietrich Bonhoeffer that Nelson has turned time and again for inspiration and guidance. Upon his retirement in 1996 from full-time teaching at North Park Seminary, *The Covenant Companion* published an interview with Nelson entitled "Bonhoeffer's Troubadour."[27] The moniker is appropriate, for, as Nelson himself com-mented two decades earlier, Bonhoeffer's writings were already providing "major inspiration and stimulation for my own theological and devotional ventures."[28] Bonhoeffer has been for Nelson his theological companion and mentor, someone who, in Nelson's words, is "readily identified with serious Christian discipleship, as well as with heroic resistance to political tyranny and structural evil."[29]

As Burton Nelson has studied the life and thought of this Christian martyr, he has concentrated in particular on three scholarly areas: (1) Bonhoeffer's oral history, the accounts and reminiscences of family and friends who knew him and his context; (2) Bonhoeffer's spirituality, the shape of his own discipleship; and (3) Bonhoeffer's contribution to a post-Holocaust theology, in particular, what the church today needs to learn from its earlier failed response to the plight of the Jews.

Nelson considers one of the highlights of his own career his collaboration with Bonhoeffer's twin sister, Sabine Leibholz, in a revision and updating of her book *The Bonhoeffers: Portrait of a Family* (published in 1994 by Covenant Publications). For Nelson, Bonhoeffer's witness and actions can only be understood as part of his remarkable family's solidarity in collective resistance to Hitler and the evil system that developed around him. In addition to Sabine, Nelson has spent significant time with Renate Bethge, Bonhoeffer's niece, and her husband, Eberhard, who became during the war period Dietrich's closest friend and confidant. Nelson first met the Bethges when they came to Chicago in 1966 to teach for a term, and their families have had extended times together over the years.

Of particular interest are the three weeks Nelson spent in the Bethges' small town near Bonn, Germany. He spoke with the Bethges about Bonhoeffer by the hour and studied Bonhoeffer memorabilia. He read the underlining and marginal notes in Bonhoeffer's confirmation Bible, which he continued to use for many years, his daily devotional books, which Bonhoeffer annotated while in prison, and a generous assortment of papers and letters. From this personal exposure to Bonhoeffer's life, Nelson wrote of the rhythm of Bonhoeffer's spiritual life, one marked with both solitude and fellowship, prayer and action, the Christian year and life's inbreaking. Nelson concluded with these words: "Spirituality is too important to be left to chance. It is more often than not meaningful and radiant by cultivation and constant attention. So it was with Bonhoeffer. So it is with those who find in his spirituality an inspirational model for today."[30]

In addition to his interaction with the Bethges and Bonhoeffer's twin sister, Sabine, Nelson's repeated interviews with Jean Lasserre, one of Bonhoeffer's four close friends from his year at Union Seminary in 1930-31, have proven valuable for understanding the early Bonhoeffer. Lassere's life of faithfulness, expressed in his commitment to peace and nonviolence, intersected well with Bonhoeffer's own public concerns. Particularly at the Fano Conference in 1934, where both Lasserre and Bonhoeffer played key roles, their interaction proved significant. Nelson narrates that, according to Lasserre, "it is possible that at Fano, [Bonhoeffer] was more advanced on the path of 'pacifism' than I was."[31] It was at Fano that the World Council of Churches decided to side with the Confessing Church in Germany rather than the so-called "German Christians," thus clearly standing in opposition to the Nazi regime for the first time. What was at stake, as Nelson documents both from the records and from depositions taken from persons who participated in the proceedings, was the very nature of not only that church but the whole *Oikoumene*.[32]

For Burton Nelson, the study of Dietrich Bonhoeffer has never been a mere academic exercise. What has been of interest to him is the impact of Bonhoeffer's life and thought for the church today. In this German churchman and theologian Nelson found someone committed to "the centrality of Jesus Christ in the Church's proclamation and life," someone with "a deep, daily, and devoted discipleship," and someone dedicated to "the pursuit of justice, equality, human rights, and neighbor-love." In Bonhoeffer Nelson found a soul mate whose passion for Christ was expressed concurrently in both a spirituality and a servanthood. Nelson is fond of quoting Bonhoeffer's words from 1935, "Only he who cries out for the Jews may sing Gregorian chant."[33] It was during the time that Bonhoeffer was privy through his brother-in-law Hans von Dohnanyi to the inside story of the Nazis' barbarism and brutality toward the Jews that he penned his two classics of religious devotion and spirituality, *The Cost of Discipleship* (1937) and *Life Together* (1939). Context and confession, justice-seeking and devotion, were conjoined in this man. Writes Nelson, "Covenanters, among others, need this fervent reminder."[34]

Over the last four decades, and complementing his study of Dietrich Bonhoeffer, Burton Nelson has devoted primary attention as well to understanding the Holocaust, particularly the church's response to it. He is currently a member of the Church Relations Committee of the Holocaust Memorial Council and Museum in Washington, D.C., and teaches each fall at Oxford University in England as a visiting scholar in post-Holocaust theology. The moral paralysis that characterized the church, both in Germany and in the United States, during the rise and fall of the Hitler regime is both tragic and sobering. In Nelson's words, "the Holocaust itself represents the gross failure of religion (in particular, the churches) to penetrate the structures of society. As a result of that failure, the message of God's transcendence and sovereignty was all but muted." What was needed, continues Nelson, "was a vast outpouring of protest, indignation, resistance, prophetic judgment, stubborn defiance, compassion, courage—of 'being for others' (Bonhoeffer)."[35]

STILL MORE TO COME!

Although Burton Nelson has retired from full-time teaching, his work continues unabated. In the recent *Covenant Companion* interview, Nelson expressed the hope of completing two books in the upcoming years.[36] One is the long-awaited volume on Bonhoeffer's spirituality, provisionally titled *The Spirituality of a Martyr*. Nelson has published a sample of Bonhoeffer's poems and sermons in other places, and his Bonhoeffer anthology contains a strong sampling of sermons, letters, lectures and addresses, and poems. But what is awaited is his selection and commentary that will provide perspective on this man of prayer and action. Nelson is working on a second volume, as well, one that will assess the impact of Bonhoeffer's life and theology in the Church worldwide as we move into the twenty-first century. As background for this project, Nelson has written to a hundred parish pastors in twelve different nations who have been influenced, like Nelson, by Bonhoeffer. We can await with anticipation this continuing development of Burton Nelson's scholarship. Given that his father continued to be active in his work even into his nineties, we have reason to believe that "the best is yet to come."

ENDNOTES

1. Interview with F. Burton Nelson, "Bonhoeffer's Troubadour," *The Covenant Companion* 85(February 1996): 8.

2. Frank Burton Nelson, *The Ecumenical Movement and the Problem of World Peace*, Ph.D. diss., Northwestern University, 1965.

3. F. Burton Nelson, "New Frontiers in African Theology," *Evangelical Review of Theology* 14 (July 1990): 224.

4. Carl Philip Anderson, "Comment," *The Covenant Quarterly* 19, no. 1 (February 1961): 48.

5. F. Burton Nelson, "Comment," *The Covenant Quarterly* 19, no. 2 (May 1961): 48.

6. F. Burton Nelson, "Comment," *The Covenant Quarterly* 37, no. 1 (February 1979): 1.

7. *Towards a Common Understanding and Vision of the World Council of Churches* (Geneva: World Council of Churches, June 1993).

8. F. Burton Nelson, "We Live in a Broken World," *The Covenant Companion* 51 (July 27, 1962): 6-7.

9. F. Burton Nelson, "Comment," *The Covenant Quarterly* 38, no. 1 (February 1980): 1.

10. F. Burton Nelson, "Comment," *The Covenant Quarterly* 43, no. 2 (March 1985): 1.

11. F. Burton Nelson, quoted in James R. Hawkinson, "Confirmation: New Courses on the Way," *The Covenant Companion* 59 (January 15, 1970): 10.

12. Ibid., 11.

13. F. Burton Nelson, "Go to School Where You Are," *The Covenant Companion* 60 (November 1, 1971): 14-15; F. Burton Nelson (with Donald W. Dayton), "The Theological Seminary and the City," in *The Urban Mission*, ed. Craig Ellison (Grand Rapids: Eerdmans, 1974), 114-21; F. Burton Nelson, "The Summer at Covenant Harbor," *The Covenant Companion* 60 (November 15, 1971): 1.

14. F. Burton Nelson, "Church History in the Church," *The Covenant Quarterly* 19, no. 1 (February 1961): 22-30.

15. F. Burton Nelson (with Ronald L. Magnuson), "A Bookshelf on Christian Citizenship," *The Covenant Quarterly* 23, no.1 (February 1965): 33-39; F. Burton Nelson, "The Lordship of Christ over Our Daily Work," *The Covenant Quarterly* 21, no. 1 (February 1963): 17-27; F. Burton Nelson, "A Bookshelf on Christian Worship," *The Covenant Quarterly* 21, no. 3 (August 1963): 34-43; F. Burton Nelson (with Arthur A. R. Nelson), "An Ecumenical Bookshelf," *The Covenant*

Quarterly 26, no. 3 (August 1968): 41-48.

16. F. Burton Nelson, "Dietrich Bonhoeffer," *The Covenant Companion* 59 (August 1, 1970): 8-9, 20; F. Burton Nelson, "Christian Faith and Public Policy: The View from Below," *The Covenant Quarterly* 40, no. 2 (May 1982): 31-40; F. Burton Nelson, "New Frontiers in African Theology," *Evangelical Review of Theology* 14 (1990): 209-24.

17. Nelson, *The Ecumenical Movement and the Problem of World Peace*, 340.

18. F. Burton Nelson, "A Call to Church Unity," in *The Orthodox Evangelicals: Who They Are and What They Are Saying*, ed. Robert E. Webber and Donald Bloesch (Nashville: Nelson, 1978), 195, 207.

19. F. Burton Nelson, "What Do We Mean When We Say a Person Is a Fundamentalist?" *The Covenant Companion* 48 (October 16, 1959): 4-6; "What Do We Mean When We Say a Person Is an Evangelical?" *The Covenant Companion* 48 (October 23, 1959): 10-11; "What Do We Mean When We Say a Person Is a Liberal?" *The Covenant Companion* 48 (October 30, 1959): 8-9; "What Do We Mean When We Say a Person Is Neo-orthodox?" *The Covenant Companion* 48 (November 6, 1959): 10-11, 20.

20. F. Burton Nelson, "This Is the Church: The First Fifteen Hundred Years," *The Covenant Companion* 50 (October 13, 1961): 6-8, 20; "This Is the Church: The Lutherans," *The Covenant Companion* 50 (October 20, 1961): 4-5; "This Is the Church: The Presbyterians," *The Covenant Companion* 50 (October 27, 1961): 8-9; "This Is the Church: The Episcopalians," *The Covenant Companion* 50 (November 3, 1961): 8-9; "This Is the Church: The Methodists," *The Covenant Companion* 50 (November 10, 1961): 8-9; "The United Church of Christ," *The Covenant Companion* 50 (November 17, 1961): 8-9; "This Is the Church: The Baptists," *The Covenant Companion* 50 (November 24, 1961): 10-11; "The Disciples of Christ," *The Covenant Companion* 50 (December 1, 1961): 8-9; "New Frontiers in Mergers," *The Covenant Companion* 50 (December 8, 1961): 8-9; cf. F. Burton Nelson, "The Church of South India: A Report," *The Covenant Quarterly* 22, no. 3 (August 1964): 31-39.

21. Nelson, *The Ecumenical Movement and the Problem of World Peace*, 11.

22. W. A. Visser 't Hooft, quoted in ibid., 16.

23. F. Burton Nelson, "The Gospel and the Ten Commandments," *The Covenant Companion* 49 (September 23, 1960, through December 16, 1960), nine issues. A recent political cartoon in *Newsday* shows Charlton Heston as Moses with tablets in one hand, a gun in the other, and an NRA button on his robe. The caption reads,"Charlton Heston in the Nine Commandments." Nelson arrived at his nine articles in another way, combining the first two commandments in his discussion.

24. F. Burton Nelson, "The New Morality According to Joseph Fletcher," *The Covenant Companion* 55 (May 6, 1966): 4-5, 30.

25. F. Burton Nelson, "William Stringfellow: Prophet to Our Time," *The Covenant Companion* 54 (January 1, 1965): 8-10.

26. F. Burton Nelson, "Barmen 1934: A Lesson in Christian Faithfulness," *The Covenant Companion* 73 (May 1984): 10-12.

27. "Bonhoeffer's Troubadour," *The Covenant Companion* 85, no. 2 (February 1996): 8-10.

28. F. Burton Nelson, "A Sabbatical Pilgrimage," *The North Parker* 42 (May 1976): 9.

29. F. Burton Nelson, "An Evening with the Twin Sister of Dietrich Bonhoeffer," *The Covenant Companion* 76 (August 1987): 20-21.

30. F. Burton Nelson, "Bonhoeffer and the Spiritual Life: Some Reflections," *The Covenant Companion* 67 (June 1, 1978): 5. Reprinted in the *Journal of Theology for South Africa* 30 (March 1980): 38.

31. F. Burton Nelson, "The Relationship of Jean Lasserre to Dietrich Bonhoeffer's Peace Concerns in the Struggle of Church and Culture," *Union Seminary Quarterly Review* 40, nos. 1 and 2 (1985): 79.

32. F. Burton Nelson, "The Holocaust and the Oikoumene: An Episode for Remembrance," in *Faith and Freedom*, ed. Richard Libowitz (Oxford: Pergamon Press, 1987), 71-81.

33. Dietrich Bonhoeffer, quoted in F. Burton Nelson, "Dietrich Bonhoeffer and the Jews: An Agenda for Exploration and Contemporary Dialogue," in *The Holocaust Forty Years After*, ed. Marcia Littell, Richard Libowitz, and Evelyn Bodek Rosen (Lewiston: Edwin Mellon Press, 1989), 88.

34. "Bonhoeffer's Troubadour," 9.

35. F. Burton Nelson, "The Holocaust and the American Future," *Radix* 12 (January-February 1981): 5, 7.

36. "Bonhoeffer's Troubadour," 9-10.

BONHOEFFER AND
RESISTANCE TO NAZISM

Living in Opposition[1]

Eberhard Bethge

Living in opposition"? What does that really mean? Put simply, is every refusal, no matter what its nature, good and correct? Does every rebellion break up the encrusted staleness of church, state, and society so that we breathe more easily?

I could tell of steps that one finally dared to take and which, given the new situation, brought about an unparalleled renewal—private, social, professional, spiritual, ecclesial—and yielded new points of view. As Bonhoeffer says at the beginning of his book *The Cost of Discipleship*, "For acquired knowledge cannot be separated from the existence in which it is acquired."[2] Inversely, however, this statement also means: without making any change in one's existence. But now we say: without opposition, blindness reigns. Or even: without opposition, people remain condemned to stupidity.

To be sure, to make an ideal of stubborn refusal is not sufficient either. As for myself and my friends during those turbulent decades, I noticed that there existed something like a pathological need to be in the minority. It was as if we had a sense of well-being only if we found a connection with the opposition—to the left of center, naturally! Our first question, therefore, still remains: what opposition, when and where, and against whom? In this, we have to inquire about its circumstances, its time of occurrence, its conditions, its supporters, and those to whom it appeals. From that derive its particular form and its certainty; its plural "life," its ambiguous, yes, even its rebellious image—eventually a shocking form of opposition, so that changes in one's "life" can still be expected. Here are a few personal retrospectives.

For me and my friends, biographically, the time for our own decisions arrived, or rather, the time for finding our independent stand coincided with the fatal year of 1933. We were not quick-witted Berliners set in our ways, but country boys from the province of Saxony, without a world press or radio. In this same year, a strange image took hold of us, the contradictions of which we did not at first notice.

Politically, in early summer we manifested a readiness to devote ourselves to the rising tide of Nazism, to participate in the general enthusiastic regimentation of the universities, to join in the protest marches against the Treaty of Versailles. No democratic tradition existed in our households. Our authorized theological faculty in Halle-Wittenberg was "Erlangen-Lutheran" at that time. No Barthian worked on a barrier against the dominant control of the German dictatorial, "common good" ideology. We considered betrayal of the Fatherland something very evil, and we imagined that we knew who had betrayed the Fatherland and who had not.

In terms of church, however, we looked on ourselves in the church-run training schools of Halle, oddly enough, as entirely with the minority that was about to become an active, dissenting group. Perhaps we were already under the influence from afar of Karl Barth. Our opposition was sparked by the frenzied nazification of the faith, theology, structure, and business of the church that had been set in motion. Noisy, even violent confrontations took place in those church-run training schools. And all of that occurred even though, examined from the vantage point of today, each of us was a more or less hidden anti-Semite. Nonetheless, we soon began our opposition with expressions of disobedience against church authorities. The beginning of this living in opposition was characterized by considerable self-assurance. No, we declared! An adoption of the civil ordinance's so-called Aryan Paragraph into the church was not to be permitted. We resisted without any hesitation the notion that blood, instead of baptism, was now the constitutive basis for belonging to the church community. There were other impossible demands that, to be sure, we did not yet recognize at all, such as the readiness to provide documentation from church records in the parish offices with the purpose of proving the Aryan descent of civil servants.

And so it happened that one and a half years after Hitler's "seizure of power," and one good year after the great election victory of the nazified "German Christians," we took the step into the illegality of the "Dahlemites." (In October 1934 the Confessional Synod of Berlin-Dahlem called upon pastors and parishes no longer to obey the church authorities of the National Socialist Party, although they were in charge of the keys and cash boxes!) Concretely stated, this meant ejection from the endowed traditional training institutions, removal from the payrolls of the People's

Church [Volkskirche], and impediments against performing marriage ceremonies. Given these accompanying consequences, we practiced theology differently, read the sources, the Bible and confessional writings, in a different light (cf. accounts from Finkenwalde), and found ourselves remarkably ready to commit ourselves to tasks that we shared in common.

All this does not yet constitute knowledge of that which nowadays we are able to appreciate, namely, that our credo continued to manifest anti-Jewish elements, that we pursued a theology of power even in the Confessing Church. This was in the sense of an attitude that *we* are now the ones and not *you*, the Jews; this is what is called the theology of contempt in the United States. There was no awareness that, with the so-called Crystal Night, 9 November 1938, and our silence about it, our previous form of living in opposition had proved itself to be blind, deaf, and mute when it came to the persecution of the Jews, so that nowadays Jews justifiably see and believe us to be close to rather than removed from Nazism.

Nonetheless, the fact remains: there existed in the so-called struggle between the church and the state a demonstrable and persisting phase in which living in opposition—a well-founded opposition, to be sure—made speaking up publicly a matter of the past. At least for a while! Profession, pulpit, and salary were put at risk, and prison walls became a stark reality to be endured from the inside.

But then a basic experience caught up with us, one that we of course began to understand only much later: the experience that a life in opposition in that particular form of ecclesial illegality was bound to crumble when the dichotomy of 1933 remained, namely, that split between saying a political "Yes!" to National Socialism and the "No!" voiced by the church.

The crimes in our history escalated. What was set in motion by the Wilhelmstraße, the Brown House, and the Prinz-Albrecht-Straße condemned the previous form of our living in opposition to insignificance. Quite different words, deeds, and, above all, risks, as well as enlisting the aid of strange allies, became necessary. The unequivocal formula of opposition of Barmen in 1934 conveyed hardly anything of genuine rejection of the criminal government. And, by merely being repeated, it became unwittingly a factual stabilizer of the crimes ascribed to that government. Barmen can never exist without the Stuttgart Confession of Guilt, October 1945. Its non-ambiguity could only be claimed if there were risks of still unknown ambiguities. Bonhoeffer knew precisely the seriousness of this when, in 1940, he got involved in the conspiracy. He described the situation concretely in his Christmas essay to his family and fellow conspirators in 1942:

We have been silent witnesses of evil deeds; we have been drenched by many storms; we have learned the arts of equivocation and pretense; experience has made us suspicious of others and kept us from being truthful and open; intolerable conflicts have worn us down and even made us cynical. Are we still of any use?[3]

My life after 1935 brought me close to this man who, particularly after 9 November 1938, was struggling to understand his life in opposition [to Nazism] as that of exercising responsibility to overcome the evil and thereby to accept this as a life worth living. This developed through tentative steps taken both forward and backward, which only very few of his contemporaries and friends recognized for what they really were. To be more precise, few people were permitted to know their full import. There were obviously moments of being sidetracked; there were also detours and paths on which one could go astray, but these were all done away with by 1940 in the midst of the conspiracy to overthrow Hitler, from which there was no turning back. One day Bonhoeffer found himself in the twilight zone of being fully involved as a double agent. This was so effective that, for a few days, when Bonhoeffer wanted to visit Karl Barth in Basel, Switzerland, in 1942, even Barth was puzzled over how this German pastor could possibly obtain a passport and currency and travel into Switzerland. Could he now really still be the one who in 1933 had led a life in opposition to Nazism? Was it possible that he now belonged to the "stabilizers" of the criminal system that was National Socialism? And because it was a matter of conspiratorial actions, did he not even then have to be silent and accept for too long a time some evil developments, such as those which, to cite one example, comprised the decisions that approved and organized the deportations of Jews to Auschwitz? Indeed, the manner in which this living in opposition changed its shape now assumed enigmatic, if not questionable, but practical expression in his life. Bonhoeffer was clearly conscious of this when he wrote his poem "Jonah."[4]

We ourselves have been deeply moved by the remembrance of the "White Rose" resistance group. Those students of the White Rose were among the brightest, and even until today, the most unambiguous and most encouraging manifestation of a life in opposition in this century of German history. They have offered an indisputable witness to the way in which readiness to give one's life for such a noble cause has even in our present times created new life. The names of Hans and Sophie Scholl, as well as those of their co-conspirators, are the only ones of the German Resistance movement that have found incorporation into the Washington Holocaust Memorial. And while listening to their story, we are moved to acknowledge that sacrifices like theirs bring life out of death.

To be sure, I confess that something else in all this occurs to me, namely, the agonizing situation of the conspirators in Berlin during those months of winter 1942-43. Precisely at the time when Judge Freisler had Hans and Sophie Scholl executed, those conspirators in Berlin were in the middle of the very carefully prepared and comprehensive phase of a putsch that ended in the month of March with two unsuccessful assassination attempts on Hitler: 13 March, when the bomb with a timed fuse was placed in Hitler's plane in Smolensk (involved were Tresckow, Dohnanyi, and Schlabrendorff); and 21 March, when Major von Gersdorf was supposed to explode a hand grenade near Hitler in the Zeughaus in Berlin. Not only did all these attempts take too long, but they also came too late. Hitler's monstrous machinery of murder could continue running without any impediment, and the eventual execution of the Scholls could not be prevented.

The examples I cite show how living in opposition must expect at times an almost strange contrariness with each individual. One must expect to do the exact opposite of the reality one aims at. Thus, also in 1943, in contrast to normal times and circumstances, extraordinary, even super-extraordinary forms of opposition had to be ventured. The events in Munich caused indeed a profound stir within the conspirators in Berlin. Now they had to contend with uncoordinated students disturbing their most complicated planning and preparations shortly before the real coup d'état was to be set in motion! What a dilemma to have to stand idly by and watch silently the murder of those to whom one felt evidently closest. Yes, even more, Falck Harnack related later how during those months he tried to bring together the Scholl circle with that of the Bonhoeffers. It did not come to that. Indeed, under no circumstances ought it have come to that! The inner logic of such different forms of living in opposition in Nazi Germany during the war in the winter of 1942-43 did not permit it. On the contrary, contacts and considerations of support were even painstakingly to be avoided or, more precisely, to be denied. In the name of the coming coup d'état, one had now to pretend that one was pro-Nazi. There could be nothing worse, back then, than if exposures of connections to Munich and to the Scholls were to occur and thus endanger the main plot against Hitler.

Actually, *horribile dictu*, the carrying out of the death sentences in Munich on 22 February 1943 brought about a sigh of relief because no connection to the Scholls was proved. Consequently, the threat of possibly endangering the plans for overthrowing Hitler and the Nazi government in Berlin was somewhat lessened.

Back then I was thinking theoretically. If members of the Scholl Circle were alive today, they could rightfully reproach the Berlin Circle of resistance for having neither protested nor intervened on their behalf. On the contrary, the Berlin resisters had carefully avoided every contact and had not wanted to have even the slightest hint that they had anything to do with the Scholls. And so, indeed, the matter stood. Bonhoeffer knew what he was talking about when he said of his group, "We have been silent witnesses of evil deeds," when he talked about "the art of equivocation and pretense" and the "intolerable conflicts," as well as of the fact that they owed "plain, honest, straightforward people" the "truthful and open" word.[5]

In the case of Bonhoeffer and his friends, one and a half years after March 1943, there were even more mass murders at Auschwitz. Also, the best of the resistance fighters could no longer escape the stigma of having been accomplices in criminal actions. Nobody could any longer appreciate anything of their living in opposition, and, in fact, the degree of their guilt kept increasing.

That is why we read in Bonhoeffer's letter the day after the failed assassination attempt of 20 July 1944, in the face of his own imminent death, that long unnoticed sentence stating that he was, nonetheless, "grateful and at peace thinking about present-day issues."[6] That is to say, thinking about the previous day, with the destruction of all their personal and political hopes, as a yet irretrievable "station on the way to freedom." Yes, unsuccessful and lost! But finally, before all the world, liberated from their oppressive complicity with the blasphemous, humanity-despising, murderous thugs of their own nation.

And now, finally, an answer to the introductory question: What kind of opposition is that from which come life and renewal? The question is aimed in the direction of responsibility. But, in addition, we are speaking of the responsibility, which nobody escapes, for events past and for events still to come. As Bonhoeffer wrote in 1942:

> The ultimate question for responsible people is to ask not how they are to extricate themselves heroically from an affair, but how the coming generation is to live. It is only from this question, with its responsibility towards history, that fruitful solutions can come, even if for the time being they are very humiliating.[7]

Such a responsibility soberly examines the conditions, the moment, the supporters and goals of the opposition set in the service of freedom. It does not expect, as we do today, everything done through computer analyses, but it does expect much from the faith of the community of believers. At the same time, this kind of responsibility looks for the judgment of those who really know the situation. It does not shy away from taking on the guilt that goes along with taking the risks without which there can be no living in opposition. By assuming this responsibility, we do not make a misjudgment in matters of self-appraisal, but open ourselves to the critical function of faith. It is for this reason that the responsible person can sustain defeat as well as success.

It is not surprising, therefore, that we read the following in Bonhoeffer's Christmas essay of 1942:

> Who stands fast? Only those whose final standard is not their reason, their principles, their conscience, their freedom, or their virtue, but those who are ready to sacrifice all this when they are called to obedient and responsible action in faith and in exclusive allegiance to God—the responsible persons who try to make their whole life an answer to the question and call of God. Where are these responsible people?[8]

ENDNOTES

1.Translated from the German text, "Leben aus dem Widerspruch," by Hans Mollenhauer, emeritus professor of German and French, North Park University; translation revised and edited by Geffrey B. Kelly.

2. *CD*, 55.

3. *LLP*, 16.

4. See *TF*, 521.

5. *LPP*, 16, 17.

6. Ibid., 370 (translation altered).

7. Ibid. (translation slightly altered).

8. Ibid. (translation slightly altered).

Theological Motives in Dietrich Bonhoeffer's Decision to Participate in Political Resistance

Andreas Pangritz

BONHOEFFER'S RETURN TO GERMANY: A "CALL OF THE CONSCIENCE" OR OBEDIENCE TO THE "CONCRETE COMMANDMENT"?

In December 1943 Dietrich Bonhoeffer wrote from prison to Eberhard Bethge:

> Now I want to assure you that I haven't for a moment regretted coming back in 1939—nor any of the consequences, either. I knew quite well what I was doing, and I acted with clear conscience. I've no wish to cross out of my life anything that has happened since, either to me personally . . . or as regards events in general. And I regard my being kept here . . . as being involved in Germany's fate, as I was resolved to be."[1]

In other words: At the moment of his return to Germany, Bonhoeffer had decided to share the destiny of Germany no matter what the consequences would be; he had decided "to share the trials of this time with my people,"[2] as he wrote to Reinhold Niebuhr at the end of July 1939.

According to the passage quoted from the prison correspondence with Eberhard Bethge, Bonhoeffer had made his decision to return from the United States to Germany in summer 1939 "with clear conscience" (orig. "*in voller Klarheit und mit bestem Gewissen*"). However, reading the traces of the painful process of decision making in his American diary, we may be surprised observing that nothing was "clear" to Bonhoeffer at the moment of decision; and his "conscience" does not seem to have played any significant role in this context.

On the contrary, on 20 July 1939, the day of decision, Bonhoeffer notes, "It is remarkable how I am never quite clear about the motives for any of my decisions. Is that a sign of confusion, of inner dishonesty, or is it a sign that we are guided without our knowing, or is it both?" And then he continues,

> Today the reading speaks dreadfully harshly of God's incorruptible judgment. He certainly sees how much personal feeling, how much anxiety there is in today's decision, however brave it may seem. The reasons one gives for an action to others and to one's self are certainly inadequate. One can give a reason for everything. In the last resort one acts from a level which remains hidden from us. So one can only ask God to judge us and to forgive us.[3]

One would hesitate to call this uncertainty a "clear conscience." Rather, it seems that the reasons that motivated Bonhoeffer became clear to him only after the decision already had been made. In any case, it is not by chance that the notion of "conscience" is not mentioned in the context of Bonhoeffer's diary. In this reticence we may discover a theological concept that radically departs from the way in which modern Protestantism has conceived an ethic of conscience. Already in his second dissertation on *Act and Being* Bonhoeffer describes the "conscience" as an attempt of Adamitic humanity to justify itself in its "self-satisfied loneliness." It belongs to the devil.[4] And again in *Creation and Fall* Bonhoeffer rejects the assertion that the conscience is the voice of God inside the sinner; on the contrary, he claims, it is the defense of the sinner against God's voice.[5] And still, in one of the first drafts for his *Ethics*, in the chapter "Ethics as Formation" (summer 1940), Bonhoeffer depicts "the man of *conscience*" participating in the "great masquerade of evil."[6] He

> fights a lonely battle against the overwhelming forces of inescapable situations which demand decisions. But he is torn apart by the extent of the conflicts in which he has to make his choice with no other aid or counsel than that which his own innermost conscience can furnish. Evil comes upon him in countless respectable and seductive disguises so that his conscience becomes timid and unsure of itself, till in the end he is satisfied if instead of a clear conscience he has a salved one.[7]

No wonder, then, that "ethics as formation," according to this chapter, "means the bold endeavor to speak about the way in which the form of Jesus Christ takes form in our world. . . . Concrete judgments and decisions will have to be ventured here. Decision and action can here no longer be delegated to the personal conscience of the individual. Here there are concrete commandments and instructions for which obedience is demanded."[8]

It has nevertheless become nearly commonplace to praise Bonhoeffer as a "hero of conscience" and to describe the conspiracy of 20 July 1944 as a "revolt of conscience." However, the centrality of the (Christian) conscience in the traditional discussion around the right of resistance can be regarded as an expression of theological individualism which is symptomatic for a church of the middle classes, a development of church and theology against which Bonhoeffer was opposed. In his letter from prison to Bethge (30 April 1944), Bonhoeffer insists that the time when people could be told "who Christ really is, for us today" "by means of words, whether theological or pious, is over, and so is the time of inwardness and conscience—and that means the time of religion in general."[9] Larry Rasmussen is right in observing: "He grew more and more convinced of the importance of calculating consequences and ever less enamored with the voice of impassioned conscience as sufficient authorization of action."[10]

But, if it was not his Christian conscience, where did Bonhoeffer hear the "concrete commandment" asking for obedience? Is it perhaps the voice of the Scriptures? It is true, Bonhoeffer permits the Bible—by means of the Herrnhut *Losungsbüchlein*—to decide about him in a somehow disconcerting, nearly fundamentalistic way. So we read in his American diary at the date of 26 June 1939, "Today, by chance, I read 2 Timothy 4:21, 'Do your best to come before winter.' . . . It is not a misuse of Scripture if I take that to be said to *me*."[11] But does the Bible speak less ambiguously than the conscience, as long as one does not force it by means of the Herrnhut *Losungen* to an unbiblical, fundamentalistic "clearness"? Or, asked the other way round: What gives the biblical phrase such an unambiguous force that Bonhoeffer cannot help simply taking it as a concrete commandment for him personally, today?

The American diary speaks of "Germany, the brethren" (13 June 1939; first day after the arrival in New York),[12] whose voices speak the more intensely the less Bonhoeffer receives messages from them. And again: "the brethren over there and their work" (18 June).[13] Once Bonhoeffer calls it "dreadful homesickness" (15 June), then "longing for work" (16 June 1939). It is clear: this is not the inner voice of his Christian conscience; these are voices from outside appealing to his responsibility, to whom Bonhoeffer listens—Germany, the brethren. But what qualifies their voices as "concrete commandments"? What does Bonhoeffer really mean in noting:

> It is unbearable over here for a German; one is simply torn in two. To stay here during a catastrophe is quite inconceivable,

unless it is ordained. But to be responsible oneself, to have to reproach oneself, for having come out unnecessarily, is certainly crushing. We cannot separate ourselves from our destiny.[14]

Bonhoeffer, the patriot who does not leave his people alone in a "difficult period" of their "national history"[15]—this would be a simplistic political interpretation of his decision, contradicted by some other motives we will have to deal with.

Bonhoeffer's latest note on the notion of "conscience" handed down to us reads, "Conscience, the voice of the general and the necessary. But agreement, command, recognition by another person is more convincing than a good conscience."[16] The structure is always the same: Bonhoeffer is not interested in listening to an inner voice, even be it that of the conscience. He wants to obey another voice, a commanding voice coming from outside: the biblical *Losungen*, Germany, the brethren, now another person. The problem is the formality of this structure: Could "another person" also mean the Führer?

The question is less eccentric than it seems at first glance. In a later draft to his *Ethics* ("The Structure of Responsible Life"; summer 1942) we can read, "Thus the call of the conscience has its origin and its goal in the autonomy of a person's own ego. . . . The great change takes place at the moment when the unity of human existence ceases to consist in its autonomy and is found, through the miracle of faith, beyond the person's own ego and its law, in Jesus Christ." And indeed, Bonhoeffer continues,

> The form of this change of the point of unity has an exact analogy in the secular sphere. When N(ational) S(ocialism) says: "My conscience is Adolf Hitler" that, too, is an attempt to find a foundation for the unity of one's own ego somewhere beyond oneself. The consequence of this is the surrender of one's own autonomy for the sake of an unconditional heteronomy, and this in turn is possible only if the other person, the person to whom I look for the unity of my life, fulfills the function of a redeemer for me. This, then, provides an extremely direct and significant parallel to the Christian truth, and at the same time an extremely direct and significant contrast with it.[17]

The front line is clear enough. Nevertheless, the sinister parallelism within the contrast raises the question, Who is to decide if Hitler is the "redeemer" or Christ? Who is to decide about which "other person" has the right to determine my conscience, to pronounce commandments which unconditionally are to be obeyed?

WHO IS "THE OTHER"? ETHICAL RESPONSIBILITY AND POLITICAL RESISTANCE

In his treatise on *Rechtfertigung und Recht* (1938; "Justification and Justice") Karl Barth proposed a theological justification of political resistance without any reference to the notion of "conscience." Starting from a christological foundation, he discovers a certain affinity between spiritual justification and secular justice, between the gospel of Jesus Christ and democracy: "From its very origin and from its concrete encounter with Christ and with his church" the state can "administer justice, protect justice, and thus . . . give a free and secure way to the gospel of justification."[18] Barth interprets the "subjection" to the will of the authorities, which Paul in Romans 13:1 allegedly demands from Christians, as simply "paying somebody the respect due to his position." This would be the self-evident other side of the "priestly service" of the Christian congregation with respect to the state, which is primarily exercised in intercession prayers. By no means would "due respect" to the authorities have the meaning of "affirming and voluntarily supporting the intentions and enterprises of the authorities, even when these are oriented to suppress rather than protect the proclamation of the gospel of justification."[19] In this case, the Christian "respect" to the authorities would assume a "critical form."[20] Thus it is not simply by chance, according to Barth, that within regions influenced by the Christian Church in the long run governments prevail which can be described as more or less "democratic, i.e. based on responsible participation of every citizen."[21] "The phrase of the alleged equal affinity or non-affinity of any possible form of government to the gospel," Barth emphasizes, "is not only shabby but simply wrong. It is true that you can go to hell in a democracy and be redeemed under a mob rule or dictatorship. But it is not true that a Christian can affirm, wish and strive for mob rule or dictatorship as seriously as for democracy."[22]

Barth does not hesitate, therefore, to make a plea for tyrannicide, referring to the Zurich reformer Zwingli and to the *Confessio Scotica*. In Zwingli's *Schlussreden* (1523) we can read that "a faithless government, which has abandoned the rule of Christ, must be *dismissed with the help of God*." And the Calvinistic *Confessio Scotica* (1560) makes it the task of the Christian "to support the life of the good people, *to oppress the tyrant,* and to defend the weak against the violence of the malicious."[23]

Bonhoeffer probably knew Barth's essay, and it is likely that he was encouraged by it to participate in political resistance even without support by the church.[24] Yet, Barth's way of reasoning is not his. In the context of a church, which interpreted the Lutheran doctrine of the two kingdoms in a highly conservative and authoritarian way, Bonhoeffer could not see very much sense in stressing the "affinity" between the spiritual and the secular. Even his own understanding of Romans 13 in *The Cost of*

Discipleship comes along in such a traditional Lutheran and authoritarian way[25] that in 1943 he would have no difficulty in referring to it during his trial at the *Reichskriegsgericht*.[26] Another reason why Bonhoeffer could not fully agree with Barth's conception may be seen in the political attitudes of the anti-Nazi conspirators. The majority of them were not just "democratic" in a Western sense, or at least "democratic" only with some qualifications. Their concepts of how to reconstruct Germany after a successful "coup d'état" tended toward Romanticism and authoritarianism.

Obviously, Barth's "democratic" reasoning in favor of political resistance is—in Bonhoeffer's view—still affected by the utopian expectations of historical progress in the years immediately after World War I, when the intention was to establish a democratic administration in Germany for the first time. In contrast to this perspective, Bonhoeffer seeks "conservative" grounds for political resistance, a foundation which would be able to save a society running self-destructively to the abyss.[27] So we read at the end of the chapter called "Inheritance and Decay" (1940) in his *Ethics:*

> Two things alone have still the power to avert the final plunge into the void. One is the miracle of a new awakening of faith, and the other is that force which the Bible calls the "restrainer," *katechon* (2 Thess. 2:7), that is to say the force of order, equipped with great physical strength, which effectively blocks the way of those who are about to plunge into the abyss. . . . The "restrainer" is the force which takes effect within history through God's governance of the world, and which sets due limits to evil. The "restrainer" itself is not God; it is not without guilt; but God makes use of it in order to preserve the world from destruction.[28]

It was not the imminent defeat of Germany which troubled Bonhoeffer most. Rather, he experienced Hitler's military successes as a catastrophe, which had to be restrained. Therefore he claimed the allied armies as "restrainers" in the biblical sense, as well as the circle of military conspiracy within the German Abwehr.

"The very fact that things are just 'going on' is the catastrophe."[29] Bonhoeffer obviously shared this insight formulated by the Jewish philosopher Walter Benjamin during his exile in Paris in the late thirties. The catastrophe is not an imminent danger of the future; it is already going on in the present. And this is the point where Bonhoeffer sees the church becoming guilty: The church has failed to accept the role of the "restrainer" and "to jam a stake between the spokes of the wheel" of a disastrous history.[30] Instead of this, even the Confessing Church had proclaimed that participation in Hitler's criminal war was a "patriotic duty."

Thus, Bonhoeffer in the run of 1941 feels compelled to formulate a "Confession of Guilt," where we read:

> The Church confesses that she has witnessed the lawless application of brutal force, the physical and spiritual suffering of countless innocent people, oppression, hatred and murder, and that she has not raised her voice on behalf of the victims and has not found ways to hasten to their aid. She is guilty of the deaths of the weakest and most defenceless brothers of Jesus Christ.[31]

According to Eberhard Bethge, there can be "no doubt that Bonhoeffer's primary motivation for entering active political conspiracy was the treatment of the Jews by the Third Reich."[32] "With this terminology, 'the brothers of Jesus Christ' Bonhoeffer by the very act of confessing his own and his church's guilt enters into deep solidarity with the victims of the Holocaust; and he shows at the same time a respect, or a self-imposed restraint, towards the victims, the Jews."[33]

Probably in the same moment when he formulated this confession of guilt Bonhoeffer inserted into the chapter on "Inheritance and Decay" the following phrase: "An expulsion of the Jews from the West must necessarily bring with it the expulsion of Christ. For Jesus was a Jew."[34] With the beginning of the war the problem was no longer "expulsion." It now became more and more clear that the so-called "final solution," the extermination of the European Jews, really was being executed. Now each moment of hesitation to "restrain" the catastrophe would mean another moment of guilt.

Compared with Bonhoeffer's longing for "Germany, the brethren" in his American diary (1939), the shift in accent is remarkable: Now it is not primarily the destiny of "Germany," not even the solidarity with the "brethren" of the Confessing Church, which turn out to motivate his political decisions, but it is the destiny of the Jewish "brothers of Jesus Christ." Western history as such depends on their destiny. As Bonhoeffer writes in "Inheritance and Decay," "Western history is, by God's will, indissolubly linked with the people of Israel, not only genetically but in a genuine uninterrupted encounter. The Jew keeps open the question of Christ."[35]

At the end of July 1939, Bonhoeffer had justified his decision to return to Germany in a letter to Reinhold Niebuhr:

> I will have no right to participate in the reconstruction of Christian life in Germany after the war if I do not share the trials of this time with my people. . . . Christians in Germany will face the terrible alternative of either willing the defeat of their nation in order that Christian civilization may survive, or willing the victory of their nation and thereby destroying our civilization. I know which of these alternatives I must choose; but I cannot make that choice in security.[36]

Even more explicit is the recollection of Willem A. Visser 't Hooft, who, during Bonhoeffer's journeys to Switzerland on instruction of the conspiracy group within the German Abwehr in 1941 and 1942, repeatedly met him in Geneva. When Visser 't Hooft asked him in September 1941, "What are you praying for in the present situation?" Bonhoeffer answered, "If you want to know it, I am praying for the defeat of Germany, because I believe this is the only possibility to pay for the suffering which my country has brought upon the world."[37]

It seems to be obvious from this recollection that Bonhoeffer's political attitude differed from the attitude of other members of the resistance movement who had joined the conspiracy in order to prevent the defeat of Germany. I want to illustrate this difference by an episode from Bonhoeffer's journey to Sweden on behalf of the Abwehr in spring 1942. On 31 May 1942 he met his friend Bishop George Bell in Sigtuna. Hans Schönfeld, member of an ecumenical research center in Geneva who was cooperating with the resistance group Kreisauer Kreis, had come to Sweden as well in order to present a "memorandum" of the German opposition to George Bell. In this "Statement by a German Pastor" Schönfeld maintains that "the internal circumstances are becoming now peculiarly favourable to a coup d'état." He suggests that "it would help and quicken this process toward the change of power . . . if the Allies would make it clear whether they are prepared for a European peace settlement. . . . If otherwise the Allies insist on a fight to the finish the German opposition with the German Army is"—according to Schönfeld—"ready to go on with the war to the bitter end in spite of its wish to end the Nazi régime." Among other ambiguous demands that, in view of the military situation, indicated the vision of a unified Europe under German hegemony, the Schönfeld "Statement" announces the willingness of the German opposition to "co-operate with all other nations for a comprehensive solution of the Jewish problem."[38] At a time when the so-called "final solution" of the Jewish question already was underway, there was—in this perspective—a "Jewish problem" waiting for solution.

In his account of the meeting, however, Bishop Bell recollects:

> Here Bonhoeffer broke in. His Christian conscience, he said, was not quite at ease with Schönfeld's ideas. There must be punishment by God. We should not be worthy of such a solution. Our action must be such as the world will understand as an act of repentance. "Christians do not wish to escape repentance, or chaos, if it is God's will to bring it upon us. We must take this judgment as Christians."[39]

It is obvious from this account that Bonhoeffer—in contrast to the major part of the opposition—does not reject the Allied demand of "unconditional surrender."[40] In view of the German guilt piling up day by day, there is no time left for negotiations. Immediate action is demanded. And obviously Bonhoeffer has no difficulty with regarding the Allied armies as well as the conspiracy group as instruments in the hand of God helping to execute his judgment.

In his *Ethics* Bonhoeffer attempts to reflect theologically the experiences of the conspiracy. He does not use the concept of "conscience" in this context; in his ethical thinking, "responsibility" is the crucial concept. Thus we read in the second version of the draft called "History and Good," written probably after the return from Sweden in summer 1942: "We give the name responsibility to this life in its aspect as a response to the life of Jesus Christ."[41]

It seems that the ethical part of Karl Barth's *Church Dogmatics* II/2, of which Bonhoeffer had read the galley proofs during his stay in Switzerland immediately before his journey to Sweden, had some influence on Bonhoeffer's concept of "responsibility." It sounds nearly like Barth in his *Church Dogmatics*[42] when we read in Bonhoeffer's draft, "This concept of responsibility is intended as referring to the concentrated totality and unity of the response to the reality which is given to us in Jesus Christ. . . . Responsibility means, therefore, that the totality of our life is pledged and that our action becomes a matter of life and death."[43]

This concept implies what Bonhoeffer calls "the structure of responsible life," which is "conditioned by two factors; life is bound to humanity and to God and a person's own life is free. . . . Without this bond and without this freedom there is no responsibility."[44] With respect to ethics, Bonhoeffer translates these two factors into "deputyship" and "acceptance of guilt." Jesus in his "real deputyship" is "the responsible person *par excellence*." Thus, "deputyship, and therefore also responsiblity, lies only in the complete surrender of one person's life to the other person."[45] This selflessness includes also "the readiness to accept guilt and freedom."[46] Again Jesus is the model:

> As one who acts responsibly in the historical existence of human beings Jesus becomes guilty. . . . Jesus took upon Himself the guilt of all human beings, and for that reason everyone who acts responsibly becomes guilty. . . . Through Jesus Christ it becomes an essential part of responsible action that the person who is without sin loves selflessly and for that reason incurs guilt.[47]

At this point the conscience gets its right within the context of the ethics of resistance. However, what Bonhoeffer calls "natural conscience" must be "overcome by the conscience which is set free in Jesus Christ. . . . Thus it is Jesus Christ who sets conscience free for the service of God and of our neighbour; He sets conscience free even and especially when a person enters into the fellowship of human guilt. . . . The conscience which has been set free is not timid . . . , but it stands wide open for our neighbour and for his concrete distress."[48] In this context Bonhoeffer can even formulate a phrase like "Jesus Christ has become my conscience."[49]

"PARTICIPATING IN THE SUFFERINGS OF GOD IN SECULAR LIFE"

The passage on "compassion" in the essay "After Ten Years," written for his fellow conspirators in December 1942, can be read as a kind of summary of Bonhoeffer's considerations on responsibility in his *Ethics*.

> We are not Christ, but if we want to be Christians, we must have some participation in Christ's large-heartedness by acting with responsibility and in freedom when the hour of danger comes, and by showing real compassion that springs, not from fear, but from the liberating and redeeming love of Christ for all who suffer. . . . The Christian is called to compassion and action not in the first place by his own sufferings, but by the sufferings of the brothers, for whose sake Christ suffered.[50]

One aspect of this compassion is political, as Bonhoeffer during his imprisonment notes in the "Thoughts on the Day of Baptism" of his grandnephew (May 1944):

> It will not be difficult for us to renounce our privileges, recognizing the justice of history. We may have to face events and changes that take no account of our wishes and our rights. But if so, we shall not give way to embittered and barren pride, but consciously submit to divine judgment, and so prove ourselves worthy to survive by participating generously and unselfishly in the life of the community and the sufferings of our fellowmen. . . . "Seek the welfare of the city . . . and pray to the Lord on its behalf" (Jer. 29,7).[51]

The identification with the life of the community is pulled from the political into theological light in the last letter to Eberhard Bethge before the failure of the coup d'état (16-18 July 1944). Now Bonhoeffer writes on "participation in the sufferings and powerlessness of God" himself in the "secular life." Bonhoeffer interprets to his friend a line of the poem "Christians and Pagans":[52] "The poem . . . contains an idea that you will recognize: 'Christians stand by God in his hour of grieving'; that is what distinguishes Christians from pagans."[53]

And Bonhoeffer explains this "standing by" in what follows as "participation":

It is not the religious act that makes the Christian, but participation in the sufferings of God in the secular life. That is *metanoia*: not in the first place thinking about one's own needs, problems, sins, and fears, but allowing oneself to be caught up into the way of Jesus Christ, into the messianic event, thus fulfilling now Isa. 53. . . . This being caught up into the messianic sufferings of God in Jesus Christ takes a variety of forms in the New Testament. . . . The only thing that is common to all these is their sharing in the suffering of God in Christ. That is their "faith." There is nothing of religious method here. The "religious act" is always something partial; "faith" is something whole, involving the whole of one's life. Jesus calls humanity, not to a new religion, but to life.[54]

The announced explanation of "this life" in "participation in the powerlessness of God in the world" can be found in the following letter to Bethge, the letter from 21 July 1944, the day after the failure of the plot: "One must completely abandon any attempt to make something of oneself. . . . In so doing we throw ourselves completely into the arms of God, taking seriously, not our own sufferings, but those of God in the world—watching with Christ in Gethsemane. That, I think, is faith; that is *metanoia*; and that is how one becomes a human being, a Christian."[55]

In his "Outline for a Book" (August 1944), Bonhoeffer finds the most provocative formulation of the thought, nearly identifying in the way of mysticism Christian life with Christ himself:

Our relation to God is not a "religious" relationship to the highest, most powerful, and best Being imaginable—that is not authentic transcendence—but our relation to God is a new life in "existence for others", through participation in the being of Jesus. The transcendental is not infinite and unattainable tasks, but the neighbour who is within reach in any given situation.[56]

Thus the formulations of "being involved in Germany's fate" and "sharing the trials of this time with my people" reveal as their theological meaning another content, i.e., "participation in the being of Jesus"! But how can both meanings be related with one another? Is it legitimate to identify one form of participation with the other, as Bonhoeffer seems to suppose?

Wolf Krötke has proposed to understand the "Being for others" as "a *human analogy* of God's concrete being in Jesus Christ."[57] Certainly this is not wrong. But does not Bonhoeffer go further, speaking of "being caught up" into "the way of Jesus Christ" or into "the messianic sufferings of God in Jesus Christ"? The identification with Jesus remaining silent in front of Pilate and saying not one word or with the Servant of God in Deutero-Isaiah, who, according to Isaiah 53:7, "did not open his mouth," being "led like a sheep to the slaughter," goes very far here. It is therefore not surprising that Krötke gets the "impression" that "according to Bonhoeffer's logic the church in its secular life should completely renounce from *speaking of God* and be satisfied with 'participating' (!) 'in the secular tasks of the life of the human community.'"[58] But what exactly does Krötke mean by "being satisfied"?

According to Krötke, "the answer that speaking of God and the Christian's relationship with God belong to the 'arcane' remains unsatisfying."[59] In line with the theological tradition, he emphasizes, "Human actions in themselves and as such always speak an ambiguous language, so that it cannot be advisable to see in the Christian's secular life a testimony of Christ speaking for itself."[60] But is it sufficient after Auschwitz simply to repeat the dogmatic tradition?

If I am not mistaken, in the run of his participation in the conspiracy against Hitler Bonhoeffer developed a decidedly different understanding: He did not shrink from ambiguities.[61] Decisive for him was: The responsible action and the suffering as its consequence have to precede speaking and reflecting. So we read in the "Thoughts on the Day of Baptism":

> For you thought and action will enter on a new relationship; your thinking will be confined to your responsibilities in action. With us thought was often the luxury of the onlooker; with you it will be entirely subordinated to action. "Not every one who *says* to me 'Lord, Lord!' shall enter the kingdom of heaven, but he who *does* the will of my Father who is in heaven", said Jesus (Matt. 7:21).[62]

With action thus attaining primacy over against the word, a Christian life will "be limited to two things: prayer and doing justice among the people."[63]

Krötke regrets that Bonhoeffer had not had the time for "an extensive reflection on the question how we now out of such a life also ought to speak of God." It is unlikely that this lack, as Krötke suggests, is due to the fact that Bonhoeffer was "kept on the move" by his discovery of the "being for others."[64] Everything has its time. And the time of conspiracy and incarceration certainly was not the time of "now also to speak of God." Rather, it was a time asking for "responsible actions," for "the deed which"—in the words of Bonhoeffer's lecture on "The Nature of the Church" (1932)—"interprets itself,"[65] a time of "waiting for God's time" ("Thoughts on the Day of Baptism"), a time of "being caught up into the messianic sufferings."

But the ambiguity of Bonhoeffer's actions, which in his work for the office Ausland/Abwehr can be grasped with hands, how can it be justified as "participation in the being of Jesus"? How can it be interpreted as a "self-speaking testimony of Christ"? The answer can hardly be found in theological formulas of the dogmatic tradition; rather, it is found in the reference to the "responsible action" itself. William J. Peck is right in emphasizing: "Deeds must precede words." Bonhoeffer therefore, according to Peck, "took back his sentence about the curse laid on the name of the Jews, in the only way in which he could take it back, by entering into solidarity with the victims of the Holocaust through his death."[66]

Bonhoeffer's reference to the song of the suffering Servant of God in Isaiah 53 interprets the suffering of Christ in a structural parallelism to the suffering of the people of Israel. According to Isaiah 53:2 f., the Servant of God "had no beauty, no majesty to draw our eyes, no grace to make us delight in him. . . . We despised him, we held him of no account, a thing of which men turn away their eyes." In correspondence to this song, it would be important in the first place not to turn away from the sight of the suffering. Eberhard Bethge writes in his essay on "Dietrich Bonhoeffer and the Jews": "Isaiah 53 is 'now' . . . fulfilled in the representative suffering of Israel for the nations. Not just in ancient times, 'then', but 'now' in the present there is a 'life of participation in the powerlessness of God in the world.' In this way the Jews really 'keep open the question of Christ'."[67] This is the meaning of Bonhoeffer's remark on the "messianic event" that Isaiah 53—the song of the suffering Servant of God—is *now* being fulfilled.

Reading these passages in Bonhoeffer's correspondence, Bethge got the impression that perhaps Bonhoeffer was "nearer to Jewish tradition than he knew himself."[68] In any case, as Bethge suggests, these words "fully bring together the messianic passion event of Christ and that of Israel, as well as the events of the present day."[69] In this context it seems to be nearly impossible not to remember a dreadful scene in Elie Wiesel's *Night:*

> One day when we came back from work, we saw three gallows rearing up in the assembly place, three black crows. Roll call. SS all round us, machine guns trained: the traditional ceremony. Three victims in chains—and one of them, the little servant, the sad-eyed angel. . . . The three victims mounted together onto the chairs. The three necks were placed at the same moment within the nooses. "Long live liberty!" cried the two adults. But the child was silent. "Where is God? Where is He?" someone behind me asked. At a sign from the head of the camp, the three chairs tipped over. Total silence throughout the camp. On the horizon, the sun was setting. . . . Then the march past began.

The two adults were no longer alive. . . . But the third rope was still moving; being so light, the child was still alive. . . . For more than half an hour he stayed there, struggling between life and death, dying in slow agony under our eyes. And we had to look him full in the face. . . . Behind me, I heard the same man asking: "Where is God now?" And I heard a voice within me answer him: "Where is He? Here He is—He is hanging here on the gallows."[70]

Perhaps Dietrich Bonhoeffer was not only "nearer to Jewish tradition than he knew himself," but also nearer to this rupture within Jewish tradition.

We do not know anything unequivocal about the inner reasons, the reasons of conscience, that caused people to join the political resistance. In many cases these reasons may have been as ambiguous as the situation itself, which conditioned the actions of the conspiracy. Clearer than the inner life of the conspirators and clearer than their concepts for a new constitution of Germany, which because of the failure of the coup d'état were never carried out, speak their actions. And now we should not so much remember the failed actions, the possible results of which no one can know exactly, but the successful ones which really were carried out.

In this context it seems appropriate to recall one of the activities of the conspiracy group, which in larger historical perspective might appear as irrelevant. I think of the so-called Operation 7, which simply consisted in the attempt to rescue a small number of human lives. By this conspirative activity in September 1942—at a time, thus, when the mass deportations of Jews already were running—the Bonhoeffer-Dohnanyi group within the Abwehr succeeded in sending a group of fourteen people of Jewish faith or Jewish descent across the Swiss border into security, camouflaged as spies of the Abwehr.[71]

The question has been asked whether, by this successful rescue activity, the conspiracy group had not threatened the more important project of the plot to kill Hitler. A postwar correspondence between Hans Bernd Gisevius and Fritz W. Arnold, who spoke for those rescued, clarifies the theological dimension of Operation 7: In the beginning of 1946, Gisevius maintained that the Ausland/Abwehr office had become "extraordinarily unsuitable for such things." It was "completely occupied with preparing the assassination attempt. He therefore described it as "highly questionable to let oneself be diverted from this great goal by any independent action, even if the intention was well-meant."[72] Fritz W. Arnold replied that he was convinced that "rescuing one human life—one grain of sand in an ocean of murdered—was much more important than any plot, independently of how great the goal was."[73] In reaction to this letter, Gisevius could not see any sense in continuing the correspondence, because, as he put it, Arnold was arguing in a "talmudic" way.[74] Unfortunately, Gisevius did not explain what he was intending by "talmudic." But it is clear that in his opinion this must be something even more stupid than "normal" theological thinking. However, it was such "talmudic" thinking that obviously motivated Bonhoeffer—in contrast to other members of the resistance movement, like Gisevius.

It is not by chance, then, that Operation 7 was one of the points why Bonhoeffer was prosecuted and finally sentenced to death. Thus Bonhoeffer became a martyr not simply as a political resister, but especially as a rescuer.

If there was something exemplary in the context of the political resistance against Hitler, it was not so much the failed coup d'état, but rather this action of human "participation," this operation of practical solidarity. This rescue activity justifies speaking of the conspirators as martyrs, as "examples of grace" for us.[75]

ENDNOTES

1. *LPP*, 174.
2. Dietrich Bonhoeffer, letter to Reinhold Niebuhr, July 1939; quotation from *TF*, 504.
3. *TF*, 496.
4. Dietrich Bonhoeffer, *Akt und Sein*, vol. 2 of *DBW2*, 137 f.
5. Dietrich Bonhoeffer, *Schöpfung und Fall*, vol. 3 of *DBW2*, 120 f.
6. Cf. *LPP*, 4.
7. *E*, 66.
8. Ibid., 88.
9. *LPP*, 279.
10. Larry Rasmussen with Renate Bethge, *Dietrich Bonhoeffer—His Significance for North Americans* (Minneapolis: Augsburg Fortress, 1990), 50.
11. *TF*, 498f.
12. Ibid., 493.
13. Ibid., 495.
14. Ibid., 497 (translation altered).
15. Cf. K.-M. Kodalle, *Dietrich Bonhoeffer. Zur Kritik seiner Theologie* (Gütersloh, 1991), 73f., who sees Bonhoeffer succumb to the *Sogkraft der Volksverbundenheit* of the time (the term seems to be nearly untranslatable).
16. July 1944; *LPP*, 343 (translation altered).
17. *E*, 243 (translation altered).
18. Karl Barth, *Rechtfertigung und Recht*, 2d ed., ThSt 104 (Zurich, 1979), 20. In his *Ethics* Bonhoeffer characterizes the topic as "preparing the way" for the "ultimate" within the "penulitmate" (*E*, 133 f.).
19. Ibid., 38f.
20. Ibid., 40.
21. Ibid., 44.

22. Ibid., 44 f., note 30b.

23. Ibid., 44 f.

24. Cf. Bonhoeffer's letter to G. Leibholz (3 March 1940) illegally smuggled via Switzerland to Oxford, in *GS* 3, 35.

25. Cf. Dietrich Bonhoeffer, *Nachfolge*, in *DBW2*:4, 256-59.

26. Cf. *LPP*, 60: "If anyone wants to learn something of my conception of the duty of Christian obedience towards the authorities, he should read my exposition of Romans 13 in my book *The Cost of Discipleship*. The appeal to subjection to the will and the demands of authority for the sake of Christian conscience has probably seldom been expressed more strongly than there. That is my personal attitude to these questions."

27. No wonder Bonhoeffer's "conservatism" in search of a thological foundation of political resistance provoked Barth's "democratic" suspiciousness. As Barth informed Bonhoeffer via Charlotte von Kirschbaum, he was distrustful of "any attempt to rescue Germany by the means of further 'national' enterprises from its immeasurable misery." Among these "'national' enterprises" he explicitly counted "also the attempts which possibly would be made by the military generals." Cf. Ch. v. Kirschbaum, letter to Bonhoeffer (17 May 1942), in Dietrich Bonhoeffer, *Schweizer Korrespondenz* 1941-42. *Im Gespräch mit Karl Barth*, TheolExh Nr. 214 (Munchen, 1982), 18.

28. *E*, 108.

29. W. Benjamin, *Das Passagen-Werk*, Fragment n. 9 a1, Frankfurt a.M. 1982, 592: "Daß es 'so weiter' geht, *ist* die Kastastrophe."

30. Dietrich Bonhoeffer, "The Church and the Jewish Question" (1933), in *TF*, 139 f. (translation altered).

31. *E*, 114.

32. Eberhard Bethge, "Dietrich Bonhoeffer and the Jews," in *Ethical Responsibility: Bonhoeffer's Legacy to the Churches* (Toronto/Leviston: Edwin Mellen, 1981), 76.

33. Ibid., 80.

34. *E*, 90.

35. Ibid., 89.

36. *TF*, 504.

37. W. A. Visser 't Hooft, "Begegnung mit Dietrich Bonhoeffer," in *Das Zeugnis eines Boten. Zum Gedächtnis von Dietrich Bonhoeffer* (Geneva, 1945), 7. Cf. already Visser 't Hooft's note after his encounter with Bonhoeffer in spring 1941: "Inside the Confessing Church there is a certain difference of conviction with regard to the stand which the Church should take. . . . With regard to the attitude to the war, it is generally recognized among believing Christians that a victory of their government will have the most fateful consequences for the Church. . . . On the other hand, they consider that a defeat of their country would probably mean its end as a nation. Thus many have come to believe that whatever the outcome of it all will be, it will be an evil thing for them. One hears, however, also voices which say that after all the suffering which their country has brought upon others they almost hope for an opportunity to pay the price by suffering themselves" (cited in Eberhard Bethge, *Dietrich Bonhoeffer. Theologie, Christ, Zeitgenosse*, 4th ed. (Munchen), 819.

38. Cf. H. Schönfeld, "Statement by a German Pastor at Stockholm (31 May 1942)," in *GS* 1, 380.

39. Cf. George Bell, "The Church and the Resistance Movement" (1957), in ibid., 405. Cf. also Bell, "The Background of the Hitler Plot" (1945), ibid., 395.

40. Cf. *DB*, 856.

41. *E*, 222.

42. In *Die Kirchliche Dogmatik II/2* Barth circumscribes the concept of "responsibility" as follows: "It is the notion of responsibility, in which we have to recognize the most exact description of the human situation in front of God's sovereign decision. We live in responsibility, i.e. our being, our will, our acting and suffering is—if we know of it or not—a permanent response to God's word spoken to us as commandment. . . . It is a permanent response to this question." Karl Barth, *Die Kirchliche Dogmatik II/2* (1942), 713.

43. *E*, 222.

44. Ibid., 224 (translation altered).

45. Ibid., 225 (translation altered). Cf. 225 f.: "Selflessness in responsibility is so complete that here we may find the fulfillment of Goethe's saying about an acting person being always without conscience."

46. Ibid., 240.

47. Ibid., 241 (translation altered).

48. Ibid., 244 (translation altered).

49. Ibid.

50. *LPP*, 14 (translation altered).

51. Ibid., 299 (translation altered).

52. Cf. the poem "Stations on the Road to Freedom" in ibid., 370 f.

53. Ibid., 361.

54. Ibid., 361 f. (translation altered).

55. Ibid., 369 f. (translation altered).

56. Ibid., 381.

57. Wolf Krötke, "Teilnehmen am Leiden Gottes. Zu Dietrich Bonhoeffers Verständnis eines 'religionslosen Christentums,'" in *450 Jahre Evangelische Theologie in Berlin*, ed. G. Beiser and Chr. Gestrich (Gottingen, 1989), 443: "eine *menschliche Entsprechung* zu Gottes konkretem Dasein in Jesus Christus."

58. Ibid., 444: "Eindruck . . . , daß die Kirche in ihrem weltlichen Leben nach B.s Logik auf das *Reden von Gott* ganz zu verzichten und sich mit dem 'Teilnehmen' (!) 'an den weltlichen Aufgaben des menschlichen Gemeinschaftslebens' zu begnügen habe."

59. Ibid.: "Die Antwort, daß das Reden von Gott und das Gottesverhältnis des Christen ins 'Arkanum' gehöre, bleibt unbefriedigend."

60. Ibid., 445: "Mensliche Taten reden für sich und als solche immer eine zweideutige Sprache, so daß es nicht geraten sein kann, im weltlichen Leben des Christen ein sozusagen für sich selbst sprechendes Christuszeugnis zu sehen."

61. There is no reason to believe that words are less ambiguous then actions. On the other hand, Bonhoeffer was convinced that there are deeds which "interpret themselves."

62. *LPP*, 298.

63. Ibid., 300 (translation altered).

64. Krötke, "Teilnehmen am Leiden Gottes," 452: "wie aus einem solchen Leben heraus nun von Gott auch zu reden ist."

65. Bonhoeffer, "The Nature of the Church," in *TF*, 91: "The primary confession of the Christian before the world is the deed which interprets itself. . . . The deed alone is our confession of faith before the world."

66. William J. Peck, "Response," in Bethge, *Ethical Responsibility*, 100.

67. Bethge, "Dietrich Bonhoeffer and the Jews," 84f.

68. Ibid., 87.

69. Ibid., 84.

70. Elie Wiesel, "Night," translated from the French by Stella Rodway, in *Night. Dawn. The Accident. Three Tales* (New York: Hill and Wang, 1972), 71 f.

71. Cf. W. Meyer, *Unternehmen Sieben. Eine Rettungsaktion für vom Holocaust Bedrohte aus dem Amt Ausland/Abwehr im Oberkommando der Wehrmacht* (Frankfurt a.M., 1933).

72. H. B. Gisevius, letter to Fr. W. Arnold (5 January 1946): "höchst bedenklich, sich durch irgendwelche Einzelaktionen, mochten sie auch noch so gut gemeint sein, von diesem großen Ziele ablenken zu lassen"; cited in ibid., 457 f.

73. Fr. W. Arnold, letter to H. B. Gisevius (9 January 1946): "daß ein gerettetes Menschenleben—ein Sandkorn im Meer der Ermordeten—schwerer als jedes Attentat, und habe es einem noch so hohen Ziele gegolten, wiegt"; cited in ibid., 590 n. 670.

74. H. B. Gisevius; cf. ibid.

75. Eberhard Bethge, sermon on occasion of a memorial service on 20 July 1994 in Berlin, *EvTh* 54 (1994): 486.

Bonhoeffer, Gandhi, and Resistance

Larry Rasmussen

B onhoeffer's favorite prophetic figure in the early 1930s was Mohandas Gandhi. Indeed, he actively sought and eventually secured an invitation to join Gandhi's ashram.[1] It had to be put aside when the call to direct Finkenwalde reordered his priorities.

The invitation from Gandhi was for a trip planned for 1935. In preparation, Bonhoeffer read widely and undertook a study project. Yet this was not the beginning of his fascination with India. The interest was a long-standing one, and different reasons are given on different occasions. At times a simple search for knowledge and wisdom is expressed, as he sought to find a way amidst the turmoil created by Nazism's rise to power in 1932.[2] At other times Bonhoeffer was seeking the gospel in different words and deeds in the face of his conviction that Western Christendom was on its deathbed.[3] Still other times his curiosity was directed toward finding a means of resistance legitimate for Christians. Such a time came in 1934 when Bonhoeffer concerned himself "very intensely with the questions of India,"[4] drew up the study project, and obtained the invitation from Gandhi. He corresponded about these matters with Reinhold Niebuhr, among others. Niebuhr discarded the letters about the study project, but he had recollections that merit recording. He told Bonhoeffer he felt it unwise to study with Gandhi for the following reasons: Gandhi was an ethical liberal with philosophical footings at great distance from those of a sophisticated German Lutheran theologian; furthermore, Nazi Germany was no place to attempt nonviolent resistance. Bonhoeffer had written Niebuhr about learning Gandhi's techniques for possible use in Germany, and Niebuhr replied that Gandhi's success depended upon British political liberalism. Hitler's creed and deeds bore no resemblance to British ways and means. The Nazis would suffer none of the pangs of conscience about using violence that the British did. Organized passive resistance would end in utter failure.[5]

Yet Bonhoeffer was not dissuaded, and he proceeded with plans for the excursion to Gandhi's ashram. While they never materialized, the question of their meaning edges into reflection on Bonhoeffer's own resistance. For the complex of his Christian pacifism and political resistance, what was the reason for the gaze toward the East?

There is a hint in a letter from Bonhoeffer to Niebuhr. The date is July 1934, shortly before the ecumenical meeting in Fanö and thus shortly before Bonhoeffer's strongest statement on pacifism.

After communicating his dissatisfaction with the compromising tack of the opposition churches in the Church Struggle (*Kirchenkampf*), Bonhoeffer writes:

> The dividing line lies elsewhere, namely with the Sermon on the Mount. And now the time has come when the Sermon on the Mount must be brought to mind again on the basis of a partially restored Reformation theology—although, to be sure, with a different understanding of the Sermon than the Reformation's. And precisely at this point the present opposition will divide again. Before we reach that juncture, everything is only preparation. The new church which must come about in Germany will look very different from the present opposition church.
>
> Incidentally I plan to go to India very soon to see what Gandhi knows about these things and to see what needs to be learned there. I am awaiting a letter and invitation from him any day now. Do you perhaps know important people there to which you could recommend me?
>
> I am presently busy with a manuscript which concerns itself with the Sermon on the Mount, etc. [*The Cost of Discipleship*]. I have read the first half of your *Moral Man*, etc. with the greatest of interest and want to finish it during vacation.[6]

This letter, the contents of which are also substantiated in a letter to Erwin Sutz,[7] makes a crucial line clear, even if almost in passing: the Sermon on the Mount is Bonhoeffer's scriptural resource for the church's resistance. *The Cost of Discipleship* is a tract for the times and Gandhi is linked with the Sermon and churchly opposition as a possible instructor. What "Gandhi knows about these things" is the reason for wanting to set out for India at this time.

Next a confession about the change in his life in the early thirties must be noted; the letter is from Bonhoeffer to Elizabeth Zinn, to whom he had been engaged at that time. "The revival of the Church and of the ministry became my supreme concern. . . . I suddenly saw as self-evident the Christian pacifism that I had recently passionately opposed. . . . My calling is quite clear to me. What God will make of it I do not know."[8]

The renewal of the Church and, inseparable from that in the 1930s, the Church's opposition to Nazism within its ranks and without—here is the cause of the thirst for Gandhi's wisdom and ways. The question then is, why Gandhi?

It is doubtful that Bonhoeffer was convinced by Niebuhr's emphasis upon the gap between Gandhi's philosophy and Bonhoeffer's theology. In the 1932 address on self-assertion, Bonhoeffer in effect summarizes *both* Gandhi's law of life and that of the *theologia crucis:* "Through love and suffering we enter the All and overcome it."[9] Jesus Christ is the supreme revelation of this law of life, but the Indian holy man has given it powerful expression in our time.[10] Bonhoeffer, always in quest of "who Jesus Christ is for us today," caught a vision that perhaps here in Gandhi and his India was the gospel in other words and deeds. Even though Bonhoeffer's Christology was intensely ecclesial during these years, Gandhi cut a figure that Bonhoeffer could only align with his own Jesus of agapeic suffering. In the face of Bonhoeffer's conviction that Western Christendom was tossing about in the throes of its own death, the search for the form of Jesus Christ today happened upon especial illumination from the East. Still, the episode remained a search and the flight of a vivid theo-political imagination rather than an embrace, whatever the drawing power of Gandhi's "theology" and his creative resistance to British imperialism.

This tableau of Gandhi as Bonhoeffer's Christology possibly incarnated "for us today" locates the contact point of the deep attraction to Gandhi. But it does not yet fully clarify the tie to resistance alluded to in the letter to Niebuhr and discussed in other correspondence between them. So the question persists: why Gandhi?

Bonhoeffer's intense study and meditation on the Sermon on the Mount had revealed "Christian pacifism . . . to be a matter of course." For Bonhoeffer this meant a radical obedience to the commanding Christ of the Sermon, a Christ whose commands must be concrete within the matrix of unrelenting work for church renewal and uncompromising opposition to Hitler. With such convictions and goals in such a matrix, the quest for genuine "*Christsein*" included the quest for *the political shape of the Sermon on the Mount,* or, stated somewhat differently, *the politically credible articulation of the gospel.* As Herbert Jehle, who shared Bonhoeffer's attraction to India at this time, put it, "His interest in India was to see how the Sermon could be translated into our political action" (meaning that of the Church Struggle participants).[11] And, as *The Cost of Discipleship* makes clear, the credible articulation of the gospel for political life meant nonviolence as the legitimate political course for the disciple. Thus Bonhoeffer's attraction to Gandhi now included the desire to learn the techniques of nonviolent action. The baseline here is from the passion for peace so visible in Bonhoeffer's ecumenical work and the discovery of the Sermon on the Mount to Christian pacifism and a new interest in the methods of a long-intriguing figure.

As the letters to Elisabeth Zinn and to Niebuhr and the conversations with Jehle indicate, Bonhoeffer's obsession with a political, credible articulation of the gospel was focused almost wholly on the Confessing Church's action. The envisioned employment of Gandhi's techniques was not for the solution of German social problems in general. Bonhoeffer does not contemplate recruiting followers from varying ranks of society through some nationwide appeal. Rather, he seeks to arm the Confessing Church for its battles with the state and the *Deutsche Christen* and for its efforts to speak "for the voiceless," the innocent victims of Nazi criminality. The intended appropriation of Gandhi was above all for ecclesial purposes. It was only secondarily for broader civil ones, even when the two could not be wholly delinked under the state church conditions in the Germany of those years.

In this connection, it is helpful to call to mind Bethge's comment, "In clearly distinguishing between the political struggle and the church struggle, Bonhoeffer differed little at this time [London, 1933-35] from his theological friends in Berlin. Active responsibility for the production of a political alternative to the Nazi state, or at least for vigilant observance of the democratic constitution, he saw as being incumbent on those who were eligible by reason of their calling and position in the state machine."[12]

Whatever Bonhoeffer's theory of the state and governance, it did not bother him that the churches' opposition necessarily contained a political dimension. The political *Gestalt* of the Church must truly be Christian, however, and for Bonhoeffer at this time that included the nonviolence of the Jesus of the Sermon on the Mount. Nonviolence was one of the marks of the disciple's way of life—and of death.

Bonhoeffer did not expect the way of nonviolent resistance to bypass suffering. On the contrary, he anticipated encountering physical punishment and, as a letter to Sutz indicates, even felt that battles short of that were preliminary skirmishes only preparatory for bloodier days.[13] "And I believe all Christendom should pray with us that it will be a 'resistance unto death,' and that people will be found to suffer it. Simply suffering— that's what it will be about."[14] In other words, Bonhoeffer was not convinced by Niebuhr's argument that Germany was no place for nonviolent resistance, because he expected no different treatment from the Nazis than Niebuhr did! Suffering would indeed come. But only by risking suffering would evil be overcome.[15] Bonhoeffer's pacifism of the *theologia crucis* was, in any case, not easily dissuaded by political considerations of consequences even when this pacifism sought a viable, concrete, political form for discipleship. In fact, as the Fanö address states clearly, the question of consequences is the Serpent's; it is not the disciple's, who endures all in vicarious, believing suffering.[16] So Gandhi, and not Niebuhr, offered the more probable political articulation of the gospel for the pacifist of the Church Struggle. Nonviolent resistance seemed the political *Gestalt* that "today" conformed to Christ's form in the world.

To summarize: In their correspondence, Niebuhr advised Bonhoeffer against studying with Gandhi because of Gandhi's philosophical and ethical liberalism and because Germany under Hitler showed no prospects whatsoever for politically successful nonviolent resistance. Yet Bonhoeffer was not dissuaded even though he held Niebuhr in high esteem as a Christian ethicist. In asking why Bonhoeffer continued with his plans, we noted that as early as 1932 Bonhoeffer draws strong parallels between the Messiah of suffering love and the Indian "Messiah." Bonhoeffer's constant search for the present form of Jesus Christ came upon this intriguing figure in the East just at the time Bonhoeffer was more and more convinced that Christendom in the West, Christ's traditional form here, was on its deathbed. The christological contact point was so strong that Bonhoeffer was not convinced by Niebuhr that Gandhi's "theology" and forms of resistance were distant from the Jesus of the Sermon on the Mount and the *theologia crucis*. But this christologically rooted fascination with Gandhi was not the end of Bonhoeffer's interest. The self-proclaimed Christian pacifist, grounded scripturally in the Sermon and seeking church renewal, entered the church struggles with all his energies. Now he saw in Gandhi the instructor, not only for the techniques of meditation and the communal life of disciples, but for resistance in the church struggles themselves. Niebuhr's argument about the impracticality of such resistance was simply not on the same plane as Bonhoeffer's theology of faith-filled or agapeic suffering. Bonhoeffer sought the political shape of the Sermon on the Mount in a way that included the nonviolence commanded of disciples by Jesus. So Gandhi again fascinated Bonhoeffer. The two never met—except to die at the hands of the violence they abhorred.

ENDNOTES

1. Gandhi responded to Bonhoeffer's request in a letter of 1 November 1934 as follows:

> Dear friend,
>   I have your letter. If you and your friend have enough money for return passage and can pay your expenses here, say, at the rate of Rs. 100 per month each, you can come whenever you like. The sooner the better so as to get the benefit of such cold weather as we get here. The Rs. 100 per month I have calculated as the outside limit for those who can live simply. It may cost you even half that amount. It all depends upon how the climate here agrees with you.
>   With reference to your desire to share my daily life, I may say that you will be staying with me if I am out of prison and settled in one place when you come. But otherwise, if I am travelling or if I am in prison, you will have to be satisfied with remaining in or near [one] of the institutions that are being constructed under my supervision. If you can stay in any of the institutions I have in mind and if you can live on the simple vegetarian food that these institutions can supply you, you will have nothing to pay for your boarding and lodging.
>
> Yours sincerely,
> [Gandhi]

Text cited from *Dietrich Bonhoeffer London: 1933-35*, Dietrich Bonhoeffer Werke 13 (Chr. Kaiser Verlag, 1994), 213-14.

2. *GS* 1, 32.
3. Ibid., 61.
4. *GS* 2, 182.
5. Interview with Reinhold Niebuhr, New York City, 7 March 1968.
6. Dietrich Bonhoeffer, letter to Reinhold Niebuhr, 13 July 1934.
7. *GS* 1, 39-41.
8. Quoted from *DB*, 155.
9. *"Das Recht auf Selbstbehauptung,"* in *GS* 3, 262.
10. Ibid.
11. Interview with Dr. Herbert Jehle, Charlottesville, Virginia, 1 March 1968.
12. *DB*, 256.
13. *GS* 1, 40.
14. Ibid.
15. *CD*, 157-58.
16. *GS* 1, 216-17.

Bonhoeffer's Exclusivism[1]

Robert Bertram

B urton Nelson, whose friends are legion, is the soul of inclusiveness. Is it any wonder that the Dietrich Bonhoeffer whom Nelson has so winsomely commended for *his* inclusiveness—of the voiceless, the marginated, the reviled—should likewise come off as almost everyone's friend? At least, *post mortem* he does. It takes one like Nelson to spot one like Bonhoeffer. As conveyors of "a wideness in God's mercy," they are two of a kind. That being so, it is all the harder for me to argue, as I now must, that Dietrich Bonhoeffer, for all his inclusiveness and probably because of that, was also and first of all *exclusive* in the extreme, an accuser and rejecter of some of the most estimable people: not only the Nazis and their sympathizers in the church, the *Deutsche Christen*, but eventually fellow Christians in his own confessional movement as well. It is not for nothing that Bonhoeffer was resented as a separatist, virtually a sectarian. To say that must sound peevish, like *Schadenfreude*, in a *festschrift* for Burton Nelson, one of my own most tolerant friends.

It doesn't make things easier that my discovery of Bonhoeffer's exclusiveness can be blamed in part on Burton Nelson himself. For it was he, bless him, who encouraged me to try to make sense of that complicated mare's nest which he personally had almost despaired of untangling, namely, the organizational "flow chart" of German churches in the *Nazizeit*. Flow? It was more like occlusion, reflux, so conflicted were the ecclesiastical crossfires and overlaps. Take one example, the Deutsche Evangelische Kirche. At first the DEK was not really a "church," but rather a voluntary national federation of autonomous, confessionally diverse *Landeskirchen*. So was *that* why the minority who gathered at Barmen to protest were really a splinter group from the DEK: not just because, back home, some of them (not all) had lost control of their own *Landeskirchen* to the new majority in their provinces, the *Deutsche Christen*, but also because the latter were now going national and were co-opting the whole DEK, reshaping it from a voluntary federation into an obligatory *church* for all the *Landeskirchen*?

But if this nationalizing of the provincial churches into a monlithic *Reichskirche* was so objectionable, why did some of the very Barmenites (not all), especially at their second meeting at Dahlem, agree that the DEK *should* become a national church—except that they, these Dahlemite confessors rather than the *Deutsche Christen*, should lay claim to *being* that national church? And why did just these confessors, the "radicals" at Dahlem whose *Landeskirchen* had been "destroyed" by *Deutsche Christen*, now turn on their fellow Barmenites whose *Landeskirchen* had succeeded in withstanding the *Deutsche Christen* "intact"? Why did confessors from the destroyed churches disparage confessors from the intact churches as unworthy of the name "confessing *church*," dismissing them as merely a "confessing *movement*"—and not really "confessing" at all, but merely "confessional"? And so on.

And why, it hurts to ask, was dear Bonhoeffer one of the most exclusivist of these excluders? It is an unhappy duty to have to admit that this bitter intra-church jumble—Nelson was right: it dare not be blinked— puts Bonhoeffer in a distinctly unfavorable light. And for his exclusivism, some would say separatism, he in turn suffered mortifying exclusion. Right within his own confessing movement he did, also among its ecumenical supporters. He laments to friend Bethge that he had become "the most reviled" person within the whole movement. However, I don't wish to minimize his exclusivism, let alone apologize for it. Quite the contrary, I hope to show that this exclusionary thrust in Bonhoeffer's lived theology is intrinsic to his confession. Recall that the Barmen Declaration itself had begun, in its very first thesis, with Christ's stark uniqueness, Christ alone and none other. Any other "revelation," the Barmenites declared, "we reject" as "false doctrine," let the chips fall where they may. Years later, in what becomes a key passage in his *Ethics*, Bonhoeffer reiterates this "exclusive claim of Christ" as basic to his own formative religious "experience" and invokes Jesus' own sweeping antithesis, "Whoever is not for me is against me" (Matthew 12:30).

True, the even more telling part of Bonhoeffer's "experience" was Christ's *inclusiveness*, his "totality." "Whoever is not against us is for us" (Mark 9:40). Indeed, it may be that Bonhoeffer suffered at least as much exclusion from within his own ranks because of whom he *included*, namely, such dubious humanists as his fellow conspirators and, worse yet, his guilty people, "Germany." Unfortunately, this second, wondrously evangelical thrust in Bonhoeffer's confession, his inclusiveness, cannot be accommodated within the space of this present essay. Like a second shoe, it will have to wait for a future writing, God granting time.[1]

Meanwhile, already in this first half of the project, may I suggest that Bonhoeffer's exclusive/inclusive dialectic provides an interpretation of Barmen that is not only intimately his own but also is intentionally *Lutheran*, something he very much wanted to be. How well he succeeded in this intention, whether his Lutheran construals were too Barthian, whether he may even have misread the facts, are all valid question. One fact is clear: those who gathered at Barmen petitioned their own confessional communions (Lutheran, Reformed, United) to respond to their declaration with "responsible interpretations [of it] from their respective confessional positions," and even such a conservative Lutheran critic of Barmen as Heinz Brunotte admits that Lutherans too shirked this request. Bonhoeffer did not. His exclusive/inclusive stance, so I suggest, offers at least one "responsible interpretation" of the Barmen Declaration, especially of its crucial first and second theses, and does that explicitly in terms of Luther's theology of law and gospel and of "two kingdoms." For that, Bonhoeffer paid a price.

REPRIORTIZING THE CHURCH'S AUTHORITIES

It is a "time for confessing," the Formula of Concord calls it, whenever the church is in danger of abdicating its unique authority, the gospel, to an overreaching secular authority. The secular pretender may be the state or the people as a whole or the secular power of the ecclesiastical institution itself or, most likely, all of these together. Against these usurpers the church's confessors must testify, even when the state is immensely popular, as under Hitler, even when the people are a defeated and voiceless nationality, as the Germans were then, even when the church's own leadership sides with this yearning ethnic folk and their revolutionary government. Against these encroaching secular powers the confessing church must testify, not in order to nullify secular authority, but in order rather to restore the church to its own distincitve priorities, where the authority of Christ's gospel is alone supreme and where secular authority, even if that also is Christ's, is strictly subordinate.

In our time, the confessional statement most noted for its reprioritizing of churchly authorities is the Barmen Declaration of 1934. And by now Bonhoeffer has become one of the most visible witnesses for that declaration. That seems at first an unlikely role for him, for he did not attend the synod that issued the declaration. In fact, he seems not to have been invited. Also, he more and more identified with only one wing of the Barmen movement, the so-called Dahlemites, and even with them more and more as their critic. Yet, for all his increasing exclusiveness (and excludedness), Bonhoeffer does provide what the confessors at Barmen explicitly asked for: a "responsible interpretation" of their declaration from their three respective confessional traditions, Lutheran and Reformed and United. As I've mentioned, I see Bonhoeffer as offering such a "responsible interpretation," and, if so, as an intentional Lutheran. For the moment, though, that confessional label is not what is important. What is, is the theological issue at stake, Barmen's own single most contested issue: the reprioritizing of churchly and civil authorities. Granted, just wording the issue that way may already betray a Lutheran bias. In any case, that is the issue which Bonhoeffer's *verantwortliche Interpretation* does seem to address.

Furthermore, as also mentioned, Bonhoeffer's interpretation, by his life no less than by his writings, had the effect of dramatizing the Barmen Declaration's exclusiveness—in Lutheran terminology, its "law." The declaration's opening thesis announces, "Jesus Christ . . . is the one Word of God which we have to hear, . . . trust and obey in life and in death," such that any other "source of [church] proclamation . . . besides this one Word of God" "we reject . . . as false doctrine." Bonhoeffer became notorious for his rejecting, and his rejecting not only of a "doctrine," but of the doctrine's adherents, church people. If one of the chief features of God's "secular" authority is the pronouncing of judgment, critically and if need be excludingly, then Bonhoeffer exemplifies how the church, not only the state, employs this authority too.

Still, in Bonhoeffer's Lutheran tradition, God's exclusivist word, the law, is meant to be only penultimate, not ultimate. Law is that critical authority by which God governs the "old" secular order, where people are to expect fairness, what is their due, but merely that. I say "merely" fairness, for in the end the law, mere fairness, is bad news. Finally, no sinner can stand that much fairness. By contrast, God's ultimate authority, the gospel, is not all that fair by the standards of the law and is actually a whole new kind of fairness. It is the good news of God's cruciform mercy in Christ through the Church, mercy that is not exclusive but indiscriminately inclusive. It is with this gospel inclusivity that Bonhoeffer construed Barmen's second thesis, that "Jesus Christ is the assurance of the forgiveness of all our sins, so . . . also God's mighty claim upon our whole life." In Bonhoeffer's view, this "total" claim of Christ could embrace even the most secular—and sinful!—of secular authorities: compromisers, oath-breakers, deceivers, professional killers. Indeed, Bonhoeffer became one with them, guilt and all—guilt, notice, before God—yet all the while as an agent in Christ's atoning. And for whom, finally? For the severely excluded, the guilty German people. The Church of Christ alone has authority for such scandalous, atoning inclusivity.

Thus, those who are excluded from the Church and from God are not the sinners, as such, but rather those who persist in imposing God's secular, legal authority as ultimate, thereby rendering both kinds of authority, both secular and churchly, impossible. Bonhoeffer attacked this inverting of authorities, this ecclesiastical majoring in minors, not only in the "German Christians" but also in current Lutheran distortions of Luther's theology of "two kingdoms" and, more and more, in what he branded as "enthusiasm" and "ecclesiastical theocracy" in his own confessing movement and, most embarrassingly (for me), in American Protestantism. For Bonhoeffer there is between God's two authorities an undeniable two-ness, which theocrats suppress, as well as an essential inseparability—a "polemical unity." But none of this "unity" between two such opposed authorities can happen except through shared suffering, which is finally Christ's own. A fuller elaboration of all this, as I've said, must await a future opportunity. But for now may I repeat, Bonhoeffer's "responsible interpretation" of Barmen strove to recapture for his times Luther's theology of two kingdoms, law and gospel. And how? By confronting the concrete theological issue at hand, namely, the need to reprioritize the church's two authorities, its authority to exclude and its authority to include. But first, back to the beginnings at Barmen.

FROM BARMEN TO DAHLEM: A NARROWING

The "Theological Declaration on the Present Situation of the German Evangelical Church" (DEK) was a protest by an ad hoc group within DEK. Calling itself a "Confessional Synod," the group protested the takeover of DEK by that church body's powerful new majority, the revolutionary, pro-Nazi German Christians. This impromptu synod was reacting against the new German Christian church leaders at least in part because of their National Socialist ideology of Germanic race and space, "blood and soil." That was at the time the popular new program for ethnic-national liberation.

Yet, at least as offensive as the German Christians' "false doctrine" was their attempt to nationalize DEK, a voluntary federation of church bodies, into a single Reich church. This national church was to be controlled by the state under a Reich bishop appointed by Hitler. That forcible assimilation (*Gleichschaltung*) under the national government threatened DEK's traditionally autonomous territorial churches and church confessions (Lutheran, Reformed, and United), not to mention the Roman Catholic Church.

The mixture of motives behind the Barmen Declaration, motives of doctrine but also of governance, was so complex and volatile that the confessors themselves could not agree on what their declaration entailed practically. Eventually they so differed from one another on the issue of governance, specifically on how the church's governance relates to the state's, that that difference itself assumed the force of doctrinal division among them. That their common foe, the German Christians, were *mis*prioritizing their authorities, the secular over the spiritual, the confessors were well enough agreed. That the most immediate threat, therefore, was to the authority of the churches, on that point too the confessors were united—united, notice, not against the National Socialist state as such, but against the state's lackeys in the church, the German Christians. In fact, the confessors seemed agreed even on this, that the German Christians' politicizing of the church's authority, the gospel of Christ, thereby violated DEK's own constitution. And since that constitution had been incorporated under civil law, the German Christians, ironically, were thus at odds with the civil government itself.

However, beyond the Barmen confessors' common front against the inner-church threat of the German Christians there was far less consensus, indeed there was deepening disagreement, on a practical alternative for relating ecclesial authority to civil. The split between the confessors became increasingly public in the months following Barmen as they had to contend less and less with the inept German Christians and more and more directly with a hostile state. Remember, that state enjoyed broad support among the people (*Volk*) whose churches were thought of as the people's churches (*Volkskirchen*). Already at the time of Barmen, Bonhoeffer, writing from his self-imposed exile in a London pastorate, ventured a prediction. He foresaw that the church conflict (*Kirchenkampf*) that was then festering, a largely internal church-political conflict, would turn out in the long run to have been merely a "preliminary skirimish" (*Vorgeplaenkel*) compared to the second, really decisive "battle for Christendom" (*Kampf um das Christentum*) that still lay ahead.

Just how preliminary Barmen was, how insufficient for the main battle ahead, how internally undecided on the key issue of spiritual and secular authority, becomes apparent only by hindsight. The text of the declaration, taken by itself, looks ever so confessionally solid and forthright, especially in its singular witness to Christ. Its six theses, each with a scriptural lead-in and with a corresponding antithesis, are lean and to the point, as is the important preamble. And doesn't that preamble stress that "as members of Lutheran, Reformed, and United churches we may and must speak with one voice in this matter"? Isn't it also true, as all popular histories of Barmen record, that in the end the synod's almost 140 delegates from all over Protestant Germany adopted the final revision of the declaration unanimously?

Given this highly publicized unanimity, Barmen's publicists have long seemed reluctant to acknowledge the stormy interconfessional differences that churned just beneath Barmen's surface. And, given that defensiveness, the recent historical revisionism that is now setting the record straight must sound to traditional interpreters like sour grapes, like a hermeneutic of suspicion bent on exposing family secrets. That reactionary non sequitur, that dissent is inadmissible except as an admission of schism, is a fallacy which Bonhoeffer himself tried to correct, unsuccessfully.

Does it really detract from the Barmen Declaration that Karl Barth's boast, that he had drafted it virtually alone with no help from the Lutherans on the drafting committee, now turns out to be a gross oversimplification of Barmen's prehistory? If even the late Klaus Scholder, one of the most eminent of *Kirchenkampf* historians, could have been swayed by Barth's claim, isn't it a tribute to Scholder's students that they rescued his posthumous publication from that error, thanks to the latest documentary discoveries by Nicolaisen? The same discoveries reveal that Barth himself, at the last moment before the final draft went before the synod for its vote, consented to rewrite Thesis Five, on church and state, to include the crucial point insisted upon by the Bavarian Lutherans.

The Bavarians' point was, just as a totalitarian state must be condemned for arrogating to itself the function of a church, so must any church be condemned which takes to itself the function of a state. That broad indictment could apply not only to the German Christians, but also to any Barmenites who might hope to coerce Lutherans into a new kind of national "Union" church. (The majority of delegates at Barmen were from the Evangelical Church of the Old Prussian Union, one of the largest Protestant bodies in the world, a corporate giant with a history of state-enforced "Union" between Lutherans and Reformed.) The antithesis that the non-Union Bavarians insisted on adding to Thesis Five could apply also to those Barmenites (and Barthians) whom Bonhoeffer would later reproach as "ecclesiastical theocrats." In any case, it surely does no harm to learn that Hans Asmussen, himself one of the declaration's drafters and the one appointed to explain the text to the assembly, included this acknowledgment in his closing remarks: "In no small way are we indebted to the perseverance of our Bavarian brothers, who did not relent until this new formulation was put forward." Here the minutes record "spirited applause."

In fact, the record shows applause even for a Bavarian Lutheran whom Asmussen had not intended to commend, Werner Elert. Not only was Elert not present at the synod, he soon became one of its sharpest critics, for a while even favoring a third front against both the German Christians and the "Unionists." Politically, he hoped for a church that could identify with the ethnic-political liberation of the people. He has been likened to a liberation theologian, a title that is anachronistic but not altogether untrue. Theologically, his major complaint against the Barmen Declaration was not against its fifth thesis, but against Thesis One—Barth's favorite—and Thesis Two: against the first because it restricts revelation to

Christ and denies to the world any revealed law, and against the second because it then compensates by reducing Christ to a new lawgiver.

As for the declaration's Thesis Five, Elert was amused by how it now contradicts Thesis One: it seems to admit after all, though grudgingly, that beyond "Jesus Christ as the one Word of God," the secular political order is also from God. Elert's critique hardly endeared him to the confessing movement. Scholder calls him "prickly," the selfsame adjective that has been applied to Bonhoeffer. But it is significant that Asmussen's quoting of Elert before the Barmen assembly, obviously pejoratively, could nevertheless earn Elert a hand.

On the other hand, maybe the applause was meant to be *against* Elert. In any case, the evidence continues to show how unresolved were the synod's differences, particularly on the prickly issue of secular and spiritual authority. True, in the end the confessors did vote for the declaration "with one voice." Even that, however, they did with a portentous proviso: that the declaration be transmitted to the three different confessional bodies "for the purpose of providing responsible interpretations from their *respective confessional traditions.*" Bonhoeffer's confessional tradition was Lutheran, but he was a Lutheran in the Church of the Old Prussian Union. That dual role would impair his credibility in both communions.

The proviso calling for separate "interpretations" does not portend an intra-Barmen conflict. But that conflict was not only interconfessional, Reformed versus Lutheran versus Union. No, the ensuing divisions within the "Confessing Church" (*Bekennende Kirche*), as the confessional movement came to be called, stemmed also from another difference. The member churches represented at Barmen were suffering quite different fates back home. The German Christians' takeover had succeeded in some territorial churches, for instance those of the Old Prussian Union, more than in others, for instance Bavaria and Wuerttemberg, whose established Lutheran churches were successfully frustrating the German Christian takeover and so were still more or less "intact."

The "destroyed" churches, by contrast with the intact ones, were having to create emergency administrations and funding and networks of their own in defiance of their new German Christian, state-supported overlords. Suddenly cut off from the traditional church tax (*Kirchensteuer*) for pastors' salaries, publication, and theological education, and hard pressed by antagonistic civil governments, these destroyed churches more and more believed that their hard-won independence entitled them alone to be the "Confessing *Church.*" By contrast, their fellow confessors in the intact churches were scorned for being more "privileged" because they were still "legal" (though barely) in their home territories. These intact churches were therefore thought to be ecclesially inferior and at best a "confessing *movement*" or "*front*," or, worse yet, not even a "confess*ing*" but merely a "confess*ional*" front.

The intactness of the intact churches irked not only their fellow confessors in the destroyed churches, but also, of course, the frustrated German Christians in those intact territories, like Bavaria and Wuerttemberg. There the *confessing* churches were still the legally *established* churches, not yet forced underground as "free" churches to maintain their confessional status. But there also, with covert support from Hitler, the German Christians were intensifying their efforts to destroy these confessing churches as well by forcing them into the one Reich church, so far unsuccessfully. For instance, one September evening after the Barmen synod, the German Christians of Bavaria chose Nuremberg, a hotbed of Nazi partisanship, for a mass demonstration in the city's Adolf Hitler Platz. They were calling for the removal of the Lutheran bishop of Bavaria, Hans Meiser, whom they denounced as a leader of the confessing movement.

On that same evening in Nuremberg, church people loyal to Bishop Meiser, having been denied a permit for a counterdemonstration, crowded instead into their churches—three churches full. Right outside were the German Christians and their crowds, fortified by the uniformed SA. Inside the three churches, each congregation awaited its turn for the bishop to arrive and preach. An eyewitness recounts the following:

> From around 6:30 P.M. until 11:30 P.M. people sat and stood in the Lorenzkirche—the old hymns of faith resounded throughout the nave and rang out so loudly that the doors had to be shut by the police. . . . Nuremberg has experienced a church revival. Christ is our Lord. He is confessed on the streets, in the houses around, in bakers' and butchers' shops. We stand firmly together.

The bishop's supporters included Party members as well as non-Party members, unaware as yet of the contradiction. But the Party leadership was getting the message: if people had to choose, they "would not hesitate to turn their backs on the Party."

The German Christians and their Reich church administration tightened the screws. Next they tried firing Bishop Meiser, and, failing that, they brought in the political police to put him under house arrest and a ban of silence. He responded with a public declaration: "We summon our pastors and communities to offer no obedience to this church government." The state president of Bavaria, who was descended upon by his own Party members warning him that 95 percent of the farmers from their region supported Meiser, concluded that they "are not afraid of any force and would prefer to have themselves branded as martyrs." "All this," says Scholder, "was without doubt one of the . . . most remarkable pro-test demonstrations ever experienced in the Third Reich." At about the same time, in the neighboring state of Wuerttemberg, a similar attempt was made to depose the Lutheran bishop there, Theophil Wurm, for his leadership in the confessing movement. As in Bavaria, the Wuerttemberger bishop and his pastors and congregations prevailed intact, but again by recourse to what amounted to civil disobedience.

Quickly a second confessional synod convened, a sequel to Barmen, this time in the Berlin suburb of Dahlem. With Bishops Meiser and Wurm under house arrest at the time, it was reasonable for the delegates to assume that *all* the confessing churches, even the intact ones in Bavaria and Wuerttemberg, had now finally been destroyed. That mistaken as-sumption (for events soon disproved it) was all that the so-called radical minority at the Dahlem synod needed to get their way. For at that junc-ture it did seem that at any moment the Hitler government would offi-cially incor-porate the Reich church into the Reich government, and all terrirorial churches with it, including the heretofore intact ones. Little did anyone guess that within days the Bavarian and Wuerttemberger popu-lace would prevail after all, that their two bishops would be released and even invited for a meeting with the Fuehrer, and that the German Chris-tians would be discredited along with their Reich bishop and any pros-pect of a Reich church.

But meanwhile at Dahlem, the synod delegates (those who stayed) voted, far from unanimously, that the Confessing Church was announc-ing an "emergency" church law, in effect a countertakeover of DEK re-placing the German Christians and instead putting the confessors in charge. All cooperation with the German Christians was forthwith to be severed. One incredulous delegate asked how such a confessors' takeover could make sense, since in his entire home territory of Thuringia all the churches together "have only a thousand members in the Confessing Commu-nity." Pastor Martin Niemoeller, on the other hand, insisted that there not even be joint Scripture study with the German Christians. In the end it was voices like Niemoeller's, from the United Church, and Barth's, from the Reformed, that prevailed at Dahlem. And it was into hands like theirs, the new Council of Brethren and its inner Council of Six, that the Dahlem synod now entrusted the leadership of the Confessing Church—and thus, presumably, of the true DEK. But this was done without strong consensus on the part of the Dahlem delegates.

By November 1934, hardly two weeks after Dahlem, the synod's fragile consensus began to come apart openly, specifically over the synod's sharp separation from German Christians and from the Reich church. In opposition to this exclusivist claim that Dahlem and its Council of Breth-ren must monopolize the leadership of DEK, other veterans of Dahlem now created instead the "First Provisional Church Government of DEK." This temporary, pluralist approach to governance met the regulations of the Reich church, yet also represented those upstart Lutheran churches like Bavaria and Wuerttemberg which meanwhile had prevailed intact. Indeed, the idea of the Provisional Church Government was officially negotiated with the state by none other than the president of the Council of Six and was supported by a majority of the Council of Brethren despite Niemoeller's and Barth's (temporary) resignations. Bonhoeffer sided emphatically with Niemoeller, who was the Bonhoeffer family's unofficial pastor in Berlin, and with Barth, to whose theological influence Bonhoeffer owed much. One wonders whether Bonhoeffer, who again had not been present at Dahlem, knew how divided the opinion at that synod had actually been.

But weren't Niemoeller and Barth right? Didn't this new compromise, the First Provisional Church Government, violate Section III of Dahlem's Message, "that in matters of the church's . . . teaching and order, the church" was "called to judge and decide alone, regardless of the state's right of supervision"? No doubt. On the other hand, the same Dahlem Message, Section IV, did defer to the Reich government asking it to recognize the church's right to self-determination. It was clear that the church wanted recognition by the secular authorities. Should the church want that? If the state acceded to the message's demands, fine. But if not, then what? How important is it for the church to have legal title, if only for its independence? Yet must it win its independence at the cost of becoming exclusive and sectarian, no longer a church of the people? But is a church of the people also of the people's political aspiration? How inconclusive Barmen had been on these questions, for all of its apparent "unanimity," Dahlem was now exposing by its glaring lack of unanimity.

THE CHURCH'S AUTHORITY TO EXCLUDE, BUT WHOM? WHOM ALL?

Enter Bonhoeffer, specifically Bonhoeffer the "Dahlemite," the "radical," the "legalist," the "sectarian"—in a word, the exclusivist. For eventually all these epithets were applied to him, and all in connection with his interpretation of Barmen—and Dahlem. That is what made him a Dahlemite: he insisted on interpreting Barmen strictly *in light of Dahlem*. No one could honestly make Barmen's confession of faith, Bonhoeffer claimed, unless they complied with Dahlem's prescriptions for church governance. And the one church governance that was binding was Dahlem's Council of Brethren, not the post-Dahlem First Provisional Church Government, which Bonhoeffer condemned as a betrayal and a capitulation to state interference. Even though he had attended neither synod at Barmen or Dahlem, nor was his absence widely lamented, he esteemed Barmen's

Declaration and, as its organizational follow-through, Dahlem's Message as inviolable. Together they were for him definitive of the authentic Confessing Church and, at its boundaries, of who could and could not be saved.

Maybe Bonhoeffer would have acknowledged, as recent critics of Dahlem have, that "the narrow principles of Dahlem . . . were accepted fully within the Confessing Church only by a small minority." Certainly Bonhoeffer counted himself in that minority. But just as certainly, he would not have conceded a criticism like Scholder's. Though Scholder could admire the resolutions that Dahlem passed, he objected to how they were legalistically universalized. "It was wrong to turn these resolutions, born out of an emergency situation, into a law for all churches and communities [even the Bavarian and Wuerttemberger Lutherans] without distinction, [as] the basis on which it was decided whether or not they belonged to the Confessing Church." For only a few days later, Scholder observed, the resolutions would have been stated differently, the Lutheran bishops of southern Germany would have been able to cooperate, and Dahlem "would have been understood everywhere as the synod of the whole Confessing Church and not just . . . of its radical wing." Bonhoeffer belonged to that "radical wing."

Why did he? Why, on what confessional grounds, could he defend such exclusion of even his fellow confessors? It wasn't only that they were perpetrating injustice. Who wasn't? And since when is the church to be restricted only to the just? The breaking point, I am suggesting, came when injustices that in mercy might have been borne with in hopes of correcting them hardened instead into *de facto* church policy, when the evangelical patience of the Christian community came to be extorted by law, enforceable law, in fact civil law. Whether in fact that happened, or to what extent it did, is open to historical inquiry. It is the confessional issue at stake which I wish to pursue here. To do that, we follow Bonhoeffer to Finkenwalde in Pomerania, where he learned new ways of being Lutheran, some of which would endear him to almost no one.

It was less than a year after Barmen when Bonhoeffer returned to northern Germany from his London exile to become director of a seminary at Finkenwalde on the Baltic coast. This was one of five underground seminaries newly opened by the Confessing Church of the Old Prussian Union. They were the work of the new Brotherhood Councils of Dahlem, opposition seminaries to the established Old Prussian Union faculties now controlled by German Christians.

There was, of course, no need of such "illegal" seminaries in the Lutheran intact churches, where the confessing movement still controlled official theological education, however precariously. This created additional friction between intact and destroyed churches, all still within the same larger confessing movement. The seminaries of the destroyed churches disdained the intact ones as "privileged" and not really "church." The intact faculties accused the destroyed ones of "pharisaism" and "legalism." That made life more miserable for both camps. Also it obscured to each of them the sacrifices and bravery of the other, though both of them were resisting a common enemy of the gospel.

Fortunately, Bonhoeffer's seminary at Finkenwalde has been spared much of that undeserved obscurity. Thanks to the reporting by its most eloquent spokeperson, Eberhard Bethge, Bonhoeffer's student and best friend and biographer, we know of the awesome Christian heroism of the Finkenwalde community. Not only that, it was remarkable for its accomplishments in pastoral formation under very straitened conditions, and all within the two and a half short years before it was closed by the Gestapo. The record of Finkenwalde, I think, is itself part of Bonhoeffer's "responsible interpretation" of Barmen. It may even be that Finkenwalde could not have made the Barmen witness it did, especially on the reprioritizing of authorities, had it not been for Bonhoeffer's alleged legalism, objectionable though that also may have been.

Bonhoeffer's work at Finkenwalde was not made easier by the fact that it was located in Pomerania—not easier, but perhaps more theologically responsible. Pomerania was a church province of the Old Prussian Union which, in protest against the German Christian takeover there, had duly mounted its own "Dahlemite" counter-church government through a provincial Council of Brethren. However, the Pomeranian confessors still prided themselves on their Lutheranism. For Lutheran Bonhoeffer, who did the same, that by itself would have been no problem. The trouble was, these Pomeranian fellow confessors of his felt a close affinity with the Lutherans in the intact church of Bavaria, specifically with Bavarian Lutheran theologians on the faculty at Erlangen like Althaus and Elert. As Bethge reports, these "two theologians' criticism that the Barmen theses had erred in following Barth's rejection of 'original revelation' in creation and history had met with a large measure of agreement here." Consequently, it was hard to enforce the measures legislated by Barmen and Dahlem, at least in any Barthian understanding of them. The result for Bonhoeffer was that, in that Lutheran context, he was made to appear "isolated and radical."

At the same time, when it came to the question of who was being more Lutheran, Bonhoeffer was not about to take a backseat, even at the point where his Lutheran critics thought him most radical. For him it was anything but a matter of indifference whether his position did justice to Luther's Reformation and the Lutheran confessions. On the contrary, he consistently invoked that tradition in his own support against "the so-called Lutherans." Aggressively he accepted the same confessional accountabilities as did those Lutherans who so differed from him on church-political issues. But were he and they really all that different theologically?

The Lutheranism of the Finkenwalde Bonhoeffer extended not only to his Christology and his theology of the Lord's Supper, where his Lutheranism is sometimes acknowledged by his followers today, though not always enthusiastically. More and more his Lutheranism surfaced also on those very issues which most sharply divided Lutherans from Barthians: law and gospel, two kingdoms, secular and spiritual authorities. At Finkenwalde Bonhoeffer was being distanced both from Lutherans and, more and more, from Barthians as well. Because of his Lutheranism? Not altogether for that reason, certainly. But that hypothesis—the Lutheran reason for his alleged legalism and sectarianism—does bear investigating. Bethge reports that at Finkenwalde, "study was centered almost wholly on the confessional writings," which "at that time aroused . . . passionate interest," and that "with each term more and more time was allocated to these classes than to any other subject." One of the confessional themes that aroused such interest was the theme of "adiaphora." In the Lutheran confessional writings the classical discussion of adiaphora appears in the Formula of Concord of 1577, specifically its tenth article. More on this later. For now, let it be noted that it was first at Finkenwalde that the Formula of Concord became virtually a "discovery" for Bonhoeffer, and also for his ordinands. In his later courses at Finkenwalde it was to become a "predominant theme." "He loved the *Formula Concordiae*." His personal copy abounds in underlines and marginal notes.

One passage in the Formula of Concord, Article Ten, must have struck Bonhoeffer as especially compatible. He emphasizes it with double marking: "To dissent from the consensus of so many nations and to be called schismatics is a serious matter. But divine authority commands us all not to be associated with and not to support impiety and unjust cruelty." "To dissent" to the point of being called "schismatic" was an agony Bonhoeffer was learning firsthand, and he was finding confessional warrant for the experience in the Lutheran declaration on adiaphora.

What earned him such reproaches as "schismatic" and "leaglist" was an article he published in the summer of 1936 on the subject of church fellowship. The article included this offending sentence of his: "Whoever knowingly separates himself from the Confessing Church in Germany separates himself from salvation." That scandalous quotation, Bethge reports, "spread like wildfire throughout the German churches." In the retelling it was soon caricatured into "Those without a Red Card [membership card in the Confessing Church] won't go to heaven." Within months Bonhoeffer was, as he said, "the most reviled man of our persuasion."

What had occasioned Bonhoeffer's provocative article, first presented as lectures to his Finkenwalde students, was the worsening situation right within his own Confessing Church. This church was dwindling not only in financial support and in numbers and in pastorates for its "illegal" ordinands, but also in its spiritual resolve to remain separate. The more credible alternative even for some members of the Councils of Brethren, yes, even for ordinands from Finkenwalde, was to reconsider their former exclusiveness and to join forces instead with the so-called Church Committees. These committees were now the latest attempt to salvage the leadership of DEK by accommodating both the concerns of the National Church and the concerns of the confessing movement. Enviably, the intact churches of Bavaria, Wuerttemberg, Baden, and Hanover managed to stay clear of these committees. The destroyed churches in the Old Prussian Union, like Pomerania, did not. Regardless, for Bonhoeffer it was the quite separate, dwindling Confessing Church that remained the only true church of Christ in Germany, from which members "separated" (his word) only on pain of their damnation.

One need not be naïve to grant that Bonhoeffer, whether or not he was right, was also misunderstood. Also there may be reason to believe that he was misinformed, for example, about how united (rather, disunited) the decision at Dahlem had actually been. Hence he may have been wrong about its authority as a binding council of the church united by the Holy Spirit. Moreover, he may have been mistaken about how "privileged" the intact churches really were, thus underestimating their confessorhood. In other words, he may have had his facts wrong about the exact scope of the "Confessing Church," and in that factual respect may himself have "separated" from the authentic Confessing Church those who had not separated themselves. That may or may not make him schismatic. It still need not follow, however, that his exclusionary statement, "Whoever knowingly separates himself from 'the Confessing Church' in Germany separates himself from salvation," was false or legalistic in its confessional intention. On the contrary, it was Bonhoeffer's intention thereby to *combat* legalism, and in so many words.

Those who misunderstood Bonhoeffer's intention legalistically included not only his detractors, but his defenders, whom he tried to disabuse or, when that failed, had to disclaim. These sympathizers with Bonhoeffer, right within the Confessing Church, even within the Finkenwalde community, imported their own legalistic preconceptions into his intention, though they did so well-meaningly. Bethge reports that the Finkenwalde seminarians were at first hard pressed to defend their teacher's controversial article, and themselves had to learn that in that article his foremost accent had in fact been a "*denial* of the whole legalistic view [of the] church," namely, the view "that the Church was to set her own boundaries and determine their extent."

Bonhoeffer's point had been quite the opposite. The church, he argued, was now having boundaries set *for* her, "drawn against her from outside," for instance, when seminarians were pressured by "outsiders" to withdraw from the Finkenwalde community. Once that happened, must not these outsiders' self-imposed boundaries be recognized as the real boundaries they then became, for those outsiders? Then the self-imposed boundaries became barriers, not to membership in some human organization, but to the body of Christ, barriers to Christ himself? That is the way Scholder, too, read Bonhoeffer's intention: he "began from the gospel call to salvation which did not itself set limits, but came up against limits." Yet Scholder also saw that Bonhoeffer's colleagues in the Confessing Church did not always read matters the same way: "The claim of the Confessing Church to be the sole church of Jesus Christ hardened into a confessional orthodoxy which inevitably put [an end] to any evangelical freedom." *That* sort of exclusiveness, as Bonhoeffer himself would later say, is the direct antithesis of evangelical freedom. It is the "timid impulse to draw narrow limits." Bonhoeffer, probably not altogether without fault of his own, incurred the charge of legalism by his very efforts to the contrary, to guard the church against legalism and for freedom.

Terms like *legalism* and *freedom*, premised as they are upon more basic terms like *law* and *gospel*, return us to the Formula of Concord, which had become a preoccupation of Bonhoeffer's at Finkenwalde. The Formula's tenth article, as we noted, purportedly deals with the subject of adiaphora, judging from the title. But only purportedly, for in fact the article deals with those circumstances when adiaphora are *not* adiaphora any longer. Ordinarily in the church there are always adiaphora, those controversial practices and teachings about which the members of the community differ and, if God's word is not being compromised, should be free to differ. The practices in question might even be offensive to some members, but if these members are "the strong," as Paul calls them, they ought to use their strength to bear with the failings of "the weak," rather than flaunt their freedom and thereby pressure "the weak" to conform against their own convictions.

However—and this is the point of Article Ten—there are limits to such adiaphoral freedom. There are times when the weak ones exploit this freedom as a subterfuge for forcing their "weak" ways upon the community, thus blackmailing the strong and in fact perverting Christian freedom into bondage. That is exactly what Bonhoeffer saw happening in the congregations where a strong pro-German spirit prevailed, by itself understandable, but where the pastor was pressured to leave because he was "non-Aryan." Even that, so Bonhoeffer told his seminarians, *might* be a conceivable course of action, however regrettable. But it dare not be allowed if the gospel's freedom was being breached. Presumably a similar breach occurred when Finkenwaldians, who were vulnerable to begin with, were being subjected to superior pressure from "the weak," namely the Church Committees. Especially was that happening when the Church Committees, which might have been tolerable in theory, seemed more and more to be harboring the very state which, as Bonhoeffer foresaw, was Antichrist itself, the determined enemy of Christendom.

When such a time comes, says the Formula of Concord X, that is a "time for confessing." For then the freedom of the gospel has been twisted into its opposite: legalistic coercion and the enslavement of consciences, the very torment which Bonhoeffer was witnessing in his seminarians and, beyond them, in Christian Germany generally. Following the cue of the Formula, Bonhoeffer scribbles in the margin, "The DCs' [German Christians'] policy on the Jews is false doctrine"—not merely sin, a violation of God's law, but heresy against the gospel. Another marginal note reads, "By its incursion into adiaphora what is being inserted is a legalistic [*gesetzliches*] understanding"—that is, of the gospel.

At such times, says the Formula, "we should not yield to adversaries even in matters of indifference, nor should we tolerate" them. That is the language not of gospel inclusivity but of judgment, which the Church's authority also obliges it to pronounce. This exclusionary authority is not unique to the Church, but, even though it contrasts with the gospel, it is essential to the Church. "It is written, 'For freedom Christ has set us free; stand fast therefore, and do not submit again to a yoke of slavery' (Gal. 5:1)." Paul's gospel metaphor of the freed slave's right to rebel is drawn from civil law, but he employs the metaphor in the service of that very different, nonlegal authority, the gospel of freedom, which now takes precedence. Exclusion ("do not submit again") serves the higher, prior authority of inclusion ("Christ has set free" even us slaves).

Employing Luther's two-kingdoms terminology, Bonhoeffer summarizes the exclusionary thrust of his article on church fellowship: the church "will be doing alien work [law] in order to carry out more efficiently its proper task [gospel]." But the law, "alien" as it may be to the gospel, is not legalism, which is a distortion *both* of law and of gospel. Granted, an Erlanger Lutheran like Elert might not at all have agreed with how Bonhoeffer *applied* this reprioritizing of authorities in the situation at hand. Still, with the reprioritizing itself he could—or should— scarcely have agreed more, particularly in view of its source in that "Gnesio-Lutheran" symbol, the Formula of Concord X.

But Bonhoeffer's article that reflects this reprioritizing of churchly authorities, the authority of gospel as "proper" over the authority of law as "alien," was after all an article only on *church* fellowship. It dealt merely with *intra-ecclesial* reprioritizing. What does that have to do with the church's external relation to the *state*? Does it follow from the reprioritizing of the gospel over law that the church takes priority over the state? That question will have to wait for a future essay, one that explores in some depth how Bonhoeffer understood that other, very different authority of the church, its authority for *inclusion*, the "*total* claim of Christ." By way of anticipation we may say this much: when a state presumes to have *that* kind of authority, when it pretends to be "totalitarian," it is no longer the state, but Antichrist. But then, when that does happen, who *is* the state in the interim? Not the church, certainly. But then who? Good question. For that involves not just the "preliminary skirmish" of the *Church* Struggle, but the very "Struggle for Christendom" itself. More on that later.

In the meantime, lest we be misunderstood to be minimizing the importance of the *Kirchenkampf*, a reminder is in order. As late as 1942 Bonhoeffer, by then a member of a political plot against Hitler, was asked by members of another plot, "The Freiburg Group," to project a plan for the Protestant church of Germany should it survive the war. Even at that late date, when church life in Germany was nearing its nadir and the state's hostility to Christianity was by then undisguised, Bonhoeffer wrote, "It is possible to settle the relations between state and church only if the *Kirchenkampf* is settled." However true it may have been that the struggle *within* the church to reprioritize its own authorities was merely a *Vorgeplaenkel* compared to its coming great conflict with the Nazi state, for Bonhoeffer the "preliminary skirmish" still came first.

ENDNOTE

1. Since this essay is the first half of a longer work in progress, no reference notes have been incorporated. I offer this essay in its present form as a tribute to Burton Nelson, who has done similar research in the area of Dietrich Bonhoeffer and the German Church Struggle.

BONHOEFFER'S SPIRITUALITY

Dietrich Bonhoeffer and Christian Spirituality

John D. Godsey

T he focus of this essay is on the life and thought of Dietrich Bonhoeffer, a German Lutheran theologian who was put to death by
the Nazis at age thirty-nine because of his involvement in the
resistance movement against Hitler. The witness of his life and the power
of his writings have made him one of the church's most influential theologians and spiritual leaders of the latter half of the twentieth century.

My own interest in Bonhoeffer began during my last year in seminary, when I read an abridged edition of his book *The Cost of Discipleship*,
the first of his writings to be translated into English. His powerful testimony to what it means to be a disciple of Jesus Christ challenged me to
think more deeply about my own spiritual journey, and I ended up writing my doctoral dissertation on *The Theology of Dietrich Bonhoeffer* at the
University of Basel in Switzerland. From then to the present day I have
read and reread and wrestled with the writings of Bonhoeffer, and through
numerous seminars have helped others to do the same. Before we move
to our consideration of Bonhoeffer's understanding of Christian spirituality, I want to present a brief sketch of his life.

BONHOEFFER'S LIFE

Dietrich Bonhoeffer and his twin sister, Sabine, were born in Breslau,
Germany, on February 4, 1906, the sixth and seventh of the eight children of a prominent physician and his wife. In 1912 the family moved to
Berlin, where the father was appointed professor of neurology and psychiatry at the University of Berlin. Dietrich was reared in this educated,
cultured family, which embodied the best of the German liberal tradition

that prized personal integrity and civic duty. In his own person he combined the analytical objectivity of his father and the piety and practical realism of his mother. He was a man who loved life and rejoiced in human ties and human pleasures, in home and friendship, in literature, music, and art. He was an accomplished pianist and a better-than-average tennis player, and because of his charm, his humor, his character, and his gifts, he was a man in whose company it was a delight to be.

When at age fourteen he decided to study theology and become a minister, his brothers and sisters tried to dissuade him, arguing that the church was a poor, feeble, *petit bourgeois* institution. He replied, "In that case, I shall reform it." He studied first at Tübingen and then in Berlin, where he completed his doctoral dissertation on *The Communion of Saints* at age twenty-one. For a year he served as vicar in a German-speaking congregation in Barcelona, Spain, after which he returned to Berlin and wrote his habilitation dissertation, *Act and Being*. The school year 1930-31 was spent as a Sloan Fellow at Union Theological Seminary in New York City, and in the fall of 1931, after a short sojourn in Bonn to hear Karl Barth, he began lecturing in systematic theology at Berlin. At the same time, he became chaplain to students at a technical college and was appointed youth secretary of the World Alliance for Promoting Friendship through the Churches, an ecumenical organization that ultimately merged with the Life and Work movement.

After Adolf Hitler became chancellor of the Third Reich in 1933, Bonhoeffer joined in founding the Confessing Church, which opposed the Nazi attempt to co-opt the church and to impose upon it its racial policies. When his own Church of the Old Prussian Union accepted the so-called Aryan Clause, which prohibited anyone of "Jewish" blood to hold office in the church, he left Germany in protest and accepted the pastorate of two German-speaking congregations in London. From there he worked for the Confessing Church by interpreting to the outside world what was happening in Germany. In 1935 he was called back to Germany by the Confessing Church to establish and direct a seminary in Pomerania for its ministerial candidates. During this period of teaching at the Finkenwalde seminary he wrote *The Cost of Discipleship*. After the seminary was closed by the Gestapo in 1937, he wrote *Life Together*.

Through the auspices of Reinhold Niebuhr, Bonhoeffer was able to leave Germany in the summer of 1939 and return to New York, where he was to lecture at Union. He remained a little over a month, but when he realized that war was imminent, he decided to go back to his homeland in order to live through the experience with his people. Soon thereafter he joined the resistance movement against Hitler and was employed as a civilian by the Abwehr, the military intelligence agency whose leaders were at the heart of the resistance. In January 1943 he became engaged to Maria von Wedemeyer, the daughter of a family he had known in Pomerania.

Bonhoeffer was arrested by the Gestapo on 5 April 1943 and was incarcerated at Tegel Military Prison in Berlin. In September 1944 he was transferred to the Gestapo prison in the Prinz Albrecht Strasse, in February 1945 he was moved to Buchenwald, and finally on 9 April 1945 he was hanged at the Flossenburg Concentration Camp in Bavaria. His brother Klaus and two brothers-in-law, Hans von Dohnanyi and Rudiger Schleicher, were also put to death as conspirators. His unfinished *Ethics* and *Letters and Papers from Prison* were published posthumously.

This outline of Bonhoeffer's life is all too brief. It does not do justice to the variety and richness of his experience, but it makes clear that he lived through and, to some extent, was shaped by one of the most troubled periods in twentieth-century history, namely, that which encompasses the rise of National Socialism in Germany, the German Church Struggle of the 1930s, the Holocaust, and the Second World War.

SPIRITUALITY DEFINED

Now to the question of spirituality. First of all, what is it? As I understand it—I think I am reflecting Bonhoeffer's view—Christian spirituality has to do with the formation of the self by the Spirit of God into the likeness of Jesus Christ, who in his own person is the true and real human being. It is God's Spirit encountering and transforming our sinful selves into the selves we were meant to be *Coram Deo*, before God. Thus, spirituality has to do with our identity, with who we are at the deepest level of our being, with that self that we call "spirit" or "soul," which cannot be simply identified with either our body or our mind, but incorporates and vitalizes and unifies both into the individual, total persons we indeed are. It is the "I" when I say "I am." But it is an "I" that even we never wholly discern. Only God knows us as we truly are.

The paradoxical truth about ourselves, however, is that the "I" that we are is never simply the "I" that we ourselves form. We become who we are through our encounter with others. We are *social selves* whose identity is formed by allowing others to enter into our space and, so to speak, become part of us. Bonhoeffer made this clear in his dissertation, *Sanctorum Communio* (or *The Communion of Saints*). One becomes a person, he argued, when the "I" is confronted by the "Thou" of another that places an ethical demand upon the "I" to respond. That is, we humans are created by God to be relational beings, related to God and to other human beings and called to respond to "the other" in a free, responsible way.

Bonhoeffer emphasized this basic relatedness and this "freedom for others" in his early academic lectures on Genesis 1-3, published later in a book entitled *Creation and Fall.* In the passage (1:26 f.) depicting humans' being created in the "image of God," Bonhoeffer says this means that we are created to be free and that freedom means "being free for the other." Creature is related to creature: "Male and female God created them." To live in a free, loving relationship with an "other" is to live in the likeness of God, whose inner trinitarian relationship of love is graciously extended in creating and loving the world in and through Jesus Christ.

The problem with us humans, according to Bonhoeffer, is the problem of *sin*. And what is sin? Sin is that egocentric condition that results from the abuse of our God-given freedom. Instead of using our freedom to live for God and our neighbors, we mysteriously and inexplicably turn away and choose to live for ourselves. We become self-centered rather than God-centered, and that self-centeredness becomes a power that reigns over all our thinking and all our doing. Sin corrupts the very heart of our being. Or, as Luther put it, sin is "the heart turned in upon itself" (*cor incurvatum in se*).

The results of sin against God, who has created us to live in communion and commanded us to freely love the other, are tragically fatal. As Bonhoeffer saw it, the sinner is no longer *imago Dei*, in the image of God, but becomes *sicut Deus*, "like God"—the one who lives out of himself or herself, creates his or her own life, is his or her own creator, his or her own judge of good and evil. In self-centered freedom, sinners take charge of their own lives and end up in bondage to self-will. The self rules, and estrangement results—estrangement from God, from other human beings, and even from one's true self. Since God is the only source of life, the sinner ends up trying to live without the requisite for life. The result can only be death: death to the spirit, death to the true self. So we are "dead men walking"—to quote the movie title—walking in an eerie masquerade on a road that leads nowhere but to death.

Given this fateful scenario, which Bonhoeffer in his dissertations and early teaching elaborated so forthrightly, is there any hope for humankind? Is it possible to loosen the ties of corrupting self-love and regain the freedom to be the persons God meant us to be, persons who love with and for others in a peaceful and righteous community? By ourselves, given our proclivities, it is not possible, but *with God* all things are possible. And we now arrive at the heart of Bonhoeffer's theology.

Ecce homo! Behold the man! Not just any human being, but the human being of God's own choosing: the Son, the Word of God who became flesh, the One who humbled himself and became like us in order that we might become like him, the One who makes it possible for sinners who have forfeited their true selves to have their selves redeemed and reconstructed into what God desires them to be.

I know of no theologian whose thought is any more Christ-centered than Bonhoeffer's. He agreed with Luther, who pointed to Jesus and declared, "This man is God for me." In his lectures on Christology during the summer semester of 1933, the summer after Hitler came to power and before Bonhoeffer left Berlin for a London pastorate, he told his students that the proper question concerning Christ is "Who?" not "How?" That is, one begins by asking *who* it is that confronts us *today* in the word of the church and calls us to faith, not with the insoluble and abstract question of *how* Jesus Christ can be both God and man, two natures in one person.

This living Christ *is* the historical Jesus: the incarnate, crucified, and resurrected one. In Jesus Christ the world is reconciled with God. The *incarnation* means that God loves the whole world, all human beings without exception, and *lived* that love as a genuine human being. The *crucifixion* declares God's judgment on human sin; God in Jesus bears the guilt and shame and death that sinful humankind deserves in order to bring peace and reconciliation. The *resurrection* means that God overcomes death and wills a new life for human beings. In Jesus Christ the *new human being* has been created, and by participation in his new being we are made new. He now is the mediator between the old and the new, the center of human existence and human history, even the center between God and nature. For Bonhoeffer, Jesus Christ is God's gracious "Yes" to the world, and henceforth we can never have the world without God or God without the world. We can no longer think that one sphere is sacred and one sphere is secular. There is only one enduring reality: the reconciliation of the world by God in and through Jesus.

From Bonhoeffer's Christ-centered theology emerged two basic emphases. The first is *the centrality of the church*, which for Bonhoeffer is not only the community of faith in God through Jesus Christ, but the actual presence of Christ on earth. Christ is present in the word of proclamation, in the sacraments enacted, and also in the community itself. Christ takes form in the individual members of the church as their old sinful selves are transformed into the image of the Christ, the new humans who exist for others. As Bonhoeffer wrote in *The Cost of Discipleship*, "when Christ calls a man, he bids him come and die" (99)—die to the old self and come to new life following Christ in the costly but joyful way of the cross. No "cheap grace" will do (that is what Bonhoeffer called the grace we bestow on ourselves in order to live the Christian life as cheaply as possible). The church, then, is for Bonhoeffer absolutely essential, because it reveals and embodies the wonderful word of God's love for the world.

The second emphasis is on *the worldliness of Christian faith*. The church does not exist for itself, but for the world. Christians do not exist for themselves, but for others. They live ex-centric lives, for they live in and for Christ, and Christ is to be found in the midst of our needy world: among the outcasts, the hungry, the homeless, the despised—in short, among those who suffer. Our God is a suffering God, and we are called to suffer with God in a world still reeling from sin and despair, from injustice and conflict. To quote from Bonhoeffer's book entitled *Ethics*, "To allow the hungry person to remain hungry would be blasphemy against God and one's neighbor, for what is nearest to God is precisely the need of one's neighbor."[1] When Bonhoeffer was in prison, his thoughts about the this-worldliness of faith became even more radical, and he polemicized against the notions of religiosity that seek to avoid worldly involvement by privatizing faith or by creating an abstract, otherworldly God whom we can call upon to solve problems that we, as mature Christians, ought to solve.

I have tried to highlight some of the essential ingredients of Bonhoeffer's thought: its social concreteness, Christ-centeredness, and this-worldliness, and its overall call for lifelong discipleship. In conclusion, I will briefly indicate how this relates to Christian spirituality—Bonhoeffer's and ours.

CHRISTIAN SPIRITUALITY: BONHOEFFER'S AND OURS

Spirituality has to do with formation, and formation always occurs in the midst of one's community and the events of one's life. Christian formation, therefore, takes place in the milieu of many influences and experiences. In Bonhoeffer's case, the formative influences of family and German culture cannot be exaggerated. I have already alluded to these in my sketch of his life, and I will only add here that the unstinting support of his large and talented family, including his in-laws, was crucial for him and remained so to the end. As for the liberal atmosphere of the Weimar Republic, it was almost decimated by the advent of National Socialism under Hitler, a totalitarian regime that quickly took away basic rights of German citizens, made anti-Semitic racism its social trademark, and fostered militarism as its national policy.

Bonhoeffer's theological education in Germany, first at Tübingen and then in Berlin, was fairly typical for the time. But I think he subsequently underwent some educational and ecclesiastical experiences that were extraordinary and that shaped him in important ways. The most momentous of these were (1) his year as an assistant minister or curate in a German-speaking congregation in Barcelona, Spain, where he encountered an entirely different ethos and also saw firsthand the problems that beset small-time businessmen and their families in a foreign climate; (2) his year-long sojourn as a student at Union Theological Seminary in New

York City, where he was jolted by the informality of dormitory life, intrigued by the theology of the "Social Gospel," and, most importantly, aroused by the suffering of blacks in Harlem, where he spent weekends teaching Sunday school at the Abyssinian Baptist Church; (3) his experiences in the fledgling ecumenical movement as a youth secretary for the pacifist-leaning World Alliance for Promoting Friendship through the Churches and later as a member of the Commission on Life and Work; and (5) his year and a half as a pastor in London, where he became a close friend of the influential Bishop of Chichester, George Bell.

Bonhoeffer's two greatest spiritual challenges still lay ahead: the Church Struggle and the conspiracy against Hitler. Whether a coincidence or not, Bonhoeffer's lifestyle began to change about the time of the rise of Nazism. His biographer and closest friend, Eberhard Bethge, says, "The theologian became a Christian." He began a regular discipline of daily meditation on the word of God in Scripture and prayer. He was especially challenged by Jesus' Sermon on the Mount and what was demanded of one who took discipleship seriously. This discipline stood him in good stead as he became embroiled in the struggle of the German Protestant Church against the Nazi government's intrusion into its life. Adamantly opposed to the Nazi attempt to impose on the church the "Aryan Clause," which prohibited any Christian with so-called Jewish blood from being a pastor, Bonhoeffer helped found what came to be known as the Confessing Church, which made its theological declaration of allegiance to *Christ alone* at Barmen in 1934 and thereafter set up its own church structures independent of the Reich Church.

In 1935 the Confessing Church recalled Bonhoeffer from England to establish a seminary in Pomerania for its ordinands. At an old schoolhouse in the village of Finkenwalde he introduced a new kind of theological education into Germany. Based partly upon what he had learned from visiting Anglican monastic communities before he left England, he fashioned a communal life that mixed the academic and the spiritual: a life that featured silent meditation on a passage of Scripture to begin the day, communal worship comprising Scripture readings, singing, and prayer after breakfast and in the evening, and classes and fun times to round out the day before bedtime silence. During the Finkenwalde experiment Bonhoeffer published *The Cost of Discipleship*, and after the school was closed by the Gestapo in 1937 he wrote *Life Together*, which detailed what it meant to live a life together under the word of God. He stressed that "self-justification and judging belong together in the same way that justification by grace and serving others belong together."[2] For our purposes, it is interesting to list the services or ministries that Bonhoeffer thought one owed to others in a Christian community: (1) the ministry of *listening* (too often we want to do all the talking); (2) *active helpfulness* (taking time to do small acts of service); (3) *bearing with others* (bearing the burden of another, which often calls for forbearance); (4) *speaking the word of God* (a free word from person to person when the situation calls for it, an admonition if a brother or sister falls into sin). Beyond these four services, Bonhoeffer advocated the introduction of aural confession, especially in preparation for the Lord's Supper—not a confession of everyone to a priest, but the confession of sin by one person to another person in the community under the premise that both live under the cross. And, oh yes, there was a general rule that Bonhoeffer emphasized: never speak ill of a brother behind his back.

Bonhoeffer was an intransigent advocate of the Confessing Church, but when most of its pastors were conscripted and it became less effective, he faced an even greater challenge. After a brief visit to the United States in the summer of 1939, he opted to forego safety and return to a disintegrating situation in Germany on the brink of war. Through his brother-in-law Hans von Dohnanyi, chief legal counsel for the Military Intelligence Service (Abwehr), he learned of the growing resistance to Hitler's war policies among high-ranking military officers and of a conspiracy, coordinated by the head of the Abwehr, to kill Hitler and sue for peace. Asked to use his ecumenical contacts to further the cause of the resistance movement, Bonhoeffer joined the Abwehr as a civilian employee and made several trips to Switzerland and Sweden on its behalf—an action that eventually caused his imprisonment and death.

How could a Christian and pastor like Bonhoeffer join the conspiracy? His question was, how could he *not* do it? In light of Hitler's extermination policies against Jews, Gypsies, and other so-called undesirables, and in light of Hitler's aggressive war policies, Bonhoeffer chose to do something rather than nothing, chose what he considered to be the lesser of two evils. He once wrote that if a madman is driving down the street hitting and maiming people on the way, it is not enough to bind up the wounds of the victims; one must stop the man from driving at all by putting a spoke in the wheel of the car.

Bonhoeffer's final writings from prison—letters to family, his friend Eberhard Bethge, and his fiancée, Maria—are fascinating, for he never stopped reading and thinking, never ceased asking who Jesus Christ is for us *today* in a world-come-of-age that is no longer religious in the old ways. He had time to take stock of Christianity in the modern age and to express surprising conclusions about the nonreligious or this-worldly character of faith.

In a letter written on 21 July 1944, the day after the failed attempt on Hitler's life, he wrote to Bethge, "By this-worldliness I mean living unreservedly in Life's duties, problems, successes and failures, experiences and perplexities. In so doing we throw ourselves completely into the arms of God, taking seriously not our own sufferings, but those of God in the world—watching with Christ in Gethsemane. That, I think, is faith; that is metanoia; and that is how one becomes a human being and a Christian."[3] In the same letter he included a poem he had written entitled "Stations on the Way to Freedom." There were four stations: Discipline, Action, Suffering, and Death.

In one of the last letters he wrote to Bethge, dated 3 August 1944, he sent an "Outline for a Book" he hoped to write. After asserting that our relation to God is not a "religious" relationship to the highest, most powerful, and best Being imaginable, but a new life in "existence for others" through participation in the being of Jesus, who was there only for others, Bonhoeffer wrote this about the church:

> The church is the church only when it exists for others . . . The church must share in the secular problems of ordinary Life, not dominating but helping and serving. It must tell persons of every calling what it means to live in Christ, to exist for others. . . . It must not under-estimate the importance of human example . . . ; it is not abstract argument, but example, that gives its word emphasis and powers.[4]

In conclusion, if you and I want to undergo that spiritual transformation into the persons God calls us to be, I think Bonhoeffer would give us this advice:

In your private life, be disciplined in your reading and meditation on the word of God in Scripture, in prayer and intercession.

In your church life, join in the life of the community, being attentive to the preached word and the administered sacraments, being active in its mission of loving service to the world, and building up the fellowship through the ministries of listening, active helpfulness, bearing and forbearing, and, when it seems called for, speaking the word of God to another.

In your public life, be an everyday disciple of Christ by entering into the sufferings of God at the hands of a godless world, courageously existing for others and thereby exhibiting in the ordinary affairs of secular life God's will for righteousness.

I leave you with two quotations:

From Bonhoeffer: "Christ opened up the way to God and to one another."[5]

From Jesus: "Whoever seeks to save his life will lose it; and whoever loses it will save it," (Luke 17:33)—and live.

ENDNOTES

1. *E*, 137.
2. *LT*, 94.
3. *LPP*, 370.
4. Ibid., 382 f.
5. *CD*, 269.

On Being a Christian Today: Dietrich Bonhoeffer's Personal Faith

Mary Glazener

I want to look at the theme "Are We Still of Any Use?" in the light of the relationship of Bonhoeffer's personal faith in Jesus Christ to the witness of his life. It is in the reflection of his lived-out faith that we can truly understand and appreciate his theology, and find guidance for being Christians today.

From early childhood Bonhoeffer showed a deep interest in theological questions. His twin sister, Sabine, records that at age four he asked their mother, "Does the good God love the chimney sweep too?" The Bonhoeffer home in Breslau, where the family lived the first six years of the lives of Dietrich and Sabine, was located across the street from a Catholic cemetery. With their noses pressed against the windowpane, the children watched with awe as the hearses, drawn by black-draped horses, moved slowly into the graveyard. This fascination with death and eternity continued when they moved to Berlin, especially during the First World War, as their older brothers and cousins were fighting and dying at the front. Dietrich and Sabine secretly practiced an exercise in concentration on the word *eternity* until their heads would swim.[1] At age twelve, already a good pianist, he composed a cantata on the sixth verse of Psalm 42, "My soul is cast down within me," a psalm on which he later preached.

At the early age of fourteen, the boy Dietrich announced to his family, including his unenthusiastic father and older brothers, his intent to study theology. He admitted later in a letter written in early 1936 to Elisabeth Zinn, the girl to whom he was unofficially engaged for a number of years (confirmed to me in an interview at her home in Heidelberg in September 1979), that it was ambition that led him to this decision.

We have a revealing piece that he wrote in 1932, in "the period of up-heaval in his theological and inner life,"[2] that mercilessly exposes this ambition and the accompanying vanity that he hated in himself.[3] The piece harks back to his school days, when in his Greek class the teacher asked what he wanted to study. He answered quickly, "Theology."

> Now he was the *center of attention.* Did he appear as he had wished, his features serious and resolute? . . . The moment swelled to pleasure, the classroom expanded to the infinite. There he stood in *the center of the world as the herald and teacher of his knowledge and ideals;* now they must all hear him in silence, and the approval of the Eternal rested on his words and his head. But again he was ashamed of himself. He well knew his contemptible vanity.
>
> How often he had sought to master it. . . .
>
> (Seeing the distrust of his fellows, he questions himself.) . . . Don't they believe the sincerity of his commitment? Do they know something about him of which he is unaware? . . .
>
> *A leaden stillness hangs over the crowd, a dreadful silent mockery.* No, that cannot be. . . . They have no right to disdain me. You do an injustice—all of you. He prays.
>
> God, say yourself if I am serious about you. Destroy me this very moment if I lie. Or punish them all; they are my enemies, your enemies. . . . I know myself that I am not good. But I know it myself—as you do, God! *I do not need the others. I, I, I will conquer.* . . . God, I am on your side!
>
> Do you hear me? Or don't you hear? To whom am I speaking? To myself? To you? To these others here?
>
> Who is speaking? My faith? My vanity?
>
> God, I will study theology. . . . They all heard it. There is no turning back.[4]

In the letter to Elisabeth Zinn he said that he "had often preached, had seen a great deal of the Church, and talked and preached about it—but had not yet become a Christian," and that "at that time I turned the doctrine of Jesus Christ into something of personal advantage for myself."[5]

PERSONAL STRUGGLES

This letter and his writing of *The Cost of Discipleship* came during the years at Finkenwalde, when he was having the most difficulty with the depression that he called *accidie tristitia*. He refers to this time in the famous letter of 21 July 1944 in *Letters and Papers from Prison*, when he says, "I thought I could acquire faith by trying to live a holy life."[6] One day, in my research for *The Cup of Wrath*, I came across in the *Gesammelte Schriften* a letter Dietrich had written to Eberhard Bethge from Misdroy, a beach on the Baltic, where he had taken the seminarians on retreat. He told of a serious problem he was having with some of the men regarding their behavior with some women there, and said he was wishing for Eberhard's advice. Then he said, "It made me think of the evening when you were with me in my room and I didn't want to listen to you, and of the help you gave at that time. Keep praying with me for the brothers. Much depends on it. And pray for me, I need it so much."[7]

This jumped out at me. I wanted to know to what he was referring. So I called Eberhard Bethge in Germany. He knew immediately what I was talking about, and said that that evening was a time of a severe attack of Bonhoeffer's depression. Bethge referred me to a piece in *Gesammelte Schriften* called "Von der Dankbarkeit des Christen" (Of the thankfulness of the Christian) and intimated that I might find help there for an understanding of what was said. "Dankbarkeit," written in 1940, was indeed revealing, especially in the light of Bethge's hint that it was autobiographical. "Gratitude is humble enough to let something be given to itself," Bonhoeffer writes. "The proud one takes only what is due him. He refuses to receive a gift. He prefers earned penalty to unearned kindness. He prefers to go under in his own strength to living out of grace."[8] From this incident I was able to learn a great deal about the relationship between Dietrich Bonhoeffer and his friend Eberhard Bethge, and something of the fertile ground in which Bonhoeffer's theology grew and developed.

Elisabeth Zinn Bornkamm (sometime after she and Dietrich broke up, she was married to the theologian Gunther Bornkamm) told me in her home in Heidelberg that she suggested to Dietrich that he talk with his psychiatrist father about his problem with *accidie tristitia*, but he said, "No, I couldn't bother him with that." Bonhoeffer's upbringing made it difficult for him to open up to the other person. He was taught—it was strongly impressed upon him—that one did not burden the other person with one's problems. One did not make a show of one's feelings so as to elicit sympathy. So that, while stimulating intellectual exchange and theological discussion came easily for him, on the human level the kind of opening up of heart and soul that brings true intimacy did not come naturally. He longed for a "spiritual father" and came close to that in Bishop Bell, but lacked the "friend that sticketh closer than a brother" until Eberhard Bethge came along.

The "proffering" of sympathy and understanding that Bonhoeffer found in Eberhard Bethge had a saving and freeing dimension for him. For each of them this relationship involved making himself available to the other, "being there" for the other, "being Christ to the other," "bearing one another's burdens." In Tegel Dietrich writes to Eberhard of "our strong spiritual affinity . . . our long spiritual fellowship."[9] Over the years this friendship undoubtedly helped Bonhoeffer overcome the *accidie tristitia*.

Bethge suggested another place in Bonhoeffer's theology that is autobiographical and illuminates his *accidie tristitia*. In the fourth chapter of *Temptation* Bonhoeffer discusses *Desperatio* and says, "The temptation to despair (*accidie*) . . . robs the believer of all joy in the Word of God, all experience of the good God; in place of which he [Satan] fills the heart with the terrors of the past, of the present and of the future. Old long-forgotten guilt suddenly rears up its head before me, as if it had happened today. Opposition to the Word of God and unwillingness to obey assume huge proportions, and complete despair . . . overwhelms my heart. . . . Man now demands an experience, proof of the grace of God." Bonhoeffer calls this the sin of "ingratitude in the face of everything that God has done for us up to this moment," and he quotes Psalm 50:23: "Forget not what good he has done you. Whoso offereth the sacrifice of thanksgiving glorifieth me, and to him . . . will I show the salvation of God." He points to "our hopelessness, as though our sins were too great for God . . . as though God did not still purpose great things even with me." Then he says, "I must recognize in all this that I am here thrust by Satan into the highest temptation of Christ on the cross, as he cried: 'My God, my God, why hast thou forsaken me.' But where God's wrath broke out, there was reconciliation. Where I, smitten by God's wrath, lose everything, there I hear the words: 'My grace is sufficient for thee; for my power is made perfect in weakness' (2 Cor. 12:9)."[10] From the letter from Misdroy and this piece I was able to create an important scene for *The Cup of Wrath*.

When I visited the Bethges in Lynchburg, Virginia, ten or twelve years ago, Eberhard told me that the attacks of *accidie tristitia* usually followed, not times of disappointment and defeat, but times of high success, especially success with influencing others—his students, for instance. When he saw in himself the ability and tendency to dominate their thinking, when they moved so readily out of their own free sphere into his bright realm, and when he caught himself enjoying that, then the demons crept up and invaded his spirit.

Clifford Green deals with this extensively in his dissertation, *The Sociality of Christ and Humanity: Dietrich Bonhoeffer's Early Theology,* and shows conclusively in Bonhoeffer's theology the autobiographical dimension of this problem of the power of the ego. Green concludes, "It is precisely by dealing with dominating power in his theological and personal pilgrimage that Bonheoffer is able to arrive at that Christian celebration of human strength and maturity which is so conspicuous in the prison writings." [11]

Over a period of time, Bonhoeffer was able to translate these experiences into concrete expressions of what it means to have faith. The question was not "What *must* I believe?" but "What do we really believe in such a way that we stake our lives on it?" And of the Church: "The Church must share in the secular problems of ordinary human life, not dominating, but helping and serving. It must tell men of every calling what it means to live in Christ, to exist for others." [12]

In Tegel prison, we have indications that he was able to hold the demons at bay. He wrote to Eberhard, to whom he had told more about it than anyone else, that "I told myself from the beginning that I was not going to oblige either man or devil in any such way. . . . I hope I shall always be able to stand firm on this." In the famous poem "Stations on the Road to Freedom," written soon after the failure of the 20 July coup, when he knew his fate was sealed, he wrote that he had committed his cause to stronger hands and now he "may rest contented." This is reinforced in the poem "Powers of Good," written to his mother from the Gestapo basement shortly before he was taken away, the next to the last word we have from him there. He begins with the words "With every power for good to stay and guide me / comforted and inspired beyond all fear," then goes on to say in verse three that if "the cup of grieving" must be drained "to the dregs . . . we will not falter, thankfully receiving all that is given by thy loving hand." [13]

It was during the height of the *accidie tristitia* at Finkenwalde that Bonhoeffer suggested to the seminarians that there should be oral confession, one brother to another. Eberhard Bethge tells of this experience: "It was in that first half year when I was candidate there that Dietrich asked me to listen to him. That was of course a most shaking experience for me, whether I was able, or had the mandate to do it, or whether I could stand it, because in those days it was still the relation of this great gifted Dietrich, and who was I? But what it was, I think, was that he wanted to have an uncomplicated person, and I think he wanted to humble himself." Then Eberhard tells that, despite his anxiety, he was able to do it. "He found his way and I found my way."

Bonhoeffer made no liturgical rules about this. "It all came quite naturally . . . but when it came to very personal and central things, he was anxious not to do something artificial, any kind of show . . . because in this experience there must be a turning away from any kind of stance . . . he was so much afraid of vanity, of showing off."

THE USE OF SCRIPTURE

In this interview Bethge tells that, at the beginning of the seminary at Zingst, Bonhoeffer had designated the half hour after breakfast for a period of meditation and said, "Everyone goes to his study place, sits there by himself, not talking at all. It is a total time of silence, meditating on a very short part of Scripture." Eberhard Bethge confesses that he had "never heard of such a thing before . . . and found it rather hard." Bonhoeffer encountered considerable resistance from the ordinands, so that once when he was away for a time on Confessing Church business, they let the practice lapse. Bethge relates that "he came back, and he was very sorry about it . . . sorry that we had so soon destroyed the whole practice already, and we felt a bit ashamed. . . . Then it came out. 'You are asking the people in the congregation to listen to your sermon, to what the Scriptures say through that sermon, but when do you listen yourself, that it is saying something to you? This half hour is . . . to discover what the words of God through Scripture say to you in your situation now. This silence is necessary to listen to what this word may say to you personally.'" They countered that it was unevangelical legalism. "Then he became a little bit furious," Bethge continued, "and said, 'This is rather a bad thing, if you are mixing up legalism with discipline. It is not the same. This is a matter of your growing maturity. . . . First you are yourself there, open to God's Word, and this makes it a matter of coming of age, of becoming an independent human being, and especially as a pastor being prepared now to meet people with other problems—to have this hour of silence.' . . . But he was not legalistic about it. He said, 'if you can't manage, please don't disturb the others by walking around.' He didn't go around and look to see whether we did it or not, but he did it himself, and sometimes we could see him in his room sitting totally concentrating—if we walked around, and some of us did at first. We were not very obedient all the time."[14]

Two of those students, Jochen Kanitz and Otto Dudzus, told me the meditation they learned from Bonhoeffer had helped them during the war in the fearful, lonely hours in the trenches. I believe that Bonhoeffer himself learned it well and that this, along with his obedience to the call of Jesus, even to the risking of his life, made it possible for him to say from prison, "I'm often surprised how little . . . I grub among my past mistakes and think how different one thing or another would be today if I had acted differently in the past; it doesn't worry me at all. Everything seems to have taken its natural course, and to be determined necessarily and straightforwardly by a higher providence."[15]

All of Bonhoeffer's writing from beginning to end reveals his reverence for the Bible and its importance in his life. Anyone who reads *Letters and Papers from Prison* must be struck by the number of references to

Scripture found there. As Professor Patrick D. Miller, of Princeton Theological Seminary, says, "Bonhoeffer lived and thought out of the deep well of Scripture."[16] It was during the "period of upheaval"—1932, referred to earlier—that Bonhoeffer delivered a lecture at an ecumenical conference in Gland, Switzerland, called "The Church Is Dead," in which he said, "Has it not become terrifyingly clear . . . that we are no longer obedient to the Bible? We are more fond of our own thoughts than of the thoughts of the Bible. We no longer read the Bible seriously, we no longer read it against ourselves, but for ourselves . . . we must read the Bible in quite a different way, until we find ourselves again."[17]

That he was "finding himself again" becomes quite clear in the letter to Elisabeth Zinn, when he tells her of the "unchristian" way he had approached his work in earlier times, the paucity of his prayer life, and his overweaning ambition. "Then," he said, "something happened, something that has changed and transformed my life to the present day. For the first time I discovered the Bible. . . . It was a great liberation."[18]

Bonhoeffer and his brother-in-law Rudiger Schleicher carried on a friendly debate about the liberal interpretation of the Bible, the interpretation current in Germany at the time and with which Bonhoeffer was thoroughly familiar when, even as a boy of fifteen, he had walked the paths of the Grunewald with neighbor Adolf Harnack and talked theology. In a remarkably personal letter to Schleicher in 1936, Bonhoeffer expresses in detail his own different approach to the Bible. "First," he says, "I want to confess quite simply that I believe the Bible alone is the answer to all our questions, and that we only need to ask persistently and with some humility in order to receive the answer from it." He points out to his friend that we cannot simply reach our own conclusions about God; if so, we will always find a God who fits in with our wishes. If, on the other hand, we let God say where he is to be found, "then that will truly be a place which at first is not agreeable to me at all. . . . That place is the cross of Christ." He states firmly that "the entire Bible, then, is the Word in which God allows himself to be found by us." In the most personal statement in the letter, he says, "I do not want to give up the Bible as this strange Word of God at any point. I intend with all my powers to ask what God wants to say to us here. Any other place outside the Bible has become too uncertain for me. I fear that I will only encounter some divine double of myself there."[19]

In *Christ the Center* Bonhoeffer takes into account historical criticism in looking at the Bible. "One must be ready to accept the concealment within history and therefore let historical criticism run its course. But it is through the Bible, with all its flaws, that the risen one encounters us. It is this encounter and the presence of Jesus with and in his Church that 'bear witness' to Jesus himself as there in history, here and now. . . . It is the risen one who himself creates faith and thus knows the way to himself 'in history.'"[20]

This openness to the Bible as God's word to him is what kept Bonhoeffer on track as he sought to know Christ "in truth and reality." As *The Cost of Discipleship* is biblically based, so are *Ethics* and *Letters and Papers from Prison*. We can take seriously his words from prison about *The Cost of Discipleship*: "I still stand by what I said,"[21] and conclude that the theological formulations in *Letters and Papers from Prison* and in *Ethics* are an expansion of these earlier concepts, not a turnaround. As an example, his premise in *Letters and Papers from Prison* of the meaning of being a Christian as "participating in the sufferings of God in the world" is foreshadowed in *The Cost of Discipleship* in such phrases as "The disciple is a disciple only in so far as he shares his Lord's suffering and rejection and crucifixion"[22] and "The wounds and scars [the Christian] receives in the fray are living tokens of this participation in the cross of his Lord."[23]

DISCIPLESHIP

From Tegel, Bonhoeffer was looking back on that difficult period of the most serious attacks of depression. At that time, in his great need, he was trying to "learn to have faith" by means of total obedience to the "superpowerful figure" of Jesus. In Tegel he had learned that Jesus wants also to be the brother who walks beside him and helps him "accept that he himself, with his own power and his own weakness, might be a source of strength for others."[24] The "danger" he saw in *The Cost of Discipleship* may have been an overemphasis on obedience that could give the impression that one could "acquire" faith, although in the book he tried to make clear that there must be a balance between faith and obedience. He says that the "simple obedience" he speaks of should not be interpreted as a "doctrine of human merit" and clearly states that "the step into the situation where faith is possible is not an offer which we can make to Jesus, but always his gracious offer to us."[25] Also, "we can only take this step aright if we fix our eyes not on the work we do, but on the word with which Jesus calls us to do it."[26] And again, "Salvation through following Jesus is not something we men can achieve for ourselves—but with God all things are possible."[27]

He never repudiated his insistence in *The Cost of Discipleship* on taking the Sermon on the Mount seriously, nor his faith in the life, death, and resurrection of Jesus Christ, which he attests to in numerous writings, both early and late. Bethge confirms that Bonhoeffer "was not looking for an object of study," but, with his question "Who is Christ?" and his later question, "Who is Christ for us today?" he was willing to risk a personal encounter, regardless of the cost.[28] In the introduction to *The Cost of Discipleship* Bonhoeffer says, "In the last resort what we want to know is . . . what Jesus Christ himself wants of us."[29]

All of Bonhoeffer's writings point to the fact that, for him, Christ was central and it is faith in him that "sets life upon a new foundation" and "justifies my being able to live before God. . . . Faith means being wrested from my imprisonment in my own self, being set free by Jesus Christ."[30] There can be no doubt that this statement is autobiographical, as is one that precedes it: "To be conformed with the Incarnate, with him who was made man, was crucified, and rose again, is to have the right to be the man one really is. Now there is no more pretence, no more hypocrisy or self-violence, no more compulsion to be something other, better and more ideal than what one is. God loves the real man. God became a real man."[31]

Preaching was the great event of Bonhoeffer's life. He considered it of such importance that he always took the homiletics classes in the seminary. So he was deeply distressed as he witnessed the pastors of his Confessing Church gradually succumbing to Nazi pressure. He could not bear to see the word of God watered down and perverted so as to shield the church and its leaders from any retaliation by the Nazis. In the letter to Eberhard from Misdroy he tells of attending church there. After the "purely German Christian sermon" he went into the sacristy and confronted the preacher: "Why do you not preach Christ? Why do you let us go hungry?" The man was at first defensive, then suddenly changed in a bland capitulation, saying, "But I cannot preach what I do not have." Dietrich says to Eberhard, "A shattered pastor. It is very sad."[32] And in New York in 1939, after a blistering criticism of a service at Riverside Church, which he called the "deification of religion," he tells of attending Broadway Presbyterian the next Sunday, where he was "very glad" about the sermon, which he found "entirely biblical."[33]

In 1938, after the fiasco of the oath to Hitler and the ploy of legalization took their toll, some of the remaining faithful pastors began to lose heart and asked, "Haven't we been battered, questioned, and locked up enough? Oughtn't we to salvage our remaining resources?" Bonhoeffer's answer was, "We are promising ourselves nothing at all from those resources. What God intends to batter, we are quite willing to see battered. We have nothing to salvage. We have not attached our hearts to organizations and institutions, not even our own. . . . But we trust confidently that God will salvage his Word, and us with it, in his miraculous way. That is the only stock of resources on which we intend to take our stand."[34]

Even so, he did not lose faith in the Church. Deep into the war in 1942, when he was already making trips outside Germany as a courier for the Resistance, he wrote in an incomplete draft "Of a Proclamation from the Pulpit after a Political Overthrow," "God has not forgotten his church. In his unfathomable mercy he calls his faithless tormented servants to repentance, to a renewal of life according to his holy will. . . . In the midst of a Christendom that has been smitten with guilt beyond measure the word of the forgiveness of all sins through Jesus Christ and the call to a new life in obedience to God's holy commandments must once more be proclaimed. . . . We call to preaching."[35]

It is "existence for others" that is the answer to the overarching and evolving question of Bonhoeffer's life: "Who is Jesus Christ for us to-day?" His new christological title for Jesus became "Jesus Christ, the man for others." Eberhard Bethge makes clear that this is not a replacement title. "In worship, confession, apologetics, teaching, and everyday conversation, we find him using the wide range of christological titles found both in the New Testament and in the Fathers. . . . He never renounced or repudiated (these): but he read, applied, and selected them in his own way, and went so far as to offer a new one."[36] Relationship, both with God and with others, had been a basic concept from the early writings. In *Creation and Fall* he says, "In the language of the Bible, freedom is not something man has for himself but something he has for others. No man is free 'as such.' . . . Being free means 'being free for the other.' . . . Only in relationship with the other am I free"; and with regard to God, "God does not will to be free for himself but for man. God in Christ is free for man. . . . The freedom of the Creator is proved by the fact that he allows us to be free for him."[37]

All this leads to and undergirds the response Bonhoeffer made to the terrible question of whether to take part in the plan to assassinate Hitler. It was perhaps the most difficult decision of his life, yet when the time came he was prepared to meet it. He was not able to justify openly his decision, because that would have been to endanger all those others involved, but in *Ethics* and in "After Ten Years," the essay he wrote for his friends and co-conspirators that appears at the beginning of *Letters and Papers from Prison*, we can see clearly what he was thinking. In the former he turns first to "the origin of all responsibility," Jesus, who "is not concerned with Himself being good (Matt. 19:17); he is concerned solely with love for the real man. . . . Jesus does not desire to be regarded as the only perfect one at the expense of men. . . . As one who acts responsibly in the historical existence of men Jesus becomes guilty. It must be emphasized that it is solely His love which makes Him incur guilt." If, in a historical situation of "extraordinary necessity," man tries to escape guilt in responsibility, if "he sets his own personal innocence above his responsibility for men [in this case, the Jews being murdered], he is blind to the more irredeemable guilt which he incurs precisely in this."[38] In "After Ten Years" he closes the paragraph on "Civil Courage" with the statement, "Civil courage . . . depends on a God who demands responsible action in a bold venture of faith, and who promises forgiveness and consolation to the man who becomes a sinner in that venture."[39] It is interesting to note that in the next paragraph, "Of Success," he uses the word *responsible* and derivatives thereof seven times. So responsibility in relationship with God and with the other person becomes for Bonhoeffer the way in which one is free and the way in which one finds the balance between faith and obedience.

He wrote these words knowing that his arrest was most likely imminent, and followed them with a remarkable affirmation of faith in the sovereignty of God in history: "I believe that God can and will bring good out of evil, even out of the greatest evil. For that purpose he needs men who make the best use of everything. . . . I believe that God is no timeless fate, but that he waits for and answers sincere prayers and responsible actions."[40]

The question now is, "What would Bonhoeffer say to us today about our usefulness?" I believe he would see more than ever the danger of squandering our usefulness and weakening our witness by a tendency to construe the Bible and even his own writings to fit our own constructs and to forward our own agendas. I believe that he would say the same to us that he said to his students at Finkenwalde: "We take it for granted as we open the Bible that we have a key to its interpretation. But then the key we use would not be the living Christ, who is both Judge and Saviour, and our use of this key no longer depends on the will of the living Holy Spirit alone."[41] He would score "religious" Christianity (he defined "religion" as man-made, "faith" as from the Spirit), the individualistic "my-Lord-and-me and me-and-my-Lord" kind of piety that leads to a misrepresentation or diminishing of certain parts of the Bible, like the Sermon on the Mount, and the fundamentalism that leads to defensiveness and exclusiveness. He would have us remember that "the 'religious act' is always something partial; 'faith' is something whole, involving the whole of one's life."[42] He would also take to task liberal theology for conceding to the world "the right to determine Christ's place in the world; in the conflict between the church and the world it accepted the comparatively easy terms of peace that the world dictated."[43]

He would probably confront us for our permissiveness and admonish us, even more strongly than he did his contemporaries, with the need for "costly" discipleship. He would say that we are weakening our witness when we fail to show our young people the way around, out of, or away from the cesspool that makes up much of our culture. Maybe he would tell us first to get out of it ourselves—certainly to do all we can in Christian responsibility to clean it up.

He would be displeased and would tell us straight out of our tendency to misuse his writings to make them say what we want them to say to fit our theological orientation. He would probably repeat to us that "the Church must come out of its stagnation" and that "it is only in the spirit of prayer that any such work can be begun and carried through."[44] On the pretext of being "honest," we take little thought of the Bible and do not seek earnestly and humbly what God is saying to us today in his word. This is totally against the spirit of Bonhoeffer and is also probably one of the chief causes of the decline of the mainline churches.

The remarkable letter of 21 August 1944 tells us that the

> key to everything is the "in him." All that we may rightly expect from God, and ask him for, is to be found in Jesus Christ. . . . If we are to learn what God promises, and what he fulfils, we must persevere in quiet meditation on the life, sayings, deeds, sufferings, and death of Jesus. It is certain that we may always live close to God and in the light of his presence, and that such living is an entirely new life for us; that nothing is then impossible for us, because all things are possible with God; that no earthly power can touch us without his will, and that danger and distress can only drive us closer to him. It is certain that we can claim nothing for ourselves, and may yet pray for everything; it is certain that our joy is hidden in suffering, and our life in death; it is certain that in all this we are in a fellowship that sustains us. In Jesus God has said an Amen to it all, and that Yes and Amen is the firm ground on which we stand.[45]

ENDNOTES

1. Sabine Leibholz-Bonhoeffer, *Portrait of a Family* (Chicago: Covenant Publications, 1994), 32.

2. *DB*, 25.

3. Ibid.

4. *SCH*, 156.

5. *DB*, 154-55.

6. *LPP*, letter of 21 July 1944, 369.

7. *GS* 2, 502.

8. Ibid., 418.

9. *LPP*, letter of 11 August 1944, 385.

10. *CF*, 124-26.

11. *SCH*, 148.

12. *LPP*, "Outline for a Book," 382-83.

13. Ibid., 400.

14. Interview with Eberhard Bethge in the Bethge home by Mel White, called "Interviews for a Bonhoeffer Film," 10 August 1976. A copy was given to me by Bain Boehlke, producer of the documentary *Dietrich Bonhoeffer: Memories and Perspectives*.

15. *LPP*, letter of 22 April 1944, 276.

16. Patrick D. Miller, "Dietrich Bonhoeffer and the Psalms," lecture given 5 March 1994 at a Bonhoeffer conference at Nassau Presbyterian Church in Princeton.

17. *NRS*, 181.

18. *DB*, 154-55.

19. Dietrich Bonhoeffer, *Meditating on the Word*, ed. David McI. Gracie (Cambridge: Cowley Publications, 1986), 43-46.

20. *CC*, 72-74.

21. *LPP*, letter of 21 July 1944, 369.

22. *CD*, 96.

23. Ibid., 99.

24. *CG*, 146.

25. *CD*, 94.

26. Ibid., 72.

27. Ibid., 94.

28. *CG*, 148.

29. *CD*, 37.

30. *E*, 121-22.

31. Ibid., 81.

32. *GS 2*, 502.

33. Ibid., 300-1.

34. *DB*, 517.

35. Dietrich Bonhoeffer, *I Have Loved This People*, 45, as quoted in *Worldly Preaching, Lectures on Homiletics,* by Bonhoeffer, ed. Clyde E. Fant (New York: Crossroad, 1991), 40.

36. Eberhard Bethge, "Bonhoeffer's Christology and His 'Religionless Christianity,'" *Union Seminary Quarterly Review*, Fall 1967, 70-71.

37. *CF*, 37-38.

38. *E*, 240-41.

39. *LPP*, 6.

40. Ibid., 11.

41. *CD*, 69.

42. *LPP*, letter of 18 July 1944, 362.

43. Quoted in *Worldly Preaching*, 66.

44. *LPP*, letter of 3 August 1944, 378-79.

45. Ibid., letter of 21 August 1944, 391.

Christological Concretion and Everyday Events in Three of Bonhoeffer's Sermons
A CONCEPTUAL PATTERN OF THEOLOGICAL DISCOURSE[1]

James Patrick Kelley

W e have argued that what we call a "christological dialectic" is a central conceptual structure presented in Bonhoeffer's early student papers, his dissertations, and his university lectures.[2] According to this view, all Christian reflection must take the form of paradoxes. This is so because Christians must speak of a God who has fully revealed himself in human history in the person of Jesus as the Christ and continues to do so today. All their theological statements, therefore, will always be wrongly understood if they are taken as specific assertions of empirical facts or historical descriptions and interpretations of these facts. Neither, however, can any genuinely Christian theology be conceived so as to avoid all accountability for the veracity of some such concrete, factual assertions. Christian theology must include in its formulas both some descriptive discourse and also some language expressing faith's special experiences and understanding of the world. If this be problematic, and it is in several important ways, so be it! Any Christian theologians who have sought to resolve this problematic paradox are simply wrong to do so. For the paradox roots in the fundamental understanding of God to which Christians testify. So far, Bonhoeffer's views are perfectly lucid, consistent, and orthodox.

A special aspect of this dominant theme of Bonhoeffer's theology centers upon the fact, emphasized especially in his lectures on Christology from 1933 but always presupposed in his theology, that Christ is both different from other historical persons and at the same time himself fully a historical person.

Christ's difference derives from his ability to be a concrete figure in past history and also to be not merely remembered, but immediately and objectively present for us here and now. Bonhoeffer stressed the concretion of Christ's presence, so that he alone is not merely subjectively recalled and then, perhaps, used as a model for moral or pious activity by those who follow him today. On the contrary, he is himself objectively present today as well as in the past. Perhaps it is only the stress he places on this point that sets Bonhoeffer's views to any great extent apart from the christological reflection of many others.[3]

Our present interest is in tracing just how Bonhoeffer goes about making good on this claim. How is it that Christ is so fully present here and now "for us" that he can be sensed and that his presence can be reported in the form of a paradox, one side of which is expressed by references to publicly perceived objects and descriptions of their concrete, worldly circumstances?

A multitude of Bonhoeffer texts suggest themselves for discussion at this point. This fact itself indicates how pervasively such a basic pattern is presupposed for all his theology. But here we concentrate upon three especially lucid passages from early sermons in which Bonhoeffer's consistent answer to the question about Christ's presence is given in stark outline.[4]

Sermons generally are suited to exposition of the affective and active side of theology. Bonhoeffer's preaching is unusually forceful in its ability to bridge between past revelations reported in the Scriptures and the most concrete implications for reshaping present attitudes and actions.[5]

But this quality was by no means confined solely to his sermons. Bethge quotes a letter from Otto Dudzus, for example, one of more than two hundred who attended Bonhoeffer's lectures on Christology in 1933:

> He looked like a student himself when he mounted the platform. But then what he had to say so gripped us all that we were no longer there to listen to this very young man but we were there because of what he had to say even though it was dreadfully early in the morning. I have never heard a lecture that impressed me nearly so much.[6]

Again, such observations could be multiplied concerning other non-sermonic materials. But here we focus upon three typical passages from Bonhoeffer's sermons.

His homily on Psalm 63:3 ("For thy goodness is better than life") on the occasion of the Harvest Festival (4 October) 1931[7] exemplifies his concern to make the presence of Christ *pro nobis* concrete in relation to worldly experience. It will serve also to illustrate his method of achieving this concretion.

The language of the opening paragraph is characteristically in past tenses. It speaks of the psalmist and his time long ago. The sort of cry he uttered then is categorized:

> It is the triumphal cry [*Jubelruf*] of the distressed and abandoned, of the weary and overburdened; the cry of longing uttered by the sick and the oppressed; the song of praise among the unemployed and the hungry in the great cities; the prayer of thanksgiving prayed by taxgatherers and prostitutes, by sinners known and unknown.[8]

The abstraction of such class terms as are repeated here is well known. No names occur in this passage. Persons are simply lumped together into nameless groups, sharing common characteristics. They lack individual particularization and concretion.

At this point a question abruptly focuses the discussion on those who are presently listening to the sermon: "But is it really true? No, it is not, not in our world, not in our age. It is only true of the unreal world of the Bible, which frightens and angers us with its strangeness. Or perhaps the verse does not seem so particularly remarkable after all. Perhaps we think that it is perfectly self-evident."[9] A change results from Bonhoeffer's rhetoric at this point, but it is not yet a shift from abstractions to concretion.

The sermon is still focused upon the imagination of the congregation, and he explores this form of abstraction for a time. He leads his audience to imagine how the psalmist must have felt. He has lost everything. About all he has left is life itself, to which he stubbornly holds. But God even "storms this last citadel."[10] God would take away even life itself! Imaginatively the audience follows Bonhoeffer's suggestion of how they feel the psalmist must himself have felt long ago, so that some begin to actually feel that they too are similarly threatened. Then they object.

Bonhoeffer recognizes and states their objection to such treatment: "What sort of exaggerated and wild talk is this? You can't talk about the goodness of God in that way. That I'm in good health, that I've still got work and a house, that's what God's goodness means to me and that's what I should thank him for."[11]

Now the preacher shifts to a different, less imaginative form of discourse: general descriptions of concrete circumstances prevailing at this moment in the political and economic life of Germany. The sermon suddenly becomes unavoidably fixed on present worldly affairs as it describes and refers attention to these objective conditions.

> Today we celebrate our harvest festival in particular circumstances and with specific thoughts in mind. The harvest has not brought what we hoped for. Every hour of rain in August and September meant hours of hunger and privation in the coming winter for

hundreds of children and adults. . . . But on top of this comes
. . . unemployment. We must be prepared for the fact that this
winter seven million people in Germany will find no work, which
means hunger for fifteen to twenty million people. Another twelve
million or so in England, twenty or more in America, while at
this very moment sixteen million are starving in China and the
position is not much better in India. These are the cold statistics
behind which stands a terrible reality (*eine grausige Wirklichkeit*).[12]

Here are still only general statistics. But we begin to have our attention
fixed upon present, concrete circumstances, not feelings about what happened in the past. Such numbers are generalizations of many concrete,
descriptive statements of the form "This person is unemployed and hungry." The preacher's concern with worldly, concrete reality cannot any
longer escape his audience. "Should we overlook these millions of people
when we celebrate our harvest festival in church? We dare not."[13]

In the next moment Bonhoeffer shifts again to encourage the congregation to imagine how it will be for them in the immediate future.

When we sit down this evening to a full table and say grace and
thank God for his goodness, we shall not be able to avoid a strange
feeling of uneasiness. It will seem incomprehensible for us that
we should be the ones to receive such gifts and we will be overwhelmed by such thoughts and will think that we have not in
any way deserved these gifts more than our hungry brothers in
our town.[14]

Once more the attention of the audience centers not upon concrete,
present, objective conditions, but upon their own imagined, future feelings. Again a question is presented, which changes the drift of the discussion.

What if, precisely at the moment when we are thanking God for
his goodness towards us, there is a ring at the door, as so often
happens these days, and we find someone standing there who
also wants to thank God for some small gift, but to whom such a
gift has been denied and who is starving with his children and
who will go to bed in bitterness? What becomes of our grace in
such moments?[15]

This scene is hypothetical, and it is also set in the imaginary, now the
future. Such imagined events need not occur as objective realities. But
these imaginary, future events were in fact occurring in Germany "so
often . . . these days."[16] They are not completely unreal possibilities, these
particular conjurings of mind. Again, the sense of concretion, immediacy,

and objectivity of this imaginative language threatens as no purely imaginary scene could do. The language of the sermon has again left the world of semantic abstractions behind. One could very well actually hear the doorbell's sound and encounter the one who rings it later today "at the moment when we are thanking God for his goodness towards us." This language relentlessly, again, refers one's thinking to specific worldly events.

What process have we traced at work in this sermon? Patently, it is an example of what may be called the language of primary experience of Christian faith. But it presupposes and itself reflects the same basic pattern of understanding of the revelatory reality of Christ that Bonhoeffer had outlined in the second order theological discourse of his 1933 academic lectures and his student papers in systematic theology. Christ is God's revelatory reality in history. He is actually encountered both in the concrete world and in the special experience of faith.

The sermon begins with the psalmist's encounter with this God in the past; his experience is one in which faith is related to his own political and social calamity. Eventually, that past thanksgiving is correlated with the German Harvest Festival of 1931. Again, faith's special experience is seen as necessarily correlated with one's broader encounter of economic conditions and meetings with persons in the everyday world. Bonhoeffer's sermon ties every abstract term to concrete experience by relentlessly specifying its concrete implications in relation to worldly activities.

It is a familiar process. Sometimes it even occurs in sermons. Here it manifests the christological dialectic in terms of which his whole theology is structured. Since Christ is experienced as God's self-revelation both in special experiences of faith and in the world at large, one must regularly identify, even in contexts where the congregation has taken time out from daily concerns to assemble to renew their special encounter with him, the worldly relevance and implications of their faith. And this must be done so that the most specific worldly events are clearly viewed as occasions of encounter with the revelatory reality of God himself. Concretion is an essential quality of the language of faith. In this respect the primary religious language of the sermon and the second order theological discourse of Bonhoeffer are at one.

A second example, from a somewhat later period, is worth examining. In 1934 Bonhoeffer was in England as pastor of two German-speaking congregations in the London area. At St. Paul's Church, one evening sermon each month was customarily given in English. One of Bonhoeffer's sermons on these occasions dealt with 2 Corinthians 12:9: "My strength is made perfect in weakness."[17] It provides a second illustration of Bonhoeffer's dogged quest for concretion in the language of his theology so that, by specifying its meanings, everyday, perceivable, worldly events become part of his broader theological discourse. Again, the fact that Christ as the revelatory reality of God is encountered in the world at large as well as in special activities of the faithful is clearly his controlling supposition.

Bonhoeffer rightly begins by noting the problem of definition that is at stake in this paradoxical text. Does Paul here have in mind "physical or mental or moral weakness"?[18] Bonhoeffer declares that most of us would rather avoid this sort of question, because it makes us feel confused and uncomfortable. "But God does not want us to put our heads into the sand like ostriches, he commands us to face reality as it is and to make an honest and definite decision."[19] Therefore, he proceeds:

> Why is this problem of weakness so all important? We answer: have you seen a greater mystery in this world than poor people, old people, insane people, people who cannot help themselves but who have just to rely on other people for help, for love, for care? Have you ever thought what outlook on life a cripple, a hopelessly sick man, a man exploited by society, a coloured man in a white country, an untouchable may have?[20]

Here again is the familiar process of specifying increasingly concrete meanings for abstract expressions. Confronted with the problem of definition of the abstraction "weakness," Bonhoeffer identifies, as his first step in the process, several meanings that are lower level abstractions: "physical weakness," "mental weakness," or "moral weakness." Each of these expressions, however, itself remains vague and abstract until it is in turn associated with references to exemplary cases of actual persons who, observed, might be called "weak" in one or more of these ways.

So the specification continues. Those who are weak have "to rely upon other people for help, for love, for care." They are first identified as classes sharing observable characteristics: "poor people, old people, insane people." Then Bonhoeffer switches to single cases: "a cripple, a hopelessly sick man, a man exploited by society, a coloured man in a white country, an untouchable." We begin to identify more and more concretely the meaning of "weakness" in terms of concrete references and descriptions. "This cripple is weak." "This hopelessly sick man is weak."

This increasing specification of the implications of abstract terms, thus increasingly identifying them with observable worldly circumstances, is one of Bonhoeffer's key techniques for relating the two paradoxical sides of the revelational reality to which his Christology points. For Bonhoeffer, it is just in such specific, observable realities of the everyday world that one actually encounters the God of Jesus Christ as the one present *pro nobis*. It is for this reason that Bonhoeffer again and again so consistently introduces such worldly specifics into what are clearly theological contexts. Every attempt, therefore, to confine one's encounter with Christ to special contexts of explicit church life must fail, since Christ's reality is actually encountered also in the broader life of the secular world.

Bonhoeffer had presented a more theoretic and detailed discussion of the historical reality of the divine self-revelation in Jesus as a man who lived a long time ago in his 1933 academic lectures on "Christology." There he had asserted that God was at the same time fully historical in this self-revelation and yet one whose reality is beyond purely historical verification. Playing upon the personal quality of Christ's reality, he insisted that one should only ask "who he is," presupposing his presence fully within history and yet as one who is more than any purely empirical or historical investigation itself can comprehend. Furthermore, no "how can he be who he is" questions can be introduced into a genuine theology. Merely to pose such questions is already to be lost in their problematic and empty implications. His answer to those who may remain too acutely attuned to such problems is a simple assertion that Christ is actually already present personally with the questioner, who cannot, therefore, reduce his or her knowledge of Christ to what can be constructed from such historical research. This indeed might appear to be closely similar to one's knowledge of any other person present with anyone today. Christ's reality seems to be different only in the fact that references cannot be made directly to a separate datum accessible to all observers, as, for example, at least some can be made to the physical body of another present person. In his dissertation Bonhoeffer had claimed that the "collective personal reality of such persons" who are part of a genuine community (*Gemeinde*), however, is what is referred to when one speaks of encounter with Christ present *pro nobis*. Such an observable presence admittedly does not solve all questions about how one can encounter other personal realities, human or divine. But it does nullify some of their force for any person who thus encounters God directly in the concrete events that relate one to his or her neighbor.[21]

In this 1934 sermon Bonhoeffer presents a similar view. Christ is present concretely in one's neighbor whom he sees in need of help. The immediacy and concretion of Christ's presence are given in the experience by which one knows his own neighbor, who may indeed take no part at all in faith's special experiences. Questions about how this can be are thorny enough whenever one entertains them, but they are trivial and irrelevant to one who is actually thus actively experiencing Christ's presence.

One must keep in mind how unwavering Bonhoeffer was concerning the fact that the norm for identifying Christ's presence in the world is given in his more specifiable form as the Word and the Sacrament of the church.[22] Here his own sermons, however, consistently force one to recognize just how this normative presence is to be experienced. As the special Word proclaimed to the assembled congregation, Christ is always concretely present in the reality of the most sensory events of the past, the present, and the future. So Bonhoeffer's own proclamation of Christ's presence *pro nobis* is always cast in terms of the interplay between the language of the most concrete descriptions of and references to the everyday world and the special theological formulations of the Christian tradition.

The more concrete language of these two sermons is predominantly in the past or present tenses. "Two and a half millennia have now passed since the ancient Jewish saint, far from Jerusalem and his homeland, devoured by misery in body and soul, surrounded by mockers and enemies of his God, pondered the strange and wonderful ways God had led him."[23] Anyone alive at the time of the Hebrew exile in a position to see and hear this "Jewish saint" could have provided this information. No special religious experience would have been required.

"Today we celebrate our Harvest Festival."[24] Again, here is a report that could easily have been made by anyone present on the occasion of this sermon's delivery. Occasionally, the time passes to the immediate future. "What if, precisely at the moment when we are thanking God for his goodness towards us, there is a ring at the door . . . and we find someone standing there who also wants to thank God for some small gift."[25] This statement also, though hypothetical, is capable of being translated into statements reporting conditions observable by anyone whose senses were operative and in a position to observe the houses to which these worshipers were to return a bit later on that October day in 1931. Along with the special language of faith, Christians' theological discourse must always also include such concrete descriptive formulas, since it must speak of God's self-revelation as a revelatory reality in the world.

Yet a third sermon from this period is oriented more generally on this future, concrete situation in which the presence of Christ is expected to be encountered. On 24 July 1932, Bonhoeffer preached in Berlin's Holy Trinity Church. On the Ninth Sunday after Trinity the service commemorated the close of the summer semester at the university. His text was John 8:32b: "The truth shall make you free."

This year had been Bonhoeffer's first as a lecturer in the theological faculty and as an ordained pastor to students at the Technische Hochschule and the confirmation class in the Wedding neighborhood of Berlin's inner city. It was also for him a kind of almost frantic ecumenical activity, both within Germany and abroad. It can only be described as a hectic time for him. And it ended in the broader, threatening circumstances of political unrest related to the "Brining crisis," which would only be fully resolved with Hitler's appointment as Reichskanzler late in the next January. Bonhoeffer had just returned to Berlin from a Franco-German ecumenical youth conference in the Westerwald, and he apparently rushed away soon after his sermon for another ecumenical youth conference on world peace, this one in Czechoslovakia. He left it early to return to Berlin in time to be able to vote in the crucial Reichstag election on the following Sunday. What would later be called the "Church Struggle" was yet to emerge. The political and economic realities facing Germany at this time were already extremely complex and problematic, and many persons chose simply to withdraw from the struggle to deal with them. But Bonhoeffer's own clear focus of the attention of his congregation at this point upon the need to face these realities is again intense in this sermon.

He began by simply reading his text. Then he proceeded to characterize its quality.

> That is perhaps the most revolutionary word of the New Testament. For that reason, it is not directed to the masses, but, on the contrary, will be understood only by the few real revolutionaries. It is an exclusive word. For the crowd it remains a mystery. They make an empty slogan [*Phrase*] out of it. That is the most dangerous thing, for such empty slogans totally deaden the revolutionary.[26]

Bonhoeffer's stance is immediately familiar. One who would understand the biblical word must recognize that it is directed towards concrete, even revolutionary circumstances. Only those "few real revolutionaries" will grasp its significance. Wishing to avoid the concrete actions in which the revolutionary is willing to engage is theologically wrong. Simply to talk in abstract, "phraseological" terms, as the masses do when they repeat such words as slogans emptied of real meaning, is common enough, but it only increases the dangers to which Germany is currently exposed.

Again here Bonhoeffer views Christian reflection as having to do with concrete activity addressed to concrete situations, not as a matter of "pure talk" or purely subjective feelings or attitudes. The crowd, after all, who do not face the demands of the gospel, make its language into a purely abstract, verbal game.[27] The gospel requires the sort of talk that is common to serious revolutionaries, a combination of general hopes and specific programmatic proposals for action to bring these hopes closer to reality. Again here, the pattern of Bonhoeffer's christological dialectic is clearly his controlling perspective.

His next step is to describe, again in quite concrete terms, a situation that "everyone has experienced."

> A group of adults is gathered. In the play of conversation a topic which is personally embarrassing to the group cannot be avoided. An agonized discussion of it finally occurs, which is full of deception and anxiety. A child, by chance there who does not un-

derstand the situation fully, knows something which all the others indeed also know but have avoided. The child is astonished that the others appear not to know what it knows and blurts it right out. A paralyzed shock makes its way around the circle. The child is again astonished, happy that it was right about the topic. Something irreparable has taken place. The conversation has been totally deprived of its deception and anxiety.[28]

Again here one finds virtually a paragraph of the most concrete description of a drawing room situation which has no special religious dimension at all. The awkwardness of this polite discussion, which cannot proceed without offending the sensibilities of those present, is clearly identified. The "inoffensive offense" of blurting out the painful topic, provided this disclosure comes from childish innocence and ignorance of what was going on in the circle until then, is graphically pictured.

No sooner has Bonhoeffer finished sketching this scene so vividly, however, than he moves away from it. Such a moment is a mere capsule dose of the larger medication which the mass of Christians in Germany desperately need in the summer of 1932. The truth which the gospel describes and requires directs those in the congregation again and again to pay attention even to embarrassing political and economic facts.

While it is easy enough to speak of freedom in some ways to Germans at present, Bonhoeffer goes on to say, it is not easy at all to speak as the biblical message does. He notes,

> In today's Germany there may be many who, like the imprisoned Israelites at one time, deeply absorbed in themselves, dream of nothing else than freedom. They have great visions of the image of freedom and grasp after it, until they awaken and the picture fades away. Indeed, it is easy today to speak thus of freedom.[29]

To speak of freedom in terms solely appropriate for visions or dreams, which immediately are destroyed when one awakens to face the complex demands of one's daily round, is easy enough. But that is not the freedom of which the gospel speaks and which it requires of Christians. "But it is very difficult to speak of freedom as the Bible does."[30] Instead of a pure vision, there one is offered a truth that empowers one to become free and to actively engender freedom. Of the one who comprehends this sort of freedom Bonhoeffer says: "The one who loves because he was made free by the truth of God is the most revolutionary person on the earth. He is the one who overturns all values. He is the dynamite of human society. He is the most dangerous person."[31] On this forcing conclusion Bonhoeffer's sermon climaxes.

Clearly, here he again understands Christian consciousness as necessarily requiring one to grapple with the thorniest social issues, at least some of which require massive restructuring of the available economic and political institutions, more than mere reform. In terms that already strikingly prefigure those he later used in the midst of the Church Struggle,[32] Bonhoeffer here again called upon his congregation to face fully and actively the complex and confusing demands of their concrete, secular situation. Only thus will they be able to experience the truthful, realistic freedom of life in Christ.

Bonhoeffer closed his sermon with a prayer:

> All of us, each individual for himself and all together, feel the oppressing encumbrance of our chains. God, we cry out after freedom. But, O God, protect us that we may not imagine a false picture of freedom and so remain in falsehood. Grant us the freedom which throws us totally upon you, upon grace. Lord, make us free with your truth, which is Jesus Christ. Lord, we wait upon your truth.[33]

Again one hears the clarion note of the Christian's responsibility to face all facts, no matter how unpleasant or secular, and to act upon them so as to make concrete changes in the public sphere of social life.

In this sermon the reality of Christ *pro nobis* is viewed more eschatologically. Christ is the one who wills creative change for all who consciously live under his lordship. To pray for his own realization is also to engage in activities that change present social structures so they more adequately promote and encourage genuine freedom. To be free is to be able to pray for the coming of such a Lord into one's own life. To experience his presence means just to be able to face realistically and truthfully the concrete situation in which one lives and to engage in tangible efforts, which in God's grace will force social institutions themselves to awaken from their present compromises with visionary, unrealistic, dreamful fantasy.

Again, Bonhoeffer here stresses the social reality of one's experience of Christ. And in the interplay between his special language of Christian faith and expressions that describe particular everyday experiences, whether they be polite social conversation or political and economic issues, he presents his understanding of the gospel. His abstract vision of "freedom" as it ought to be as the revelatory reality of Christ also becomes the tangible future of the world, which revolutionaries work to make real. This real freedom of Christ keeps breaking into the awkwardness and pure abstraction of most persons' intellectualized freedom, as the child's remark breaks through the unreal and uncomfortable tangents into which everyday, mannerly conversation sometimes turns. But this real freedom, evidenced in everyday circumstances even as it is revealed in Christ, also therefore requires realistic, truthful, and detailed analysis of those circumstances as well as committed effort to act to bring about the implications for social change that result from this analysis. No mere discussion, no completely abstract or phraseological language will suffice for such purposes.

This work has traced a conceptual pattern whereby Bonhoeffer's consistent "christological dialectic" is expressed in three sermons. Here and elsewhere in his writings it provides a demanding incentive for Christians to face social realities frankly, even when they become threatening or frustratingly obtuse. It also both affirms the vision of a better social order and motivates persons of Christian faith to engage in actions that appear likely to transform present institutions and conditions of everyday life into greater future conformity with this vision. While Bonhoeffer does not himself directly propose any detailed program of social reform for Germany, he is clearly calling upon all Christians to seek to work out such programs. To engage in such programming and political and economic reform is in fact to experience the reality of Christ's presence *pro nobis* as "truthful, realistic freedom" and to avoid the fantasy that transmutes the concrete demands of faith into merely intellectual or contemplative abstraction. His broader theology regularly juxtaposes what we have found here: two different but dialectically interrelated forms of conceiving reality. The one can only be abstract and imaginative in its orientational richness. In Bonhoeffer's view, however, such imaginative structures can only serve Christian spirituality when it also dares to use the most concrete descriptive and referential discourse to indicate what responsible actions faith requires those who would be faithful to undertake.

ENDNOTES

1. The author's friendship with Prof. Burton Nelson through many years has meant a deepening of his knowledge of Bonhoeffer's life and theology and of Burton's pastoral depth. The present work, a revision of a section of an unpublished Ph.D. dissertation on "Revelation and the Secular in the Theology of Dietrich Bonhoeffer" (Yale University, 1980), is offered here as a token of respect for the faith, theology, and sermons of both of these men.

2. Many agree that Bonhoeffer's theology displays a consistent concentration upon Christology and seeks to make the implications of Christian faith concrete and clear. The present analysis is an effort to explicate these recurrent central themes by examination of three early sermons. The full statement of this argument for Bonhoeffer's early works is in "Revelation and the Secular," 178-203.

3. Above all, Bonhoeffer here agrees with Karl Barth.

4. A similar analysis of the manner in which the paradoxical conceptual structure of Bonhoeffer's christological dialectic appears in his other writings is pre-

sented in "Revelation and the Secular," 215-341.

5. See Clyde E. Fant's discussion of Bonhoeffer's preaching in part 1 of *Bonhoeffer: Worldly Preaching* (Nashville: Thomas Nelson, Inc., 1975).
6. *DB* [E.T.], 164; *DB*, 265.
7. *GS* 4, 17-25; *NRS*, 125-32.
8. Ibid., 17-18; 125 (German term supplied).
9. Ibid., 18; 125.
10. Ibid., 19; 126.
11. Ibid., 20; 127.
12. Ibid., 20-21; 128.
13. Ibid., 21; 128.
14. Ibid.
15. Ibid.
16. Ibid.
17. *GS* 4, 179-82.
18. Ibid., 179.
19. Ibid.
20. Ibid., 179-80.
21. Obviously, from the way Bonhoeffer specifies the concrete presence of Christ in these sermons and elsewhere, he cannot mean by *Gemeinde* only the members of a congregation gathered for worship or mutual concerns. He repeatedly specifies that anyone known to be in need is the one in whom Christ's presence is encountered. One does not always meet such persons in church.
22. This normative priority is clearly laid down in the ontological language of *Akt und Sein*, for example, where the church is presented as the sole place "where *Dasein* is understood" (s. 88; *AB*, 118). Bonhoeffer here uses *Dasein* to signify the concreteness of all existence. The church as an existing community is one part of the world of *Dasein*, but only one part. Yet in the church the concrete being of the whole existing world is consciously understood. In part 3 below we shall see how this view of the church's understanding of all reality is modified somewhat in Bonhoeffer's latest writings, but never disavowed. However, its later groundings take on a decidedly less explicitly ontological and systematic form.
23. *NRS*, 125; *GS* 4, 17.
24. Ibid., 128; 20.
25. Ibid., 128; 21.
26. "Das ist vielleicht das revolutionärste Wort des Neuen Testaments. Es richtet sich darum nicht an die Massen, sondern es wird begriffen von den wenigen echten Revolutionären. Es ist ein exklusives Wort. Es bleibt der Menge ein Geheimnis, sie macht eine Phrase daraus. Das is Gefährlichste; denn die Phrase stempft das Revolutionäre gänzlich ab" (*GS* 4, 79; translated by the present author).
27. The present author, in "Revelation and the Secular," shows how Bonhoeffer consistently avoided all concepts that he regarded as purely "*phraseologische*," since he wanted to speak about concrete realities.
28. "Ein Kreis von erwachsenen Menschen ist zusammen. Im Laufe des Gespräches kann ein Thema, das einigen Anwesenden persönlich peinlich ist, nicht vermieden werden. Es kommt zu einer gequälten Aussprache, die voller Lüge und Angst ist. Ein Kind, das zufällig dabei ist und die Lage nicht erfasst, weiss irgendetwas, was zwar alle anderen auch wissen, aber scheu verdecken. Das Kind wundert sich, dass die anderen das nicht zu wissen scheinen, was es weiss, und sagt es rund heraus. Ein starres Entsetzen geht durch den Kreis—das Kind wundert sich und freut sich, dass es das Richtige gewusst hat. Es ist etwas Irreparables geschehen. Das Gerede

voll Lüge und Angst ist jäh abgeschnitten" (*GS*, 79-80; translation by present author).

29. "Es mag im heutigen Deutschland manche geben, die, wie einst die gefangenen Israeliten, tief in sich versunken von nichts anderem träumen als von der Freiheit, die in grossen Visionen ihr Bild sehen und nach ihm greifen, bis sie erwachen und das Bild zerrinnt. Jawohl, es ist heute leicht, von der Freiheit so zu reden" (ibid., 82; translation by the present author).

30. "Aber es ist sehr schwer, von der Freiheit so zu reden, wie die Bibel es tut" (ibid.; translation by the present author).

31. "Der Mensch, der liebt, weil er durch die Wahrheit Gottes frei gemacht ist, ist der revolutionärste Mensch auf Erden. Er ist der Umsturz aller Werte, er ist der Sprengstoff der menschlichen Gesellschaft, er ist der gefährlichste Mensch" (ibid., 86; translation by the present author).

32. One thinks especially of the notion of "costly grace," a central theme of *Nachfolge*, as Bonhoeffer understood the cost to be expended not only in protecting the privileges of the Church against state restriction, but also in behalf of all victims of political, economic, and social injustice, whatever might be their religious allegiance or lack of it.

33. "Wir alle, jeder einzelne für sich und wir als Gesamtheit, fühlen die drückende Last unserer Ketten. Gott, wir schreien nach der Freiheit. Aber, o Gott, bewahre uns, dass wir kein lügnerisches Bild der Freiheit erträumen und in der Lüge bleiben. Gib du uns die Freiheit die uns ganz auf dich, auf die Gnade wirft. Herr, mache uns mit deiner Wahrheit, die Jesus Christus ist, frei. Herr, wir warten auf deine Wahrheit" (*GS* 4, 87; translation by the present author).

Responsible Sharing of the Mystery of Christian Faith: *Disciplina Arcani* in the Life and Theology of Dietrich Bonhoeffer

John W. Matthews

I t is the intent of this essay to describe the concept of *disciplina arcani*[1] in the early church and to show how Dietrich Bonhoeffer understood the concept. Furthermore, specific implications will be drawn regarding the importance of the concept for our own day. It is not at all surprising that Dietrich Bonhoeffer found this ancient concept helpful, because the context of his life was in several ways similar to that of the early church. The twentieth-century threats to Christian faith from National Socialism, the German Christian heresy, and religious banality in the German National Church (Volkskirche) were in some ways very similar to the ancient threats of overt pagan hostility, the Gnostic heresy, and religious banality in the post-Constantinian church. Although Bonhoeffer's extant writings reveal only three specific references to it,[2] the concept of *disciplina arcani* was central to Bonhoeffer's entire theological orientation. The "early" Bonhoeffer understood *arkandisziplin*[3] to be "responsible sharing of the mystery" of Christian faith primarily in the context of the Church focused in word and sacraments. The "later" Bonhoeffer matured toward an understanding of *arkandisziplin* as the "responsible sharing of the mystery" of Christian faith also in the context of the secular community through prayer, righteous action, qualified silence, and the nonreligious interpretation of biblical concepts in a world come of age. An understanding of Bonhoeffer's maturation regarding this concept lies at the heart of an appreciation of his theological contribution and is important in sharing the Christian mystery responsibly in our day.

DISCIPLINA ARCANI IN THE LIFE OF THE EARLY CHURCH

The concept of *disciplina arcani* has its roots in the New Testament community. The Scriptures describe a concern to protect and responsibly share the gospel of the kingdom, inaugurated in Jesus the Christ, against profanation. "And he said to them, To you has been given the secret of the kingdom of God, but for those outside everything is in parables" (Mark 4:10-11). Similarly, we read in Matthew's Gospel: "Do not give dogs what is holy; and do not throw your pearls before swine, lest they trample them under foot"(Matthew 7:6). The writings of Paul reveal a similar concern in his distinction between human wisdom and the wisdom of God:

> Yet among the mature we do impart wisdom, although it is not a wisdom of this age or of the rulers of this age, who are doomed to pass away. But we impart a secret and hidden wisdom of God, which God decreed before the ages for our glorification. None of the rulers of this age understood this; for if they had, they would not have crucified the Lord of Glory. (1 Corinthians 2:6-8)

This concern for "responsible sharing of the mystery" continued into the life of the early church, as evidenced in the writings of Tertullian, Origen, Basil, Ambrose, Gregory of Nazianzus, Jerome, Chrysostom, Augustine, Innocent I, and Cyril of Alexandria. Cyril of Alexandria (A.D. 412-44) wrote about the need for carefully guarding the mysteries of Christian faith:

> These mysteries, which the Church now explains to thee who art passing out of the class of Catechumens, it is not the custom to explain to heathen. For to a heathen we do not explain the mysteries concerning Father, Son, and Holy Ghost, nor before Catechumens do we speak plainly of the mysteries; but many things we often speak in a veiled way, that the believers who know may understand and they who know not may get no hurt. (Catech. Vi,29)[4]

> St. Augustine and St. Chrysostom, in like manner, frequently stopped short in their public addresses, and after a more or less veiled reference to the mysteries, continued with: "the initiated will understand what I mean."[5]

In the early church, the catechumenate was the primary means of practicing *disciplina arcani*. The catechumenate was a formal program of instruction and activity for initiating persons into the Christian faith in a guided and gradual fashion. "Systematic organization of the catechumenate shows a clear pastoral awareness of the importance of serious introduction to the sacramental world of Christianity."[6] Following an initial period of examination which determined whether one was sincere, there were steps of instruction and practical training in what it meant to be Christian. The catechumens were under careful scrutiny regarding their worthiness to share in the mystery of Christian faith. Three years was the normal time required to complete catechetical instruction in preparation for Christian baptism.[7]

Overt pagan hostility appears to have been the initial threat to the Christian mystery which occasioned a need for *disciplina arcani*. Although Christians before A.D. 70 enjoyed a relatively secure position as "relatives" of Judaism, the conflict between the Christian Church and the Roman culture became increasingly violent. The major persecutions of Decius (A.D. 250-51) and Diocletian (A.D. 303-04) were part of an overall attempt to eliminate the sacrilegious Christians from society. The persecutions of Caracalla, Maximus, Gallus, and Valerian further displayed overt pagan hostility, necessitating a more careful guarding of the Christian mystery *against* persecution and profanation.

Gnostic Christianity, with its doctrine of efficacious initiations, is usually identified as a second context in which *disciplina arcani* arose. As the early church reflected upon the mystery it possessed and sought to share it responsibly, the church found it necessary to distinguish its beliefs from similar concepts in Gnosticism. The mystery of God Incarnate in Jesus the Christ was substantially different from the docetic mystery of Gnostic thought. Initiation as practiced through the catechumenate bore little resemblance to the philosophical exercises for the "spiritual ones" being introduced to Gnosticism. Since, for Christians, "The Word became flesh and dwelt among us"(John 1:14), salvation was understood as available not only to those who had the intellectual capacity to receive such knowledge from the pleroma beyond, but "to all who received him, who believed in his name, he gave power to become the children of God" (John 1:12).

Religious banality, which followed Constantine's Edict of Milan in A.D. 313, presented a third threat occasioning a need for *disciplina arcani*. The threat facing the Church after A.D. 313 was less physical or heretical and more psychological and behavioral. Apathy and religious banality resulted from Christianity's being endorsed as the official religion of the state without the condition of personal conviction or loyalty.

> Since under Constantine the Great at the beginning of the fourth century Christianity became a state religion, masses of pagans flowed into the Church, and this danger had for the Church a

double misunderstanding: a devaluation of its holy possessions of faith (*arcanum*) to banalities of religious convention and in the causal correlation with the secularization of Christian life through which "the masses only desired external Christianity."[8]

Disciplina arcani was practiced in the early church to protect and responsibly share the incarnational presence of God in Jesus Christ, which was "in the world but not of it" (John 17). The institution of a catechumenate reveals "the mentality of a Church conscious of her responsibility, who took her moral ideal seriously and courageously laid down clear conditions for those who wanted to become her members."[9]

ARKANDISZIPLIN IN THE THEOLOGY OF DIETRICH BONHOEFFER

Bonhoeffer wrote from Tegel prison on 5 May 1944, "That means that an *arkandisziplin* must be restored. Through which the mysteries of Christian faith are protected against profanation."[10] Three questions arise from Bonhoeffer's observation: First, what are the mysteries of Christian faith to which he referred? Second, what threats in his day caused him to believe these mysteries needed protection? Third, how did he propose that this protection might be accomplished? The answers to these questions reveal just how central *disciplina arcani* was to Bonhoeffer's entire theological orientation.

The mysteries of Christian faith, for Bonhoeffer, are the ways in which Jesus Christ was and is incarnationally present in the world. "If we now ask about the *arkanum*, which is guarded in the *disziplin* of life together, it can clearly be stated: it is Jesus Christ himself."[11] "The proclaimed Word is the incarnate Christ himself."[12] "The one who has been made flesh, made man, is in the sacrament in the form of a stumbling block."[13] "The Church is the presence of God in the world."[14] Bonhoeffer understood the presence of Jesus Christ in this threefold Lutheran manner: the word, the sacraments, and the Church. In his christological lectures presented during the summer of 1933, Bonhoeffer delineated what he believed to be the central mystery of Christian faith:

> Jesus is the Christ present as the Crucified and Risen One. . . . Christ is present in the Church as a person. . . . Only the Risen One makes possible the presence of the living person. . . . Only because Jesus Christ is man is he present in time and place. Only because Jesus Christ is God is he eternally present everywhere. . . . This presence has a three-fold form in the church, that of the Word, the sacraments and the community.[15]

There were at least three threats to these mysteries which, according to Bonhoeffer, occasioned the need for protection against profanation: National Socialism, the German Christian heresy, and religious banality in the German National Church (Volkskirche).

Concerning the threat of National Socialism, Arthur Cochrane writes, "It ought to have been obvious from the start that when Hitler proclaimed an ideology as a political faith with totalitarian claims upon the whole life of men, and demanded for himself absolute obedience, National Socialism and Christianity were mutually exclusive."[16]

The real threat of National Socialism lay in its worship of another god. In place of the kingdom of God established by Jesus Christ and transcending racial boundaries was the thousand-year Reich created by Hitler and intent on the inclusion of only those persons of Aryan descent. The mystery of Christian faith—the incarnational presence of God—was being confronted by the incarnational presence of Satan, Adolf Hitler.

Concerning the threat of the German Christian heresy, Karl Barth wrote,

> Our protest is directed against the teaching of the German Christians. . . . Our protest . . . cannot begin only at the Aryan paragraph. . . . It must be directed fundamentally against the fact (which is the source of all individual errors) that, besides the Holy Scriptures as the unique source of revelation, the German Christians affirm the German nationhood, its history and its contemporary situation as a second source of revelation.[17]

The real threat of the German Christian heresy lay in its affirmation of a "second source of revelation." Similar to the ancient heretical threat of Gnosticism (requiring additional philosophical enlightenment) was the German Christian heretical threat requiring belief in God's additional revelation through the leader (*Fuhrer*) of a master race (*Herrnrasse*). The mystery of Christian faith, grounded in the unique revelation of God "once and for all" (Hebrews 10:10), was being confronted by an additional, and contrary, reality.

Concerning the threat of religious banality, Bonhoeffer himself wrote,

> It is under the influence of this (cheap) kind of "grace" that the world has been made "Christian," but at the cost of secularizing the Christian religion as never before. . . . The Christian life comes to mean nothing more than living in the world and as the world, in being no different from the world for the sake of grace. . . . The result was that a nation became Christian and Lutheran but at the cost of true discipleship.[18]

The real threat of religious banality within the German National Church was that the complete presence of Jesus Christ in grace and judgment was replaced by merely civic and political obedience. In the uncritical marriage of church and state, the truth was sacrificed on the altar of expedience. When the acceptable thing to do became Christian, then the "Christian" thing was to do what was acceptable.

We are given significant help by Bonhoeffer on how the protection against profanation might be accomplished. In light of the three aforementioned threats, he often wrote about the necessity for "responsible sharing of the mystery" in the life of the church. On the occasion of a retreat for Confessing Church pastors in May 1937, Bonhoeffer delivered a paper entitled "The Power of the Keys and Church Discipline," in which his concern was summarized:

> The promise of grace is not to be squandered; it needs to be protected from the godless. There are those who are not worthy of the sanctuary. The proclamation of grace has its limits. Grace may not be proclaimed to anyone who does not recognize or distinguish or desire it. . . . For its own sake, for the sake of the sinner, and for the sake of the community, the Holy is to be protected from cheap surrender.[19]

Equally eloquent was his earlier concern for "costly grace."

> Costly grace is the treasure hidden in the field. . . . It is the pearl of great price. . . . Costly grace is the Incarnation of God. . . . It has to be protected from the world, and not thrown to the dogs. . . . Cheap grace is the preaching of forgiveness without requiring repentance, baptism without church discipline, communion without confession. . . . We must therefore attempt to recover a true understanding of the mutual relation between grace and discipleship.[20]

Jorg Meier has correctly understood that, for Bonhoeffer, the essential activity of the Church is to "specifically carry out the protection of the integrity of the present body of Christ by correct preaching, right administration of the sacraments, and proper communal life."[21] The Confessing Church came into being in 1934 in direct response to the threats that National Socialism posed for this essential activity of the church. Bonhoeffer never tired of defending the church's God-given authority and commission to preach the gospel correctly and live Christian life authentically. His early and ongoing concern was that the "mystery of Christian faith" be protected and responsibly shared in the context of the church community.

The maturation of *disciplina arcani* in the theology of Dietrich Bonhoeffer is revealed in a letter to his friend Eberhard Bethge, dated 30 April 1944:

> What is bothering me incessantly is the question what Christianity really is, or indeed who Christ is, for us today. . . . What do a Church, a community, a sermon, a liturgy, a Christian life mean in a religionless world? . . . How do we speak . . . in a "secular" way about "God"? . . . What is the place of worship and prayer in a religionless situation? Does the secret discipline . . . take on new importance here?[22]

While Bonhoeffer's concern for "responsible sharing of the mystery" in the context of the church community never diminished, we can observe in his later years an insistence that the church's ultimate identity in Christ never be separated from its penultimate solidarity with the world.[23] He shared with other members of his family a deep love for and commitment to the world into which he was born. His theology consistently reflected a deep desire to relate the eternal Christ to the temporal culture. Bonhoeffer's vision for this "new importance" of *arkandisziplin* included particular ideas about Christian prayer, righteous action, qualified silence, and nonreligious interpretation of biblical concepts.

Arkandisziplin meant, for Bonhoeffer, that Christian prayer is "undemonstrative action":

> Prayer is the supreme instance of the hidden character of the Christian life. It is the antithesis of self-display. . . . Prayer does not aim at any direct effect upon the world; it is addressed to God alone, and is therefore the perfect example of undemonstrative action.[24]

Prayer is conversation with God for the purpose of affirming one's ultimate identity with Christ and one's penultimate solidarity with the world. In prayer Christians are incorporated into the kingdom of God, recognize that God knows their every need, intercede for the entire world, and are organized with other Christians into instruments of God's will.[25] Christian prayer, while undemonstrative, is active in that it places one in a proper posture before God, one's neighbor, and oneself. "Responsible sharing of the mystery" begins in prayer by discouraging merely personal agendas, divine manipulation, self-seeking piety, and strictly individualistic faith.

Arkandisziplin meant, for Bonhoeffer, that righteous action and qualified silence are essential elements of authentic witness. Bonhoeffer wrote, "Our Church, which has been fighting in these years only for its self-preservation, . . . is incapable of taking the word of reconciliation and redemption to mankind and the world. . . . Our being Christians today will be limited to two things: prayer and righteous action among men."[26] In his fragmentary work on *Ethics,* Bonhoeffer addressed the topic of righteous action, although under the heading "The Structure of Responsible Life":

> The structure of responsible life is conditioned by two factors; life is bound to man and to God and a man's own life is free. . . . The obligation assumes the form of deputyship and of correspondence with reality; freedom displays itself in self-examination of life and of action and in the venture of a concrete decision. . . . Responsible action includes both the readiness to accept guilt and freedom.[27]

Deputyship in correspondence with reality that is lived in freedom and the readiness to accept guilt could well summarize Bonhoeffer's convictions regarding righteous action.

Qualified silence was, for Bonhoeffer, a necessary counterpart to righteous action. From his father he learned that "silence is also an important form of speech."[28] "No good at all can come from acting before the world and one's self as though we knew the truth, when in reality we do not. . . . Qualified silence might perhaps be more appropriate for the church today than talk which is very unqualified."[29] At certain times and in certain places the Church finds itself knowing the ultimate Word of reconciliation in Jesus Christ, but being unable to relate it to the penultimate reality of given situations. "Truth is too important for that, and it would be a betrayal of this truth if the church were to hide itself behind resolutions and pious so-called Christian principles, when it is called to look the truth in the face and once and for all confess its guilt and its ignorance."[30]

Arkandisziplin meant, for Bonhoeffer, the necessity of a "non-religious interpretation of biblical concepts in a world come of age." Although this phrase has often been abused and misunderstood to simply affirm the secular humanism of our day, the "language of a new righteousness and truth,"[31] which he strove to create, is essential for "responsible sharing of the mystery." Bonhoeffer wrote on 30 April 1944:

> We are moving towards a completely religionless time; people as they are now simply cannot be religious any more. . . . Our whole nineteen-hundred-year-old Christian preaching and theology rest on the "religious *a priori*" of mankind. . . . But if one day it becomes clear that this *a priori* does not exist at all . . .[32]

Bonhoeffer's critique of the "religious *a priori*" had its beginning in Karl Barth's radical distinction between religion and Christian faith. "Every sermon he gave in Barcelona indicated what he had learnt from Karl Barth . . . of opposition to religion . . . religion meaning that human activity that seeks to reach the beyond, to postulate a divinity, to invoke help and protection, in short: religion as self-justification."[33]

His criticism of religion was primarily aimed at outdated ideas and expressions of Christian faith such as other-worldly metaphysics, rigorous individualism, the compartmentalism of life into sacred and profane spheres, an image of God simply as a rescuer in time of trouble, arrogance and privilege associated with belonging to the church, and religious tutelage which fostered childlike dependence.[34] Bonhoeffer felt that these outdated religious ideas associated with Christian faith created unnecessary stumbling blocks for authentic discipleship and hindered "responsible sharing of the mystery." His plea for a "non-religious interpretation" was a call for credible expressions of Christian doctrines and realities in the world which had "come of age."

Bonhoeffer's affirmation of the "world come of age" complemented his critique of the religious *a priori*. He understood the world's coming of age to be a natural, important, and divinely willed movement[35] under the lordship of Jesus Christ. The "world come of age" (*die mundige Welt*) was not understood by him to mean that humanity had arrived at a state of moral or scientific perfection, rather that the world's maturity (*mundigkeit*) implied mature responsibility. The world no longer looked to God as a *deus ex machina* from the posture of childlike dependence. On 8 June 1944 Bonhoeffer wrote,

> Efforts are made to prove to a world thus come of age that it cannot live without the tutelage of "God." . . . But what if one day they no longer exist as such, if they . . . the so-called "ultimate questions"—death, guilt—to which only "God" can give an answer . . . too can be answered "without God"? . . . The attack by Christian apologetic on the adulthood of the world . . . seems to me like an attempt to put a grown-up man back into adolescence, i.e. to make him dependent on things on which he is, in fact, no longer dependent.[36]

It was the combination of a world come of *age* with humanity's slowly dying religious *a priori* which led Bonhoeffer to affirm the need for a reinterpretation of biblical concepts in a nonreligious way. "Responsible sharing of the mystery," which begins in prayer and expresses itself in righteous action and qualified silence, now interprets itself theologically in authentic and credible (nonreligious) ways.

Dietrich Bonhoeffer's life and theology can be viewed as an encounter with the question "Who is Christ for us today?"[37] The answer to this dynamic question was not, for him, confined within the chapters of Christian dogmatics, nor ever finally realizable at any one point in history. The presence of Christ needs to be "seen and adored"[38] anew in each life situation. From his earliest days Bonhoeffer understood that Jesus Christ was the God-man present in the community of the Church through the word and sacraments. Yet, and equally significant, he struggled to know the presence of Jesus Christ also at the center of secular history. When Dietrich Bonhoeffer, in 1939, became formally associated with the conspiracy plotting the death of Adolf Hitler, he did so not apart from, but in the grace and judgment of Jesus Christ. In the responsible actions of the conspirators he recognized the presence of Jesus Christ, active at the center of secular history. His solidarity with those who were conspiring for Hitler's death authenticated his conviction that "the church is the church only when it exists for others."[39] "At the end of his prison letters Bonhoeffer proposed his answer to the question, 'Who is Christ for us today?' 'Jesus, the man-for-others' is in fact a new christological title for Bonhoeffer."[40] For Bonhoeffer, the Church is true to itself and credible in the world only when it exists "for others." Bonhoeffer's life and theology are living examples of *disciplina arcani.*

RESPONSIBLE SHARING OF THE MYSTERY OF CHRISTIAN FAITH

Christian Edification: The Relationship of Believing and Being. When the mystery of Christian faith is responsibly shared, Christian edification takes the form of realization. Sanctification is more akin to "being" in Christ than "becoming" like Christ. Christian edification is not what humanity intends to accomplish for God, but the realization of what God intends to accomplish through and for humanity. *Disciplina arcani* assists the Church in knowing that to believe in Jesus Christ is to realize its "being" in Christ. Christian edification understands church community to be a reality received with gratitude rather than an ideal for which to strive. *Disciplina arcani* assists the Church in guarding, protecting, and responsibly sharing the reality of God's incarnational presence in, with, and under every human community.

Christian Education: The Relationship of Believing and Knowing. When the mystery of Christian faith is responsibly shared, Christian education takes the form of describing and discussing the historical Christian kerygma as well as the contemporary reality of God's presence in Jesus Christ through the word, sacraments, and church community. *Disciplina arcani* assists the Church in its educational ministry by encouraging serious reflection on the content of our faith as well as the contexts of our lives. Insofar as cognitive experience affects Christian self-understanding and faith, *disciplina arcani* assists our "rightly handling the word of truth" (2 Timothy 2:15).

Christian Ethics: The Relationship of Believing and Doing. When the mystery of Christian faith is responsibly shared, Christian ethics takes the form of responsible action. Ethical behavior in the Christian community is validated not by the intrinsic virtue of certain deeds from a human perspective, but by the promise of Christ that he is present. "As you have done it to one of the least of these my brethren, you did it to me" (Matthew 25:40). *Disciplina arcani* reminds the church that in, with, and under "merely" human deeds of compassion and justice, God is present. Further, *disciplina arcani* affirms that under certain circumstances, a "qualified silence" bears the most authentic witness to Christ's presence.

Christian "Evangelism": The Relationship of Believing and Witnessing. When the mystery of Christian faith is responsibly shared, Christian witness takes the form of authentic existence. *Disciplina arcani* reminds the Church that its life in Christ is a witness. Bonhoeffer's vision of Christian discipleship in the world come of age necessarily alters traditional ideas about evangelism programs and stresses instead the need for authentic existence: being, knowing, doing the ministry of Christ. In the world come of age, responsible, loving deeds for the neighbor become the means through which the Holy Spirit draws persons into the community of faith. The maturity of the world (*mundigket*) requires that deeds, not words, primarily convey the authenticity of Christian discipleship. While children are often told what to think and do, adults must observe for themselves and responsibly decide. *Disciplina arcani* reminds us that we are "ambassadors for Christ, God making his appeal through us" (2 Corinthians 5:20).

Dietrich Bonhoeffer's life and theology bear authentic witness to the reality of God's presence not only in the church community through the word and sacraments, but also at the center of history and human existence and as mediator between God and nature.[41] Through "correct preaching, right administration of the sacraments, proper communal life,"[42] as well as prayer, righteous action, qualified silence, and the nonreligious interpretation of biblical concepts, *disciplina arcani* is accomplished no less in our day than in the early church or in Nazi Germany.

ENDNOTES

1. The term *disciplina arcani* refers to an early church concept of "responsible sharing of the mystery" of Christain faith—the historic and present Christ—so that the Incarnate One was guarded against profanation. However, *disciplina arcani* did not become a *technicus terminus* until the seventeenth century, when, in the context of a heated theological debate, it was used to rationalize the "apostolic" roots of certain Catholic teachings in spite of their absence in any written record. Examples of teachings purported to be apostolic, yet absent from early records, are transubstantiation and the veneration of images and saints. Tetzel argued against the Jesuit Emanuel von Schlestrate that there were no such teachings kept secret before the year A.D. 200 (*The New Schaff-Herzog Encyclopedia of Religious Knowledge*, 1949 ed., s.v. "*Arcani Disciplina*," by Norman Bontwetsch).

2. *GS* 4, 239; *LPP*, 281, 286.

3. The term *arkandisziplin*, which Bonhoeffer himself used when referring to *disciplina arcani*, is somewhat misleading. Both terms have often been inaccurately rendered "arcane discipline" or "secret discipline," which fail to substantivize *arcani* (secret or mystery). *Arcani* is a substantivized adjective serving as a noun; *disciplina* ought to be more broadly understood as "responsible sharing," not simply discipline. Bonhoeffer's own careless appropriation of this term has resulted in many enthusiasts welcoming his "secret discipline" as a pious counterpart to the worldly, nonreligious, secular interpretation of biblical concepts. In fact, the nonreligious interpretation of biblical concepts is not a counterpart but an important implication of *disciplina arcani*.

4. *Encyclopedia of Religion and Ethics*, 1908 ed., s.v. *"Arcani Disciplina,"* by Edward T. Horn, 676.

5. *The Catholic Encyclopedia*, 1909 ed., s.v. "Discipline of the Secret," by Arthur S. Barnes, 32.

6. Karl Baus, *Handbook of Church History*, Vol. 1: *From the Apostolic Comunity to Constantine* (New York: Herder and Herder, 1965), 215.

7. Ibid., 276-77.

8. Jorg Meier, "Weltlichkeit und Arkandisziplin bei Dietrich Bonhoeffer," *Theologische Existenz Heute* (Munchen: Christian Kaiser Verlag, 1966), 64.

9. Baus, *Handbook of Church History*, 277.

10. *LPP*, 286.

11. Gisela Meuss, "Arkandisziplin und Weltichkeit bei Dietrich Bonhoeffer," *Die Mundige Welt III* (Munchen: Christian Kaiser Verlag, 1960), 84.

12. *GS* 4, 240.

13. *CC*, 55.

14. *NRS*, 154

15. *CC*, 43-47.

16. Arthur C. Cochrane, *The Church's Confession under Hitler* (Philadelphia: The Westminster Press, 1962), 36.

17. Karl Barth, *The German Church Conflict* (Richmond: John Knox Press, 1965), 16.

18. *CD*, 45-60.

19. *WF*, 151.

20. *CD*, 47.

21. Meier, "Weltlichkeit und Arkandisziplin bei Dietrich Bonhoeffer," 69.

22. *LPP*, 279-81. In line 6 of the above quotation, *was bedeutet* is incorrectly rendered "place." Bonhoeffer's concern here is not with the legitimacy or location of worship and prayer, but rather with the meaning or significance of these activities. Earlier in the same quote *was bedeutet* is translated "mean" and more closely describes Bonhoeffer's intent. This incorrect rendering has led several writers to "place" arkandisziplin in juxtaposition to worldliness in Bonhoeffer's theology rather than understand worldliness as an important implication of the "meaning" of *arkandisziplin*. *Disciplina arcani* represents significantly more than an inward, private, devotional counterpart to an outward, public, ethical, nonreligious interpretation of biblical concepts.

23. *E*, 120 ff.

24. *CD*, 181.

25. Ibid., 185, 183; *LT*, 85-87; Dietrich Bonhoeffer, *The Communion of Saints* (New York: Harper and Row, 1963), 134.

26. *LPP*, 300.

27. *E*, 224-41.

28. Renate Bethge, "Elite and Silence in Bonhoeffer's Person and Thoughts," a discussion paper presented at the meeting of The International Bonhoeffer Society for Archive and Research held in February of 1980 at Oxford University, 8.

29. *NRS*, 160.

30. Ibid.

31. *LPP*, 300.

32. Ibid., 279-80.

33. *DB*, 775.

34. Ibid., 774-82.

35. *LPP*, 360-61.

36. Ibid., 326-27.

37. Ibid., 279.

38. *WF*, 75.

39. *LPP*, 382.

40. Eberhard Bethge, "Bonhoeffer's Christology and His 'Religionless Christianity,'" *Union Seminary Quarterly Review* 33:1 (Fall 1967): 75.

41. *CC*, 62-67.

42. Meier, "Weltlichkeit und Arkandisziplin bei Dietrich Bonhoeffer," 69.

BONHOEFFER AND
JEWISH-CHRISTIAN RELATIONS

"…they burned all the meeting places of God in the land"[1]

Jane Pejsa

My thesis is quite simple, namely: In our great rush to memorialize the places of Dietrich Bonhoeffer's life and ministry, we ought also to take note of the neighboring sites where once stood the synagogues and Jewish cemetery chapels. Their wanton destruction on Kristallnacht, 1938, turned out to be God's urgent call to his servant Dietrich Bonhoeffer.

Certainly all of us know well Bonhoeffer's stance on the "Jewish Question," beginning already in 1933 and sharpening as the years went by. Along with this went his gradual disappointment in his own Confessing Church. Clearly the final straw in this disappointment was the calamity of 9 November 1938—Kristallnacht.

These events are, in general, well known. During a single night of flame and terror, the synagogues and cemetery chapels all across Germany were torched, the cemeteries vandalized, Jews arrested or worse, and their businesses wantonly destroyed. Even in Pomerania, where the Confessing Church fared better than elsewhere, all fifteen synagogues were destroyed that night. And recall that Dietrich Bonhoeffer at the time was in Pomerania with his seminarians.

You all know how the Bonhoeffer story played out: This being the second half of the week, he was with one group of seminarians in the village of Gross Schlonwitz just outside Schlawe. Not until after the weekend did he return to the superintendent's house in Koslin, where the second group of seminarians was living. From them he learned all that had happened. Clearly the young men were on the defensive, admitting they had stayed in their rooms when the Koslin synagogue was torched.

It is recorded that Bonhoeffer expressed his severe disappointment with them. He also wrote "9.XI.38" into the margin of his Bible at Psalm 74, underlining the words "they burned all the meeting places of God in the land. We do not see our signs: there is no longer any prophet, and there is none among us who knows how long."

Afterwards Bonhoeffer wrote a letter to all the Finkenwalde alumni. Again he cited the Hebrew scriptures, specifically Psalm 74 and Zechariah 2, with the admonition that "he who touches you touches the apple of his eye."

I believe that the Kristallnacht pogrom marks the critical turn in Bonhoeffer's life journey. He began to distance himself from the Confessing Church, for circumstances were leading him rather to view his own fate as intertwined with that of the Jews in his land.

So where does this all bring us? For sure it brings us to this decade of memorials—memorials to the life and death of Dietrich Bonhoeffer, memorials to the Jewish Holocaust, and memorials to the many millions of other victims who were slaughtered during this time of Nazi terror.

Indeed, Dietrich Bonhoeffer's life has something to say about all of these victims. I maintain that it has a great deal to say about the Jews in Pomerania, about their synagogues and about their cemeteries: for on Kristallnacht Bonhoeffer was there. He understood what was happening—"they burned all the meeting places of God in the land"—and he carried this burden with him through the few remaining years of his life.

What does this have to do with memorials? you might well ask. The land where Bonhoeffer's seminary so briefly flowered is no more. This is Poland—western Pomorze—a new land with inhabitants for whom Kristallnacht and Dietrich Bonhoeffer have little meaning.

Yet Pomerania is alive, if not well, in the memories of the German children who once dwelled there—children of the Third Reich. For almost sixty years, they who once lived in places like Finkenwalde, Koslin, and Schlawe have carried the burden of Kristallnacht. These last surviving witnesses to that fateful event are now mostly grandmothers and grandfathers living in Germany. What I find quite astounding is the fact that they are for the first time putting on paper their fragmentary childhood memories of Kristallnacht. These reminiscences are a growing library in the archives of the *Pommersche Zeitung* at Hannover. Let me read just a few snippets:

"I saw the broken windows and the burned-out synagogue. I did not comprehend what was being done to these people. Where are they now? What ever became of them?"

"The red brick wall that enclosed the Jewish cemetery was toppled with a maul; the gravestones were broken and the trees were all cut in half."

"On the way to school I saw the burned evidence. A cabinetmaker had furnished the sawdust and the proprietor of an auto repair shop the gasoline. The torch had probably been destroyed in the fire. On the synagogue gate one could still read the words 'And they came out of the city and lamented at the walls of Jerusalem.'"

"Across from my school stood the synagogue which was set afire in 1938. Well into the first years of the war we could see the ruins of the building from our classrooms. . . . In the summer of 1943 or 1944, Russian prisoners of war were put to work disposing of the ruins and cleaning up the roof tiles. Once I pushed a piece of my lunch sandwich through the fence, and as a result I was given a sound thrashing by my school headmaster. Later the prisoners were put to work in the cemetery, breaking the Jewish grave markers into gravelsize stones."

"After school we went into the Jewish cemetery. . . . During the night, the gravestones had been toppled and the chapel totally burned out. The charred funeral hearse stood in front of the ruins. In the morning our teacher began to rail against [Germany's] defeat on the ninth of November 1918. He went on to justify the deeds engineered by the SA the previous night. The Jews were the cause of our misfortunes, said he."

These many years later it is not difficult to imagine these scenes and the many others that have been recorded over the past three years—reminiscences from a time when the witnesses were ten to twelve years old. What becomes problematical for me is that some of these scenes played out within shouting distance of places that are today the cornerstones of the Bonhoeffer legacy—Finkenwalde, Koslin, and Schlawe.

So back to my original thesis: A veritable memorial-frenzy is now underway to mark those places of Bonhoeffer's life that now lie in Poland. The first memorial was mounted in 1995—a major bronze plaque in the church at Slawno (Schlawe) near the sites of the Gross Schlonwitz and Sigurdshof Collective Pastorates. Then, in May of 1996, a group of Americans erected plastic markers at Szczecin Zdroje (Finkenwalde), at Koszalin (Koslin), and at Tychowo (Sigurdshof). Later in the year a joint committee of Germans and Poles, amid great fanfare, erected a bronze plaque to mark Bonhoeffer's birthplace in Wraclaw (Breslau).

I believe Bonhoeffer himself would judge it grossly inadequate to remember him without simultaneouly acknowledging those of God's people whose plight first opened his eyes. In Koslin and in Schlawe, the synagogues and the Jewish cemeteries lay not more than five minutes from the places where Bonhoeffer and his seminarians lived and worked. Were Bonhoeffer among us, I am sure he would be the first to seek out the remnants of these "meeting places of God" in order to uncover the stones and in some way memorialize them.

It would be very difficult to identify these holy places—the synagogue and cemetery sites—were it not for the aging children of the Third Reich. These days they are traveling to Poland in droves and visiting their childhood hometowns. What I find so remarkable is that, along the way, they are searching out *and recording* the synagogue sites as well as the sites of the Jewish cemeteries. But time is running out, for the last of those who witnessed Kristallnacht are in their early seventies.

Due to circumstances of history, most Poles who dwell in Pomorze today know nothing of this history. Yet they are people of immense goodwill, and they want to reach out. This I know for sure.

So, when we remember Bonhoeffer and honor Burton, let me place an idea before you. I suggest a joint effort within the International Bonhoeffer Society. It involves the English Language Section, also the German Section and the newly established Polish Section. Working together, we can erect permanent markers at Finkenwalde, at Koslin, at Gross Schlonwitz, and at Sigurdshof—not only at the sites where Bonhoeffer lived and taught, but also at the sites of the nearby synagogues and cemeteries, whose destruction in 1938 surely pointed the way in his last years.

I see this as a project to be completed early in the year 2000, in time for the grand Berlin Bonhoeffer conference: to jointly research, design, craft, and erect some eight bronze plaques with text in three languages. Such a project has the potential of enhancing the Bonhoeffer legacy while building wondrous bridges, both international and ecumenical.

Let's do it!

ENDNOTE

1. From Psalm 74, verse 8.

SUMMARY OF SOURCES

Bethge, Eberhard. *Dietrich Bonhoeffer, Man of Vision—Man of Courage.* Trans. Eric Mosbacher, et al. New York: Harper and Row, 1977.

Pejsa, Jane. "Destroyed Jewish Communities." 26th Annual Scholars' Conference on the Holocaust and the Church, March 1996.

———. *To Pomerania in Search of Dietrich Bonhoeffer: A Traveler's Companion and Guide for Those Who Venture East of the Oden River, Seeking Markers of Bonhoeffer's Life and Ministry,* 1925 through 1943. Expanded 2d. ed. Minneapolis: Kenwood Pub., 1996.

Scheller, Rita, ed. *Pommersche Zeitung.* 1994, 1995, 1996.

Zimmerman, Wolf-Dieter, and Smith, Ronald Gregor, eds. *I Knew Dietrich Bonhoeffer.* Trans. Kathe Gregor Smith. New York: Harper and Row, 1966.

Bonhoeffer and the Jews: Implications for Jewish-Christian Reconciliation[1]

Geffrey B. Kelly

The failure of the German churches to counteract, or even to muster a more effective and widespread moral indignation at, the blatant criminality of the Nazi government in the 1930s has been well attested, church declarations of their innocence or invincible ignorance to the contrary notwithstanding. We are now in the period of sixty-some years later, and for many this may again evoke sorrowful, even angry memories of the near triumph of evil in the Hitler era. The question is still pondered: Were the churches accomplices or victims during the rise to prominence of Adolf Hitler and the ensuing atrocities attributed to him? Many churches bristle at the suggestion that they were complicit in the evils of that time. In fact, in 1984 they celebrated the fiftieth anniversary of the Barmen Declaration, a highpoint in the German church resistance, such as it was, to Nazism. I will look at Barmen in this essay, but not to argue, as some have, that this is the balm which preserved Christian church honor in those dishonorable times. I will, instead, note the shortcomings of Barmen in an effort to sharpen the focus of our final section, the future of an honest Jewish-Christian dialogue.

It is a disturbing irony of history that Dietrich Bonhoeffer has been honored as a heroic martyr by the very church he himself declared to be guilty of the blood of the Jews and other innocent victims of Nazism. His defense of the Jews has, in fact, often been invoked as evidence that the Christian churches did not act with sufficient courage or fortitude to counteract the escalating oppression of the Jews under the Hitler government. He argued that direct church action was called for by its mission to radiate the prophetic presence of Jesus Christ to a country stirred as never before to hatred of a vulnerable minority, the Jews, as well as to so-called Christians seemingly indifferent to acts of aggression against innocents of all types, including Jews by virtue of their race and religion and political dissenters because of their threat to the dictatorship.

THE GERMAN CHURCH STRUGGLE

Much of Bonhoeffer's defense of the Jews is set in the context of his involvement in the German church struggle of the 1930s. While there are many directions an analysis of this struggle could take, we will concentrate on only two aspects: the implications for Christian faith of immoral actions aimed at terrorizing and later exterminating the Jewish population of Germany and the occupied territories, and the present-day significance for the Christian churches of the genocidal Nazi onslaught on the Jews as a people. The German church struggle was, initially, over a matter of principle: whether a so-called racial purity could be made a condition for church ministry, and, second, whether the church's public vocation should be to serve as a moral conscience and a critical voice in defense of the victims of the government's unjust laws and repressive actions. When the church failed to declare its solidarity with the Jews or to speak up in their defense, Bonhoeffer accused it of complicity in the acts of injustice, brutality, and murder that ensued.[2]

THE ANTI-JEWISH LEGISLATION

At the time of Hitler's accession to power on 30 January 1933, Bonhoeffer had himself been wavering over a decision to devote his life to the teaching profession at the university or to direct his energies toward a parish ministry. He was equally attracted to the academic podium and the church pulpit; in his own life, they would complement each other. The passage of the state laws sanctioning discrimination against Jews and bearing on what seemed to him at the time the even larger issue of the freedom of a Christian church to be a church independent of state domination, however, gave his life and ministry a new sense of purpose. After the passage of the Aryan legislation on 7 April 1933, he was the first scholar-pastor to attempt an analysis of the consequences of the discriminatory laws for the relationship of the church to the Nazi government. His analysis of the issues took the public form of a controversial address to the clergy of Berlin entitled "The Church in the Presence of the Jewish Question" (*Die Kirche vor der Juden Frage*). The Aryan legislation recently passed had the obvious aim to systematically exclude Jews from civil service positions and to deny them the right to participate freely and fully in the educational, cultural, and religious life of Germany.

The legislation should not have come as a complete surprise. On the first of April a one-day government-organized boycott of Jewish stores was staged throughout Germany. The church's timid reaction to the boycott and the recently passed discriminatory laws bothered Bonhoeffer. His personal problems with his church were embedded in the frustrations of trying to convey to church leaders a sense of their personal responsibility to use their power and moral suasion to defend human rights in the name of Jesus Christ. His efforts were to prove fruitless. The churches seemed to have become, in his eyes, mere agents of the state. For his part, he was attempting to make resistance to the unjust laws a vital part of the church's public policy. It was in this context that Bonhoeffer presented his opinions on the "Jewish Question."

THE CHURCH AND THE JEWISH QUESTION

This controversial talk rambled around the issue of state acts toward the Jews and the legal issues involved. When we separate the predictable, theologically tainted assertions about the Jews being punished by God and their eventual "homecoming" possible only through conversion to Christ from the specific core of how the church should react to the legislation, we can detect the concrete practicality that became commonplace in Bonhoeffer's later writings. Leaving aside all the conventional rationalizations, the central issue remained: what should the church do? Passive acceptance of the Nazi persecution of the Jews was, he believed, an intolerable threat to the integrity of the Christian churches. If Bonhoeffer's initial observations on the Jews in Germany repeated ages-old Christian stereotypes, now exposed for their inherent mendacity, he did succeed in drawing the attention of his fellow clergymen to an issue they would have preferred to ignore. After all, the Jews were not Christians, and the suggestion that anti-Jewish attitudes and actions could be a prelude to the diminution of the church's moral authority would have seemed preposterous. But, for Bonhoeffer, the whole stability and integrity of civil and ecclesiastical authority were at stake. Not just the church, but survival of justice in governance was being threatened. In Bonhoeffer's words, "The state which endangers the Christian proclamation endangers itself."[3] The clergy and their leaders, on the other hand, seemed stunned into silence by the swiftness with which the Nazis set their policies into motion.

Admittedly, Bonhoeffer's talk and published essay are not only tinged with unfair characterizations of the Jews, but also are too closely aligned with Luther's doctrine of the "two realms." They were, therefore, somewhat problematic in their declaration of the church's deference to the state in legislative matters in a period that would call for starker confrontation. He still naïvely sees the possibility of changing the legislation through the power of moral suasion and newly crafted, rectifying laws to override the injustice. What is more significant, however, is that Bonhoeffer outlines what then was a daring course of *action* for the church when few dared to speak out, let alone act. At the least, he insisted, the church could question the legitimacy of the governmental legislation. Second, the church had an "unconditional obligation to the victims of these actions, *even if they do not belong to the Christian community.*"[4] Finally, the church might have to do more than bandage the victims strewn beneath the wheel; it might have to "jam a spoke in the wheel" of the state through direct political action. In Bonhoeffer's view, this last step could occur only when the state had failed in its role, either by imposing an excess of law and order or by sanctioning too little of it. Nazism had sinned in both directions, and so Bonhoeffer saw the church approaching the point where it would be called to "protect the state *qua* state from itself and to preserve it."[5]

Only later, when the possibility of reversing the "legalized" steps being set in place by Nazi ideologues seemed hopeless, would Bonhoeffer openly advocate overthrowing the state as a means of "protecting the state from itself." The first focus here, in this earlier phase of his defense of the Jews, is still starkly ecclesiastical, though the clause cited above indicates that he had begun to see the whole issue as involving the church in a decision where the humane and gospel-mandated compassion intersected. What should the church do when some of its members, Christians of Jewish ancestry, had become, for racist reasons, victims of discrimination even within their own churches? What paths of action were left open in the face of the arrogant, bullying interference of state in church affairs? Only secondarily does concern for human rights *qua* human emerge as a church issue in the dramatic segment that he added in consultation with his family and after seeing more fully the implications for the Jewish community of the Aryan legislation. Prior to that, in the body of the talk, Bonhoeffer speaks strongly of the need for individuals and humanitarian groups, apart from the church, to remind the state of the possible immorality of its policies and to act as the accusers when the state offends against public morality.

Bonhoeffer's efforts to bring the church out of its confused timidity and into the practical sphere of responsible action and compassionate public policy are cautious and restrained. When the Nazi restrictions on the Jewish citizenry were imported into church politics through the infamous "Brown Synod," Bonhoeffer and like-minded others would take the first steps to form a separate "confessing church." The significance of Bonhoeffer's talk and essay runs deeper than its obvious exhortation to protect the baptized Jews among church members. One must see the essay in proper context. Originally Bonhoeffer's paper was to constitute an argument against the demeaning status that would be forced on baptized Jews. The boycott against Jewish merchants and the civil service legislation of 7 April 1933 prompted him to revise his text and to compose a whole section to deal with the injustices of the state against the Jewish citizenry, regardless of their baptized status. It was this section, as Bonhoeffer's biographer has pointed out, that caused such a stir in the audience that some left in disgust. Admonition of a state, help to the victims regardless of their religious affiliation, and possibly jamming the spokes of the wheel of state were far too much for the more conservative and order-loving among the ministers. Only with the publication of the essay in English in the 1960s did the awareness of Bonhoeffer's historically and theologically conditioned adherence to the typical anti-Judaisms of the churches surface.[6]

This ideologically skewed theology, not the main points Bonhoeffer wished to make, provided the grist for writers like Stanley Rosenbaum and, more recently, Stephen Ray to conclude that Bonhoeffer was merely the best of a bad lot of theologians. In our book, *A Testament to Freedom*, Burton Nelson and I tried to point this out in a footnote where we criticized Rosenbaum for his failure to see the whole picture of Bonhoeffer's defense of the Jewish victims of Nazi hatred, and for a detectable tendentiousness in his presentation. For that, Stephen Ray, a Yale scholar, reproved us for what he called blustering on our part. Leaving aside the *ad hominem* style of Ray's accusation, we stand firm in our conviction that both Rosenbaum and Ray miss the essential point of Bonhoeffer's essay and that neither one offers any solid contextual evidence for their conclusions. Ray focuses on the last step of Bonhoeffer's proposed course of action for the churches to assert that Bonhoeffer's prime intent is to preserve the state and the church rather than respond to the cries of the victims. Ray writes, "It is the difference between the victims, in this case the Jews, being the final cause of the *statu confessioni* [*sic*] or simply the efficient cause. As an efficient cause the Jews are reduced to something of a heuristic device for gauging the rightness of the path upon which the state has embarked."[7] This conclusion is based on questionable premises.

First of all, Bonhoeffer's use of the word "victim" (*Opfer*) to designate those affected by the recent racist laws was carefully chosen by him. No other theologian of the time had been able to see the state's actions as *victimizing* a distinct, unjustly targeted minority of its citizens. The state is thereby branded as an *oppressor* entity. Through his addition of the phrase "even if they do not belong to the Christian community," Bonhoeffer puts accountability for helping these victims on the church itself. He does not give the church room to wriggle out of its responsibility. The church has to do more than protest; it can never countenance unjust, repressive laws by a government, however legitimate its power may be. The church must engage in direct political action; it must "jam a spoke in the wheel" of state. The point of this segment of the essay is not, as Ray avers, to gauge the rightness or wrongness of the path that state has legislated. It is, rather, a call to the church to act responsibly, even to brusquely intervene in state affairs.

Further, Ray appears to be ignorant of the recent research in Germany by Christoph Strohm and Christine-Ruth Müller that pertains to the essay in question.[8] Strohm produces solid evidence that, although Bonhoeffer did not on principle advocate direct political action on the part of the church as an absolute right, he nonetheless did argue that, in extreme cases, such as repression of the civil and human rights of minorities, the church was bound to take such steps as were necessary to restore the rights of those targeted by the discriminatory laws. Strohm points out that this was a position held in common with his brother-in-law, the jurist Gerhard Leibholz. For Bonhoeffer, it was Christ, the center of both church and state, who mandated the church in these instances to do something against the state, which was endangering at the same time both a significant portion of its citizenry and the Christian faith. The government of Germany, in this view, was in the process of losing its legality through its racist excesses.

Müller's research shows how, from the very beginning, Bonhoeffer and his brother-in-law Hans von Dohnanyi opposed the persecution of the Jews in a manner that was unequivocal and consistent. She fills in many of the contextual gaps in which Bonhoeffer can be seen as gradually able to shift away from the burdens of anti-Judaism stereotyping by means of the compassion aroused within him for the victims of his government's vicious racism. Through documentary evidence, she notes that whenever Bonhoeffer calls for Christians and their churches to be advocates for their "brothers," he means *unbaptized Jews*. She sets her findings against the backdrop of the churches and various circles of resistance to Hitler being burdened with the traditional anti-Semitism of the rest of German society. Protests on behalf of the Jews were scattered and ineffectual for a church that held the distorted view of Jews, considering them a people inimical to Christian and Germanic values. Bonhoeffer was, in fact, breaking new political ground for the church.

BONHOEFFER'S EARLY DEFENSE OF THE JEWS

For Bonhoeffer, the "Aryan paragraph" legislation was an occasion demanding that the church declare a *status confessionis*, an obligation to confess its faith and take concrete action against this latest menace to the Christian faith itself. He was moved, therefore, in July 1933 to write an "Appeal to the Ministers of the Old Prussian Union," in which he pointed out the following:

> The Aryan clause in the form contained in the first program of the "German Christians" is a *Status Confessionis* for the church.

Nothing is more dangerous than for us to allow ourselves to be hoodwinked by statements as to its relative harmlessness. The constantly repeated effort to befog the questions relative to it, is intended to keep us from seeing clearly the fact, by the very substance of which the church is endangered, and thus wrest out of our hands the decision for which we are responsible to the church alone. . . . The excluding church is erecting a racial law as a prerequisite of Christian communion. But in doing so, it loses Christ himself, who is the goal of even this human, purely temporal law. . . . With exclusion of the Jewish-Christians from the communion of worship, he who realizes the nature of the church must feel himself to be excluded also.[9]

Bonhoeffer represented a group within the church that included his close friend Franz Hildebrandt, an ordained minister of Jewish ancestry disbarred from exercising his ministry by the new laws; this group clearly and early on understood the scope of these anti-Jewish laws and their implication for the Christian churches and the future of German society.

That Bonhoeffer intended, not to defend some political theory, nor to squeeze a more refined theology of Judaism from the church, but to produce concrete, political action is made clear in this excerpt from a letter to Erwin Sutz on 11 September 1934. He tells Sutz that, "once and for all, we need to do away with the theologically grounded restrictions in regard to action by the state—after all, it is only fear. 'Open your mouth for those who have no voice' (Prov. 31:8).—Who still knows that in the church today; that this is the least requirement of the Bible in such times?"[10] The phrase from Proverbs will be repeated by Bonhoeffer several times in the course of the church struggle, to explain his own dangerous solidarity with the dispossessed of his wayward nation. Earlier he had complained to Sutz that people in Germany who should know better appeared lost in dealing with the Jewish Question. "The Jewish Question troubles the church very much and here even the most intelligent people have entirely lost their heads and their Bibles over it."[11] Bonhoeffer's biographer reports, further, that Bonhoeffer extended his concern to all German Jews, whether or not they had accepted baptism. He cites the resolution that Bonhoeffer helped hammer out at an international conference in Sofia during Bonhoeffer's involvement as youth secretary in the ecumenical movement of the 1930s. This resolution is unique for its exposé of the official anti-Semitism ravaging Germany at that time. "We especially deplore the fact that the state measures against the Jews in Germany have had such an effect on public opinion that in some circles the Jewish race is considered a race of inferior status."[12] In a move fraught with risk, Bonhoeffer delivered a copy of the resolution to the German embassy in Sofia.

Several weeks after having written up for publication his article on "The Church in the Presence of the Jewish Question," and before the ecumenical conference in Sofia, Bonhoeffer deliberately violated the "Law against High Treason" by sending information to Rabbi Stephen Wise on the Nazi repressive movements against the Jews of Germany. Paul Lehmann, who was visiting with Bonhoeffer at the time, acted as intermediary in delivering the message. Bonhoeffer had met Rabbi Wise during his stay in America in 1931 and knew of his ties to President Roosevelt. Enlisting the aid of Rabbi Wise seemed to Bonhoeffer a logical move to inform influential circles in the United States of the persecution then underway in Nazi Germany. Although Roosevelt took no concrete, public action, he did write to Rabbi Wise expressing "the sorrow of our Jewish fellow citizens over the savagery of the Nazis against their helpless victims."[13] Bonhoeffer's bold action can be contrasted with the steps taken by several church leaders with ecumenical contacts who requested their sister churches in the United States and England to oppose the anti-Hitler propaganda then being disseminated, and to be reassured that peaceful calm reigned in Germany and any prisoners were always being well treated.[14]

Bonhoeffer's unequivocal stand in support of the rights of baptized Jews is attested by his closest friend of that time, Franz Hildebrandt, who recalled that, for Bonhoeffer,

> the course for the church was clear . . . from the beginning and remained clear to the end; there could be no compromise with the brown hordes of Nazism and no patience with ecclesiastical diplomacy. . . . He reasoned, in view of the so-called "Aryanization" of the clergy under the Nazi laws, that he could not be in a ministry which had become a racial privilege. I cannot recall or imagine any other man to have taken this line of solidarity with those of us who had to resign their pastorates under that legislation.[15]

Hildebrandt's statement is reinforced by a passage from a letter that Bonhoeffer sent to Karl Barth explaining why he could not accept a pastorate in Berlin and why he had, in fact, left the scene of the church struggle to accept a London pastorate, though he knew Barth would disapprove.

> I was offered at the same time a pastorate in the east of Berlin; my election was certain. Then came the Aryan Clause in Prussia and I knew that I could not accept the pastorate I longed for in this particular neighborhood without giving up my attitude of unconditional opposition to the church, without making myself

untrustworthy to my people from the start, and without betraying my solidarity with the Jewish Christian pastors—my closest friend is one of them and is at the moment on the brink; he is now coming to me in England.[16]

Even prior to this letter, Bonhoeffer had been active in agitating for the convocation of a general council which could formulate a definitive confession of faith in the name of the Christian unity now threatened by Nazism's uncanny ability to penetrate church policies and indirectly impose its insidious ideology in the name of some good desired by the churches, such as protection from atheistic Bolshevism and the so-called international Jewry. Bethge reports that Bonhoeffer's suggestion to convoke a council, delivered at a meeting between the German Christians and the "Young Reformers" on 22 June 1933, was dismissed as anachronistic, "like routing out ancient halberds from dusty ecclesiastical armories."[17] The suggestion that a council root out the new heresy also smacked of an infringement on that "open-mindedness" and tolerance which were the boast of twentieth-century Protestant liberalism. Yet the idea of a council was itself to be somewhat realized a year later in the Barmen and Dahlem Synods, though what was accomplished at these councils and later in the ecumenical gatherings of the 1930s was but a slim shadow of the radical steps and uncompromising declarations that Bonhoeffer dreamed of provoking.

By now, Bonhoeffer fully realized that the struggle was not merely an internal church squabble; it was one that would entail dramatic conflict with the government. In the church assemblies of July, he and Franz Hildebrandt pushed the view that bishops and clergy should proclaim what would amount to a "spiritual interdict" on all religious services so long as state commissars controlled the affairs of church. The reaction of the pastors was less than sanguine. Few recognized the potential of spiritual interdict as a powerful weapon of coercion against dictatorship. Some saw in the proposal only the intransigence of Bonhoeffer and Hildebrandt. It struck most of the clergy as either laughable or subversive. One can only surmise the effect such an action would have had on Nazi policies. Later, during the war, that very tactic proposed by Bonhoeffer was, in fact, adopted by the Norwegian church in the aftermath of actions against Provost Fjellbu and Bishop Berggrav. There followed a pastors' strike and wholesale church resignations. As a step toward restoring morale in the German army, Berlin was moved to intervene in favor of the bishops. Ironically, it was Bonhoeffer and Count Helmut von Moltke, later executed for his role in the Kreisau circle, who were sent by the Abwehr, the German military intelligence, to assess the situation and the danger to German troops. Bonhoeffer, drawing from his experience in 1933, used the occasion to encourage the Norwegian church not to cave in to Nazi persuasion to reopen the churches for the sake of public morale.

BETHEL AND BARMEN: THE CONFESSIONS OF FAITH OF THE CONFESSING CHURCH

By summer 1933, those who appreciated the dangers to the church posed by the racist legislation of April and the growing dominance of the German Christians, whose church policy was becoming more and more aligned with Nazi ideology, began to organize themselves into what would in September become the Pastors Emergency League and later the Confessing Church. The idea of a German Reich Church became a rallying point for the German Christians at their National Conference on 3 and 4 April 1933. The impetus to formulate a confession of faith, rather than a mere counterprotest, came from Bonhoeffer himself after the overwhelming victory of the German Christians in the church elections of 1933, and after the first anxieties created by the Aryan Clause. Bonhoeffer was behind the impetus from two sources, the Young Reformers Movement, of which he was a part, and the German Christian Student Union, to formulate a new confession to deal with the present crisis. Bonhoeffer and Herman Sasse, a pastor and professor-theologian at Erlangen, were commissioned, therefore, to retire to the religious center at Bethel to draft such a confession. They did this in August 1933. The first draft, containing a special section focused on the Jewish Question, was the work of Bonhoeffer.[18] It constitutes the strongest statement of the problem, surpassing even the more general declarations of Barmen in its undiplomatic specificity.

With respect to the future of a Jewish-Christian dialogue, the Bethel Confession is significant, not because of any success it had in sensitizing Christians to the discrimination Jews faced in Nazi Germany, but for the way it expresses new beginnings in the Christian Church's attitude toward the Jews. For this reason alone, Bethel could stand as a corrective to the general principles so forcefully affirmed at Barmen some six months later. As a document of the church struggle, this confession is additionally important in that it brings into the open the theological clash between the German Christians and the Young Reformers group, represented by Bonhoeffer, Sasse, and Vischer. The fact that the intended target of the confession is the German Christians, with their announced sympathies for the Aryan Clause in the church, might mitigate somewhat the sticky religious stereotypes of Judaism that the authors still held. We still find mention of the Jews being blamed for having rejected their Messiah, the Christ. We also see repeated the "disinheritance" theory: in Christ, the Christian Church has displaced the Jewish people of the "old" covenant. There is, likewise, the inevitable claim of the Christian Church's mission to convert the Jews to Christianity. On this latter point, however, a qualification is needed. As William J. Peck has pointed out, one mustn't overlook Bonhoeffer's intention to "keep the church open to the conversion of the Jews at a time when there was pressure to exclude them and thereby put racial limits on the fellowship of the church."[19]

Similarly, the disinheritance theory is couched in terms that reject the so-called world mission of a "chosen master race" now able to establish a "national church" with a purely Aryan composition. Bonhoeffer's sarcasm in this section of the confession is unmistakable. He denies that the place of the Jewish people of the Old Testament had been "taken by another *nation*." Here his intent is to counteract the bloated claim that Nazi ideologues had been called to be God's agents in casting God's choice of Israel aside and bringing into being a new chosen people of impeccable Aryan lineage, a new messianic kingdom, as the nazified Teutonic mythology would have it.

What is also significant about this confession is its reaffirmation of God's choice of Israel in wholly theological terms and its insistence that God has not retracted that choice. "The 'holy remnant,'" Bonhoeffer insists, "can neither be absorbed into another nation by emancipation and assimilation . . . nor be exterminated by Pharaoh-like measures. This 'holy remnant' bears the indelible stamp of the chosen people. . . . No nation can ever be commissioned to avenge on the Jews the murder of Golgotha."[20] In one stroke, Bonhoeffer was rejecting that most unjust of all the imagined grievances of the Christian churches against the Jews, that they had killed Jesus Christ. That accusation has been the pretext for much of the violence done over the centuries by Christians against Jews. The aim here is principally to smoke out the German Christians, to force them to declare their real intent in subscribing to Nazi ideology, and to expose their innate heretical bent in this matter. As he wrote to his grandmother at the time, "We want to try to make the German Christians declare their intentions. Whether we shall succeed I rather doubt." He stated his fear that they were heading toward a grandiose national church that could never be reconciled with genuine Christianity. "The question really is: Germanism or Christianity? The sooner the conflict comes out into the open, the better."[21] In the confession he argued that the presence of Jewish Christians was "a sign that the barrier between Jew and Gentile had been broken down and that faith in Christ may not be perverted into a national religion or a racially determined Christianity."[22]

Despite its shortcomings, this document is a clear repudiation of Aryanism and the Nazi aims to rid the German nation and church of any Jewish presence and influence. This confession criticized the attitudes of church leaders who themselves subscribed to the nation's racist policies and, what is startling, given the long history of Christian invective against Jews, emphasized God's continued fidelity to Israel and the indestructibility of the Jewish people. In their boldest form, these were claims considered seditious and contradictory to the official Nazi line. Bonhoeffer's text exposes his obvious disdain for the church's concern not to offend the Nazi overlords. Persuading other churchmen to sign on to the document was another matter. It was circulated to a group of some twenty experts, including known sympathizers with the German Christian cause Paul Althaus and Adolf von Schlatter. As a result, its most biting segments in defense of the Jews were so watered down that Bonhoeffer himself refused to sign the final, toothless document.[23]

His frustration at this failure to confront the state and the German Christians more starkly, and the increasing number of provincial synods that adopted the Aryan Clause, were factors in his decision to leave Berlin in the fall of 1933 and accept the pastorate of two German-speaking parishes in London. Looking back on that period, Heinz Edouard Tödt has observed, "In 1933 Bonhoeffer was almost alone in his opinions; he was the only one who considered solidarity with the Jews, especially with non-Christian Jews, to be a matter of such importance as to obligate the Christian churches to risk a massive conflict with the state—a risk which could threaten their very existence."[24]

Bonhoeffer's fears were soon realized. The German Christians, who supported Hitler's policies in their churches, had taken control of key positions in the Protestant Church of Germany (Evangelische Kirche Deutschlands, or EKD), composed of Lutheran, United, and Reformed elements. In September 1933 the Old Prussian General Synod meeting in Wittenberg would become, to the shock of Bonhoeffer and his like-minded colleagues, a paramilitary spectacle, as many of the delegates appeared in their brown uniforms, giving the Nazi salute and sporting the swastika. Ludwig Müller, who had been appointed by Hitler in April to be his confidential advisor and plenipotentiary in matters pertaining to the Protestant churches, was confirmed as national bishop. The Aryan paragraph was adopted as the Church Law Relating to the Legal Position of Clergy and Church Officers, effectively limiting the ministry to those who would give unconditional support to the Nazi government and who were of pure Aryan descent. The "heresy" of the German Christians was now out in the open and would be called such by Bonhoeffer. What the Reich Church stood for was made clearer by some of their most extreme spokesmen. Dr. Reinhard Krause, for example, speaking at a massive rally of German Christians at the Sports Pavilion in Berlin just after Hitler's policies were affirmed in a national plebiscite in November 1933, proposed to the ministers that they "free themselves from all un-German tendencies in worship and in creed, especially from the Old Testament and Jewish morality." Four months later, Herman Grüner, a spokesman for the German Christians, formulated six theses, the second of which made the startling claim that "Hitler is the way of the Spirit and the will of God for the German people to enter the church of Christ." Another thesis made the outrageous claim that "National Socialism is positive Christianity in action."[25]

More fully aware than ever before of the dangers to Christianity of these preposterous distortions of the nature of the Christian Church and the gospel teachings of Jesus Christ, and the threat represented by limiting ministerial service to those only who were "politically correct" and racially pure, a group of opposing pastors, led by Karl Barth and Martin Niemöller, formed themselves into the Pastors Emergency League. They organized a Confessing Church synod to be held 29-31 May 1934 at Barmen-Wuppertal. There, representatives of nineteen provincial churches were unanimous in stating their opposition to policies advocated by the German Christians and their nazified Reich Church. One important phrase would become the battlecry of the Confessing Church in the church struggle and make many of the signers marked men with the Gestapo: "We repudiate the false teaching that there are areas of our life to which we belong not to Jesus Christ, but to another Lord."[26] The allusion to Adolf Hitler should have been obvious to any reader of the declaration. The Confessing Church thus took its stand on the matter of principle: its demand for the freedom to be the Church of Jesus Christ.

Although Bonhoeffer was unable to attend the synod of Barmen, he looked back on the declaration as a strong affirmation that church order was bound solely to Jesus Christ and not to the regnant political ideology. Further, he saw his own stand vindicated, namely, that the church should not be constrained to suit its convictions to the dictates of patriotic politics and popular public opinion. If this was the strength of Barmen, its weakness lies in its seeming insensitivity to the plight of the Jews, evidenced in its failure to mention them or to link this persecuted people with the denunciation of the infectious national idolatry and the spirited defense of church rights and order. Elsewhere and during the commemorative celebrations of the fiftieth anniversary of the Barmen Declaration, I voiced the unpopular judgment that I considered the document "something Hitler could live with." The churchmen at Barmen could now claim that they had said their piece and could continue on their ways with consciences untainted because by their words they had sided with the word of God and condemned the displacing of God in good German lives. Some who revel in the memory of Barmen and who are justly proud that the church did at last take a stand against the national idolatry are still not sensitive to this omission of the Jewish issue. Karl Barth, the author of the document, would himself later acknowledge and regret the missed opportunity. The church, he wrote, did not take "the road which might have led to an unprecedented new encounter with the Jews."[27]

THE ECUMENICAL MOVEMENT AND ANTI-NAZI ACTIVITY

Taking the best reading of the declaration as his cue, however, Bonhoeffer became an outspoken champion of Barmen as a rallying point for the anti-Nazi stand of the Confessing Church. In his ecumenical contacts, therefore, he channeled his energies toward having the Confessing Church officially recognized as the only valid representative of the Protestant churches of Germany in gatherings of the World Alliance for Promoting Friendship among the Churches. He began a campaign against the heresy of the German Reich Church and demanded its ouster from the ecumenical body. Because of his implacable insistence on a totally unequivocal condemnation of the heretical Reich Church, and his refusal to share space allotted to both church groups, he was considered by several delegates somewhat of a young fanatic. Bethge describes the difficult position in which Bonhoeffer was placed by his insistence on a rigorous attitude toward the Reich Church. "Bonhoeffer's position was a peculiar one," his biographer writes. "In spite of his whole-hearted partisanship, his brethren in the German Confessing Church had come to look upon him as an outsider because of his perpetual concern with the Sermon on the Mount. Yet among his ecumenical friends, to whom the Sermon on the Mount was of prime importance, he had become a stranger as a result of his insistence on the Confession and the need to repudiate heresy."[28]

Radical and obstinate though he was, Bonhoeffer had succeeded in attracting some of the most influential ecumenists to his causes, notably Bishop Bell and Bishop Ammundsen, through whose influence the Confessing Church eventually received official recognition at the World Alliance. Bonhoeffer had become an irrepressible advocate for world peace at these ecumenical conferences. In one memorable sermon at the morning service of 28 August 1934 in Fanø, Denmark, he challenged the delegates finally to act as the universal Church of Jesus Christ and "speak out so that the world, though it gnash its teeth, will have to hear, so that the peoples will rejoice because the church of Christ in the name of Christ has taken the weapons from the hands of their sons, forbidden war, proclaimed the peace of Christ against the raging world." Earlier in the same sermon he had proclaimed that the "church of Christ lives at one and the same time in all peoples, yet beyond all boundaries, whether national, political, social, or *racial*."[29] His argument is simplistic but derived, for all its simplicity, from the gospel claim that Christians are to acclaim Christ present in the least of their brothers and sisters, particularly in those who suffer from the woes of systemic injustice. "They cannot take up arms against Christ himself—yet this is what they do if they take up arms against one another."[30] It will not be long before that same argument is used to defend Jews against persecution. To hurt Jews is to hurt none other than

Jesus Christ.

We see this identification with the Jews affirmed in christocentric language in Bonhoeffer's spiritual classic *The Cost of Discipleship*. Towards the end of this book, in describing the "image of Christ" and where this image of Christ is to be found, he remarks unequivocally, "Those who are now attacking the least of the people are attacking Christ."[31] The allusion to the Jews, whom Bonhoeffer called at that time the "least of the people," was unmistakable to those who had sat at Bonhoeffer's lectures and knew to whom he was referring. This euphemism was employed at a time when explicit mention of the Jews could bring on the full wrath of the Nazi security forces. Even before writing those words, Bonhoeffer reminded his seminarians—as he later would his readers—that the "Beatitude of Mercy" is characterized by those who are able to renounce

> *their own dignity* for they are merciful. As if their own needs and their own poverty were not enough, they take upon themselves the needs and humiliation and sin of others. They have an irresistible love for the down-trodden, the sick, the wretched, the degraded, the oppressed, for those who suffer unjustly, for the outcast, and for all who are tortured with anxiety. . . . In order that they may be compassionate they cast away the most priceless treasure of human life, their personal dignity and honor.[32]

In speaking and later writing those words, Bonhoeffer was aware of the aspersions cast on those who would make common cause with the beleaguered Jew in Nazi Germany. To be called a "Jew lover," to be branded as an unpatriotic, disloyal citizen, to be a sympathizer with the enemies of the people's noble Führer and his dreams for the Third Reich and the glorious millennium this would usher in, was indeed to renounce one's own dignity.

In the excitement that followed Bonhoeffer's sermon at Fanø, his student Otto Dudzus remarked that "Bonhoeffer had charged so far ahead that the conference could not follow him. Did that surprise anybody? But on the other hand: could anybody have a good conscience about it?"[33] History would prove this assessment an exaggeration. Many had a good conscience about Germany's pell-mell rush to war and its invocation of a policy of violence, revenge, and terror against its enemies, real and imagined.

FRUSTRATIONS IN MOUNTING A CHURCH RESISTANCE

Bonhoeffer's own naïve hopes for a forceful intervention by the World Alliance on behalf of world peace, and for a declaration of solidarity with the prime victims of Nazi Germany's vindictive, genocidal policies, were doomed to failure. Neither the ecumenical movement nor the Confessing Church lived up to the promise of decisive action against the Nazi government. The ecumenical movement, which Bonhoeffer regarded as the most powerful source of hope for the preservation of Christianity in Germany and the world, eventually would become indecisive and unwilling to interfere further in "Germany's internal ecclesiastical affairs." Bonhoeffer would continue to needle his church into assuming ever more unyielding attitudes toward the Reich Church, but accommodation seemed to be more the order of the day. Hitler would bait the trap of compromise with the emotional appeal to loyalty to the Fatherland, blind, obedient patriotism, and Teutonic military glory, perhaps proving once again Samuel Johnson's cynical definition of patriotism as "the last refuge of a scoundrel." In Hitler's time, however, patriotism was presented as the only valid proof of one's honorable citizenship and personal valor.

Bonhoeffer saw himself struggling not simply in the political rat holes of Hitler's racist policies, which he opposed from their inception, but in the more crucial and complex areas of the demands of genuine Christian faith and fidelity to the Christian gospel itself. Outside that gospel there could be no salvation for the Christian. The weak, playing-it-safe tactics of the Confessing Church, which had attempted to throw all risky decisions involving opposition to the political authority back to the individual consciences of the pastors, prompted Bonhoeffer's vinegary retort in the form of pointed rhetorical questions: "Will Confessing synods learn that it is important to counsel and to decide in defiance of all dangers and difficulties. . . ? Will they ever learn that majority decisions in matters of conscience kill the spirit?"[34]

The failure of the churches to mount an effective opposition to Hitler and Nazi policies can be called a failure of nerve. But that would hardly explain the actual cooperation of the churches in those adjunct services that make the running of civil government and the conduct of a war possible. Many in the churches saw no contradiction between the Christian gospel, to which a church was overtly committed, and the political conduct of churchgoers whose actions and laws were directed by manipulative leaders against a people whom that same gospel commanded believers to love. It seems evident that in the crisis years of the 1930s neither church nor state would fully understand the demands of the Christian gospel. For the church, this was more than a failure of nerve; it was a failure in identity and mission.

Bonhoeffer's personal problems with church leaders were embedded in the frustrations of trying to enlist their cooperation in forming a solid, moral counterforce to the Nazi ideology then threatening Christian faith and social justice at home and world peace abroad. As a result, he began more and more to disassociate himself from his church, which he had come to regard as more interested in its own survival than in taking a forthright stand on the malfeasance then being perpetrated by the government's security forces. This was not a church that followed the example and gospel mandates of Jesus Christ when concrete action was called for. By the mid 1930s his judgments on Confessing Church synods always seemed to depend on whether the resolutions included defense of the Jewish people, not merely the baptized among them. His biographer reports that he dampened the enthusiastic reception of many a seemingly intrepid synodal pronouncement with his own disapproval if the synod in question failed to speak out for the Jews. Church timidity on this issue was one of the reasons he joined the political resistance movement.[35]

Speaking out on behalf of the Jews soon became for Bonhoeffer the test of Christianity's own genuineness and, consequently, of the church's proper mission in a world infected by ideological perversions of justice and the denial of civil rights. Bonhoeffer often cited Proverbs 31:8 to explain his own hazardous solidarity with the Jews: "Speak up for those who have no voice." Who in Germany had enough courage to speak on behalf of those helpless victims of nationalized hatred with no one to come to their aid in any efficacious way? The phrase from Proverbs appears in a variety of contexts, most notably in his lecture on "The Interpretation of the New Testament," presented to the Confessing Church of Saxony. Alluding to the church's mission, Bonhoeffer declared:

> The service of the church has to be given to those who suffer violence and injustice. The Old Testament still demands right-dealing of the state, the New Testament no longer does. Without asking about justice or injustice, the church takes to itself all the sufferers, all the forsaken of every party and of every status. "Speak up for those who have no voice" (Prov. 31:8). Here the decision will really be made whether we are still the church of the present Christ. The Jewish Question.[36]

It is to this period of 1935, when the divisions within the German church were most bitter, that Bonhoeffer's often quoted retort belongs: "Only those who cry out for the Jews may sing Gregorian Chants."[37] The context for Bonhoeffer's remark is the preference of so many church gatherings for discussions on forms of worship and even new church music rather than facing up to the real crisis, namely, the possibility of making a concerted resistance to the Nuremberg laws or taking a courageous, if unpopular, stand on the Jewish Question. For Bonhoeffer at this time, if there was anything like a mission to the Jews, it was no longer to convert or even to preach to them of the so-called truth of Christianity. The church's mission was to reach out to these "least" of Christ's brothers and sisters. Marga Meusel expressed Bonhoeffer's sentiments very well in her memorandum after the failure of the Augsburg Synod of June 1935, which Bonhoeffer had accused of having made no clear statement condemning the persecution of the Jews.

> Where is Abel your brother? In our case, too, in the case of the Confessing Church, there can be no answer other than that given by Cain. . . . And if the church, afraid for its own destruction, can in many instances do nothing, why is it not at least conscious of its guilt? . . . Why are there no services of intercession as there were for the imprisoned pastors? The church makes it desperately hard for anyone to defend it. . . . But that there can be people in the Confessing Church who dare assume that they are entitled, even called, to preach to the Jews, whose present sufferings are our crime, is a fact that must fill us with icy fear.[38]

Having gathered evidence of atrocities committed against the Jews, Superintendent Albertz of the Steglitz Synod, who was a close friend of Bonhoeffer, sent a private, confidential memorandum to Adolf Hitler raising the issue of the persecution of Jewish citizens. This memorandum contained the remarkable claim that the Christian "commandment to love one's neighbor must still prevail over what was an officially inspired hatred of the Jews." Two of Bonhoeffer's students, Ernst Tillich and Werner Koch, published the memorandum in the foreign press.[39] Bonhoeffer's influence on and resonance with Meusel's statement can be seen in his later "Confession of Guilt" on behalf of the church.

REACTION TO CRYSTAL NIGHT

Clearly, the displacement theory, God's so-called rejection of his choice of Israel in favor of Christianity, had lost all credibility among thinking, sensitive Christians like Bonhoeffer. If anything, the fate of the Jews was now seen by him as bound inextricably to the fate of Christianity and, indeed, to the credibility of a church professing its faith in the continuing presence of Jesus Christ in the poor and the outcast. Nonetheless, the events of the infamous Kristallnacht (Crystal Night, or the Night of the Broken Glass) resurrected, even in some of Bonhoeffer's students, the anti-Jewish theory that this wanton destruction of Jewish property and random brutalizing of Jews was God's continued punishment for their "complicity" in the crucifixion of Christ. Bonhoeffer argued vehemently against those who dredged up this "teaching of contempt" for Jews that had been invoked over the centuries to "justify" sporadic pogroms and organized acts of vengeance against this innocent people. Against those who used this discredited theory as a rationale for church silence at the atrocities of Crystal Night, Bonhoeffer pointed out, "When today the synagogues are set afire, tomorrow the churches will burn."[40]

Bonhoeffer's pastoral letter to his seminarians dated 20 November 1938 alludes to this state-sanctioned torment of the Jewish people in a strategic paragraph. "During the past few days, I have been thinking a great deal about Psalm 74, Zechariah 2:12, Romans 9:4f. and 11:11-15. That takes us right into prayer."[41] Each of these references is significant for Bonhoeffer's attempt to call his seminarians' attention to the compassion, concern, and solidarity they must have with the Jews who had suffered so much during the terrible violence of Crystal Night.

The first reference, Psalm 74, contains the line "They said in their hearts, 'Let us destroy them; let us burn all the shrines of God in the land.'" Bonhoeffer's own Bible has a pencil line at Psalm 74:8 and, in the margin, the date of Crystal Night, 9.11.38 (9 November 1938), with an exclamation point. Further, Zechariah 2:12 reads, "Whoever touches you touches the apple of my eye." Romans 9 speaks of Israel having received "the adoption, the glory, the covenants, the law, the worship, and the promises." From the Jews, the apostle Paul says, came the patriarchs and the Messiah. Then, in chapter 11, to which Bonhoeffer refers, Paul argues that God had never rejected his chosen people! These words of Paul, cited in 1938, rejoin the sentiments Bonhoeffer had expressed in his earlier attempt to force the German Christians to face up to his accusation in the "Bethel Confession" of 1933 that they had perverted the gospel by their endorsement of Hitler's policy of racial and religious discrimination against the Jewish people of Germany. The Jews were not displaced by Christians, let alone the new national religion of baptized Aryans. Bethge notes that the churches' wimpish reaction to Crystal Night was a cause of immense anguish on Bonhoeffer's part. Even the Confessing Church, with rare exceptions, chose silence and shielded itself as its resistance to Nazism was further eroded. By then Bonhoeffer was being drawn into what seemed the more practical form of resistance, political conspiracy.[42]

BONHOEFFER'S ETHICS AND THE CONFESSION OF GUILT

Having joined the German resistance movement centered in the Abwehr, the military intelligence unit, Bonhoeffer was still able to devote time to beginning to write his *Ethics*, a book he once mused would be his life's final work. While engaged in direct resistance activities on behalf of the conspiracy, Bonhoeffer used his time to begin work on *Ethics*. Some of the most remarkable statements of the need for Christian solidarity with the Jews are incorporated into this text, which Bonhoeffer never lived to complete. When the deportations of Jews had begun, for example, Bonhoeffer wrote that Christian history was "indissolubly linked with the people of Israel, not only in terms of origins, but also in a genuinely uninterrupted relationship. The Jew keeps open the question of

Christ." He added that "an expulsion of the Jews from the West must necessarily bring with it the expulsion of Christ; for Jesus Christ was a Jew."[43] That extraordinary passage is unique for its emphatic linking up of Christ with Judaism and of Judaism with the fate of Christianity. Without Judaism, Christianity runs the risk of becoming, as it did in Nazi Germany, a pagan religion for a racist state. Bonhoeffer's insights here stand in contrast with those of so many of his fellow churchmen, who still clung to their sanitized religious practices, hiding behind facades of pious practice in an age that called for responsible action against a criminalized government. His words stand, too, as a direct contradiction of the Nazi religious propaganda that depicted Jesus as a pure Aryan beset by Jewish enemies during his lifetime and, astoundingly, in the present church struggle as well.

In that same section of his *Ethics*, Bonhoeffer also asserted that the Jew "is the sign of God's free and merciful choice and of the repudiating wrath of God." So much of Jewish history in the Bible deals with the stormy relationship of Israel with God, with alternating experiences of God's mercy and deliverance and with God's wrath at the idolatries and injustices to which the nation and its people succumbed, only to be recalled to Torah by the unforgettable years of exile and the sharp word of divine reproof through the prophets. This, too, had now to become for Christians a sign that their relationship with God deserved the repudiating wrath of God because of the idolatries and injustices that Christianity was as prone to as any errant Jewish people of old. Christians had not displaced Jews either in purity of doctrine or in correct ritual, and certainly not in their moral behavior—witness the idolatry and systemic injustice to which they subscribed in the Hitler era.

Perhaps no words of Bonhoeffer, outraged at the persecution of the Jews, are as daring and biting as his "Confession of Guilt" on behalf of the churches.[44] In this confession Bonhoeffer writes what amounts to an indictment of the churches for their complicity in the injustices and murders committed by the Nazis. The church, he said, must confess "itself guilty of the decline in responsible action, in bravery in the defense of a cause, and in willingness to suffer for what is known to be right." He berates the churches for standing by "while violence and wrong were being committed under cover of this name Christ." He demands that the churches confess that they have "witnessed the lawless application of brutal force, the physical and spiritual suffering of countless innocent people, oppression, hatred and murder, and have not raised their voice on behalf of the victims or found ways to hasten to their aid." His poignant confession includes a powerful phrase that could itself serve as a model for acknowledgment of the churches' responsibility for the Holocaust. The churches, he contends, are "guilty of the deaths of the weakest and most defenseless brothers and sisters of Jesus Christ." This latter phrase was Bonhoeffer's way of referring to the Jewish people. What is especially noteworthy about this confession is that it was composed, not in the gloom of the collapse of Hitler's Reich, but at the very zenith of Nazi military successes, the fall of France. While the people of Germany, including many church leaders, were milling about the streets with church bells gonging, hailing the victories of their army and the enlightened, fearless leadership of their Führer, Bonhoeffer was privately lamenting the spectacle and accusing the churches of being accomplices by their silence in the suffering on which the Nazi ideology fed.

For Bonhoeffer, it would not be sufficient absolution of guilt for the Christian churches to catalogue those brave things church people did to save Jews during Hitler's rise to power and during World War II. Nor would it suffice to single out spirited vocal defenses of the Jews, even on the part of those, like Bonhoeffer, who would later give their lives. The fact remains that, in his opinion, the church, in this test of its being the true Church of Jesus Christ by a Christlike concern for the downtrodden, was guilty of infidelity. His bitterness against his church is evident in so many of his later writings. It was a bitterness stemming from what he sensed to be both a failure of trust in God and a denial of compassion. The brothers and sisters of Christians, he would insist to his seminarians, are not only those one encounters in explicitly Christian gatherings. Rather, Christ's closest brothers and sisters in suffering were the Jews, and the test of one's own Christian faith soon became whether one would speak up or do something on behalf of these victims. Not long after he wrote those dramatic passages of his *Ethics*, his hopes for stopping the slaughter on the battlefields and in the death camps were no longer with the churches; his energies were channeled into the resistance movement.

WORK IN THE ANTI-HITLER CONSPIRACY

Bonhoeffer's role in that movement consisted not only in being a courier negotiating terms of surrender with the allies should the coup d'état be successful, but also in being a moral force encouraging the conspirators to persist in their courageous plans. In the cynical casuistry of blood and conquest, which was part of the Nazi ideology, war and murder for the sake of nationalistic pride and national security were praised, and betraying one's country was the worst crime imaginable. The sensitive men and women of the conspiracy depended, therefore, on Bonhoeffer's moral support to help them cope with the "guilt" they experienced in plotting the violence needed to successfully assassinate Hitler and overthrow the Nazi government. For Bonhoeffer, the problem became more one of accepting guilt after the manner of Christ, who himself dared to accomplish the deed of free responsibility despite the shame of his eventual execution. In the inverted Nazi morality, unquestioning patriotism and slavish obedience to the order to kill were exalted as virtues. Yet these very "virtues" could, Bonhoeffer would argue, become a betrayal of one's conscience and country. True "patriots" were, paradoxically, those Germans who worked for the defeat of their own country. The conspirators, who were attempting to cope with the moral confusion of divided loyalties and the shame of a "treasonous" move against their own government —indeed, acting to insure the defeat of their nation—were indeed persons of extraordinary courage.

The church, on the other hand, had clearly chosen the path of "patriotism" and a quietistic support of Hitler's law and order at home and nationalistic expansion by conquest abroad. Some praised the war as a crusade against atheistic Bolshevism. Countless pastors seized the opportunity to demonstrate their loyalty to the government. Many enlisted; thousands would die in the war. Only a small number of church people would give their lives in opposing Hitler's mad schemes of world conquest and eugenic "purity." In short, the churches had, like the German generals, done what Bonhoeffer called their "duty by the devil."[45] These were words Bonhoeffer wrote in an essay he sent as a Christmas 1942 present to his family and fellow conspirators in order to bolster their spirits and stiffen their resolve on the eve of the practical attempts soon to be made on the life of Hitler. He rejects the argument, later to be heard at the Nuremberg trials, of those who would claim to be only following orders.

> Here, what is commanded is accepted as what is most certain, the responsibility for it rests on the commander, not on the persons commanded. But none of those who confine themselves to the limits of duty ever go so far as to venture, on their sole responsibility, to act in the only way that makes it possible to score a direct hit on evil and defeat it. The people of duty will in the end have to do their duty by the devil too.[46]

The churches were either silent or a disappointing opposition to those who had accepted the challenge to deliver their nation from evil. The conspirators were forced to act in isolation from their churches.

In Bonhoeffer's words from that same essay, entitled "After Ten Years," the churches and church goers who knew about the atrocities and did nothing had quite simply failed to be Christian. "We are not Christ," Bonhoeffer contended, "but if we want to be Christians, we must have some share in Christ's largeheartedness *by acting with responsibility and in freedom when the hour of danger comes,* and by showing a real compassion that springs, not from fear, but from the liberating and redeeming love of Christ for all who suffer. *Mere waiting and looking on is not Chris-*

tian behavior. Christians are called to *compassion and action*, not in the first place by their own sufferings, but by the sufferings of their brothers and sisters, for whose sake Christ suffered."[47] Those who read that essay knew full well that most church leaders and generals preferred to wait and look on, and military leaders, sensing the dangers of the kind of treasonous action to be undertaken by the conspirators, were unwilling to get involved in the coup d'état, however tacitly they might have approved of the act. When the plot failed, many churches had their bells rung and prayers of thanksgiving offered for the deliverance of their beloved Führer.

Bonhoeffer's fundamental discontent with his church as well as his hopes for the future in a chastened, revitalized church are brought out with added vehemence in the prison letters. "The church," he urged in these letters, "must come out of its stagnation. We must move out again into the open air of intellectual discussion with the world, and *risk saying controversial things*, if we are to get down to the serious problems of life."[48] The churches had, in his opinion, shirked their responsibility either to speak with any vehemence or to act, and thus they had permitted ruthless acts by right-wing criminal leaders of the government to continue, supported in their claim to respectability by either church acquiescence or church silence. In his baptismal sermon written from prison, Bonhoeffer envisioned a church less triumphalist, less pietistical, and less timid. If the Christian Church were ever to regain its credibility in the post-war world, it would have to be through a new way of speaking and a new way of acting. Such a church could be reborn only by the church's living a life of prayer and action for justice. For Bonhoeffer, the only credible faith was that inspirited by compassion and shaped in service.[49] In one of his last letters before his execution, he put it very succinctly in an "Outline for a Book" he never lived to write: "The church is the church only when it exists for others. . . . It must tell people of every calling what it means to live in Christ, to exist for others." Earlier in that same outline, he said that the true test of one's faith was neither adherence to its abstract set of beliefs nor obedience to ecclesiastical statutes. Rather, it is to answer honestly the question "What do we really believe? I mean, believe in such a way that we stake our lives on it?"[50]

By participating in the conspiracy against the Nazi government, Bonhoeffer was, indeed, staking his life on his conviction that this was the only way to bring an end to the killing fields and death camps of World War II. To that end he agreed to become a double agent and to undertake five trips, all sponsored by the Abwehr, the German military intelligence unit and the center of the conspiracy, ostensibly to gather information useful to Germany but actually to inform the allies of the conspiracy and to ask terms that would make a successful coup d'état possible. Three of those journeys were to Switzerland, one was to Norway, and one, the most memorable trip, was to Sigtuna, Sweden. It was at Sigtuna that he met with his old friend, Bishop Bell of Chichester, who would act as a go-between for Bonhoeffer's resistance group with Winston Churchill and Anthony Eden for the purposes of giving detailed information of the conspiratorial activities undertaken by the Abwehr to overthrow the Hitler government, and of asking, in return for a successful coup d'état, enough breathing space following the assassination for the German generals to form an interim, de-nazified government and to surrender to the Allies.

Bonhoeffer's attitude toward those who suffered under Hitler has been recorded by Bishop Bell. In contrast to the conditions offered by other resistance movements within Germany, Bonhoeffer wanted Bishop Bell to know that he fully supported Germany's making reparations to the victims of its bellicose, genocidal actions. Bell had already heard a proposal for a mutually acceptable peace settlement from Hans Schönfeld, who unexpectedly was in the same room with Bell when Bonhoeffer arrived. Schönfeld's memorandum asked for decent terms of surrender under the threat of Germany's fighting on to the death. He then offered his group's full cooperation "with all other nations for a comprehensive solution of the Jewish problem." Bell tells of Bonhoeffer's breaking in at that point and replying that "his Christian conscience . . . was not quite at ease with Schönfeld's ideas. There must be punishment by God. We should not be worthy of such a solution. Our action must be such as the world will understand as an act of repentance. 'Christians do not wish to escape repentance, or chaos, if it is God's will to bring it upon us. We must take this judgment as Christians.'"[51] Both Bonhoeffer and Schönfeld were in agreement that a Germany purged of Hitler and Nazism would repeal the Nuremberg Laws and make full restitution to the Jewish people for the harm done to them and the property stolen from them. Fifty-four years after the end of the war, at the time of this writing, many Jews are still waiting for that full restitution.

BONHOEFFER'S ROLE IN OPERATION 7

In explaining Bonhoeffer's involvement in the anti-Hitler conspiracy, Bethge states quite simply, "There is no doubt that Bonhoeffer's primary motivation for entering active political conspiracy was the treatment of the Jews by the Third Reich."[52] In an action more directly related to rescuing Jews from Nazi Germany, Bonhoeffer became involved in Operation 7, an action that would lead to his eventual arrest and become a central focus in his interrogations in prison. Operation 7 was ostensibly an effort to rescue a small number of Jews by assigning them to service as undercover agents working in Switzerland. This would save them from the deportations of Jews from Berlin then in full swing. Their actual role would be to tell the world of the Nazi atrocities. Because the operation needed large sums of money, it attracted the attention of the Gestapo and led to the arrest of one of the Abwehr agents, who, under torture, revealed the name of Bonhoeffer. Bonhoeffer himself was deeply involved. It was his role to obtain permission for these Jews—eventually fourteen Jews would be rescued through this operation—to enter Switzerland. To that end, Bonhoeffer wrote self-incriminating letters to the president of the Federation of Swiss Churches. In the indictment against him, Bonhoeffer was also confronted with a letter he had written to Hans von Dohnanyi, requesting his help in rescuing Jewish Professor Perels. Perels survived the war.

Andreas Pangritz reports on a spirited debate between Hans Bernd Gisevius and Fritz W. Arnold on whether this Operation 7 made any practical sense at a time when all activities of the Abwehr should have been channeled into ensuring a successful assassination of Hitler. Gisevius argued that rescuing Jews in those circumstances was a commendable but highly dangerous distraction from the more important goal. Arnold countered with his own conviction that "rescuing one human life—one grain of sand in an ocean of murdered—was much more important than any plot, independently of how great the goal was."[53] Bonhoeffer's thinking was clearly more in line with Arnold's argument from compassion. Pangritz concludes that this action was one of the reasons Bonhoeffer was condemned to death, thus making him not only a political resister but also a martyred rescuer of the Jews.

Bonhoeffer's death in that cause is also one reason why Stephen Wise has taken up the cause of finally having him recognized as one of the "Righteous Gentiles" honored at Yad Vashem, the memorial to the Holocaust in Jerusalem. Despite all of the evidence of Bonhoeffer's outspoken and, at times, behind-the-scenes defense of the Jewish victims of Nazism, the director of Yad Vashem's Department for the Righteous among the Nations, Mordechai Paldiel, had continued to refuse to recognize Bonhoeffer as among the now 13,000 so honored. Paldiel claims that there is no evidence that Bonhoeffer "specifically helped Jews." Stephen Wise, grandson of Rabbi Stephen Wise, mentioned above, to whom Bonhoeffer, in violation of the High Treason Law, delivered information relative to the Nazi persecution of the Jews of Germany, has not been deterred from his seeking justice in this matter. In letters and memoranda to Paldiel, he has persisted in producing a vast amount of evidence, including an affidavit from one of the rescued Jews of Operation 7, Bethge's well-substantiated testimony on Bonhoeffer's decisive actions to protect Jews, and his skilled lawyer's impeccable logic in support of according Bonhoeffer this honor. What is more, Wise contrasts the reasons for admitting some of the noted Righteous Gentiles, such as Heinrich Gruber and Armin Wegner, to the honor with the flimsy reasons Paldiel gives for denying Bonhoeffer, whose credentials in speaking out for and rescuing Jews are even more impressive and well documented.

Paldiel's counter-arguments strike any independent observer as self-serving, tendentious, and biased. Historian Peter Hoffmann, of McGill University, likewise finds Paldiel's arguments unconvincing. Hoffmann believes that Paldiel is hopelessly prejudiced against giving any recognition to members of the German resistance movement, of which Hans von Dohnanyi and Bonhoeffer were members. Evidently he does not want to accept that this movement could have anything more in its intent than the baser motive of salvaging something for Germany from the ruins of the Third Reich. Hence Paldiel's stonewalling and evasions of the persistent demands of Wise for a full accounting of Paldiel's *real* reasons for denying the honor to Bonhoeffer. Wise's remark to the *Jerusalem Post* is worth noting: "Without the information which I am asking for, preparing a petition is like trying to apply to a private club whose charter is sealed, whose application procedures are withheld, and whose blackballing rules are absolute and unreviewable."[54] Wise is an outstanding lawyer with fervent memories of Bonhoeffer's efforts to protect Jews through his grandfather, Rabbi Wise, and with a passion for justice in this matter. Bonhoeffer could have no better advocate for the recognition he deserves at Yad Vashem.

TOWARD JEWISH-CHRISTIAN RECONCILIATION: THE END OF THE STEREOTYPES

Whether Bonhoeffer is ever honored as a Righteous Gentile at Yad Vashem is not so significant as the value of his example and writings for the future of the Jewish-Christian dialogue and a fuller reconciliation of Jews and Christians. What might signal a change in Christian Church attitudes toward the Jews victimized by the systemic racism and religious bias of the twentieth century is what Bonhoeffer wrote toward the end of his essay gift to the conspirators: "We have for once learned to see the great events of world history from below, from the perspective of the outcast, the suspects, the maltreated, the powerless, the oppressed, the reviled—in short, from the perspective of those who suffer."[55] Bonhoeffer's own life was a steady journey from the comfort of a university teaching post to the bitterness of being a minority opposition to both church and state, from the safety of a refuge in the United States to the dangerous life of a conspirator, from clerical and familial privilege to the harsh imprisonment and death of a "traitor." This view from below was the perspective of a black preacher in Harlem, of a French pacifist, of pastors concerned about political idolatry creeping into their churches, of a fellow minister with Jewish blood, of inmates at Nazi prisons and death camps. The circumstances of his life helped Bonhoeffer to see the problems of his people from the view of "the oppressed." If there was a radical shift or "conversion" in his life, it was in that period when he rediscovered the Sermon on the Mount and realized that there were "things for which an uncompromising stand is worthwhile. And it seemed . . . that peace and social justice, or Christ himself are such things."[56] In that era, the issues of peace and social justice and Christ himself converged in the persecuted Jew and the Jewish Question.

While so much of Bonhoeffer's life and theology reveals a deep-set Christocentrism and an unwavering devotion to the Christian Church, equally striking is his having identified so closely with the plight of those prime victims of Nazi villainy, the Jewish people. This has several implications for the manner in which the Christian churches still need to be liberated from those prejudicial attitudes toward Judaism that rotted their identity from their very origins as a Christian church and not as a Christ-led reform of Judaism. This is not the place to trace the history of Christian anti-Semitism, nor am I arguing that Bonhoeffer's heroic actions and sharp words on behalf of the Jews exculpate Christian churches from guilt in the Holocaust. On the contrary, there is as much a lesson to be learned from the fact that Bonhoeffer was so isolated and ultimately so ineffective in this cause as from his accusation that the Christian churches were "guilty of the deaths of the weakest and most defenseless brothers and sisters of Jesus Christ."[57]

Part of that guilt is rooted in the hostility generated by Christianity's early and apparently bitter break with Judaism. The separation of Jews and Christians was more than a theological rift. Certainly Martin Buber, in his own incisive way, has perceptively described the clash of vision that made the separation so inevitable: "To the Christian the Jew is the incomprehensibly obdurate man, who declined to see what has happened; and to the Jew the Christian is the incomprehensibly daring man who affirms in an unredeemed world that its redemption has been accomplished."[58] This is a gracious interpretation of a protracted history of invective and persecution in which Christians saw in Judaism a nagging reminder that the promise of Christianity was still unfulfilled, and in Jews a convenient scapegoat for those societal ills which contradicted that promise. That hatred of Judaism constituted a clear rejection of Jesus, who joined compassion for the outcast with a spirit of forgiveness and even love of enemies, was a contradiction hardly noticed as Christian history became tainted with the quasi-religious sanctions that made repression of the Jews seem like virtuous, even manly actions. The Jews were considered a people destined to pay forever for the death of Jesus Christ and, therefore, rejected by God and doomed to wander nationless at the mercy of peoples who would barely tolerate their presence among them.

When Bonhoeffer attempted to parry these pseudo-theological rationalizations for the misfortunes of the Jews, he encountered fierce opposition within his own church. He was reproved for his study of Ezra-Nehemiah, for example, for overlooking the issue of Jewish guilt in the murder of Jesus. But, as William J. Peck has observed, "Bonhoeffer did not hold any subgroup in the church or in world history responsible for Golgotha. . . . He [Jesus] was betrayed and killed by man, as much by the church of today as by the church of Ezra. This is Bonhoeffer's stand in opposition to the neutral theologians in a debate that leads from politics to the iconic-mythic issues of theology."[59] There is likewise a shift in Bonhoeffer's Bible studies during the period of the 1930s, in which he seemed at first to have interpreted everything from an extreme christocentric typology, only to modify this by a more respectful attempt to understand Christ himself from the vantage point of the Hebrew Scriptures. If in the beginning, and in typically Christian exegesis from the patristic period on, he could declare that the Old Testament belonged to Christ, by the time of his work in the conspiracy he could affirm that Christ belonged to the Jews.[60] Indeed, he identified with them in the ghettos and death camps.

Such an extraordinary solidarity with the Jews on Bonhoeffer's part has been noted by Pinchas Lipade, an Orthodox Jew, who not only saw Bonhoeffer's theology of the 1930s take a surprisingly Judaic turn toward the Torah and the Mishnah, but has also expressed this startling conclusion about where that theology might lead. "From a Jewish perspective," he writes, "Bonhoeffer is a pioneer and forerunner of the slow, step-by-step re-Hebraisation of the churches in our days."[61] Historian Ruth Zerner goes so far as to suggest, along the lines of Bonhoeffer's "unconscious Christianity," that Bonhoeffer himself was an "unconscious Jew."[62] It is not clear what either expression might mean other than that Christianity and Judaism converge at those points of intersection where the gospel is a Christian adaptation by Rabbi Jesus of the Jewish Torah.

In this spirit, perhaps it is time in the history of the Christian churches for Christians to cease referring to the Hebrew Scriptures as the *Old* Testament and to their own Scriptures as the *New* Testament, if by "new" is meant that the Christian Scriptures had supplanted the "outdated" Hebrew Scriptures. Christian imperialism in regard to the Bible has led either to a denigration of the Hebrew Scriptures or to a total Christification of them, by which Christianity fashions its "displacement theory" and feeds its own distortion of God's mysterious choice of the Jewish people to epitomize faith in God before an idolatrous world. No longer can a church ever assert that God has rejected Judaism in favor of Christianity. Nor can a church claim that pogroms against Jews reflect only their just punishment for killing the Christ or that Christians have a mission to evangelize Jews. These are the ecclesiastical stereotypes that were sloganeered by church leaders while their unthinking, resentful minions sought out scapegoats for their own and a nation's misfortunes. Bonhoeffer has argued the greater responsibility of those who egged on the mobs and those who, by their timidity, ignorance, or indifference, made the violent, hate-filled behavior of the mobs possible. It was Bonhoeffer who pointed out that to reject Judaism and the Jewish roots of Christianity is to reject Christ himself. Bonhoeffer argued the necessity and the benefits of seeing reality from the perspective of those who suffer. His own writings, the lessons gleaned from the vast Holocaust literature, and the availability of documentary films on the Holocaust and living history from survivors of the horrors of the death camps, along with museum exhibits such as the deeply moving, extremely unsettling Holocaust Museum in Washington, D.C., should be part of every Christian education curriculum. Not to do so would be a sin against the Christian churches' duty to educate their people about the Holocaust and to make available to every Christian believer an important lesson on the depths to which human evil can sink, and the potential for humans, graced by God, to rise above tyranny and genocide.

RECONCILIATION AND THE END OF CHRISTIAN TRIUMPHALISM

If Christianity is ever to divest itself of its anti-Judaic myths and move toward a more sincere reconciliation with Judaism, a new consciousness of its own identity is needed. For the sake of an honest dialogue between the religions, Christian theology must steep itself in rabbinical commentary on the Jews' own Scriptures, and in Jewish understanding of Christian history, something not always flattering to the Church and its myths about Christian superiority over the Jews. This could constitute the beginnings of the end of that Christian theological-ecclesial imperialism which has motivated suppression of the Jewishness of Jesus and the Jewish connections of Christianity itself.[63]

The Christian contempt for Judaism is, however, only one part of that larger problem in Christianity which has hindered genuine ecumenical dialogue at all levels: church triumphalism. Truth about God and faith has nearly always been declared to coincide with what the Christian churches teach or what they have preserved in their New Testament and in their "authentic" reading of the Old Testament. Such "truth" has been proclaimed coterminous with Christianity alone of all the world religions. Christian scorn of the Jew is born of that aggressive, excluding attitude that, because of the proclaimed divinity of Jesus Christ, claims that Christianity alone possesses the fullness of truth or knows the whole truth about God. And, for many, it is all packed into the pages of the Christ-centered, Christian-interpreted Bible, or in the teachings of a church astoundingly preserved by God's Spirit from all error. It is difficult to engage in interreligious dialogue with an ecclesiastical system whose major premise is a claim that the dialogue partner is in near hopeless (put more kindly, "invincible") error. The Christian interpretation of divine revelation is deeply mired in triumphalist pretensions, such that it is questionable whether Jesus himself could get a fair hearing on several of his teachings, were he to return to earth today as in Dostoyevsky's story of the "Grand Inquisitor." I suspect he would be dismissed as one more loud, itinerant prophet in the mode of Amos, Jeremiah, or John the Baptizer.

The rampant Christian belief in its own monopoly on the so-called truths of revelation has prompted one specialist on revelation theology to comment that the Church's difficulty in understanding Judaism is traceable to many historical and social factors, but underlying these problems is a continuing inadequacy in appreciating the nature of God's revelation. For most church leaders, revelation is "something that came in the past and stopped." This meant that "the Old Testament cannot be anything but old . . . or supplanted or at least completed by the New Testament. They cannot accept that God could still be revealing God to the Jews because they believe that God is no longer revealing God to anybody. Revelation in their view was completed, sealed, and delivered *in toto* to the Apostles in the era between the resurrection and Jesus' ascension."[64] One has only to witness the smugness with which slick televangelists explain the whole truth to their pliable audiences to see evidence of the way Christian preachers can make monopolistic claims to be the sole purveyors of God's teachings to the world. It is possible, however, that if Jews and Christians can study their Scriptures prayerfully and with mutual appreciation, "they can search together for the God in whom they both believe, the one who is glimpsed under different aspects in the lives of Jews and Christians. In such an undertaking the Christian will have to ask himself with candor where the most striking witness of the suffering servant of Yahweh has been found in the twentieth century."[65] A study of Bonhoeffer's theology would point to the presence of the "suffering servant," indeed, of Jesus Christ himself, in the long lines of victims at the gas chambers in Nazi death camps. Jesus Christ was crucified anew in the Holocaust.

The common search of Christian and Jew for the God in whom they both believe has, unfortunately, been stymied by that idol-like sense of Christianity's own claim to be superior to all other religions. The Church alone becomes, in this perspective, the sole dispenser of revealed truths and the only means of salvation in the world. Nazi imperialism is but the pagan, Teutonic counterpart of the extreme sacralization of a church for its own sake. A church worshiping itself and its own absolute, inerrant authority pays homage to an idol, however fitting the liturgical language may be to worship the God acknowledged by Christian, Jew, and Moslem alike. Christianity glories in the cross of Christ, but was often unable to see that the "crucifixion of the Jews," to borrow Franklin Littell's memorable phrase, was the shameful scheme of baptized Christians.

It is this strange church insulation against shame, guilt, and sinfulness in the past that led Christians to behave toward Jews with either the malignant apathy of conquerors or the repression and anger of the insecure bigot. The German Catholic theologian Johann Baptist Metz has pointed out that Christianity's dangerous triumphalism has inflicted an "incapacity for dismay in the face of disasters" on Christian consciousness and, therefore, an insensitivity to the message of Auschwitz for humankind.[66] We can hardly claim to interpret that "message of Auschwitz" for our own Christian churches, much less for our Jewish brothers and sisters today. But we do detect a common consciousness that might move us to listen together in perhaps a new way to God, the father of Moses and of Jesus. Recent apologies to the Jews by Vatican Council II and by Pope John Paul II are steps toward the kind of reconciliation that can only spring from a sense of sin and from a church begging for forgiveness from those oppressed by its public sins against a people once looked on as the enemy. If God can speak on the top of Mt. Sinai and from the crucified victim of Roman imperialism and priestly, aristocratic connivance, God can speak from the heart of the world itself, even the hellish world of Auschwitz. The responsibility of Jews and Christians is to respond to God's love and make this love known to others, to be, as Rabbi Jesus enjoins his followers, the salt of the earth and the light of the nations, and by their compassion to glorify their Lord God. For the Jews, the idea of the Shekinah is a way of proclaiming God's personal involvement with God's children in the world through the presence of divine love. It is an idea of God that Christians can share with Jews. That God is present among God's children is at the roots of what Bonhoeffer had described in his prison letters as God's vulnerability and suffering. God was, as a rabbinical commentary would have it, grieved at heart at the time of the flood. God wept for God's children in exile. In all their afflictions God was afflicted. This God suffers when God's children suffer. Our personal sorrow is God's sorrow.[67]

This is close to what Bonhoeffer meant by his claim that

> the God who is with us is the God who forsakes us (Mark 15:34). The God who lets us live in the world without the working hypothesis of God is the God before whom we stand continually. Before God and with God we live without God. God lets God be pushed out of the world on to the cross. God is weak and powerless in the world, and that is precisely the way, the only

way, in which God is with us and helps us, not by virtue of the divine omnipotence, but by virtue of God's weakness and suffering.[68]

God's loving, caring, even grieving presence among God's people functions for Jews as the Incarnation of Jesus Christ functions for Christians. Bonhoeffer had witnessed against a triumphalist, insensitive church seemingly impervious to the cries for help from those who in all centuries have been brothers and sisters to Jesus Christ. Christians have much to learn from their Jewish brethren. The reconciliation between Jews and Christians will become possible only when they can identify with each other in joy and sorrow, when they can foster each other's well-being, not out of a sense of patronizing condescension, but in the spirit of the one who calls them together to be equally God's people. To ask if such a reconciliation can ever be possible after Auschwitz is like asking whether Jews and Christians can pray together after Auschwitz. To this I would answer with Johann Metz, "We can pray [together] *after* Auschwitz, because people prayed *in* Auschwitz."[69]

ENDNOTES

1. This article is a totally revised version of a paper that I originally presented at the Scholars Conference, sponsored by the National Conference of Christians and Jews, New York, 1983. It is fitting that it be included in this *festschrift* and dedicated to Burton Nelson, since Burton has been badgering me ever since to revise the paper and publish it.

2. See Bonhoeffer's "Confession of Guilt," in *TF*, 362-63.

3. *TF*, 132.

4. Ibid., emphasis mine.

5. Ibid., 133.

6. Eberhard Bethge, "Bonhoeffer and the Jews," in John D. Godsey and Geffrey B. Kelly, eds., *Ethical Responsibility: Bonhoeffer's Legacy to the Churches* (Lewiston: The Edwin Mellen Press, 1981), 59-60.

7. Stephen G. Ray Jr., "Race and Christian Identity: A Consideration of Bonhoeffer's Treatment of the Jewish Question," unpublished paper presented at the annual meeting of the American Academy of Religion, New Orleans, 1996, 7-8.

8. Christoph Strohm, *Theologische Ethik im Kampf gegen den National-sozialismus. Der Weg Dietrich Bonhoeffers mit den Juristen Hans von Dohnanyi und Gerhard Leibholz in den Widerstand* (Theological ethics in the struggle against Nazism. The way of Dietrich Bonhoeffer and the jurists, Hans von Dohnanyi and Gerhard Leibholz) (Munich, 1989). Christine-Ruth Müller, *Dietrich Bonhoeffers Kampf gegen die nationalsozialistische Verfolgung und Vernichtung der Juden. Bonhoeffer's Haltung zur Judenfrage im Vergleich mit Stellungnahmen aus der evangelischen Kirche und Kreisen des deutschen Widerstandes* (The struggle of Dietrich Bonhoeffer against Nazism's persecution and annihilation of the Jews. Bonhoeffer's attitude toward the Jewish Question in comparison with the position taken by the Protestant churches and the German resistance circles) (Munich, 1990).

9. *GS* 6, 272.

10. *TF*, 412 (translation slightly altered).

11. Letter of 14 April 1933, *TF*, 410.

12. *DB*, 201.

13. Stephen A. Wise, "Why Isn't Bonhoeffer Honored at Yad Vashem?" *Christian Century*, 25 February 1998, 202.

14. *DB*, 202.

15. Franz Hildebrandt, "An Oasis of Freedom," in *I Knew Dietrich Bonhoeffer*, ed. Wolf-Dieter Zimmermann (New York: Harper, 1966), 38-39.

16. Letter of 24 October 1933, *TF*, 391.

17. *DB*, 220.

18. Müller, *Dietrich Bonhoeffers Kampf*, 31-35, 195-96.

19. William J. Peck, "From Cain to the Death Camps: An Essay on Bonhoeffer and Judaism," *Union Seminary Quarterly Review* 28, no. 3 (Winter 1973), 174.

20. *TF*, 136.

21. Letter of 20 August 1933, *TF*, 419.

22. *TF*, 137.

23. Ibid., 17.

24. Cited in Bethge, "Bonhoeffer and the Jews," 63.

25. Cited in Edwin H. Robertson, *Christians against Hitler* (London: SCM, 1962), 24-25.

26. Ibid., 50 (translation slightly altered). For the full text of Barmen's declarations, resolutions, and motions, see Arthur Cochrane, *The Church's Confession against Hitler* (Pittsburg: Pickwick Press, 1976), 237-47.

27. Cited in Eberhard Bethge, "The Holocaust and Christian Anti-Semitism: Perspectives of a Christian Survivor," *Union Seminary Quarterly Review* 31, nos. 3 and 4 (1977), 144.

28. *DB*, 298.

29. *TF*, 228-29, emphasis mine.

30. Ibid., 228.

31. *CD*, 341 (translation slightly altered). In the new Touchstone edition, this passage is located on 301.

32. Ibid., 124-25. In the new Touchstone edition, this passage is located on 111.

33. *DB*, 313.

34. *GS* 2, 314.

35. Bethge, "Bonhoeffer and the Jews," 63.

36. *NRS*, 325 (translation altered).

37. Ibid., 71-72.

38. *DB*, 405-6.

39. Ibid., 406. See also Bethge, "Bonhoeffer and the Jews," 72-73.

40. Ibid., 74.

41. *TF*, 444. This quotation is cited with the biblical texts added in ibid., 75-76.

42. Ibid., 76.

43. *E*, 89-90.

44. Ibid., 110-19. The translation here is that found in *TF*, 362-63.

45. *LPP*, 5.

46. Ibid. (translated altered).

47. Ibid., 14 (translation altered), emphasis mine.

48. Ibid., 378, emphasis mine.

49. See my chapter "Prayer and Action for Justice: Bonhoeffer's Spirituality," in John W. de Gruchy, ed., *Cambridge Companion to Bonhoeffer* (Cambridge: Cambridge University Press, 1999).

50. *LPP*, 382-83.

51. *GS* 1, 380, 405. For a more detailed account of Bonhoeffer's trip to meet with Bishop Bell in Sigtuna, see F. Burton Nelson, "Bonhoeffer at Sigtuna, 1942: A Case Study in the Ecumenical Church Service," in Godsey and Kelly, *Ethical Responsibility*, 131-42.

52. Bethge, "Bonhoeffer and the Jews," 76.

53. Andreas Pangritz, "Sharing the Destiny of His People," in de Gruchy, *Cambridge Companion to Bonhoeffer*, 274.

54. For a fuller development of this debate, see Wise, "Why Isn't Bonhoeffer Honored?" and "Who, Exactly, Is a 'Righteous Gentile'?" reprinted from *The Jerusalem Post*, 22 April 1998, 12, in the *Newsletter of the International Bonhoeffer Society, English Language Section*, no. 67 (June 1998), 1-3.

55. *LPP*, 17.

56. *DB*, 155.

57. *E*, 114; translation from *TF*, 363.

58. Cited in Alan Davies, *Antisemitism and the Christian Mind* (New York: Herder and Herder, 1969), 153.

59. William J. Peck, "The Role of the 'Enemy' in Bonhoeffer's Life and Thought," in A. J. Klassen, ed., *A Bonhoeffer Legacy: Essays in Understanding* (Grand Rapids: Eerdmans, 1981), 353.

60. Bethge, "Bonhoeffer and the Jews," 88-89.

61. Pinchas Lapide, "Bonhoeffer und das Judentum," in Ernst Feil, ed., *Verspieltes Erbe: Dietrich Bonhoeffer und der deutsche Nachkriegsprotestantismus* (Lost legacy: Dietrich Bonhoeffer and post-war Protestantism) (Munich: Kaiser, 1979), 129.

62. Ruth Zerner, "Dietrich Bonhoeffer's Prison Fiction: A Commentary," in Dietrich Bonhoeffer, *Fiction from Prison: Gathering Up the Past*, ed. Renate and Eberhard Bethge with Clifford Green, trans. Ursula Hoffmann (Philadelphia: Fortress Press, 1981), 155.

63. See, for example, the related issues raised over twenty years ago by Rosemary Reuther in her *Faith and Fratricide: The Theological Roots of Anti-Semitism* (New York: Seabury, 1974), 257-61.

64. Gabriel Moran, "The God of Revelation," *Commonweal* 85, no. 18 (10 February 1967), 501.

65. Ibid.

66. Johann Baptist Metz, *The Emergent Church: The Future of Christianity in a Postbourgeois World*, trans. Peter Mann (New York: Crossroad, 1981), 25.

67. Philip E. Devenish, "Jews and Christians Searching for God," *America* 148, no. 8 (26 February 1983), 149-52. See also my article "Sharing in the Pain of God: Dietrich Bonhoeffer's Reflections on Christian Vulnerability," *Weavings* 8, no. 4 (July/August 1993), 6-15.

68. *LPP*, 360-61 (translation altered).

69. Metz, *The Emergent Church*, 19.

BONHOEFFER'S CIRCLES

Bonhoeffer and the Role of Women[1]

Renate Bethge

D ietrich Bonhoeffer grew up in a setting where men and women had their special and distinctively different places. But also among the men and the women there were big differences. The mother had a very different place from the kitchen maid, the father a different one from the gardener. Yet all were respected adults. Children were not supposed to give impudent answers to any of them.

It is difficult to say whether the father, Karl Bonhoeffer, or the mother, Paula, née von Hase, had a more prominent place in the family. The father was a very respected personality in his work at Berlin University as the professor of neurology and psychiatry, and somehow this transmitted itself to the family as well. The children saw their father much less frequently than their mother, so his worth may have grown by his rarity. And their mother herself cared that the father's image appeared spotless, that things went the way he liked, that he had peace and quiet for his work. He really was an impressive person—but that is a different point. It was obvious that the father was very fond of the mother, was chivalrous to her, and also cared that the others behaved in the same way.

THE ROLE OF WOMEN IN HOME AND SOCIETY

Some people of the generation of my mother (Ursula Bonhoeffer) and Dietrich who had visited in the Bonhoeffer home before the war thought that their mother was the dominating figure in the family. She had eight children and quite a staff, and she organized everything. Her children and grandchildren and their education were most important to her. She was always ready to put everything at stake for them. Once her son Klaus took his fifteen-minute swimming test and did not dare to jump into the water, which was part of the test. She jumped into deep water, fully dressed and without being able to swim, as she had once heard that one would come up by oneself. Luckily, the swimming instructor was there to pull her out. How much this encounter strengthened Klaus's courage, I do not know.

The mother was strict, but she had the most wonderful imaginative thoughts for games and feasts, gifts and food for the children, as well as puppet shows to play and books to read to them. She liked to give big parties, not only for children, but also for the adults. These parties were famous because she always had some original ideas for them: special games or dances, little funny skits, and the like. Because of the unconventional and witty atmosphere of these parties, I have met people much later who still remarked with excitement about them.

The mother was the soul and the spirit of the house. I never saw her cooking or sewing, but always in discussions with much planning about family matters. Even more often (as it was during the Nazi period), she discussed political and church situations. She was the granddaughter of the church historian Karl August von Hase, who was well known at the time. Her father had also been a theologian and was a preacher to the court for a while, and her mother had been a Countess von Kalckreuth. This probably made her accustomed to a generous style of life, which she always kept.

She was a conscious Christian, although she only began attending church frequently when the Confessing Church became very important to her. When Dietrich was a minister for German congregations in London, she was the one who kept him informed about political and church events at home, very often in coded language. She liked discussions, and it is said that even on walks during the holidays she was so wrapped up in them that she hardly saw the landscape or the mushrooms, in which her husband was interested. She was consulted by everybody. What she said was listened to, and how she planned things was accepted. The way to the father had to go through her. My mother reported that when she was already married and once went directly into her father's room, her mother asked why she done that without first asking her.

In the family, an important role was played by the grandmother on the father's side. (The grandmother on the mother's side had died early.) She was energetic; in her younger years she had been involved in women's emancipation. She lived in Tübingen. When Dietrich studied there for a year, he lived with her. There are letters between them, and from her letters to him one can see what an interest she took in his plans. She also gave him important hints. She wrote to him in Barcelona in 1928, "In your place I would try to get to know the opposite world in the east; I think, for instance, of India, Buddha and his world." (As a matter of fact, Dietrich then repeatedly tried to go to India. He even got an invitation from Gandhi to stay with him for a long spell of time.) Later she lived with her son, my grandfather, in Berlin.

With the rest of the family, from the very beginning she was an outspoken enemy of the Nazis. On 1 April 1933, Hitler ordered that nobody was to buy anything in a Jewish shop, and storm troopers stood guard before such shops and stores. She just walked through the row of those watchmen, did her shopping, and came out through the row of the perplexed men, saying, "I do my shopping where I always do my shopping."

When she died in 1936 at age ninety-three, Dietrich described her in his funeral speech for her:

> She could not bear to see the rights of a person violated. . . . Thus her last years were darkened by the grief that she bore about the fate of the Jews in our country, which she suffered with them. She came out of a different time, out of a different spiritual world, and this world will not sink into the grave with her. This heritage, for which we are grateful to her, puts us under obligation.[2]

In our family, as in most families at the time, it was believed that for the woman, fulfillment was to be found in the family. If a woman had to remain without husband and children, then an occupation would be thought of as a substitute. Of course, it would have to be a meaningful occupation, which meant work in the social area or an academic profession. To work as a secretary was regarded as inadequate. Instead, a girl would have gone into a big family as a mother's helper, as Dietrich's and my mother's cousin did with us. This was in fulfillment of a female role or in preparation for having one's own household.

Of course, it was known that not every marriage went well, but it was thought that a happy marriage was the normal case. In view of the Bonhoeffer parents, that seemed obvious. So if a woman who had a sensible husband was not happy, it was seen as an exceptional case. Also, in those circles various things were done to help the daughters to a "suitable" husband and to exclude supposedly unsuitable men. This sometimes led to tragedies, but on the whole went fairly well.

Self-realization was an unknown word at that time. It would have been seen as abnormal in Bonhoeffer's surroundings if a woman had called for it. There were, of course, people at the time, including women, who lived in the sense of this word, as one can see from the life of Hanna Tillich, the wife of the theologian Paul Tillich. She tells how she planned to marry a man with the aim of leaving him after exactly one year in order to live with Tillich. This man had no idea of this, and she really did it.

Dietrich's twin sister, Sabine, attended an art school for a while. When she told her parents that her professor had said to her, "Miss Bonhoeffer, you should live more intensely," my grandmother said, "You know, this school is not the right thing for you." She took Sabine out of the school. Nobody in the family thought that this was wrong, not even Sabine herself. She told this to me with amusement some years ago.

The parents, of course, wanted all their children to develop according to their abilities, including the girls. They did much for this, providing, for instance, books and music lessons. A French governess was engaged to teach French, and governesses and schools were chosen carefully. In order to study at a university at that time, girls had to go into boys' school for the later school years. This was possible, though, and one of the Bonhoeffer girls did it.

Nearly the most important in their education was to learn from their mother consideration, to help the weaker person to his or her right, and to have open eyes for the problems of other people, including people in a different social position. My mother was the oldest of the Bonhoeffer daughters, and she later started training in social work. When she was sixteen years old, she was sent into the household of a former maid of the family. She had to look after the woman's six children and husband, who was often drunk, so that she could recover from an illness.

Naturally, such a task would never have been expected from a son. The boys had to come to help at once if something was to be carried or other such things needed to be done. But one was much more deliberate in dealing with their time. With them, always in the background there was their later profession as their main task. They were to be able to prepare themselves for it without too many disturbances. Only one of the four daughters started to study at a university, and she gave it up after three semesters, as she married. Marriage was taken so seriously that to work on top of it did not occur to anyone. It was presupposed that girls could realize themselves best in marriage. In any case, a mother had to be totally at home for any children. For the boys, of course, breaking off their studies would have been out of the question.

The Bonhoeffer mother herself had studied to be a teacher "for higher education for girls." So she taught all her children during their first school years, each one with a few little friends of his or her age. Although she had fought to be allowed to study, which was not done by girls in her day, later on it was no longer important for her. Apart from this teaching at home, she never took it up. Her life was full without it, with the eight children and the big household in which everybody was to be considered.

One can hardly imagine such a household today: there were the first and second maids for the rooms, the cook and the first and second kitchen maids, the governess for the big children and the other one for the small children, and the maid for the clothing (mainly the mother's), who also helped in the serving of feasts. Additional women were engaged for such occasions. Such a house was, of course, not an isolated place; many people went in and out. It was part of the society, and at the same time a little realm by itself. To lead it well and with a light hand was seen as something important, and as an equivalent, though different, role to a man's profession.

In 1926 Klaus Bonhoeffer in an amusing way hinted at the distribution of the roles in the Bonhoeffer family in a "Constitution" written for fun on his mother's birthday:

> Preamble: The constitution is patriarchal. . . . Owner: Privy Councillor Bonhoeffer (Prof. of medicine). Sole Business Manager: Mrs. Paula Bonhoeffer. . . . The Sole Business Manager will decide by herself on medical problems. The male descendants of the Owner receive half a vote as soon as they have passed the age of 30. [In 1926 none of the children was yet thirty years old.] The female descendants are expected, before completion of their 21st year, to find an opportunity to found a branch company.[3]

There was a remarkable academic woman in the family, Charlotte Leubuscher—unmarried, of course—who had studied economics and taught in Berlin at the Technical University, something very unusual for a woman at the time. She was a younger cousin of the mother. She often visited the Bonhoeffer house. This relative apparently was not held in highest esteem by the Bonhoeffer children since, for all her intelligence, she was too much of a teacher. My mother told me that the children made fun of her. I saw her in Berlin only when I was a small child, as she left Germany very soon after the Nazis took power, because of her Jewish father. But I came into close contact with her when we lived in London, and I was quite impressed by her unusual and witty personality. Yet I can imagine that children could not see that. It may be also that she became more open-minded when she grew older. Anyway, this woman could not serve as an example for the girls, nor did she especially impress the boys.

Most of the women more widely known were artists back then. Dietrich went to Elly Ney's piano concerts, he liked Paula Wessely and other actresses, and the painter Käthe Kollwitz interested him. Women writers played a still bigger role in public—and also for Dietrich. My husband tells that, in Finkenwalde on a Sunday afternoon, Bonhoeffer read *Die Judenbuche*, by Annette von Drost-Hülshoff, to the students. Ricarda Huch was also highly esteemed, not only because she left the Prussian Academy of the Arts when the Nazis took over, but also because of her historical books and fiction. And there are many other women writers, like Selma Lagerlöf, Ina Seidel, and Marie von Ebner Eschenbach, who were read in the family and by Dietrich as a matter of course. English women writers like the Brontës or Katherine Mansfield were not known in the family as far as I remember.

It seems to me that the book on Marie Curie written by her daughter was seen as especially valuable for the youth, maybe more for the girls than for the boys. Maybe, after all, it was meant as a possible example for us.

Later on, the lives of Dietrich's sisters looked different from that of their mother. They had four, three, or two children and still had one or two maids living in the house. Yet they had to look after all the small things in the house much more than their mother did. Through the pressure of the Nazi time, however, this was thrust into the background. I never heard any of the sisters complaining about the difficulties of their role. There were more important matters that occupied all the family then: the worry about their many Jewish friends, the growing injustice and what could be done about it, concrete considerations for the resistance, and then the war. The youngest sister, Susanne, was additionally very active in the congregation of which her husband was the minister. Only from Christine I once heard a sigh, "How privileged a man is that he can sit in peace and quiet at his desk."

It certainly had a lot to do with their mother's attitude that the thought of resistance came up so self-evidently in the family. For Dietrich's confirmation, she had written in his Bible the verse 2 Corinthians 3:6: "The letter kills, but the Spirit gives life."

Of course, in view of the letter, the resistance was illegal, but it was in accordance with the Christian spirit to stand up for the people who had to suffer the terrible wrongs of the Nazi regime. Thus, Dietrich could write in his *Ethics*: "The conscience which has been set free is not timid like the conscience which is bound by the law, but it stands wide open for our neighbor and for his concrete distress."[4]

In addition to Dietrich, his brother Klaus and two brothers-in-law— my father, Rüdiger Schleicher, and Hans von Dohnanyi—were killed by the Nazis. Thus my grandparents lost two sons-in-law.

This whole complex dominated all the years after 1933, when Bonhoeffer was only twenty-seven. There was unbelievably cruel suppression, where action was urgently needed. In this situation, thinking about the disadvantage of women would have seemed absurd in our family. Of course, we were angry about the policy of the Nazis toward women. They did not want women to learn much, but pressed them to have many children and gave them awards like cattle for breeding. But one did not need to conform to that.

Nevertheless, the bestowal of the so-called Mother's Cross perplexed the family. You received this cross if you had four or more children. So my mother and my grandmother were the only two members of the family who were eligible, and they were solemnly invited to the awards ceremony. Finally the family decided that my grandmother could afford at her age not to go, but that my mother should go to the ceremony and accept the cross. This she did, but for a long time afterward she was angry about it. Yet she told some crazy things about the celebration that gave the family something to laugh about.

BONHOEFFER'S RELATIONSHIPS WITH WOMEN

From early on, of course, Dietrich had much contact with girls and women. In his own generation he may have had more contact with girls than with boys, as among the five younger Bonhoeffer siblings he was the only boy. The three oldest brothers were a good deal older than he. With his younger sisters and their friends he took long hikes, went to museums, and liked the dancing festivities at home and in other houses. With his youngest sister's girlfriend, Anneliese Schnurmann, he started a youth club in 1932 for unemployed young people, which was soon dissolved by the Nazis, as it was seen as Communist.

During his university studies he had much contact with women. In his third semester he heard that for the exam he needed to have done Sunday school work, so he asked some of his female fellow students and his youngest sister to do such work with him in their local Grunewald church. As this sister reported, the work thrived immensely. They could hardly cope with the many children who suddenly came.

While studying at the university and afterwards, Bonhoeffer had for years a very close friendship with fellow student Elisabeth Zinn, to whom he sent all his sermons when he was a young minister in London. It is only through her that these sermons survived. This friendship came to an end when Dietrich started the preachers' seminary in Finkenwalde. As he wrote much later to his fiancée, Maria von Wedemeyer, he thought that at that time of crisis he should be totally free to work in the church.

When he was a lecturer in Berlin, there were also girls among his students. As a matter of course, he took them along to theological and ecumenical conferences. Yet in "his" preachers' seminary in Finkenwalde there were no women apart from the housekeeper. That was just the normal custom at the time. Mixed student hostels did not exist yet; they would even have been seen as immoral. Anyway, the students who came to Dietrich in Finkenwalde were sent by the Confessing Church. He had not chosen them.

Yet the feminist theologian Leonore Siegele-Wenschkewitz thinks that Dietrich fell victim to the anti-feminist educational policy of the Nazis, because you can see him in 1934 in a photo in Fanø with his male and female students, while a little later in Finkenwalde there are only male students in the photo. But this is because of the circumstances. Indeed, some then-fiancées of Finkenwalde students reported that Bonhoeffer seemed not very pleased when they came to visit. Yet I think that Bonhoeffer just did not like the attention of his pupils distracted.

In 1936 Bonhoeffer ordained a woman by the order of the Brethren Council of the Saxony Province of the Confessing Church, when women were not yet officially ordained. He did this as a matter of course, but it did not occur to him to fight for the general ordination of women or for the right of women to take over parishes of their own. Even men who were loyal to the Confessing Church could not count on a parish at all.

At that time, women could only work at a church where a man already was working as the first minister, or they could work in special fields like hospital care or prisons for women. They also were not called Frau Pfarrer, as men were called Herr Pfarrer, since Frau Pfarrer was the name of the minister's wife. All their lives they remained Frau Vikarin, even though Herr Vikar was the title of a young beginner in ministry under the main minister. If a *Vikarin* married a minister, she automatically lost her job. Through the war, that changed by itself. When the men had to become soldiers, such women practically took over the whole parish work.

During his time in Finkenwalde, Bonhoeffer became close to Ruth von Kleist-Retzow, the elderly widow of a landowner in the Pomeranian province. She was very interested in the Confessing Church and supported the seminary. In order to give her grandchildren, whose parents lived on rural estates, the possibility of going to a secondary school, she lived with them in Stettin, not far from Finkenwalde, during the school year. One of these grandchildren was Bonhoeffer's later fiancée, Maria von Wedemeyer. Frau von Kleist-Retzow attended Finkenwalde services together with her grandchildren, and those who were the right age were also confirmed by Dietrich. Maria was not yet old enough. Dietrich often had theological conversations with Frau von Kleist-Retzow. He also spent some times on her estate, where he worked on his *Ethics*.

Leonore Siegele-Wenschkewitz's observation is correct that, in Bonhoeffer's early interpretations of the creation story, he aims at a doctrine of *humanity*, not one of the sexes. Of course, he had to consider the difference between the sexes, but this difference did not lead to an order of status. He spoke about the "being there for the other" of the two, about Eve's function as an assistant to Adam, and of her being face-to-face with him. Bonhoeffer wrote, "The only other assistant or help for man in the Bible is God himself."[5]

Siegele-Wenschkewitz shows what a high value Bonhoeffer gives to the community of man and woman when he writes, "It carries in the proper sense the destination to be church."[6] He leaves out Ephesians 5:22: "You married women must subordinate yourselves to your husbands as you do to the Lord." Instead, he includes Ephesians 5:31-32:

"Therefore a man shall leave his father and mother and be joined to his wife, and the two shall become one. This mystery is a profound one, and I am saying that it refers to Christ and the church."

As an example of the opposite tendency, Siegele-Wenschkewitz then shows the sermon he wrote from prison for Eberhard's and my wedding, which was very important to Dietrich, in 1943, ten years after *Creation and Fall*. Here Bonhoeffer writes, "The wife's honor is to serve the husband; to be a 'help mate for him,' as the creation story has it" (Genesis 2:18).[7] Here the husband alone has all responsibility. The sphere of action for the wife is "the house of the husband."

We hear that this wedding sermon is often taken as an example for other wedding sermons because of some very beautiful parts in it. Yet it also gives offense because of the serving role that is given to the wife. The sermon, coming out of prison, reached us only about half a year after our wedding, and I was astonished by it. I did not recognize this attitude in Dietrich, nor did I know it from others in the family. Our real wedding sermon, delivered by Dietrich's former student Gerhard Ebeling, consisted of much of the same. I thought that this seemed to be what had to be said in the church. Also I explained this sermon to myself with the thought that Dietrich wanted to give his friend Eberhard, my husband, a better chance to make his voice audible in our big Berlin family, which was used to planning and deciding everything predominantly by women.

A CHANGING ATTITUDE TOWARD WOMEN

The Dutch theologian René Van Eyden, who has worked on "Dietrich Bonhoeffer's Understanding of Male and Female,"[8] sees our wedding sermon as the sum of Bonhoeffer's theology on marriage up to this time. In opposition to Siegele-Wenschkewitz, who saw a wider and more open understanding of the husband-wife relation in Bonhoeffer's *early* time, van Eyden sees it *after* our wedding sermon, that is, in the last year of his life.

As one point for this new, wider, more open attitude, van Eyden cites the "Thoughts on the Baptism," where Bonhoeffer recognizes that the world has radically changed. Van Eyden quotes: "All Christian thinking, speaking, and organizing must be born anew. . . . It will be a new language, perhaps quite non-religious, but liberating and redeeming—as was Jesus' language . . . the language of a new righteousness and truth.[9] Thus also toward women, concludes van Eyden.

His second, much more direct example for Bonhoeffer's changed view on husband and wife is Bonhoeffer's devotions that he wrote in his prison cell for 7 June 1944, when my husband had his short leave from the army. Those he is addressing are the same as a year before in the wedding sermon—Eberhard and me—but now there is nothing about subordination or serving. Reciprocity is everything. Here Bonhoeffer speaks about the mutual support of husband and wife for body, soul, and mind, and he sees this as the essence of marriage. Before he comes to this conclusion, Bonhoeffer says that, in view of God's words when he created Eve—"I will give you an assistant"—"this word seems too trifling to describe what marriage is."[10] Apart from his thoughts for our situation, it is easy to notice here his own affliction, as he is hoping for his own marriage and suffers from the separation from his fiancée.

I think that both Siegele-Wenschkewitz and van Eyden have correct points. Bonhoeffer did not like to speak about women being subordinated to men in his early time, before Finkenwalde, or in his very last time, after our wedding sermon. I think that the change in between had to do with his teaching in the preachers' seminary, where he had only men students and now had to teach not on behalf of the university, but on behalf of the church. This put him under obligation toward the doctrine of the church. And he put up with it, as the burning problems occupying him lay in a different field. Also, before Finkenwalde, the family life at home, in which the "subordination" of women did not fit, was still very near to him. In addition, his long-standing friendship with Elisabeth Zinn, which came to an end with Finkenwalde, would have played a part. Here, too, the thought of the "serving" wife would not have come up.

When Eberhard and I married in 1943, Dietrich had been engaged to Maria only a very short time, and a real exchange with his fiancée had not yet started. My husband had been his student, so that what Bonhoeffer had taught, he of course felt compelled to bring into his sermon as a continuation of his earlier thinking.

Furthermore, this sermon was composed in the first, very hard weeks in prison, most likely by mobilizing all his strength. In those weeks Bonhoeffer was overwhelmed with problems: he was totally isolated and could not speak with anybody, the cell and the bed were terribly dirty, he was afraid to say anything that might endanger others in the interrogations, the groans in the neighboring cells were awful, and he thought of suicide. In that situation, thinking of a new order for marriage was far off for him.

But with time his situation changed. There were some friendlier watchmen; he was not so totally isolated any more. He felt fairly equal to the situation. Now also he had contact with his fiancée, although it was rather scanty. He surely knew from the beginning that this girl was a very independent person, in spite of her nineteen, then twenty years of age. But it became more tangible for him as contact with her grew. Yet he had the strong wish that she would be in accord with him, for instance, in their assessment of books. So he wrote to my husband, when he heard that this was not the case, "I would very much like my wife to be as much of the same mind as possible in such questions. . . . I don't like it when husbands and wives have different opinions. . . . Is that another aspect of my 'tyrannical' nature?"[11] he adds humorously, yet somewhat doubtfully.

It became more and more obvious how the women outside could and did cope with the situation. Christine, after her own five weeks' imprisonment, had taken up the fight for her husband in all possible ways—in permitted, authorized channels and also in very dangerous, hidden ones. The women managed to provide Dietrich not only with urgently needed additional food, but also with smuggled news. After the visit of his sister Ursula, Bonhoeffer wrote, "It's always so comforting to find you so calm and cheerful despite all the unpleasantness you have to put up with."[12]

The women were now the strong ones, and the men in prison could rely on them. The women also could be very quick-witted; they quickly found the lies they needed to tell the Nazis, and they knew how to utter them with believable naïveté.

Even I, to whom the devotions were directed together with Eberhard, had now become a mother, even though only eighteen. At the time of our wedding, I had been only seventeen years old, a rather early bride. To all this the thought of the subordinate woman did not fit. Without direct duties toward the church, Bonhoeffer now in other fields could detach himself from some of its more narrow teachings and find new insights, which we find in *Letters and Papers from Prison*.

But again back to van Eyden. He states, similarly to Siegel-Wenschke-witz, that there is not much in Bonhoeffer's writings about the relation of man and woman. He points to the courses in pastoral care that Bonhoeffer taught in Finkenwalde between 1935 and 1939, when he said what a wedding sermon should contain. For Bonhoeffer, the first thing in it should be thanksgiving. Then it should be said that marriage is God's order. And Bonhoeffer says, "God is the master of the marriage. God does not yield from this right for anybody"—probably not for the man either, I think. In the next point Bonhoeffer says,

> Under the Lordship of God marriage also shall have its order, so that the man is the master inside the marriage while loving his wife and the wife is subject to her husband, also through loving her husband. It should be said concretely how this would look and what it means.[13]

Here I find a certain hesitation to simply impute to the woman a serving role. She is supposed to be subject to her husband, but in doing the same thing that is expected from him to her: loving him. How that should be done, Bonhoeffer leaves to the person in the concrete situation. He himself does not seem to like that topic; at least, it does not interest him much.

From Finkenwalde in 1938—that means after three years of teaching—it sounds a bit different, and we read from a Bonhoeffer interpretation of the first letter of Timothy,

> The husband is the head of the woman and of the family. He is the priest. He intercedes with God for his family. . . . For Paul the order is clear: women have full part in salvation and in the truth. But they have a different calling than the man. The honor of the woman should not be searched for in public, but in modesty and in moderation, which means in the hiddenness of the inconspicuous. She is allowed to learn, is even supposed to learn. . . . She is not to teach or to rule. Paul says: I don't permit it. Precisely in submitting she will develop more wisdom than if she would rule. This is not simple conservatism, but biblical order.[14]

From this last sentence it becomes clear that Bonhoeffer knew he contradicted present tendencies, van Eyden stresses. For Bonhoeffer it was most important to give a direct interpretation of the text. He talks about this in a lecture in August 1935, "Applying New Testament Texts." Here he talks about the wish to justify Christian faith in the present, and he warns against the method "of applying the test in a way that the biblical message is run through the strainer of one's own cognition—what does not go through, is despised and thrown away; that one cuts and trims the message until it fits into one's fixed frame."[15] Certainly Bonhoeffer did not want to do that with the Bible text concerning marriage, even though he may have found it hard.

Although Bonhoeffer often is rejected or unnoticed by feminist theologians, he had a big influence on liberation theology in South America as well as in South Africa and in other parts of the world. Some feminists still see his commitment to the oppressed as helpful for their cause. They see Bonhoeffer's characterization of Christ as "the man for others," and the conception of the powerless and suffering God, as important contributions.

Like the church, Bonhoeffer in his time did not notice that the biblical order, as it was seen then, was not in accordance with the attitude of Jesus toward women. Often Jesus questioned social and religious hierarchical orders, and he took women absolutely seriously. In spite of Paul's well-known utterances about the submission and silence demanded of women, he also said, "There is neither Jew nor Greek; there is neither slave nor free; there is neither male nor female, for you are all one in Christ Jesus" (Galatians 3:28), and, "God shows no partiality" (Romans 2:11).

Bonhoeffer touched on this problem of the difference between being at the top and being at the bottom, and on the other hand being yet equal before God, in his *Fiction from Prison,* which he wrote early in his prison time. Once Christoph, the main character, says to his friend,

> So according to the Christian doctrine all people are supposed to be equal . . . or even "the weaker and poorer, the better." That's the exact opposite, after all, of what both of us experience and think and want every day. . . . That would only lead to hopeless equalization.

And the friend also says that there must be a top and a bottom and that all depends on the right people being on top, whereupon Christoph says, "I don't understand it. Somewhere there must be a contradiction."[16] The conversation of the friends is interrupted by the action, and a solution for this problem is not given, but the problem stays throughout the script.

This *Fiction from Prison* is generally important for Bonhoeffer's view of women. But, as with our wedding sermon, the prison situation is playing a big role here. *Fiction* was also written in his early time in prison. He did not work on it later on. In it Bonhoeffer draws an almost rhapsodic picture of the self-sacrificing woman who loves to care for her house and her family. He makes Christoph's sister Klara answer, when asked if she will become a musician, "No, I never thought of that. Also, I didn't have enough of what it takes, and I don't want to do something halfway. I'll stay at home and some day I'd like to get married and have a family." And Bonhoeffer goes on,

> The simplicity and warmth with which Klara said this made it clear that she wasn't speaking of her personal happiness but of her vocation. . . . She was born a mother who had experienced the joy of a good family life from childhood and now carried it within her as a possession she could never lose.[17]

The women in *Fiction* are not simple. Klara, who estimates her talents for becoming a musician as not enough, is also self-critical. The women here have more sympathetic understanding than the men. The girlfriend of Christoph, Renate, understands his situation better than does his friend Ulrich. The women are the ones who organize the planning for the family. On the outing, Klara calls the brothers to first look for mushrooms, and they do it right away; the mother proposes a plan for a visit on the next day, and everybody follows.

Certainly, in the figure of Klara one can see a good deal of Dietrich's sisters Ursula and Sabine in her clarity and assurance, also in her certainty of judgment. But Dietrich's more aggressive sisters, Christine and Susanne,

are left out. Also Dietrich's fiancée, Maria von Wedemeyer, did not recognize herself in one of the female persons, although surely Dietrich wanted
to show her in the figure of Renate. The only woman who is described as
a critical person is the grandmother.

It is conspicuous that in the novel there are four brothers, as in the
Bonhoeffer family, but there is only one sister, although Bonhoeffer also
had four sisters. There is once a mention of a married sister, whose coat is
hanging in the hall, but that is all.

As in our wedding sermon, women appear here totally related to the
men; Bonhoeffer describes them:

> Only women from old families walk this way, women who—like
> their mothers before them—have always known themselves safe
> under the protection of their fathers, husbands, or brothers and
> safe within the realm of their families. But these women will also
> walk like that when disaster strikes and forces them to stand alone;
> that protection under which they once lived surrounds them at
> every step, even in the hour of greatest desolation, like an invis-
> ible power that no one dares to touch.[18]

As a prisoner, who with other men of his immediate family is in life-
threatening danger, Bonhoeffer knows that the women will remain strong,
and he himself wins strength through this. Yet this also—at least now—is
led back to the men. Perhaps Bonhoeffer just does not want to forget the
men, who, of course, have to do with the attitude of the women "through
generations" as the women have to do with the attitude of the men. In
Fiction, sometimes this forgetting of the man seems to disturb him. It
happens that apparently the mother spontaneously comes to Bonhoeffer's
mind, which he then corrects in reference to the father.

For instance, in the novel, he had first written that Martin had en-
treated his mother to allow him to wear a school cap. Then he changed it
to read "his father." Similarly, "You know you have a good mother" was
changed into "You know you have good parents."[19] He wants to be just
to everybody. In his evil situation, he wants to ascribe something good to
everybody. In November 1943 he writes, "Our past is always kept before
us by thankfulness and penitence."[20]

The thought of demanding or even pugnacious women is not comfortable for him now. He thinks of the women in the way they are so
important for him now, in their central role to the family and their unconditional, reliable effort for the men. The women also provided him with
whatever was possible and walked for him to the Gestapo offices. Even
here in prison they mediated for him a feeling of security. And in remembering the houses they organized, he wrote,

Most people have forgotten nowadays what a home can mean; though some of us have come to realize it as never before. It is a kingdom of its own in the midst of the world, a stronghold amid life's storms and stresses, a refuge, even a sanctuary.[21]

Here one has to think again of what Bonhoeffer at that time wrote to his parents in light of the fiction he was writing:

In general, a prisoner is no doubt inclined to make up, through an exaggerated sentimentality, for the soullessness and lack of warmth in his surroundings; and perhaps he may react too strongly to anything sentimental that affects him personally.[22]

Bonhoeffer came out of a patriarchal social structure. But in his surroundings, the women played an important role and were held in high esteem. That must have been so in wider circles. The signs of reverence that were shown to women give evidence to this. As Goethe says, "There is no outward sign of courtesy that would not have a deep ethical [moral] reason."

At the time, the homes, whose care and spirit were the women's responsibility, were a cultural center of the educated classes. They played a big role before all social life—and with it conversations, games, and music—moved out into restaurants or clubs or was more or less dropped altogether, or became strictly professional.

Life as it took place in those houses, of course, was possible only because there were enough people—mostly women—who earned their living by doing the housework. Now these women can do other things and live their own lives, but without them such houses cannot exist any more. This is only one of the many changes since Bonhoeffer's lifetime, but it is a fundamental one.

ENDNOTES

1. This essay first appeared in "Dietrich Bonhoeffer after Fifty Years," edited by Barbara Green, *Church & Society* (July/August 1995), 34-52. It is reprinted here with the gracious permission of Barbara Green. Renate Bethge dedicates this reprint to Dr. F. B. Nelson.

2. *GS* 4, 458 f.

3. Dietrich Bonhoeffer, *Fiction from Prison* (Munich: Kaiser Verlag, 1978), 131.

4. Dietrich Bonhoeffer, *Ethics*, ed. Eberhard Bethge (New York: Macmillan Company, 1955), 213.

5. *CF.*

6. Ibid.

7. *LPP*, 43-44.

8. Included in the documents of the 1988 Conference of the International Bonhoeffer Society, the Netherlands.

9. "Thoughts on the Day of the Baptism of Dietrich Wilhelm Rüdiger Bethge," *LPP*, 300.

10. *GS* 4, 592.

11. *LPP*, 148.

12. Ibid., 127.

13. *GS* 5, 413.

14. *GS* 4, 367-69.

15. *GS* 3, 304.

16. Bonhoeffer, *Fiction from Prison*, 77.

17. Ibid., 97-98.

18. Ibid., 95.

19. Ibid., 15.

20. *LPP*, 129.

21. Ibid., 44.

22. Ibid., 71.

Poore Foolische Friend: Bonhoeffer, Bethge, Vibrans, and a Theology of Friendship

Barbara Green

Eberhard Bethge was Dietrich Bonhoeffer's best friend during the last decade of his life. Most of the famous letters in Bonhoeffer's *Letters and Papers from Prison* were written to Bethge. After the war Bethge published them, the surviving pieces of Bonhoeffer's works, and later went on to write the definitive thousand-page biography of Dietrich Bonhoeffer.

Looking back on 1945 at the end of the war and the end of Hitler's dictatorship in Germany, Bethge once wrote, "The freedom, for which we had so longed, came in the form of an inescapable field of ruins and death. How could new foundations be laid in the church, in politics, in the personal sphere, when all the best people were missing?"[1] Among those killed in the war were two sons and two sons-in-law in the Bonhoeffer family, including Dietrich; four of Eberhard's cousins; both of his best childhood friends; and Fritz Onnasch, Eberhard's sister's husband, who was a member of the inner circle with Bethge at Bonhoeffer's seminary. Every day, everyone had to assume there was a good chance they would not survive the day; every day brought news of more people dying. Death was all around; it was the dominant fact of life.

Among those killed in the war was Bethge's cousin and close friend, Gerhard Vibrans. Recently Bethge and two of Gerhard Vibrans's sisters have published a significant volume of Vibrans's letters to his family and friends. They had dug out the old letters while doing research for the new critical edition of Bonhoeffer's works. They discovered anew what a treasure trove they were sitting on with Vibrans's letters, and they undertook to edit and publish them.

As one of the minority of women involved in Bonhoeffer studies, I have some hesitation about focusing on friendship among men during a time when women were excluded from the kind of theological training that all of the men enjoyed. Leonore Siegele-Wenschkewitz has helpfully pointed out that this was not a status quo inherited from the Weimar Republic era. Rather, the inclusion of women fostered during Weimar was systematically reversed by the Nazis. And that was one point where most of the Confessing Church did not fight the system.[2] This is a matter of some real pain for me, as I later became friends with women for whom exclusion during those years was a painful and defining experience in their lives. But the story itself is compelling and the material rich.

"A.Y.V." was the form of address commonly used in the circle of cousins and friends around Eberhard Bethge and Gerhard Vibrans. Vibrans—and all of them—wrote long circular letters to the friends describing the situation in the Church Struggle in great detail. The salutation in the circular letters was always "A.Y.V." The circle had picked up that form of address after an appearance they had made at the wedding of Gerhard's sister Ruth in 1930. "A.Y.V." stands for "Armer yrrsinniger Vreund," written in the medieval style of spelling, with a *Y* on "yrrsinniger" and a *V* on "Vreund." This pseudo-Elizabethan spelling for "Poore Foolische Friend" might reproduce the flavor of the medieval spelling.

The "A.Y.V.'s" must have been a wonderful circle of young people, many of them cousins, who genuinely loved each other and stood by each other through thick and thin during those tumultuous and finally tragic years. This relationship between Bethge and Vibrans (and the circle around them) was formative in Bethge's young life, shaping what became his great gift for friendship. And Bethge's great gift for friendship brought as much to his later relationship with Bonhoeffer as Bonhoeffer himself did. Bethge's friendship not only sustained Bonhoeffer during his years in prison, but helped nurture forth much of Bonhoeffer's most creative thinking. Finally, both Bonhoeffer and Bethge, late in their respective lives, did get around to reflecting directly on their friendship and what it meant for them.

During Bethge's own imprisonment in the winter of 1944-45, he wrote a memoir for his wife about his fallen cousin Gerhard Vibrans. In it he describes how they spent their school holidays together doing everything boys used to do, and how important the Vibrans household was for Bethge in expanding his own horizons. Vibrans's father was a devoted parish pastor who was doggedly loyal to the Confessing Church and suffered much abuse for it. His mother was a younger sister of Bethge's father. Gerhard was the fifth of eight children (four boys and four girls); two brothers died in childhood.

After Bethge had finished high school, the two cousins lived together during their university studies. They spent a semester in Königsberg, East Prussia, a semester in Berlin, and a semester in Vienna. Finally they returned to their "home" university in Halle to begin more serious preparation for their examinations. Bethge writes:

> Seldom was [Gerhard] alone in his room. He sat there smoking with his long colorful cigarette holder from Hungary, talking until late into the night about books, arguing about the university conflict when they fired Günther Dehn or forging a plan to turn the neighbor's room in the dormitory upside down. All that by candlelight. He had a weakness for candlelight. . . . He did not think much of his own academic achievements, but it was always his room where all our discussions took place.[3]
>
> All of the friends and cousins in Halle used to go out to Annarode on Sundays, where his father was pastor. From Saturday afternoon until Monday morning we turned the place into a loudly resounding field camp. Anyone who could even remotely play an instrument or carry a tune was welcome. We would always get our parts in the mail in advance to practice them separately. And then we would pull together a Christmas or Lenten music program. When we played it in church Sunday morning, we ourselves were the ones who probably liked it best. We would play again for fun on Sunday evenings, but we were usually too tired to do much. These weekends always ended with a moonlight hike up to the valley. Gerhard's mother always insisted that we sing "Der Mond ist aufgegangen", and then, sadly, it would be over. But we knew that the Vibrans were already thinking about doing it again, and not about the burdens of hospitality they had just finished.
>
> Gerhard loved this kind of parsonage, which was open to everyone. And he intended to have one like it himself. . . . After the wonderful year in Zingst and Finkenwalde, he went to [serve the parish in] Rosian. He was not recognized by the officials, but loved all the more in a parish not much interested in church.
>
> There he could fill his parsonage the way he wanted. One Sunday he gathered thirty male and female cousins around his table. . . . He stirred together all those who had grown apart, and no one could resist the enthusiasm with which he led the group. . . .
>
> At every festival Gerhard's father could be seen sitting in a corner during the general upheaval of preparations. He would be writing the poem for the day on the back of an old envelope. Not all of them were as good as those of Matthias Claudius, but

they did inherit some of his warmth and wit. Gerhard inherited the ability to write so easily from his father. His easy writing came out most serendipitously in his letters. Never again did I ever meet a person who could keep up with such a voluminous correspondence with friends and acquaintances, his family, and half of his congregation. And it was always fresh and interesting. He could describe wonderfully what he had experienced: whether it was buying a car, his first pastoral conference, or the invasion of Russia. But the ease with which words came to him did not reduce how hard he worked on his sermons. His feelings of responsibility for his sermons weighed heavily on him, but they kept the sermons from becoming routine.

He loved his family and never avoided any effort to take the trip at any time of the day or night. In the morning he used to sit on his bicycle, riding with no hands, leaning way back in the seat and singing for his life. Later on he would take his small car back and forth from his pastorate in Rosian to his parents' home in Annarode. It was always overloaded with brothers and sisters, people from his parish and children he collected. Whenever he appeared, people's joy in living rose a few degrees. There were some laws he zealously enforced out of love for his parents: Alcohol was forbidden and the smallest lie was met with disdain . . . but no one felt under pressure. "Ich danke Gott und freue mich" [I thank God and rejoice] was his favorite song. He introduced it to the seminary in Finkenwalde, and at the end he sang it with his last comrades in the ice on the Russian front. There he was killed on February 3, 1942.[4]

Vibrans and Bethge were being trained for pastoral ministry in the church district around Magdeburg. When they had passed their exams and their practical experience as vicars, they were sent to the preachers' seminary in Wittenberg. But Nazi sympathizers had taken control of that institution and required all students to sign a pledge of loyalty to the Reichsbishop. Bethge, Vibrans, and a few of their friends instead signed a letter refusing to make such a pledge, whereupon they were all expelled from the seminary ten days after their arrival. The Confessing Church leadership cast about for a place to put them, and finally sent Bethge and Vibrans up to Dietrich Bonhoeffer's seminary at Zingst and later at Finkenwalde on the Baltic sea coast. The two cousins had never heard of Bonhoeffer before, but they soon became twin pillars of the community Bonhoeffer built among his students. Gerhard Vibrans wrote home enormously long descriptions of all that happened. Here are a few appetizers from that chronicle:

On 6 July 1935 Gerhard Vibrans wrote to his parents (for the first time the students were confronted with Bonhoeffer's pacifism, grounded in his Christian faith):

> Last evening we talked about war and the ethical conflicts which it may bring. Viewed empirically, psychologically, there are such conflicts, but theologically there simply cannot be such conflicts. I just do not understand that last sentence, because it is meaningless for me, unreal, for the conflicts really are there.[5]

Then comes a first signal of the deepening relationship between Bonhoeffer and Bethge:

> Eberhard seems, after all, to be able to think theologically, at least he is acting that way. Now he has become the chief's clear favorite. But that is not at all good for my "Mikokse" [inferiority complexes]. The chief always says, "Brother Bethge, did you have anything further to say?" . . . Eberhard's sermon on Isaiah 53 turned out so brilliantly, that the chief just can't calm down about it. But it is very long, very disorganized and impossible to commit to memory. But the chief was so happy that the text was interpreted by the three theologians in the seminary, Kanitz, Schönherr and Bethge, along such similar lines.[6]

On 12 July 1935 Gerhard Vibrans wrote to his parents (after attending a poorly conducted worship service in a nearby village):

> We want to start holding services here [at the seminary in Finkenwalde]. We have a nice gymnasium here, which can be turned into a simple confessing church. Then, of course, we will start having trouble with the local pastor. (Did I write already that he complained to the consistory about us, that rascal?) We needed a lot of things for our chapel.
>
> Dr. Bonhoeffer, Eberhard, and I—what a rare honor for me—travelled, therefore, to Stettin and looked at all sorts of things. First we went into a modern art shop, where you could get everything. Unfortunately, we didn't find any candlesticks we liked, but we did order a large chandelier for the dining room. When we gave our address, "Confessing Church," it turned out that the shop owner belongs to it herself! Then we picked out draperies for the same room—we men! I learned a lot about all the things you have to pay attention to in selecting draperies. Then we went on to look for crosses and a communion set. We looked around for a long time in a bookstore, like we usually do. The chief bought this and that. All of us didn't like the cruci-

fixes. Eberhard didn't like the communion set, and it really was too shiny, so we went on. But before we left, Bonhoeffer asked about art reproductions from Piper [publishing house]. They showed him the Four Apostles by Dürer, and he bought them, after he had hesitated for a moment. "Should I really buy them? If you want to do something, you should do it right away, otherwise nothing will ever get done." And he laid out 80 Marks cash on the table. So now he owns them, until the seminary gets some money some day. Then he bought a folder for his sister, Susanne, who has just given birth by Caesarian section. We stopped for a while in a cafe to have iced coffee, iced chocolate, cake and so forth. Then we went to a second-hand art shop, in which we found old crucifixes, madonnas, Pomeranian images of Mary, bells, a gong, in short, a dark and mysterious world, in which the ghosts of E. T. A. Hoffmann threatened to come alive. I will let you know later what comes of it all for our seminary.[7]

On 19 July 1935 Gerhard Vibrans wrote to his parents:

We now have our own boat. When we went swimming, Bonhoeffer asked me to look around for some little rowboat to cost about 50 Marks. He also had his own inflatable boat sent here. So I asked down at the barber shop—where else could you find out about something like that? The barber asked someone else, and in an instant we had an offer. We had a wonderful time trying it out, and went swimming from it. But when we talked about it later, a lot of doubts surfaced: it was a luxury, we needed other things much worse, etc. I gave a short impassioned speech that the boat only cost us 2 Marks per person. An annual pass to the public bathing beach would cost 5 Marks per person, thus 125 Marks altogether. . . . And that cost would be for only one year, whereas our boat would float for 100 years, and would give us pleasure even when it is too cold to swim. At that point, Bonhoeffer broke off the debate, gave me the 50 Marks out of his own pocket, and the case is closed. So now I am keeper of the boat, in addition to already being the furniture mover and the pharmacist, I mean I gradually presumed to take all that on.

The letters are full of details of the Church Struggle and rumors of the mischief with which Hitler's minions were harassing the Confessing Church. Here is a sample from the same letter:

Bonhoeffer received a private rumor from his contacts in London that Ribbontrop said that it is possible that Marahrens will soon become Reichsbishop, named by Hitler. With it came a

picture of August [Marahrens], as the [Lutheran] abbot of Loc-
cum, with a bishop's crook, a tiara, and a very Reichsbishoply
expression on his face. That is the best way of waking up the
Confessing Church! Who knows what would happen then![8]

On 12 September 1935 he wrote to his A.Y.V. friends:

We are now holding services every Sunday in our own church,
which we constructed ourselves out of the old gymnasium. That
man who does church art, Gross, came up and helped us. Because of his Aryan impurity, he is in great difficulties, and he has
a lot of children. He is the third non-Aryan I have met here, and
whose troubles from the whole situation have really upset me.
Another one was Pastor Hildebrandt. . . . Hildebrandt is a non-
Aryan, a fine person, pastor in Dahlem. Because of him I got
into quite an argument with Cousin L., who was upset that a
Jew was standing in a Christian pulpit. . . . All three of them are
harassed men, whose dignity is being trampled down.

At the end of the first course, Bonhoeffer asked Bethge and a few
others to stay on in Finkenwalde to form a spiritual core for succeeding
classes of students. Gerhard Vibrans was placed in a parish in Rosian, near
Magdeburg. From there he wrote back to Finkenwalde:

Rosian, June 24, 1936

My dear Dietrich,
My artistry in writing letters is gone forever. I don't have
any time for it, even though I have only 1,500 souls in three
villages. But I want to try to put down a few lines, because a
thunderstorm is about to break and I can't go out anyway. I
really would like to know your advice.
My smaller village, Schweinitz, with 600 souls is a *very* poor
parish. But on average only about 1.5 people go to church there
every Sunday. The Schweinitz people don't even recognize
Sunday. . . . Of course, they work on Sunday. A very Christian
neighbor was chopping wood in the pastor's widow's garden
early Sunday morning. They take that sort of thing for granted
there. The church stands at the beginning of the village; the
village stretches out along a single road. At the other end and in
the middle, they don't even hear the church bell ringing. Since
services are held only every other week, the people tell me they
don't know when church is scheduled. To help that, I posted
notices on three announcement boards with an invitation to come
to church. But no one reads them. Now I am thinking I should

walk every Sunday through the village wearing my clerical robe, in order to get people to notice that it is Sunday. The danger of being misunderstood, of being seen as a clown who is inviting them to a circus is there, but not overly great. Should I even try such a thing?

The young people in the confirmation class are supposed to come to church, and if they can't come, they are supposed to be excused. The result: there are 27 of them, one is excused, 25 don't show up. They are all ashamed in front of each other to come. They also often miss their classes without being excused. Then the parents explain, without seeing anything to get excited about, that they needed their children at home. And it is true that the boys are already driving teams in the fields. There are so few field laborers that all the children have to help (even I went out to help bring in the hay). . . . What to do?

Visiting in the homes is my great worry. I just don't accomplish much. So far I have kept on opening up the Bible and praying, but I always have huge doubts. . . . Most of the time they don't fold their hands, and they are visibly relieved to be rid of me. . . . No one has refused me, they just put up with it. But that doesn't mean they have the slightest intention of going to church. . . . They say one of my predecessors said, "I'll get my salary whether or not anyone shows up for church." . . . On Trinity Sunday no one was in the church at all except the custodian. . . .

The young girls are my joy. To the great annoyance of the teacher, they like to come to the parish house. They refuse to stop coming because of the harvest and come every Wednesday. They refuse to go to the girls' Hitler Youth. The teacher thinks I am collecting the reactionaries. But their reaction is not against the party, but against his person. . . .

No one has a clue about church politics. They don't know here who or what a Reichsbishop is. . . . Confessing Church? Not a chance! Only a few have heard of the German Christians, but confuse them completely with other groups. . . . Sometime I would like to say some outrageous heresy in my sermon—no one would say a thing. . . .

In the smaller villages there aren't any youth groups or any women's or men's groups. How do I reach people? Can't you bring the whole seminary down to this area sometime?

Your picture stands before me (you think I'm a fan of yours?) with a ping-pong paddle in your right hand. . . . One year ago today we bought the Apostles, which hopefully have *finally* found a place worthy of them. Can't we turn back the wheel of history, so that all that comes back? Well, as long as Eberhard is with you, I'm not too worried about you. But what happens if Eberhard has to leave? Then the sun would stand alone again in the heavens, a lonely star. I could send you endless lamentations to prove to you how the wifelessness of my existence here makes it a joyless one. And you are going to lose your bet that I would get married in two years. That is fate, but Zander thinks it is laziness.

Well, dear Dietrich, I've kept you and me all too long, but I've enjoyed it. Nervously you will put down these pages, and I can hear you whispering, "You idiot."

You get along well with my cousin, you hear? I will pay you for it with loyalty. With many greetings, your unspeakably grateful Gerhard.[10]

Bonhoeffer answered immediately from Finkenwalde:

June 27, 1936

I was unbelievably happy to get your letter. You have no idea how happy I am that you exist and that you are there for all of us and for me. We often speak of you. You don't deserve such a hard piece of work! We should come sometime to help you, or at least to be together, which may give you more confidence. . . .

Your report about Schweinitz, where by the way a distant relative of mine is a German Christian, a party member and a doctor, leaves me feeling as helpless as you do. I have just written to [your superintendent] that I think things need to be reorganized. If a village doesn't want to hear our message, then we should just go someplace else. There are limits. But for now you have to keep trying. . . . I do think you are on the right track. . . . I still think that if you keep visiting people faithfully, slowly they will start coming back to the church. If there are only two or three there, I wouldn't go up into the pulpit, but I would do it more like a Bible study. . . .

Well, I really can't say very much. Only this, that I follow your every step and want to help you whenever you need me. . . . Don't let your wifeless-therefore-joyless existence get you down. I still think I am going to win my bet. Let's not touch on whether or not such war-time marriages [1936!] as our brothers are now entering are the right thing.

Remembering you faithfully, dear Gerhard, your loyal Dietrich.[11]

In August 1936 Vibrans rode along as far as Switzerland with Bonhoeffer and Bethge, who were on their way to an ecumenical conference in Chamby and then on to Rome. Bonhoeffer was exhausted. Vibrans pointed out that he was getting cranky, which put Bonhoeffer into a full pout. Immediately after they separated, both men wrote letters of abject and affectionate apology and put the incident behind them. In Vibrans's letter, there is an interesting passage about the friendship already well developed between Bethge and Bonhoeffer:

> You have to admit that you and Eberhard have a really unique relationship, which is untouched by my relationship to you and to him. I really am far enough along to be able to see that without envy. But I am grateful again and again that somehow through the past I am connected with you two. Not only through the past, but through what I gained from the past, which is present and will always remain so.[12]

Vibrans's letters to his A. Y. V. friends go on to describe the deteriorating situation of the Confessing Church, his life as pastor in Rosian, his being drafted into the Wehrmacht and being sent first to France, then to Yugoslavia, and finally to Russia, to experience the invasion and that first horrible winter there. On leave after returning from France, he married Elisabeth Trebesius. Their married life consisted of those three weeks' leave and their daily letters to each other.

His description to her of his first day of the invasion of Russia is a spontaneous masterpiece of the reality of that experience. He spent the day weighed down by the radio equipment he had to carry, running, running, running, trying to keep up with the faster infantry in his unit. His horror at the hunger, suffering, and death he saw all around him is heart-breaking.

By then, his life had taken a quite different direction from his cousin Eberhard's. So we take leave temporarily of Vibrans and go back to the relationship between Bethge and Bonhoeffer.

Bonhoeffer had had other especially close friends, including Hans Christoph von Hase, Franz Hildebrandt, and Elisabeth Zinn. His relationship with Bethge was characterized by their working and living together much of the time. Bethge stayed with the seminary until it was finally closed down. Even during the time that Bethge had his own apartment in the early 1940s in Berlin, he lived more with Dietrich at his parents' home than anywhere else.

During the war years, Bethge advanced in status to member of the family by marrying Bonhoeffer's niece, Renate Schleicher. After Bonhoeffer's arrest in April 1943, they were out of touch for seven months until Bonhoeffer figured out a way to have letters smuggled in and out of the prison. Then, of course, the great outpouring of correspondence came, and it continued until Bonhoeffer was transferred to the Gestapo prison in October 1944. Bethge himself was imprisoned shortly thereafter. At that point, all direct contact broke off permanently.

Extensive reflection on his friendship with Bethge can be found in one of Bonhoeffer's prison letters. In it Bonhoeffer reflects theologically on friendship, but he doesn't fit it into a system of order. He counts it among the gifts of freedom, in contrast to the claims of responsibilities on one's life. The occasion for the prison reflection was that Bethge had protested that the family did not regularly share Bonhoeffer's letters to his parents with him. Maria von Wedemeyer, as Bonhoeffer's fiancée, saw them regularly, as did Bonhoeffer's brothers and sisters. But Bethge felt that his friendship was not recognized in the family as having the same rights of access as the family had. In answering that complaint, Bonhoeffer wrote in January 1944:

I will also see that you get my letters to my parents.

I think you made a very precise observation in this connection about friendship, which, in contrast to marriage and kinship, enjoys no generally recognized rights, and therefore depends entirely on its own inherent quality. It is really not easy to classify friendship sociologically. Probably it is to be regarded as a sub-heading of culture and education, while brotherhood would be a sub-heading under the concept of church, and comradeship a sub-heading of the concepts of work and politics. Marriage, work, state and church have their concrete divine mandate; but what about culture and education? I don't think they can just be classified under work, however tempting that might be in many ways.

They belong, not to the sphere of obedience, but to the broad area of freedom, which surrounds all three spheres of the divine mandates. Whoever knows nothing about this area of freedom may be a father, citizen, and worker, indeed even a Christian; but I doubt whether he is a complete person (and, thus, a Christian in the widest sense of the term). Our "Protestant" (not Lutheran) Prussian world has been so dominated by the four mandates that the sphere of freedom has quite receded into the background. . . . Who, for instance, in our times, can attend to music or friendship, play games or take pleasure in something with an easy mind? Surely not the "ethical" person, but only the Christian. Precisely because friendship belongs to this sphere of freedom ("of the Christian person"!?) [cf. Luther], it must be confidently defended against all the disapproving frowns of "ethical" existences, though without claiming for it the *necessitas* of a divine commandment, but only the *necessitas* of *freedom!* I believe that within the sphere of this freedom friendship is by far the rarest and most priceless treasure, for where else is there any in this world of ours, dominated as it is by the first three mandates? It cannot be compared with the treasures of the mandates; in relation to them it is *sui generis,* but it belongs to them as the cornflower belongs to the grainfield.[13]

Here is a significant articulation of Bonhoeffer's experience and theology of friendship. He had worked out in his *Ethics* a doctrine of divine mandates. It was an experiment on his part, a way of responding to the perversion of the Lutheran doctrine of Orders of Creation, which the Nazis were badly abusing to justify their racism. Bonhoeffer varied somewhat in what he included in the list of mandates. Usually he included family and marriage, work, the state or civil authority, and sometimes the church. In any case, mandates were ordained by God as part of divine order, which entailed responsibilities and obligations. He identified a sphere of human freedom outside the mandates, and put friendship in that freedom. Friendship lives only from its own genuineness, not from preordained obligation.

During the same weeks in which Bonhoeffer wrote this to Bethge, he mentioned the theme in his correspondence with Maria von Wedemeyer. They talked about their upbringing in their two families. Dietrich emphasized how good he thought it was for parents to remain parents and not to try to make themselves "equal" with their children as "friends" in a comradely way. In doing so, he spoke very positively about "the austerity in the relationship of a father to a son," and even about a "sanctity of the office of fatherhood."[14] Maria, however, contradicted him. Her own father had died eighteen months before at the Russian front. She wrote back, "I can tell you that I have only ever had one friend, and that was Father."[15] And later: "I cannot completely accept your rejection of friendship with parents. . . . I always took it for granted that when I went riding with Father, I told him *everything.*"[16]

Dietrich's division between family and friends did not really make sense to Maria, but they never had a chance to carry on that discussion to a real conclusion. Some later interpreters have wondered if she exploded the categories of the mandates with these comments, but Bonhoeffer himself would have been the only one able to answer that question.

The other main characteristic of these friendships is described by Christian Gremmels, a German Bonhoeffer scholar and editor of *A Life in Pictures.* In a 1994 essay on friendship and Bonhoeffer, Gremmels points out that during the Nazi reign of terror, the intentional nurturing of friendship was more than a retreat into a private sphere. It was a political act itself. The Nazis set out to make mistrust the dominant atmosphere in the country. Friends trusted each other as never before as an act of resistance against that Nazi political agenda. Gremmels writes:

> Personal friendship transcended the private sphere and became political, because it held onto the great ideas of the previous ages, ideas like trust, responsibility, loyalty, bravery, shame, and discipline, in opposition to the [Nazi] perversion of those ideas. Friendship was political because friendship included the knowledge that its integrity could only be reconstructed in a conspiratorial way *because* of the dominant perversion of its truths. Such friendship had to occasionally assume aspects from which it could remain free in easier times, aspects like denying its very existence.[17]

So friendship belongs to freedom. And it is intrinsically, also, a political act, an act that takes place in the larger society and transcends the barriers society puts in its way. Friendship as a loving political act might indeed transcend the limits of historical time and cultural context and speak to our time, as well.

At the end, Gerhard Vibrans's death brought a terrible grief to his friends and family. He was killed on the Russian front by a piece of artillery shrapnel that landed in his shelter. He had just gotten out his songbook and was preparing to sing hymns with his comrades. When Bonhoeffer heard the news, he wrote to Gerhard's parents:

> Dear Brother Vibrans!
> . . . The death of your dear son Gerhard has grieved me more than any other death notice during this war. I think the pain and feeling of emptiness, which his death has left in me, could hardly be worse if he were my own physical brother. Gerhard was especially close to my heart. I am impoverished by his death. How much more so must that be for you, who knew him so much better, who thus know so much more deeply what you have lost in him. . . . Since I got to know Gerhard—I give thanks to God that I got to know him—I knew that he was the sort of person, of whom there are only a few. The closer we became, the more I bowed down to him. With his integrity, his love of the truth, his selflessness, his purity, he meant more to me than I can say and than he knew. The combination of simplicity and maturity gave him the ability to win people's trust wherever he went. . . . I shall be grateful to him my whole life long for two things: for the way in which he kept Sunday holy, and for his teaching me the song

by Claudius, "Ich danke Gott und freue mich." Through him, these two things have become a living treasure for me. . . . I can no longer tell Gerhard my thanks for what he has meant to me and to our larger brotherhood. So I would like respectfully to express it to you as Gerhard's father and mother, with heart-rending memories of the lovely hours I spent together with Gerhard in your home. With sincere greetings, yours, Dietrich Bonhoeffer.[18]

ENDNOTES

1. Eberhard Bethge, *In Zitz gab es keine Juden*, (München: Kaiser Verlag, 1989), 201.
2. Leonore Siegele-Wenschkewitz, "Die Ehre der Frau, dem Manne zu dienen: Zum Frauenbild des Theologen Dietrich Bonhoeffer," unpublished manuscript, 1994, 13.
3. Bethge, *In Zitz gab es keine Juden*, 68.
4. Ibid., 70-71.
5. Gerhard Vibrans, *So ist es gewesen* (Gütersloh: Kaiser/Gütersloher Verlagshaus, 1995), 178-79.
6. Ibid., 180.
7. Ibid., 181-82.
8. Ibid., 182.
9. Ibid., 190-91.
10. Ibid., 276-79.
11. Ibid., 279-81.
12. Ibid., 287.
13. *LPP*, 192-93.
14. Dietrich Bonhoeffer and Maria von Wedemeyer, *Love Letters from Cell 92*, ed. Ruth-Alice von Bismarck and Ulrich Kabitz (Nashville: Abingdon Press, 1995), 139.
15. Ibid., 143.
16. Ibid., 149.
17. Christian Gremmels and Wolfgang Huber, eds., *Theologie und Freundschaft* (Gütersloh: Chr. Kaiser/Gütersloher Verlagshaus, 1994), 150-51.
18. Vibrans, *So ist es gewesen*, 327-28.

Writing to the Spouse from Prison: Dietrich Bonhoeffer and Vacláv Havel[1]

H. Martin Rumscheidt

In this essay I make use of a fairly common procedure in attempting to provide an interpretation of someone who, having gone from life among us, can no longer interpret himself to us. By studying a similar piece of literature, written by someone still alive and continuing to provide interpretative materials, I enter into my interpretation of the deceased person's work. Someone alive assists in understanding someone who has returned to the source of all life.

Both Dietrich Bonhoeffer and Vacláv Havel have exerted powerful influences on me and my thinking. Both are at home in the grand intellectual tradition of Europe, especially that of the Enlightenment and its striving for human freedom, truth, and integrity. While Bonhoeffer embodies the heritage of German Protestantism, especially the dimensions of it associated with Martin Luther and Karl Barth, Havel expresses himself less in the terms of his religious heritage, Roman Catholicism, and more in those of liberal idealism as it came to be shaped by the long Czech-Hussite vision of *living in truth*.

Bonhoeffer, a Prussian upper-middle-class aristocratic Christian, member of the clergy, and university professor, lived from 1906 until 1945. He died when Hitler's henchmen executed him, on the Führer's personal orders, by hanging him in a concentration camp located on the German-Czechoslovakian border, three weeks before the final collapse of the Third Reich. He had been a participant—*on the basis of his Christian faith*—in the conspiracy to assassinate Hitler. Until his actual involvement was discovered, he had been held in prison for his openly known opposition to the ideology, brutality, and paganism of Hitler's National Socialist Germany.

Havel, a Czech middle-class intellectual, playwright, essayist, and interpreter of modern culture, was born in 1936. Known for his open opposition to the ideology and disdain for humanity of Czechoslovakia's Communist government, he was imprisoned four times between 1977 and 1989 in the Ruzyně, Heřmanice, and Plzeň-Bory prisons. After the collapse of Communist rule in Czechoslovakia, he was chosen to be the country's president and, after the separation of Czechia and Slovakia, president of the Czech Republic.

In drawing on Havel to interpret Bonhoeffer, I acknowledge that it is the similarities that play a weightier role than the differences. This is especially so on account of one of the similarities not yet referred to. Both men had the opportunity to leave their native lands for places where they could have worked and developed their thinking without harassment, where prison and death were not constant threats to their existence. In 1939, when Bonhoeffer had gone to the United States, he made the decision to return to the Germany of Hitler, convinced that, if he did not, he had no right to be a participant in the rebuilding of a Germany different from the one that National Socialism had built. His return eventually led to imprisonment and his brutal murder. Havel refused offer after offer to come to the West, including the offers of his own government to expatriate him there on the condition that he stay away from Czechoslovakia, knowing that he would forfeit the right to work with his compatriots for a "new" country in the tomorrow that one day would come after the actual Socialism of the day. Such commitment to the "welfare of the city," to use the felicitous phrase of the prophet Jeremiah (29:7), to seek it in the midst of its suffering and sorrow, and to bear the consequences of doing that from within rather than from the outside and in safety, is testimony that compels me. The determination that marked their decision to return or not to leave, and the fact that they stayed the course, are two highly significant hermeneutical factors in understanding and interpreting their writings.

My attempt to interpret Bonhoeffer through Havel is not unconsciously "ecumenical." A Roman Catholic—albeit a non-practicing one—will assist in reading a Protestant; a German, the armies of whose homeland invaded and then brutalized Czechoslovakia, is studied in the light of a citizen of the conquered and betrayed nation; a person of literature helps find the meaning of a theologian.

LOVE LETTERS FROM CELL 92

I seek to interpret a work published in 1994 and 1995 in England and the United States by Harper Collins and Abingdon Press, respectively: *Love Letters from Cell 92: The Correspondence between Dietrich Bonhoeffer and Maria von Wedemeyer 1943-1945.*[2] It is the correspondence between a couple engaged to be married; nearly all of Bonhoeffer's letters to von Wedemeyer were written from prison. The editions published in Germany and England have photos of each of them on the cover; the American edition leaves von Wedemeyer off and does not signal that there were letters *to* cell 92. It also cites a German theologian's depiction of the book: "a deeply moving love story in a deadly time" (Jürgen Moltmann).

The very cover of the American edition creates difficulties for readers in understanding this work. I contacted one of the book's editors, Mme. Ruth-Alice von Bismarck, a relative of Maria von Wedemeyer, about these difficulties; she said that the English title, *Love Letters from Cell 92*, does injustice to the correspondence. In her view, "love letters" and "love story" fail the reality of this couple because such phrases are today so culture-bound as to mislead the contemporary reader. This out-of-the-ordinary correspondence is in danger of being gravely misunderstood as a result of what was, even in the best interpretation of it, an unthinking choice of titles for the English translation. Eberhard Bethge, Bonhoeffer's biographer, has spent much of his life in acquainting the church and theology, the academy and individual people's faith convictions, with the life and work of this witness for Christ. In an afterword to this book, he said that the publication "constitutes the unforeseen highlight of my declining years."[3] I cannot help wondering what is in his mind when the correspondence between two people whom he knew so well and cared about so much not only appears under the title *Love Letters from Cell 92*, but also ignores the fact that the other significant person of that correspondence sent letters *to* cell 92. The careless and distorting cover of the book necessitates that this correspondence be rescued from the unjust fate of a superficial approach—to put the matter bluntly, from an appearance of voyeurism upon a man and woman's narcissism. Those who do not know Bonhoeffer's person, his work and witness, or the dignity that marked the life of von Wedemeyer should not involuntarily become subject to the beguiling spin the unfortunate title puts on the book.

A number of years ago, I faced a similar quandary when the other volume of Bonhoeffer's correspondence from prison was being mined by what was then called "death-of-God theology." Concerned that the highly culture-bound form of the most prominent expression of that theology had caused a reading of those letters that failed the reality of what moved Bonhoeffer, I looked for a work of comparable genre to assist me in my endeavor. I found it, somewhat surprisingly, in a document from the time when the Roman Empire was collapsing: *The Consolation of Philosophy*, by Anicius Manlius Severinus Boethius, who died at age forty-two (or forty-four) as a consequence of Theodoric the Great's henchmen's tortures in 524 C.E. He wrote the work while in prison. As a *patricius* at age twenty-eight and a consul a year later, he had every opportunity to leave the

Western Empire, where intrigue and malevolence against him were a threat to his life; yet he made the decision to stay and face the consequences. I believe that Boethius and Bonhoeffer sensed the vacuousness of the Christianity of their day in the face of the decline of their respective civilizations. Both looked for a church, a faith, a theology that might survive the collapse they saw coming with such clarity and then, in the tomorrow after the collapse, revive a community less vulnerable to failing the reality of both God and humanity.[4] Living in the ominous situation into which noble minds are often drawn when the tension between might and right is no longer held in check by the wielders of might and the guardians of right, the two men (as well as Vacláv Havel, as we shall see later) wrote letters and papers in prison that give light to later generations that also seek what a South African saying expresses so well: the tomorrow that is another country.

In trying to develop a hermeneutic that both guards the Bonhoeffer-von Wedemeyer letters against a misleading orientation and provides an interpretation of what they are about, I follow a similar procedure. Is there a work that, through the process of comparison, helps us see what lives in and moves the love that, indeed, does speak in this correspondence?

LETTERS TO OLGA

I first looked closely at the magnificent memoir of Nelson Mandela, *Long Walk to Freedom*. My spouse had read to me many of the passages of the correspondence between Winnie and Nelson Mandela over those many, seemingly endless years of his imprisonment. The presence of numerous parallels between South Africa's apartheid policy and Germany's National Socialist racism suggested insights helpful in my task. But it was finally another future president's correspondence that produced the most productive comparison: Vacláv Havel's *Letters to Olga*.

These 145 letters, all from Havel and none from Olga herself, were written between 4 June 1979 and 30 January 1983 from the prisons in the former Czechoslovakia where Havel was being held. Jiří Dienstbier, one of Havel's fellow inmates, a co-signer of the famous human rights declaration known as "Charter 77," and, after the "Velvet Revolution" of late 1989, a fellow politician, once wrote that writing letters helped them bear the burden of incarceration. Under the prevailing conditions, corresponding was the only possibility of self-realization for persons accustomed to writing, he noted. Havel himself cites several reasons why writing letters had special significance for him: it was the only chance for tolerable self-realization, it allowed him to gain clarity about things, and, above all, it was the only communication with the world that was close to him and Olga. I cite Nelson Mandela to explain what I believe Havel means. Immediately after the brief and very closely monitored visits from Winnie, he would sit down and restate in a letter the substance of their conversation. "After a visit, I replayed all the details in my mind of what Winnie wore, what she said, what I said. I then wrote her a letter going over some of what we had discussed, and reminding her of how much I cared for her . . . how courageous she was. I saw my letters to her both as love letters and as the only way I could give her the emotional support she needed."[5] But next to mutual support in bearing the separation one from the other, there was, very prominently, the mutual encouragement for their common struggle to help build the tomorrow that is another South Africa.

The fifteenth-century movement of renewal in Bohemia and Moravia associated with the theologian and preacher Jan Hus and known among church historians as "the first Reformation" heralded *living in truth* as its chief virtue. At the base of the impressive statue of Hus on Staroměstské náměsti in Old Prague, his call to the people is inscribed: "Love one another and live with one another in truth." Havel's collection of essays, published in English under the title *Living in Truth*, is the essential testament to his beliefs; he explores what a humanity worthy of the noble title "human" requires. We find him talking about "the higher responsibility of every individual," "the personal answerability for one's convictions, even if that means the loss of one's freedom." "In all my writings," he says, "my starting point has always been what I know, my experience of this world I live in. . . . It has always been my hope that bearing witness to certain specific experiences of the world, I will be able to disclose something *universally* human, specific experience only being a way of saying something about being in general, about people in today's world, about the crisis of modern-day humanity—in other words, about those matters that concern us all."[6] There is a specificity that shapes his words: they come from one whose personal experience is that of having chosen one of the most demanding of freedoms: that of living in one's own country *and* then thinking and speaking as one feels called to. This freedom that generated the decision to remain in Czechoslovakia (or in Rome for Boethius and Germany for Bonhoeffer) led Havel to prison. Experience like this is not something passive, nor does it come about on its own accord. In addition, it is not something that has to do solely with consciousness; rather, it is active and humans call it upon themselves, preparing for it by accepting or rejecting the world they live in. It is, in other words, experience that commits human conscience, experience lived and witnessed to at a high price.

In the essay "Politics and Conscience," Havel says that "living in truth" is what marks people who seek "to retrieve their humanity and resume the responsibility for the world by [asserting] politics as morality in practice. [Even in the world as it is now,] those apparently powerless people who have the courage to speak the truth out loud and stand by what they say body and soul, and are prepared to pay dearly for doing so, have—astonishingly enough—greater power—however formally disenfranchised they are—than thousands of anonymous electors in other circumstances."[7] Here responsibility is duty, yes, but it is so much more: it is *destiny*.

What Havel means is this:

> I favour "anti-political politics," that is, politics not as the technology of power and manipulation, of cybernetic rule over humans or as the art of the useful, but politics as one of the ways of seeking and achieving meaningful lives, of protecting and serving such lives. I favour politics as practical morality, as service to the truth, as essentially human and humanly measured care for our fellow-humans. It is, I presume, an approach which in this world, is extremely impractical and difficult to apply in daily life. Still, I know of no better alternative. But "anti-political politics" is possible. Politics "from below." Politics of humans, not of the apparatus. Politics growing from the heart, not from a thesis. It is not an accident that this hopeful experience has to be lived just here, on this grim battlement. Under the "rule of everydayness," we have to descend to the very bottom of the well before we can see the stars. When Jan Patočka wrote about Charter 77, he used the term "solidarity of the shaken." He was thinking of those who dared resist impersonal power and to confront it with the only thing at their disposal, their own humanity. Does not the perspective of a better future depend on something like a community of the shaken which will seek to make a real political force out of a phenomenon so ridiculed by the technicians of power—the phenomenon of human conscience?[8]

Havel might well have continued here with words written forty years earlier in a German prison:

> There remains an experience of incomparable value. We have for once learnt to see the great events of world history from below, from the perspective of the outcast, the suspects, the maltreated, the powerless, the oppressed, the reviled—in short, from the perspective of those who suffer. The important thing is . . . that our perception of generosity, humanity, justice and mercy should have become clearer, freer, less corruptible. We have to learn that personal suffering is a more effective key, a more rewarding principle for exploring the world in thought and action than per-

sonal good fortune. This perspective from below must not become the partisan possession of those who are eternally dissatisfied; rather, we must do justice to life in all its dimensions from a higher satisfaction, whose foundation is beyond any talk of "from below" or "from above."[9]

Vacláv Havel is deeply rooted in Czech intellectuality and culture, its art—especially the theatre—and its readiness to offer resistance. The profound philosophical tradition of Masaryk and Patočka that is embedded in his pursuit of the high aim of responsibility which, when offering resistance, is ready to bear the consequences may well be summed up in the German words that comprise the title of Dietrich Bonhoeffer's letters and papers from prison: *Widerstand* and *Ergebung*, resistance and surrender. Havel resisted the assault on democracy by the intellectual tendency common to both National Socialism and the Communism that was factually in existence around him, whose demand for conformity increasingly dominated public discourse. He opposed the pressures of *Gleichschaltung*, or homogenization, in which culture was subverted by the denigration of the past and by a functional view of the present, and in which politics was indoctrinated by the belief that one-party rule is beneficial to the greater civil community. Havel's call for *social* or *political* responsibility has solid utopian undertones. During the "Prague Spring" of 1968, discussion centered in the vision of a more just, democratic, pluralistic, and livable society, in the vision of what East German pastor Heino Falcke four years later called "*ein verbesserlicher Sozialismus*," a socialism that can better itself.

Like the 1978 essay "The Power of the Powerless,"[10] Havel's letters from prison to his spouse, Olga, raise many subjects that stir the hearts of people in the great intellectual tradition of Europe: the nature of belief, the dehumanization that marks today's world, the struggle between "the order of life" and "the order of death," the origins of fanaticism and fundamentalism, the nature and meaning of responsibility and what it is to be "human." Havel explores a process that is central to an understanding of the twentieth century: Why and how does utopia turn into dystopia? Why are visions like Socialism no longer subject to anatomy, but, instead, to autopsy?[11] In one of the letters he speaks of his "apparent disadvantage" of having been born into an affluent, bourgeois Czech family and growing up under the Nazi and Communist regimes, both of which turned against him and his family precisely because of that background.[12] As he put it, he had to learn to see things from outside the purview of power and privilege, from "below." His best-known works from the seventies, the "Vaněk Trilogy," contributed to his fate at the hands of the *apparatchiks*. In these pieces he explores directly what voicelessness is and does; he speaks to the situation of "people who are trapped in jobs that are denigrating not because they are menial but because in order to keep them, people must demean themselves, hide their humiliation by indulging in mindless consumption, make their peace with the regime and then feel that the cause of justice is best served by their silence." One of the victims of this totalitarianism cries out: "You always got a chance, but what about me? Who's gonna stick out their neck for me? Who's afraid of me? Who's gonna write about me? Who's gonna help me? Who even gives a shit? I'm just the manure that makes your fancy principles grow." Havel knows no answer to this cry, for there is none. As he sees it, there "is only action, not 'on behalf' of those who suffer, but as one of them."[13]

The last sixteen letters to Olga were first published in a *samisdat,* or underground, edition. Using the pseudonym Sidonius (after Sidonius Apollinaris, 430-486 C.E., Bishop of Clermont-Ferrand, a panegyrist and one who dabbled in imperial politics), someone wrote a commentary on those letters and drew the suggestive parallel between them and *The Consolation of Philosophy,* by Boethius.[14] In an interview Havel said, "Olga and I have not professed love for each other for at least two hundred years, but we both feel that we are probably inseparable. It is true that you won't find many heartfelt, personal passages specifically addressed to my wife in those letters. Even so, I think that Olga is the main hero, though admittedly hidden. That is why I put her name in the title of the book. Doesn't the endless search for a firm point, for certainty, for an absolute horizon which fills those letters say something in itself to confirm that?"[15]

The letters are the medium in which Havel worked through the impassioned debate, in part caused by his conviction and imprisonment, about the meaning of human existence, the urgent questioning of what one should expect of life—whether to accept silently the world as it is presented and slip obsequiously into the place prearranged and assigned to one by others, or whether one has the conviction, courage, and strength to exercise free choice in the matter, to decide to stay in the conflicting situation and offer resistance in the name of one's humanity.[16] These "love letters" are profoundly about the true form of resistance and surrender on the part of a genuinely responsible human being who sees the possibility and necessity of a new tomorrow and is grasped by its promise, its *Zuspruch* and *Anspruch.*

INTERPRETATION

The hermeneutical signals from this Czech correspondence influence the interpretation I give the German correspondence named. They also assist in discerning what I believe is the true intent of Bonhoeffer's *theo-*

logical reflections that appear in the collection *Letters and Papers from Prison.* Sidestepping the interests of *academic* or *"scientific"* theology, Bonhoeffer seeks to develop a *worldly* theology that addresses a humanity that is, in his words, *religionless;* it is a theology that offers what Karl Barth called *political worship of God.* And as such a theologian, Bonhoeffer writes to Maria von Wedemeyer, "Our union can only be a token of God's grace and goodness which summons us to believe in God. When Jeremiah said, in his people's hour of direst need, that 'houses, fields [and vineyards] shall again be bought in this land,' it was a token of confidence in the future. That requires faith. . . . I don't mean the faith that flees the world, but the faith that endures *in* the world and loves and remains true to that world in spite of all the hardships it brings us. Our marriage must be a 'yes' to God's earth."[17] "I now feel more and more that through you and your willingness to become my spouse, I am given utterly new confidence in life. And whenever I see you again for an hour, I know I can never lose that confidence."[18] Maria von Wedemeyer replies, "It is so easy to look upon [times of trial] as a burden only, until, looking back, one suddenly realizes that one has been given a gift. What a tempting error it is to dream oneself into the future, to long for a goal and to live and to suffer with it in view. But that leaves unnoticed the little stone fragments which compose the background, the framework and nuances of a person's life, and all that is finally left is but bare outlines. Only when one lives fully in the now can one remain open to what is to come and must happen. Without this, I notice again and again, I lose my gratitude for the past and the courage to face the present."[19] When I read sentences like these and remind myself that a nineteen-year-old woman wrote them, I, for one, would want to remain silent for a long time before assigning them to the genre of "love" literature.

Bonhoeffer's reply to that letter includes sentences like these: "Neither of us had any fundamental desire for an easy life, much as we both take pleasure in life's lovely, happy times, as much as we doubtless yearn for such times today. For both of us, I believe, happiness lies elsewhere, in a more remote place that not only passes some people's understanding but will continue to do so. At bottom, we both seek tasks to perform. Each of us has hitherto sought them separately, but from now on they'll be common tasks in which we shall fully grow together."[20] *This* "love language" has the contours of something large; it is the critical connection between a relationship these two people share as woman and man, on the one hand, and their sense of responsibility for and to a social vision—a utopia—that empowers their "living in truth," on the other.

Ulrich Kabitz, the co-editor with Ruth-Alice von Bismarck of this correspondence, wrote the historical notes appended to the texts of the letters. In them he discusses the perspective that governs Bonhoeffer's work since 1937, the year the book *Nachfolge* (*The Cost of Discipleship*) appeared. It is as if Kabitz wanted to find the common denominator of everything Bonhoeffer was participating in, including the relationship with Maria von Wedemeyer. "The most urgent requirement was to discover what forces the churches could deploy as cells of resistance to inhumanity as centers devoted to the construction of a new order after the war."[21] The book *Ethics* and the essay "After Ten Years," both of which Bonhoeffer was working on at the time of his engagement to von Wedemeyer in early 1943, explore how theology, through its own renewal, could contribute to opening up a meaningful prospect for life in Germany and Europe in the tomorrow after Hitler. In a few highly concentrated sentences, Bonhoeffer writes what, in my view, embodies the clue to understanding these "love letters." I am sure that the love which so evidently held Bonhoeffer and von Wedemeyer in a profoundly moving bond was one that lived from and nurtured a vision, a "utopia," in which—*within their love for each other*—there is space to love the earth, have open, public, and critical discourse, space for "a politics from the heart," exercised in a community of "solidarity with the shaken." These are the "concentrated sentences" from the essay "After Ten Years":

> We have been mute witnesses to evil deeds, . . . we have learned the art of dissimulation and equivocation; experience has rendered us suspicious of people and we have often failed to speak the truth freely to others. Unendurable conflicts have worn us down or have turned us into cynics: are we still of use? We shall not need geniuses, cynics or people who despise others nor shrewd strategists, but simple, straight-forward people. Will our inner strength to resist what has been forced upon us be good enough and our honesty with ourselves remain sufficiently relentless that we find the way again that leads to simplicity and integrity?[22]

When it comes to seeking understanding and providing an interpretation of a text not of one's own context, particularly when that text is rooted in situations of oppression, poverty, racism, sexism, and the like, it is imperative, in my judgment, that one rely on those who have direct experience of such situations. One aspect of my experience of the world I inhabit, that of Ameropean, white, male intellectualism, is that seeking understanding and providing interpretation is far too often undertaken without any submission to voices that reveal the experiential reality of those on the "underside of history," at the "bottom of the well." What I know of the toil and "labor pain" to free the word *love* from the domain of individualism and private ecstasy tells me how easy it is in reading the letters of Dietrich and Maria, as well as those of Vaclàv and Olga, to fail these people and their vision. My argument has been that doing justice to this correspondence—but also that from Czechoslovakia—requires that they be read not as "a deeply moving love story in a deadly time," but as a deeply moving testimony of a love equal to a deadly time. For such a perspective may serve to illumine how and why strength for "living in truth" in the deadly times of public life is sustained by love that includes in itself but also far transcends the ecstasy of private life.

ENDNOTES

1. This is a revised and expanded version of an address delivered at the Seventh International Bonhoeffer Congress at Cape Town, South Africa, 7-11 January 1996.

2. Dietrich Bonhoeffer, *Love Letters from Cell 92: The Correspondence between Dietrich Bonhoeffer and Maria von Wedemeyer 1943-1945*, ed. Ruth-Alice von Bismark and Ulrich Kabitz, trans. John Brownjohn (Nashville: Abingdon, 1995).

3. Ibid., 365.

4. H. Martin Rumscheidt, "Voices from Prison: Boethius and Bonhoeffer," *Studies in Religion/Sciences Religieuses* 10/4 (1981): 463-71; or "Stimmen aus dem Gefängnis: Boethius und Bonhoeffer," *Evangelische Theologie* 44 (1984): 267-79.

5. Nelson Mandela, *Long Walk to Freedom. The Autobiography of Nelson Mandela* (Boston: Little, Brown Company, 1995), 426.

6. Vacláv Havel, *Living in Truth*, ed. Jan Vladislav (London: Faber & Faber, 1987), xiii.

7. Ibid., xviii.

8. Ibid., 155 ff.

9. *LPP*, 17.

10. Havel, *Living in Truth*, 36ff.

11. Vacláv Havel, *Letters to Olga*, trans. Paul Wilson (London: Faber & Faber, 1988),12 f.

12. Ibid., 13.

13. Ibid., 16 f.

14. Ibid., 17.

15. Ibid., 10.

16. Edá Kriseová, *Vacláv Havel. The Authorized Biography*, trans. Caleb Crain (New York: St. Martin's Press, 1993), 103.

17. Bonhoeffer, *Love Letters from Cell 92*, 64 (translation altered).

18. Ibid., 74.

19. Ibid., 79.

20. Ibid., 86.

21. Ibid., 327.

22. Dietrich Bonhoeffer, *Widerstand und Ergebung*, ed. Eberhard Bethge, et al., trans. H. Martin Rumscheidt (Munich: Kaiser Verlag, 1998), 38; cf. *LPP*, 16 f., n. 6.

Barth's "Gospel and Law" and Bonhoeffer's *The Cost of Discipleship*

Jonathan Sorum

I n 1935, while Dietrich Bonhoeffer was working intensively on *The Cost of Discipleship*, Karl Barth issued his famous challenge of the traditional Lutheran formulation "law and gospel" in an essay entitled "Gospel and Law."[1] Written just when the Nazi authorities had dismissed him from his chair at the university in Bonn and forcibly exiled him to his native Switzerland, Barth's essay was the culmination of his personal participation in the German church struggle.[2] His reversal of the usual order "law-gospel" was a provocation to his contemporaries in the German Protestant churches to rethink the hallowed Reformation doctrine in view of what he believed to be its utter failure to meet the challenge of his time.

Bonhoeffer apparently never took part in the controversy Barth's pamphlet touched off. He no doubt felt much closer to Barth's position than to that of Barth's Lutheran critics, whose view of a divine law prior to and virtually separated from the gospel provided a theological basis for the so-called German Christian movement, both in its extreme and in its more moderate forms. But how does Barth's position in this essay compare with Bonhoeffer's position in *The Cost of Discipleship*? Does Bonhoeffer actually abandon the Lutheran order law-gospel and move completely over to the Barthian side in *The Cost of Discipleship*?

Bonhoeffer was not much in the habit of speaking in terms of law and gospel.[3] Only twice in *The Cost of Discipleship* does he make explicit reference to the theme of law and gospel, and then only in passing.[4] Nevertheless, a translation of his doctrine of justification in *The Cost of Discipleship* into law-gospel terms is possible, and such a translation shows that, while agreeing with Barth's intentions, he strives to achieve them by adhering to the Lutheran order of *first* law, *then* gospel. A comparison of the two writings reveals the close agreement between the two theologians—and the fundamental difference.

BARTH'S ARGUMENT IN "GOSPEL AND LAW"

Barth's essay is an attack on natural theology, the teaching that human beings are capable of some genuine knowledge of God apart from revelation. Traditional Protestantism, especially Lutheranism, regarded the law as a general revelation of God's will, accessible to all. The gospel, on the other hand, is revealed only through the Word and announces the forgiveness of sins for Christ's sake.

Barth believed that modernist Protestantism built upon this basic conceptual foundation when it turned to the category of "religion" in order to find a place for Christianity within modernity. Religion, the modern theologians claimed, is a genuine and universal human experience and knowledge of God, to which Christianity supplies the completion and fulfillment. The gospel became the description of an individual interior experience of "grace" immune from critical scrutiny, while the actual life of the believer was ordered under the modern worldview.

The German Christian heresy, in both its extreme and more moderate forms, was the final step in this process. The idea that the law is revealed in nature, history, and society became the entry point for Nazi ideas into the church. The surest way to know this "law," so the argument went, is not so much through the individual conscience as through the collective will of one's people (*Volk*), as expressed in the leader (*Führer*). Since Christians are justified by faith, they are freed to submit to these "orders of creation" as avenues of service, even if such service inevitably involves the risk of incurring guilt. Christian sanctification means abandoning the selfish pursuit of individual moral purity and serving one's people in the realm of family, state, and *Volk*. For the people at large, meanwhile, this obedience to a larger "morality" becomes the preparation for hearing and believing the gospel as they discover the limits of morality and the need for Christ and his forgiveness. The result in Germany was that the church, including most of the Confessing Church, collapsed before the Nazi onslaught, leaving the German people largely without a concrete, visible community that proclaimed the gospel and set a limit to forces of evil.

Barth rejects the entire anthropocentric approach and seeks to start afresh with his theology of revelation. For Barth, the basic problem is that humans blur the distinction between Creator and creature. True theology begins with the determination to rigorously preserve this distinction. Humans do not in some way, even negatively, have an apprehension of

God "naturally"; any knowledge of God is a result of God's unilateral revelation. That God speaks with us at all is already grace.[5] So the content of the law must finally be grace, and it is only from grace, from the gospel, that we know the law. Therefore, the law is strictly subordinate to the gospel and understood from it; the proper theological order is *first* gospel and only *then* law. The order law-gospel, even with the best will in the world, cannot but lead to a loss of *God's* law and *God's* gospel.

In other words, the content of the law is Jesus Christ. Barth here articulates his doctrine of law and gospel in terms of his Christology. God, he emphasizes, did not *change* into flesh, but *took on* flesh. God took on a full and complete human existence in order to give us the gift of participation in divine existence. In becoming human, God took on a human shape or form in this world, and this shape or form is Christ's fulfillment of the law. We humans would have been saved if only we could have accepted that we must die for our sin and submit to God's judgment. Then we would have given God all the glory and so been saved by pure grace. But we would not. In Jesus Christ, however, *God* gave this answer to sin and God's judgment of death in our place. In short, Jesus had faith. Barth repeatedly emphasizes that it took the "eternal Word made flesh"[6] to do this. Only he can stand for us in our humanity, because he is "God's Son and therefore Himself God and therefore Himself the Judge, before whom He assumes the responsiblity for us."[7] The eternal Son offers his "assumed, obedient, and glorified humanity"[8] in place of our sinful humanity. Christian faith is not faith in our own faith (another method of religious self-assertion!), but faith in *Jesus' own faith*. Faith in Jesus' own faith spells the end of the self-asserting self, and Jesus becomes the subject, the person, of the believer: I live by Jesus' own faith (Galatians 2:20).

In law-gospel terms, then, the law, while not confused with the gospel, cannot be divided from it. Jesus Christ is the true content of the law and the only criterion for deciding what the law is. "From what God here does for us, we learn what God wants with us and of us."[9] God's creative word has the goal of the conformity of our actions with his. So grace can only come in the form of the demand for obedience. The law gives humans room in the gospel—by giving them a concrete way to believe that doesn't dissolve into a nomism or antinomianism of pure inwardness.[10] And the law gives the gospel room in our human space—by being the proclamation of God's human form in the world. As Barth writes:

> How could the Lordship of Jesus Christ be proclaimed without the proclamation in itself being a demand for obedience; the Incarnation otherwise than as command of self-denial, the cross of Christ otherwise than as a command to follow after Him and to take up one's own cross, His resurrection otherwise than as

under the admonition of the ancient Easter pericope (1 Cor. 5:7): "Purge out therefore the old leaven, that ye may be a new lump!"?[11]

Faith, then, always implies obedience. By faith, the Christian lives inside Jesus' own obedience and has that obedience as a reality in his or her life.

Barth then explains how the law convicts us of sin and leads us to Christ. The law, rightly understood, with its true content (Jesus' faith), exposes the core of human sin for the first time. Our sin is that we inevitably evacuate the law of its true content and use it for our own self-justification. The law without its true content can only be understood—or, rather, *misunderstood*—as an occasion for us to claim that we both want to satisfy its demands and are able to do so. But such a claim is the core of sin, self-assertion against God. The misunderstood law makes sin overwhelmingly sinful. Under this scheme, Christ is, at best, God's way of helping us in our self-assertion, not the end of our self-assertion against God. Far from being a preliminary to the gospel, such a misunderstood law blocks the way to the true gospel. Without its true content—Christ's "yes" to death and grace—the content of the law becomes demonic opposition to Jesus Christ. The unincarnate "Christ" who is supposed to help us can bring no comfort at all to those trapped by its merciless demands, for God is not mocked and still stands by the law, even when humans are misusing it for their own self-assertion. If the law is robbed of its true content, which is Christ, then all sorts of methods of self-assertion will take his place in it, including "in these last troubled times the so happily invented 'people's laws' that are brought forward in order to give to the law of God the content needed and desired for this purpose."[12] Barth continues:

> Once God is no more God in His law, then that law has become only too like many other laws, and He Himself only too like many other gods, for these do exist. And it will then become a fascinating pursuit to make an interchange on occasion between Him and His laws and these others.[13]

Humans remain alone and unhelped, at the mercy of these forces, with nowhere to stand in order to resist them.

Real *Anfechtung* (spiritual trial) comes when a person realizes that the problem is not the lack of willingness to do the good; the problem is that we are all too willing to do the good. That is, *we* wish to do the good instead of allowing Christ to be and do the good in us. We then realize that our good works are nothing but works of covetousness against law.

With this realization, the way is open for grace. Christ appears as the true content of the misunderstood and misused law to justify real sinners.

Here, and here alone, the order law-gospel has its place. When we see Christ as the true content of the law, then the empty law can no longer condemn and is at an end. Then the law becomes, not the demand for self-assertion and thus the instrument of God's wrath, but the declaration that God will make everything good. By the power of the Spirit, we believe that we will have Christ living in us, who already has fulfilled the law; and his fulfilling of the law, his "yes" to grace, will become a concrete reality in our lives.

The result is a church that embodies Christ's fulfillment of the law and hence stands as a witness against the world's sin:

> Indeed even the Church would not be the Church if in its very existence, as also in its doctrine and conduct, the law of God, His commandments, His questions, His admonitions, His accusations, were not visible and palpable even for the world, for state and for society; if the message of the grace of God the Trinity, as that is set forth in the three articles of the Creed and constitutes alone the task of the Church, did not become prophetic testimony to the will of God against all sinful presumption, against all lawlessness and unrighteousness of men.[14]

Here is the crucial witness the church was called to make in the face of the Nazi onslaught. Here is Barth's elucidation of Barmen.

We may note that Barth's position exhibits traditional features of Reformed theology:

1. A Christology that, within the framework of Chalcedon, emphasizes the distinction between and integrity of the divine and human natures in Christ.
2. The inner testimony of the Spirit, necessary in order to apprehend the true gospel content of the law.
3. An emphasis on the third use of the law; hence the order gospel-law.

BONHOEFFER'S LUTHERAN CHRISTOLOGY

How does this position compare with that of Dietrich Bonhoeffer in *The Cost of Discipleship*? Bonhoeffer speaks of Jesus' call to follow as a "gracious call, a gracious command, beyond the opposition between the law and the gospel."[15] Furthermore, he says, "Only the one who has faith is obedient and only the one who is obedient has faith."[16] At first glance, these formulations seem close to Barth's conception of the law as the "form" of the gospel. In fact, it is likely that Barth later lavished such high praise on *The Cost of Discipleship* in his *Church Dogmatics* precisely because he believed that it admirably articulated a view very much like his own.[17] Like Barth, Bonhoeffer rejected any notion of a natural theology. Like Barth, Bonhoeffer was interested in understanding the law and the gospel from the perspective of their unity in Christ. Like Barth, Bonhoeffer insisted that the gospel breaks through to human beings as gospel precisely in the form of a command, namely, Jesus' command to follow. Like Barth, Bonhoeffer claimed that Christ was the whole content of this command. Like Barth, Bonhoeffer taught that only an obedient church could set a limit to the sinfulness of the state and society.

Nevertheless, the difference between them is fundamental. Barth and Bonhoeffer are indeed comrades in arms in the church struggle, but they operate out of different theological paradigms, as revealed most clearly in their differing Christologies. Since *The Cost of Discipleship* is essentially Bonhoeffer's development of his basic christological position, an examination of his 1933 Christology lectures will help to clarify how he differs from Barth.

The beginning of Bonhoeffer's Christology is the encounter with the human being Jesus totally within the horizon of this earthly existence. We do not first have a concept of God and a concept of humanity that we then combine according to the Chalcedonian formula in order to understand Christ. For Bonhoeffer, the divinity is first revealed in the decision of the human being Jesus to go under the law as a curse. Chalcedon is not the narrative of the drama, but the delineation of its boundaries, instructions about what *not* to say when telling the story.[18] The incarnation is the necessary framework within which to tell the story, not the story itself.

Barth's narrative, as he would later put it in the *Church Dogmatics*, is the divine Son's sojourn into the far country and back again. From a privileged position in view of both sides of the great divide between Creator and creature, the theologian carefully describes how the Creator takes on humanity without thereby becoming confused with it. What saves us is that God carves out a space in this world where we can participate by faith in God's own human obedience. To be sure, for Barth this obedience is nothing but the cross, God's human submission to God's judgment over sin. The cross is indeed central to Barth's theology. But the cross is important because it qualifies the incarnation: God takes on *sinful* humanity, with all its consequences. The incarnation is the true drama. Because Barth's story is of the eternal Word taking on sinful humanity, the Creator taking on fallen creature, he beholds the law and gospel in their unity *a priori*: the Word of God that unites these two must be grace. Even a word of judgment is a form of *the* Word who became flesh for us. In law-gospel terms, then, the corresponding distinction is not between the law and the gospel, but between the law and the law—the misunderstood law abstracted from the gospel (which, devoid of Christ, can only be misused for human self-assertion) and the true law that is the form of the gospel, the law that is the incarnate Word.

For Bonhoeffer, on the other hand, the fundamental distinction is given by the cross, not the incarnation viewed as a cosmic narrative. The true interface between God and the world is not given in a prior distinction between Creator and creation, which then becomes a reality for us in the distinction between the divine and human natures in Christ. Bonhoeffer does not inhabit Barth's traditional two-tiered universe.[19] For Bonhoeffer, God is deeply hidden in the humiliation of the human being Jesus. The transcendent begins with the encounter with this human being (the "who" question), who finally brings the unbounded self to an end as it recognizes that it cannot order him under its own logos (by means of the "how" question).[20] The unbounded, sinful self can only kill him, in order that it can go on living with its "how" questions. But then he rises from the dead and cannot anymore be disposed of. Here, finally, the unbounded, sinful self is at an end. The incarnation alone was not sufficient to reveal transcendence: "Humans may struggle against the incarnate one; against the risen one, they are powerless. Now they are themselves the ones who are condemned and put to death."[21] As such, we find ourselves called into question: "Who are you that you can only ask about me, when I restore you, justify you and give you grace?"[22] Only God can question us so. The encounter with God happens in *being* asked, Who are you? (as only God can) and, at the same time, *asking*, Who are you? (finally dropping the "how" and "what" questions of the unbounded self).

In other words, Jesus Christ present in word and sacrament in the church is simultaneously law and gospel, but the theological order is *first* law, *then* gospel. Only when we have faced the answer to God's "Who are you?" ("I am a sinner") can we hear the answer to our "Who are you?" ("I am for you"). If Barth's fundamental distinction is between Creator and creature, Bonhoeffer's is between the one righteous One and the sinner, the divine-human One who is righteous in becoming a curse for us and the sinner revealed as such in him. The scandal is the cross—and the resurrection of *this* crucified one—not the incarnation in and of itself. "The offense of Jesus Christ is not his incarnation—that is revelation!—but his humiliation."[23] The fundamental distinction between God and humans is given in history, in the encounter with this human being in his humiliation, in his going under the law as a sinner, "in the likeness of sinful flesh" (Romans 8:3). This humiliation is enacted within the church when he is preached, offered, and given, as *pro me*. The question is not how God can be in time or how the human being Jesus can be contemporaneous with us. "God in timeless eternity is not God; Jesus limited by time is not Jesus. Rather we may say that in the man Jesus, God is God."[24] The question, then, is, Who is this one divine-human person, Jesus? And his ontological identity is that he is *pro me*. Where humanity should stand, there he stands. "He is the congregation. He not only acts for it, he *is* the congregation, in that he goes to the cross, bears sin, and dies. Therefore in him humanity is crucified, killed, and judged."[25]

The congregation is his body by virtue of receiving its existence from the one whose whole existence is to be *for* the congregation. He gives himself to faith as the center of who the believer is. But this center is also the boundary. As the one who is *pro me*, he is the fulfilled law, and so is our judge at the same time as he is our justification. Law and gospel are temporally simultaneous; they are first distinguished from one another in that they are given together, in profound unity, at the cross. And when Christ gives his existence to the congregation, his existence as the humiliated one, the one who is for the sinful congregation, the congregation (which now knows the distinction between the law and the gospel) exhibits the very same offense of the cross to the world.

> This Christ existing as congregation is the whole person, the one who is exalted and who is humiliated. His being as congregation, just as his being as word and sacrament, has the form of the offense. Insofar as it is congregation, it is no longer under sin. But it remains in the world of the old Adam, the *homoioma sarkos* [the likeness of flesh, Rom. 8:3], under the age of sin. It remains human in repentance.[26]

The distinction between Creator and creature first comes into view only in the encounter with the humiliated One at the cross. Where law is first distinguished from gospel at the cross, there the one divine-human One in his humiliation is both Creator and new creation. His humiliation *is* his divine-human existence, not an accident of his divine-human substance. In the sacrament, especially, he is *pro me*, and as such he is the "restored creation of our spirit-bodily existence."[27] Divinity is first defined by the very same criterion that defines his humanity as new creation. His going under the law, under the "likeness of sinful flesh" for us, gives the revelation both of divinity and of humanity; we are brought up short before the true mystery of transcendence (Jesus' human obedience to the cross) and are given that divine mystery to be our own humanity. We die and are raised to newness of life.

So, whereas for Barth the distinction is between the law (as misunderstood) and law (with the gospel as its true content), for Bonhoeffer the distinction is between the law and the gospel. Their unity is not known ahead of time, but given at the cross as a gift, as "outcome." And whereas Barth's beginning is the distinction between Creator and creature, the nature of each somehow being known ahead of time, Bonhoeffer first discovers the Creator-creature distinction in the one identity of the divine humanity of Jesus, an identity defined by the cross.

In his critique of Barth's "Gospel and Law," the Lutheran theologian Gerhard Forde helps us to understand the implications of this difference for Barth's and Bonhoeffer's differing conceptions of law and gospel.[28] Both Barth and Forde insist on an eschatological break in the continuity of the law, but they conceive of this break quite differently. Forde acknowledges no absolute distinction on the level of law, since even the law that comes with the proclamation of Christ finally only accuses. Furthermore, the law that comes with the proclamation of Christ is not a new law, but the final and ultimate statement of the very same law at work everywhere in this old age, for the Christ that is proclaimed is the one who was born "under the law." The law, then, is not the form of the gospel, but the form of this sinful age.

Barth seems to think that it is humans who "use" (or "misuse") the law, but Forde insists that it is always *God* who uses the law. As Forde writes,

> The point is that even though *man* [*sic*] misuses the law, *God* does not. God is, after all, the sovereign of the law; what man needs, then, is not another totally different law, but rather the faith to submit to God's use of the law and in the light of the gospel to become a proper steward of his sovereign.[29]

Therefore, the law proclaimed *in Christ* is the offer, not of an entry into what seems to be a totally new, eschatological world, as in Barth, but of entry into *this* world whose form is to live under the law, that is, under the accusing voice of condemnation. Human beings abandon their Godlike abuse of the law in their attempt to justify themselves and begin to live *under* the law as finite beings who confess their sinfulness. The unity of the law with the gospel of God's justification of the ungodly can only be maintained by faith alone, in the face of *Anfechtung*. This faith looks to Christ alone, and so in him the law truly comes to an end. But this happens by faith, not by sight. In the meantime, Christian existence means being pressed down completely into existence fully in this world, under the law. In this way, the Christian becomes conformed to Christ, the Crucified One, and has Christ's resurrection—the end of the law—by faith alone.

It would seem that Barth merely posits the antinomy of law and gospel in order to demonstrate the triumph of grace, which was already guaranteed as a matter of sure knowledge ahead of time. The would-be Christian is then left to think himself or herself into this new eschatological existence: How do I obey this new law that is the "form" of the gospel? As Bonhoeffer feared from the beginning of his encounter with Barth's theology, faith is then not nonreflective regard for Christ alone, but collapses into self-reflection upon one's "heavenly double."[30]

Bonhoeffer's position avoids sanctioning a "natural law" revealed apart from Christ—the view that Barth opposed so passionately—precisely *be-*

cause it maintains the order law-gospel. Only the church knows the end of the law in Jesus Christ, and therefore only the church knows the true law of this world. To use Bonhoeffer's later terminology, the church knows the ultimate (the justification of the ungodly in Christ) and from this position can identify the good as that which tends to keep the law purely law, ultimately always accusing and never justifying, thereby preserving the world for justification in Christ alone.[31] Sinful human beings, by definition, cannot tolerate this criterion for the good, since they must justify themselves. In agreement with Barth, Bonhoeffer maintains that it is only from revelation that we can learn the true nature of the good.

But, unlike Barth, Bonhoeffer is able to trace the profound continuity between this divinely revealed law and the best instincts of humanity at large, who know nothing of this revelation. Christians who know the distinction between the law and the gospel because they know of the end of the law in Christ become stewards of the end of the law in society at large, exhibiting a deep solidarity with the world, a true worldliness through their life under the cross. Christians do not have a privileged knowledge of some new, eschatological law, but, on the contrary, submit *even more than non-Christians* to the law of this world. It is precisely in doing this that they make their witness to the eschatological limit of the law. Christians become stewards of the proper use of God's law in society, setting a limit to the tyranny of the state while at the same time countering any church's theocratic claims by upholding the legitimate (that is, strictly limited) power of the state.

Bonhoeffer explicitly mentions this in his Christology lecture when he states that the church with its proclamation of the cross is not only the boundary and limit of the state, but also its hidden center. The cross (not the incarnation as such) is both the end of *this* world's law and its fulfillment. The church, Bonhoeffer writes,

> does not set up a new law through its acknowledgment of the cross and its proclamation, a new law that the state would have to obey. Rather, it proclaims that God's entry into history and his being killed by history has once and for all broken through and overcome [*aufgehoben*] the order of the state, while at the same time once and for all affirming and fulfilling it.[32]

Before going on to consider how he works out this christological position in *The Cost of Discipleship*, we may pause to observe that it exhibits traditional features of Lutheran theology:

1. A Christology that, within the framework of Chalcedon, emphasizes the unity of the one divine-human person of Christ.
2. The work of the Spirit as revealing Christ in his humiliation (the offense), to kill and to make alive. The Spirit does not reveal a

world hidden behind the text (the incarnation of the "totally other" God), but rather shuts off all such worlds in order to encounter the God totally in this world, hidden in the offense of the cross.

3. An emphasis on the first (civil) and second (theological) uses of the law; hence the order law-gospel.

LAW AND GOSPEL IN *THE COST OF DISCIPLESHIP*

In *The Cost of Discipleship*, Bonhoeffer does not abandon this basic Lutheran framework. On the contrary, he employs it polemically against a pseudo-Lutheranism that threatened to destroy the church and leave state and society defenseless against the onslaught of evil. He does not much use law-gospel language because the terminology itself had become compromised and would be immediately misunderstood. But he still writes from within its dialectic, and from a Lutheran point of view. When Bonhoeffer insists that only the one who is obedient can have faith, he is not positing a new law different from the law of this world, a law that is the "form" of the gospel. Instead, he is insisting again on the hiddenness of Christ under the law of *this* world, and that he is found only by those who go under this law in obedience to his command to follow him.

The so-called Lutherans of Bonhoeffer's time were, in effect, denying the humiliation of Christ. They had made him into a triumphalistic principle they could use as their ticket into the coming world. In the meantime, they had no alternative but to live completely trapped under an unlimited and hence otherworldly and antiworldly law. Bonhoeffer's formula asserting the necessity of obedience for faith rejects the error of locating Christ entirely within the consciousness of believers and declares him to be fully in the world, under the law, as the crucified and risen One.

In *The Cost of Discipleship*, obedience to Christ's call to follow is finally to hear the law as the law in law *and* gospel, that is, as a law with an end, as fulfilled law. It is to go out into the world, under the law, where Christ is, to lose oneself so that by faith Christ becomes who one is. It is by this faith that one has a resurrection, a share in the eschaton, the end of the law, thereby holding law and gospel together in their unity in Christ. The distinction between God and the world that is also the union of God and a (sinful) world is truly given only in the crucified One, and not in a prior abstract distinction between God and the world in which sin is posited only to show the inevitable triumph of grace.

Therefore, when Bonhoeffer speaks of Christ's call to follow as a gracious command, "beyond the opposition between law and gospel," he is speaking of *what faith believes under the cross* (that is, as the outcome of obedience to Jesus' call), not of a fundamental unity between law and gospel (the law as the form of the gospel) that is known ahead of time. The command is gracious precisely because it is *not* gospel (or the "form" of the gospel), but finally *merely* law, commanding a purely finite, dead work. This is the law as *God* uses it, as it is spoken by Christ, who brought it to an end by his cross and resurrection. It is the command to be, finally, what one actually is, namely, a lost and condemned sinner under the law, but *with Christ*, who is justification and resurrection for lost and condemned sinners. Only when law and gospel are held fast together in faith in Christ is law finally *purely* law and gospel *purely* gospel and their opposition overcome. This has two consequences:

First, the order is law-gospel, not gospel-law. This order, however, is the *theologically* necessary order, and not a temporal order. Law and gospel are in fact temporally simultaneous in Jesus' call to follow. But they are theologically ordered as *first* law, *then* gospel, in that for the first time the law is distinguished from the gospel as that which comes to an end in Christ. In that the law is claimed in a finite, dead work of obedience as the law that comes to an end in the gospel, as the law of *this* world and not as the way *out* of this world, the law comes to its end in Christ. Bonhoeffer's emphasis on faith that sees only Christ expresses the end of the law. What comes to expression in such obedience, then, is nothing other than Christ's fulfillment of the law at the cross. The purely finite, dead work of obedience to that law—the law that is finally not mistaken for gospel—is entry into Christ's humiliation, where, by faith, Christ's humiliation under the law for sinners is the believer's and the believer's sinful existence under the law is Christ's. This gift of the law as entry into Christ's humiliation, his substitutionary presence, is the whole content of the concept of "following," the truly evangelical *imitatio* that is the theme of Bonhoeffer's book.

The second consequence of the order law-gospel is that entry into Christ's humiliation is entry into the reality of the world. Ironically, the pseudo-Lutheran advocates of cheap grace have two different laws, just as Barth does. Barth distinguished between the misused law and the true law, whose content is the gospel. His pseudo-Lutheran adversaries, in effect, distinguished between a law within the conscience and a law within the world. If the gospel stills the accusing voice within the conscience, but does not radically judge and contain the law within the world, then it is evident that the law within the conscience is not the law within the world, and what happens within the conscience is merely a charade of self-accusation and self-forgiveness. In that case, the law as accusing voice still has unlimited scope and the victim of cheap grace remains unforgiven and unhelped, trapped in an abstraction from the world. Bonhoeffer insists on the necessity of obedience for faith precisely in order to preach the one law of this world as the law under which Christ is to be found as the crucified One. Entry into the world under the law is necessary in order to meet the God who is in the world under the law. In that the follower obeys, God uses the law to kill and the obedience is immediately lost to the follower as something the follower could claim as part of himself or herself. The law comes to an end, and the follower has Jesus alone, by faith alone. In that Christ is the *end* of the law, he is also the *goal* of the law. Outward, literal, *worldly* obedience to the law is necessary, or one does not really encounter the law *of this world*, the law that has its end in Christ. *The Cost of Discipleship* is Bonhoeffer's insistence that Christ is both the end *and* the goal of the law: only the one who has faith obeys (Christ is the end of the law), and only the one who obeys has faith (Christ is the goal of the law). Each is true because of the other, and neither is true without the other.

And in Christ, the follower is at once in the world as a steward of God's proper use of the law, which is law that is law alone and does not pretend also to be gospel. The law is the "form" of this age, not of the gospel.[33] The law is not a ladder out of this world into a new world, but the shape of life that does not anymore aspire to remake this world, but rather to love it as it is. This means that the Christian is truly worldly in the deepest sense by being vigilant to keep the law confined to this world and this age. The struggle for justice is the struggle to keep any power from justifying itself. The theologian's distinction between form and content will not help here. What is crucial here is the Holy Spirit's distinction between the word of God that only accuses and the word of God that declares the glad news of justification in Christ, a distinction that can be won only in the hard school of experience, that is, only by the one who obeys.

Perhaps Bonhoeffer was ahead of Barth in addressing the issues of the Christian's responsibility in the world because of his perspective. Bonhoeffer saw immediately that the real task of the church in confrontation with the Nazi regime was to stand up for the Jews. He did not advocate this on the basis of a supposed *Christian* law, but on the basis of Christian knowledge of the limit of the *world's* law. Is it a mere coincidence that Barth only came to the realization that defense of the Jews was the heart of the matter much later, as he himself admitted long afterward?[34]

It is from this perspective, too, that we must understand Bonhoeffer's accusation in *Letters and Papers from Prison* that Barth's position is essentially a "positivism of revelation."[35] Bonhoeffer praises Barth for his critique of religion and for seeing that Christianity is about an eschatological event, not the fulfillment of a human potentiality for knowing God. But Bonhoeffer alleges that Barth merely offers a whole system of doctrine that never at any point addresses the reality of the world in which people actually live. In other words, the law in Barth's system is a new law that comes from outside the world, and not the old law of this world. The mystery of the Christian faith is not guarded by a secret discipline at the cross, but is foisted upon people from an alien eschatological dimension. What Bonhoeffer means is that, in such a version of Christianity, Christ, along with his church, is not found deeply hidden under the law of this world, at the cross, and therefore in the deepest solidarity with the world.[36] Bonhoeffer charges that, in the last analysis, the positivism of revelation sets up a "law of faith" and thereby destroys what, "through the incarnation of Christ," should be a gift for us. Christ must not be stripped of his incognito. The church's secret discipline must keep him hidden under the form of the cross, under the law, under the form of a sinful, condemned church, in solidarity with a sinful, condemned world, so that the one who goes under the law, who obeys his command to follow him, finds him there as the end of the law, the justification of the ungodly. Then, and only then, is Christ "gift." It is not enough to give the church as the place where one's eyes are opened to see the true gospel content of the law. This conception ultimately leaves people unhelped: How do I get this correct vision of the law for myself? I am not able to obey nonreflectively, as *actus directus*. Reflection must intervene between Jesus' call to follow and my obedience. And when it does, I discover that I am not at all sure what to do. How do I appropriate for myself what could only be a divine obedience, offered by the eternal Word of God? What could that possibly mean? I find myself searching for my "heavenly double" and lose sight of Christ. "The church now stands in the place of religion—that is in and of itself biblical—, but the world is to a certain extent thrown back on itself and left to itself, and that is the error."[37] Of course, Bonhoeffer was not suggesting that Barth himself was basically wrong about what Christian obedience entails or that he failed signficantly to give leadership and direction to the church during the church struggle. He was criticizing Barth's theological conceptuality, not Barth himself.

But what about Bonhoeffer in *The Cost of Discipleship*? Does he indulge in otherworldly sectarianism in this book, leaving the world to fend for itself? It should be clear by now that obedience to Jesus' call to follow is also entry into the deepest solidarity with the world under the law. In Nazi Germany, where the law had ballooned into a tyranny whose claims knew no limits, Bonhoeffer saw very little that approached true worldliness. Hence, the worldliness of following Jesus could find very little in society with which to make common cause, and the life of following Jesus could only be "hand to hand combat" with an *unworldly* world that knew only its own unlimited law as a false gospel. Conformed to Christ crucified under the law, and certain of a resurrection in him, Christians exhibit the limited law that forms this world, thereby drawing a boundary to the world's unbounded claims. In stressing the extraordinariness of the life lived so radically under the law, Bonhoeffer counters the current "Lutheran" misunderstanding of Christian worldliness as the renouncing of any resistance to the overweening claims of an unlimited law. Nazi Germany was unworldliness with a vengeance; the small band of persecuted and powerless followers of Jesus was an island of worldliness in this ocean of chaotic violence, and thereby formed the nucleus of any restoration of decency in society at large.[38] Not coincidentally, the followers of Jesus also find themselves in solidarity with the victims of injustice, those whom the brutal law of the oppressors condemned as subhuman and consigned to marginality, slander, torture, and death. Precisely Bonhoeffer's *Lutheran* understanding of law and gospel as expressed in *The Cost of Discipleship* is the basis for his activity on their behalf in the resistance.

CONCLUSION

All of this is not to suggest that Barth and Bonhoeffer were not in profound agreement with one another in their intentions. They were. What is at issue here is the relative adequacy of their respective theologies to help them attain their shared goal of a genuine proclamation and a genuine obedience in the midst of the crisis of their time.

Barth found resources to confront the crisis in his Reformed tradition, especially in its emphasis on the sovereignty of God and the third use of the law. He produced a brilliant reappropriation of that tradition that seemed to confront the crisis squarely. At the same time, he laid himself open to the charge of merely producing a mirror image of the modernist move in theology. Instead of explaining Christianity in terms of human religion, he begins by abstracting God from human experience and then explains Christianity—God's gracious, unilateral coming into the world—as the negation of human religion. As Bonhoeffer later wrote, the critique of human religion was valid—it was a direct attack on the German Christian and modernist heresies. But it left a strangely otherworldly, abstract God to proclaim, a positivism of revelation that finally undermines God as gift *for us.*

Bonhoeffer inherited a deeply compromised tradition, but never agreed with Barth that Lutherans had conceded the game to modernity with their Christology by collapsing God into the world. On the contrary, he believed that true theology grew out of that christological tradition that finds transcendence, not in the drama of an other-worldly God entering into the flesh, but in this human being Jesus going under the curse of the law on the cross and being raised from the dead. Here Bonhoeffer found the true transcendence that would stand as a limit to the evils of overweening modernity even as it affirmed modernity's legitimate claims for this world.

It is true that, of all his works, *The Cost of Discipleship* comes closest to the Barthian position on law and gospel. Perhaps that is why he later criticized it as giving a method for attaining faith, i.e., undermining Christ as gift. But in the same passage he also said that he stood by what he wrote at that time, indicating that *The Cost of Discipleship* stands in continuity with his other writings, before and after.[39] At its heart is a vision of the Christian faith which sees the event of the cross—*within* this world, *within* the life of this human being Jesus—as the place where God meets humanity.

ENDNOTES

1. Karl Barth, *Evangelium und Gesetz*, Theologische Existenz heute, ed. Karl Barth and Eduard Thurneysen, no. 32 (Munich: Kaiser Verlag, 1935). Two English translations exist. The one quoted here is "Gospel and Law," in *God, Grace and Gospel*, trans. James Strathearn McNab (Edinburgh: Oliver and Boyd, 1959), 2-27. The other is "Gospel and Law," in Karl Barth, *Community, State and Church*, ed. Will Herberg, trans. A. M. Hall (Garden City, N.Y.: Doubleday & Company, 1960), 71-100.

2. Barth was supposed to deliver the paper as a lecture in Barmen shortly after he had been forced to move to Basle, but he was forbidden to speak and escorted back over the border by the Gestapo. K. G. Steck, preface to Barth, "Gospel and Law," 2.

3. Norbert Müller, "Gesetz und Evangelium bei Bonhoeffer," in Albrecht Schönherr and Wolf Kroetke, eds., *Bonhoeffer-Studein: Beiträge zur Theologie und Wirkungsgeschichte Dietrich Bonhoeffers* (Munich: Kaiser Verlag, 1985), 51-60, shows that Bonhoeffer can, however, be understood in terms of an understanding of law and gospel that corrects what Bonhoeffer believed was a misunderstanding of law and gospel widespread at the time, namely, an understanding that gives the law a certain independence from the gospel.

4. Dietrich Bonhoeffer, *Nachfolge*, Dietrich Bonhoeffer Werke 4, ed. Martin Kuske and Ilse Todt (Munich: Kaiser Verlag, 1989), 47, 286. The present English translation is unusable; the quotes are the present author's translation from the original German.

5. Barth, "Gospel and Law," 4.

6. Ibid., 6.

7. Ibid., 7.

8. Ibid.

9. Ibid., 8-9.

10. Ibid., 20.

11. Ibid., 10.

12. Ibid., 20.

13. Ibid.

14. Ibid., 10.

15. Bonhoeffer, *Nachfolge*, 27.

16. Ibid., 52.

17. In *Church Dogmatics* IV, 2, trans. G. W. Bromiley (Edinburgh: T. & T. Clark, 1958), 533, the original German version of which appeared in 1955, twenty years after "Gospel and Law," Barth writes, "Easily the best that has been written on this subject [discipleship] is to be found in *The Cost of Discipleship*, by Dietrich

Bonhoeffer. . . . We do not refer to all the parts, which were obviously compiled from different sources, but to the opening sections, 'The Call of Discipleship,' 'Simple Obedience,' and 'Discipleship and the Individual.' In these the matter is handled with such depth and precision that I am almost tempted simply to reproduce them in an extended quotation." A page later (535), Barth echos his earlier essay when he writes that in Jesus' command to follow, "grace has the form of command, the Gospel the form of the law." He then goes on to virtually duplicate Bonhoeffer's conception of the call to follow and the disciple's obedience. According to Barth, Jesus Christ is the whole content of the command: "For the only possible content of this command is that this or that specific man to whom it is given should come to, and follow and be with, the One who gives it" (536). The disciple must take the "first step" of simple, outward obedience that finally takes one beyond oneself (538-42) and makes a visible break with the world (543-46). Significantly, though, the obedience of the disciple is not actually Christ's obedience, the true break with the world, but only "an indication, demonstration and attestation of this break" (543). Here we already catch a glimpse of the basic difference between Barth and Bonhoeffer.

18. *CC*, 87-89.

19. See Bonhoeffer's later critique of "thinking in terms of two spheres" in his *Ethics*, ed. Eberhard Bethge, trans. Neville Horton Smith (New York: Simon & Schuster, 1955), 196-207.

20. *CC*, 30.

21. Ibid., 33-34 (translation altered).

22. Ibid., 34.

23. Ibid., 46.

24. Ibid., 45.

25. Ibid., 48 (translation altered).

26. Ibid., 59 (translation altered).

27. Ibid., 57 (translation altered).

28. Gerhard Forde, *The Law-Gospel Debate: An Interpretation of Its Historical Development* (Minneapolis: Augsburg Publishing House, 1969), 175-233.

29. Ibid., 206-7.

30. See *AB, DBW*2, 99, where Bonhoeffer critiques Barth's concept of the new person in faith: "Is the new I to be thought of in unity with the empirical total-I, or does it remain its 'heavenly double'? This is where Barth's concept of act becomes an issue. If the act of the new I has its continuity in the supratemporal, then the danger of a theology of experience is indeed wholly averted; but this occurs at the expense of the historicity of human beings and, hence, of the existential character of act." Bonhoeffer fears that, for Barth, the "I" of faith must turn from regarding Christ alone to reflect on its identity with the "not-I," that is, the new self in Christ. This reflection is a fundamental inversion of faith, which by definition is a regarding of Christ alone. Barth is still too much determined by his neo-Kantian roots, and he is still controlled by its paradigm even in negating it, in putting the minus sign outside the brackets. His new beginnning in theology still falls prey to the self's reflection on itself and its inability to think itself out of itself.

31. *E*, 120-43.

32. *CC*, 63 (translation altered).

33. Forde, *Law-Gospel Debate*, 211: "Only a living faith in Christ as the end of the law can hold the law in its proper perspective [that is, as the form of *this* age and that which accuses the sinner and *not* as the way to the new age]. Faith alone makes and keeps the law 'natural.'" Cf. Bonhoeffer's concept of the "natural" in *Ethics*,

143-51.

34. See Karl Barth, "A Letter to Eberhard Bethge," *Canadian Journal of Theology* 15 (July 1969): 201.

35. *LPP*, 280, 286, 329. As is well known, Barth himself found this charge incomprehensible. See Barth, "A Letter to Eberhard Bethge," 202-3.

36. John Godsey, in "Barth and Bonhoeffer: The Basic Difference," *Quarterly Review: A Scholarly Journal for Reflection on Ministry* 7, no. 1 (Spring 1987): 24-25, makes this point without, I think, really getting to the heart of the matter. Godsey writes, "For Barth, Christ is the God-bearer of the new humanity that marks the demise and transfiguration of the old. Questions regarding the old are relativized and, ultimately, theologically uninteresting. For Bonhoeffer, Christ, as the incarnate, crucified, and risen One—the divine lover, judge, and renewer of the world—leads his followers into the very midst of precisely this world, which is by no means to be prematurely written off" (25). Bonhoeffer, in his later prison writings, may have been put off by Barth's "invincible supralapsarianism" (24), and he always struggled to take into account the legitimate, this-worldly concerns of traditional liberal theology, but he also always aimed, no less than Barth, to re-articulate the great themes of the Reformation and resist "resignation in the face of the original Christological-eschatological beginning in favor of some kind of realization (in fact becoming more and more abstract) in a specifically human sphere" (Barth to Bonhoeffer, 14 October 1936, in *WF*, 120; quoted in Godsey, "Barth and Bonhoeffer," 15-16). Godsey could leave the impression that, whereas Barth made a 180 degree turn with regard to liberal theology, substituting a theocentric approach for an anthropocentric one, Bonhoeffer merely reverted to an anthropocentric scheme of human transformation. Bonhoeffer's concern for the penultimate is grounded entirely in God's ultimate, sovereign act of justifying the ungodly in Jesus Christ; the continuity is found only in the discontinuity. The difference between him and Barth, as we have seen, is how the two theologians define the discontinuity.

37. *LPP*, 286.

38. Of course this overtly political implication of his position could not become explicit in a book published in Nazi Germany.

39. "I suppose I wrote *The Cost of Discipleship* as the end of that path. Today I can see the dangers of that book, though I still stand by what I wrote." *LPP*, 369.

Karl Barth's Treatment of the Man-Woman Relationship: Issues for Theological Method[1]

Clifford Green

While he appreciated specific contributions of other theological contemporaries, such as Rudolf Bultmann, the theologian whom Dietrich Bonhoeffer regarded as his closest ally was certainly Karl Barth. In *Sanctorum Communio*, with its christological doctrine of revelation—Christ as the personification of the new humanity, whose social form is the church-community—Bonhoeffer from the beginning stood on Barth's side of the watershed that had been created in early twentieth-century theology. At the other end of his literary career, while working on his *Ethics*, Bonhoeffer sought to enlist Barth's help in formulating a key section on responsibility; and when he managed to get page proofs of Barth's ethics of "The Command of God"[2] during a trip to Switzerland in 1942, he identified so strongly with Barth's presentation that he took over much of the basic approach, and detailed illustrations, into his own writing.[3]

Even closer to the subject of this paper, the first work of Bonhoeffer that Barth is reported to have read is *Creation and Fall*. Indeed, Barth took over the idea of *analogia relationis* (analogy of relationship) by which Bonhoeffer expounded the *imago dei* in that book;[4] it fitted so well with Barth's own proposal for an *analogia fidei* (analogy of faith) as distinct from *analogia entis* (analogy of being). For Barth, the relationship of man and woman is a primal paradigm of human relatedness, which he also expounds in this part of the *Church Dogmatics* in terms of the relations of parents and children, and near and distant neighbors. For Bonhoeffer, even in his exposition of the relation of Adam and Eve in *Creation and Fall*, the significance of the other person lies precisely in being "other," not in the gender of the other. Sociality, not sexuality, is central to his anthropology in his theological exposition of the Genesis creation stories.

Given this combination—closeness of theological position, yet difference in approaching the relationship of man and woman—it may be instructive for students of Bonhoeffer to consider a parallel in Barth, including its problems. Since I have earlier examined Barth's treatment of this subject by analyzing passages in the *Church Dogmatics*,[5] particularly §54.2 on "Man and Woman," in III/4, I will approach the subject differently here. First, I will draw attention to some leads connected with Barth's co-worker, Charlotte von Kirschbaum. Then I will point to serious difficulties in understanding Barth on this subject that are created by the English translation. Third, I will give a summary of Barth's position, and then, finally, conclude with a critique of that position.

KARL BARTH AND CHARLOTTE VON KIRSCHBAUM

In 1987 Renate Köbler published a little book entitled *Schattenarbeit. Charlotte von Kirschbaum—die Theologin an der Seite Karl Barths*,[6] literally, "Shadow-work. Charlotte von Kirschbaum—the theologian at Karl Barth's side." The English translation is entitled *In the Shadow of Karl Barth: Charlotte von Kirschbaum*. This version of the title catches the sense of *Schattenarbeit* as work done in the shadows and not receiving the public recognition it deserves. But it obscures the point the author wanted to make, namely, that Charlotte von Kirschbaum was a theologian, not just a secretary, and that she worked beside Barth as a partner and co-worker. Unwittingly, perhaps, the English title deepens the shadow and hides the status that the German author intended to light up within that shadow. Barth himself acknowledged her crucial role. In the preface to part 3 of his *Doctrine of Creation*, Barth wrote:

> I should not like to conclude this Preface without expressly drawing the attention of readers of these seven volumes to what they and I owe to the twenty years of work quietly accomplished at my side by Charlotte von Kirschbaum. She has devoted no less of her life and powers to the growth of this work than I have myself. Without her cooperation it could not have advanced from day to day. . . . I know what it really means to have a helper.[7]

When the fragmentary final volume of the *Church Dogmatics* was published at the end of Barth's life, he again wrote in the preface of "my faithful assistant Charlotte von Kirschbaum, who had been indispensable since 1930."[8] Then, in his fullest and most succinct tribute, he spoke of her partnership in creating "the *Church Dogmatics*, in whose rise and progress she had played so great a part."[9]

In addition to her major contribution to the *Church Dogmatics* as a whole, we probably owe a good deal to Charlotte von Kirschbaum for the more constructive insights in §54 on "Mann und Frau," man and woman. Indeed, we might be permitted to wonder how much the relationship between Barth and von Kirschbaum as partners and co-workers served as a paradigm for this text.

In any case, we know that her views and Barth's on this subject are virtually the same, as we can see in her essay on "Women's Service in the Proclamation of the Word."[10] This text was originally one of several lectures delivered at a conference in France in 1949 and published later that year as *Die Wirkliche Frau*.[11] These lectures obviously deserve study to see what light they throw on Barth's position and von Kirschbaum's contribution to it.

One fruitful line for further research is a remark in the foreword. There von Kirschbaum points out that the fifth chapter, "Kritische Ausblicke," aims to distinguish her position from two others, the Catholic doctrine of woman as expounded by Gertrud von Le Fort and the existentialist feminism found in Simone de Beauvoir's *The Second Sex*.[12]

The latter is discussed in some detail by Barth.[13] On the one hand, he is appreciative of de Beauvoir's critique of male chauvinism, her unmasking "the myth of the woman," which supports it, and her avoidance of "the idealistic myth of the androgyne." Negatively, he is critical of "'the flight from one's own sex' . . . derived from the existentialism of J. P. Sartre." According to this view, sexual differentiation is not constitutive of human existence, but something to be transcended in existential freedom.

Gertrud von Le Fort (1876-1971) does not appear in the *Church Dogmatics*, so far as I can see. A popular author of historical novels and a convert to Catholicism in 1926, her book *Die ewige Frau*[14] was widely read; first published in 1934, it had gone through twenty editions or reprints by 1962 and has been translated into French, English, Spanish, Portugese, and Dutch. It drew upon Catholic dogmatics to present woman as "preserver and motherly sacrificer."[15] The gist of Le Fort's position is seen in the following statement:

> The receptive, passive attitude of the feminine principle appears as the decisive, the positive element, in the Christian order of grace. The Marian dogma, brought down to a simple formula, means the cooperation of the creature in the salvation of the world.[16]

It is not difficult to recognize the theological and anthropological grounds on which von Kirschbaum and Barth would reject this view. Indeed, it is important to keep both of these options (those of Le Fort and de Beauvoir) in mind as foils to what Barth actually does say.

DIFFICULTIES IN UNDERSTANDING BARTH

Scrutinizing the language into which Barth has been translated is perhaps as important as understanding the contemporary options to which he sought to provide an alternative. This requires some comments on the translation. In going through several hundred pages of Barth's German to check the gender bias of the English against the original, I found that the translators had consistently made the language of Barth's texts sound much more sexist than it was. *Mensch*, for example, was always translated "man" instead of "human being." Compare the following: "If we listen to what Scripture says concerning man, then at the point where our attention and thoughts are allowed to rest there is revealed an elect man, *the* elect man."[17] This should read: "If we listen to what Scripture says concerning humanity, then at the point where our attention and thoughts are allowed to rest there is revealed an elect human being, *the* elect human being."[18]

Or again, from a section on "Der wirkliche Mensch" (translated in the *Church Dogmatics* as "Real Man": "The ontological determination of humanity is grounded in the fact that one man among all others is the man Jesus."[19] This should read: "The ontological determination of humanity is grounded in the fact that one human being among all others is the human Jesus."[20]

One more example, this time on the incarnation:

And in Jesus Christ God becomes and is man, the fellowman of all men. As God he is not merely one of many such fellow-men, nor is he merely the idea of fellow-humanity. . . . He became and is man, the fellow-man of all men.[21]

This should read:

And in Jesus Christ God becomes and is human, the companion [fellow-human being] of all people. As God he is not merely one of many such companions, nor is he merely the idea of cohumanity. . . . He became and is human, the fellow-companion of all human beings.[22]

In the context of the translation issue, let me also note two other problems. One is the problem of German as a declined language where the gender form of the article is purely grammatical; this often leads to unnecessarily sexist translations.

The other is simply wrong translations,[23] and there are some notorious examples in the relevant texts. For example, where Barth writes that a woman acknowledges *keine Superiorität*, no superiority, on the part of a man, the translators have said, "She does not admit to any *false* superiority on his part."[24] This conveys the totally false impression that Barth holds to *some* sort of superiority on the part of the man, a "true" superiority instead of a "false" one.

In another passage the translators have Barth contradicting himself by arguing against "the establishment of an equality" between woman and man.[25] But *Gleichordnung* here means not equality, but "the establishment of an order of *interchangeability*." *Gleichheit*—which can mean equality, sameness, and likeness—gave the translators a lot of trouble. On III/4:169 the translation says that "there is no simple equality" between woman and man, when Barth's view is that there is no "sameness." (This reminds us of the translation that there is "no false superiority," where the adjective reverses Barth's position.) Most egregious is the rendering "they are claimed and sanctified as man and woman, each for himself [*sic*], each in relation to the other in his [*sic*] own particular place."

SUMMARY

Having sounded the alert about how translations can mislead the unsuspecting reader, I will now—at the risk of oversimplification—try to summarize Barth's position in a few paragraphs.[26]

First, his *intent* was a theology of equal freedom and responsibility of men and women. In his 1946 essay "The Christian Community and the Civil Community,"[27] Barth said that restricting "the political freedom and responsibility not only of certain classes and races, but, supremely, of that of woman, is an arbitrary convention which does not deserve to be preserved any longer."[28] Classism, racism, and sexism, said this socialist theologian, should find no sanctuary in the Christian Church or sanction in its theology.

Second, at the heart of Barth's theological anthropology is the notion of *analogia relationis*. This is the anthropological correlate of the epistemological notion *analogia fidei* to describe the method of a theology based on revelation. Here Barth follows Bonhoeffer's insight that the *imago Dei* is not to be sought in attributes of isolated individual beings, such as reason, but in their co-humanity.[29]

It is crucial to understand how this analogy works. Ultimately it holds that human existence and relations should be viewed on the model of the inner-Trinitarian life of God. In *Church Dogmatics* III/4, the paragraph §54, which begins with "Man and Woman," is headed "Freedom in Community [*Gemeinschaft*]." Stating this in terms of God as Creator, Barth writes: "God created them male and female, corresponding to the fact that God exists in relationship and not in isolation."[30] Anthropologically stated, "a human being . . . is destined to be the covenant-partner of God, and this determination characterizes human existence as being-in-encounter with one's human companion."[31] Thus the analogy is not: as God is to male, so male is to female; or again: As a human being is subordinate to

God, so woman is subordinate to man. The true analogy is this: As in Jesus Christ God is the God for and with humanity, the God of pro-humanity, so human life is life in co-humanity.

The co-humanity of man and woman is not the only case, of course, where the *analogia relationis* as *imago Dei* is seen; the other sections of §54 deal with relationships of parents and children and relationships with near and distant neighbors. So it would not be correct to say that the *sexuality*, or gender distinction, of human beings constitutes them as *imago Dei*.[32] Rather, it is human *relationality, co-humanity*, which is the basic term. Gender relations, family relations, and relations with other neighbors are all instances of the co-humanity in which the *analogia relationis* resides.

Third, it follows that Barth's interpretation of Genesis 1:27 and Genesis 5:1-2 as *analogia relationis* is a repudiation of centuries of male ideology which interpreted the *imago Dei* as the image of God in the male.[33]

Finally, what ethical conclusions did Barth draw from this theological exegesis? First, he asserted the equality of men and women and rejected the imperatives and caricatures of sexual stereotypes. Following Galatians 3:28, he asserted that women and men are one in Christ "and stand upon an equal footing."[34]

He also rejected the idea of abstractions such as masculinity and femininity per se, as though they were ontological determinations or eternal archetypes, *pace* the Jungians. Such abstractions Barth replaces with cultural relativism. "It is not a question of keeping any special masculine and feminine standards. . . . Different ages, peoples and cultures have had very different ideas of what is concretely appropriate, salutary and necessary in man and woman as such."[35]

Within this relativism, however, Barth holds firmly to sexual differentiation. The last quotation, while asserting cultural relativism, continues, "But this does not mean that the distinction between masculine and non-masculine or feminine and unfeminine being, attitude and action is illusory."[36]

The core of Barth's view can perhaps be summed up as follows:

1. Affirmation of one's own sexuality within the sexual duality of human beings;
2. the equality and freedom of women and men in reciprocal relation to each other;
3. the rejection of abstract definitions and stereotypes of masculinity and femininity in favor of a culturally relative approach to gender differentiation;
4. a model of reciprocal self-giving and mutual accountability as a basis for growing in mutual strength and maturity;
5. a doctrine of *Ordnung*, interpreted as *sequence*, not hierarchy,

comprising the relationship of man and woman, a sequence in which the man is A and the woman B, a sequence in which A and B are equal, and in which the "priority" of A is a priority of service.

CRITIQUE

Granting Barth the credit he deserves for being perhaps the only European male theologian addressing these issues in the 1940s and 1950s, I want to focus my concluding critique on two points. In doing so, the methodological issues come into view.

First, what does it mean to say theologically that men and women are "fundamentally different beings" (*grundverschiedenes Wesen*) from each other?[37] Is biology theological destiny?

And here is a crucial issue for theological methodology in a theology of revelation: What is the role of autonomous disciplines like biology, psychology, sociology, anthropology, and history in theological anthropology? Do these support the assertion that men and women are "fundamentally different beings" on *gender* grounds? Are our differences as *males and females* more decisive than our differences as *individuals*, regardless of our sex?

I would argue that a theology of revelation like Barth's must examine its statements in light of insights from such disciplines, and that it can do so without compromising its basic commitments. Further, it has its own insights and questions to offer in dialogue with secular disciplines (e.g., an individualistic psychology). But it will be chastened and probably prevented from knowing so much about "fundamentally different beings." And it will be prevented from talking about "feminine thought, feeling and conduct on the part of men"[38]—that seems to fall back into the very stereotypes Barth had so refreshingly rejected. It will probably also be prevented from making gender differentiation so important as to warn us not to "exchange . . . one's own sex for the other."[39]

To put this point theologically rather than in terms of an interdisciplinary theological method: Surely it is the *other* as a *you*, an independent subject, not the other as a person of different sex, that is crucial for Barth's theological anthropology and ethics. (From *Sanctorum Communio* onwards, including his formulation of the *analogia relationis* in *Creation and Fall*, this was Bonhoeffer's point, and it is the reason that sexuality per se was not theologically central, as it was for Barth.)

The second critical issue I wish to raise concerns the interpretation of *relationis* as an *Ordnung* of sequence. The *Ordnung* (or "system," as Keith Crim translates it in Renate Köbler's book on Charlotte von Kirschbaum) Barth understands as *sequence* in the mutual relationship of two equal beings. It is not ostensibly a hierarchical model, but dialogical; it is constituted by initiative and response. A man's "preceding" requires him to put a woman's interest above his own; a woman's "following" (*Nachordnung*) is an initiative, and certainly not slavish acquiescence to a man's will.

An example Barth gives of "preceding," of "initiative" on the man's part, is responsibility for contraception. The man must be responsible for any nuisance, inconvenience, pain, or risk. Since a woman is more burdened and at risk by pregnancy and childbirth, when it comes to contraception "she must bear the lighter burden, and he the heavier. . . . [This is] an opportunity intelligently to respect the *Ordnung* of the relationship of man and woman."[40] If we have to have Überordnung, this sort of thinking really turns it on its head.[41]

Reading Barth *in optimam partem*, my problem is with the sequence aspect, man as A and woman as B. The model, rather, has to be *mutuality*, which means both man *and* woman are responsible for *mutual initiatives* and *mutual responses*.[42] This leads us to the intrinsic methodological problem that I believe is fundamentally *exegetical* in Barth. I contend that Barth *systematizes* and hence *stabilizes* the New Testament texts on men and women. The patriarchal texts (e.g., 1 Corinthians 11:2 ff.; 14:34 f.; Ephesians 5:22), I submit, are the reason Barth designates man as A—even though his intent and exegetical dialectics are to *undermine* the patriarchalism.[43]

I think it is a more accurate and historical reading of Paul and other New Testament texts to recognize the conflicts between texts like Galatians 3:28 and 1 Corinthians 11:11-12 and those in 1 Corinthians 11:2 ff. (Christ is the head of man, the man is the head of woman) and 1 Corinthians 14:34 (women should keep silent in church and ask their husbands at home). A judgment has to be made—as Barth in fact made it!—in favor of the former and against the latter. And there are ample supports in Barth's Christology and doctrine of God for the ethic of co-humanity he sought to develop in his discussion of women and men. So he didn't have to systematize and stabilize the texts. It would have been more helpful if he had analyzed the social-cultural conditioning of Paul and other New Testament texts in the manner of feminist critiques, and then differentiated the texts rather than stabilizing them. But this would have been to go down paths analogous to Bultmann's—and we know what Barth thought about that!

ENDNOTES

1. The original version of this paper was first presented at the meeting of the Karl Barth Society of North America in New Orleans on 16 November 1990.

2. Karl Barth, *Church Dogmatics* II/2 (Edinburgh: T. and T. Clark, 1948), 509-781.

3. Compare chapter 7 on "The 'Ethical' and the 'Christian' as a Theme" in Dietrich Bonhoeffer, *Ethics* (New York: Simon and Schuster, 1995), with Barth's exposition cited in note 2; and see Larry Rasmussen, "A Question of Method," in William J. Peck, ed., *New Studies in Bonhoeffer's Ethics* (Lewiston, New York: Edwin Mellen Press, 1987), 103-38.

4. *CF, DBW* 3, 65. See in editorial note 22 the references to Barth, *Church Dogmatics* III/1:228-30, as well as III/2:220-21 and 323-24.

5. See Clifford J. Green, "Liberation Theology? Karl Barth on Women and Men," *Union Seminary Quarterly Review* 19, nos. 3 and 4 (spring and summer 1974): 221-31.

6. Renate Köbler, *Schattenarbeit. Charlotte von Kirschbaum—die Theologin an der Seite Karl Barths* (Köln: Pahl-Rugenstein, 1987). The English translation by Keith Crim was published by Westminster/John Knox Press in 1989.

7. Barth, *Church Dogmatics*, III/3: xiii. The allusion to Genesis 2:18 here is unmistakable, even though the German words are slightly different. See also Eberhard Busch, *Karl Barth* (Philadelphia: Fortress Press, 1976), 185.

8. Barth, *Church Dogmatics* IV/4: viii.

9. Ibid.

10. Köbler, *Schattenarbeit*, English translation, 93-124.

11. See Charlotte von Kirschbaum, *Die Wirkliche Frau* (Zurich: Evangelischer Verlag, 1949).

12. Von Kirschbaum refers to the "first volume" of Simone de Beauvoir, *Le Deuxieme Sexe*. The French edition (Gallimard, 1949), to which the *Church Dogmatics* also refers, was published in two volumes, *Le Fait et Les Mythes* and *L'Experience Vecue*.

13. Cf. Barth, *Church Dogmatics* III/4:162 ff.

14. Gertrud von Le Fort, *Die ewige Frau* (Munich: Kösel & Pustet, 1934). The subtitle is *Die Frau der Zeit, Die zeitlose Frau*. A French translation was published by a religious book club in 1946. The English translation by Marie Cecilia Buehrle is *The Eternal Woman. The Woman in Time, Timeless Woman* (Milwaukee: Bruce Publishing Co., 1954); the preface contains a biographical sketch by Max Jordan.

15. The German is *bewahrende und mütterlich Opfernde*, as cited in Brockhaus 11:263. Jordan summarizes Le Fort's position with phrases like "woman's constitutive desire to surrender," which is theologized in terms of Marian dogma.

16. Cited by Max Jordan in his preface to Buehrle, *The Eternal Woman*, vii.

17. Barth, *Church Dogmatics* II/2:58.

18. See Clifford Green, ed., *Karl Barth: Theologian of Freedom* (Minneapolis: Fortress Press, 1991), 185.

19. Barth, *Church Dogmatics* III/2:132.

20. Green, *Karl Barth: Theologian of Freedom*, 227.

21. Barth, *Church Dogmatics* IV/2:50.

22. Green, *Karl Barth: Theologian of Freedom*, 200 f.

23. One of my favorites gives a man the option of being a father or mother! "It is part of the creaturely status of man . . . that he is conceived and born and is thus the child of a father and mother, and that he himself in his turn can conceive and

thus become the father or mother of children" (Barth, *Church Dogmatics* II/4:240). This problem is easily avoided by translating *Mensch* properly as "human being" and then using plural pronouns.

24. Ibid., III/4:171.

25. Ibid.

26. See note 5 above for the essay on which I am drawing here.

27. This appeared one year after III/1, published in 1945, and five years before the treatment of "Man and Woman" in III/4.

28. Green, *Karl Barth: Theologian of Freedom*, 285.

29. Cp. *CF*, 63f., 94ff.; and Barth, *Church Dogmatics* III/1:194ff.

30. Barth, *Church Dogmatics* III/4:117.

31. Ibid., III/4:116 (translation altered).

32. This appears to be the contention of Sheila Briggs when she writes of Barth's "idiosyncratic understanding of the human image of God as being found in the gender differentiation between man and woman." See "Men and Women in the Theology of Karl Barth," paper presented at the Barth centenary conference, Stony Point, New York, May 1986. However, Barth's argument that the man-woman relationship is the *Grundform* of the *imago* relationship may be seen as supporting that reading. For a full account of Briggs's analysis and critique of Barth, see also her doctoral dissertation and her paper prepared for the November 1990 meeting of the Barth Society.

33. For additional exegetical implications, see Green, "Liberation Theology?" 225.

34. Barth, *Church Dogmatics* III/4:164.

35. Ibid., III/4:154.

36. Ibid. One wonders how much the Chalcedonian paradigm informed Barth's thinking about gender differentiation and relation.

37. Barth, *Kirchliche Dogmatik* III/4:165; *Church Dogmatics* III/4:149.

38. Ibid., III/4:155.

39. Ibid. For additional questions on this line, see Green, "Liberation Theology?" 227.

40. Barth, *Church Dogmatics* III/4:276.

41. Perhaps a significant indicator of Barth's own position is that he suspects in Bonhoeffer's doctrine of mandates "a suggestion of North German patriarchalism," *Church Dogmatics* III/4:22.

42. See Green, "Liberation Theology?" 229, where this criticism is elaborated.

43. René van Eyden reports that Henriette Visser 't Hooft wrote letters to Karl Barth in 1934 attacking the biblical basis of male domination. "She asked Barth if he could justify 'The man is the head of the woman,' in 1 Corinthians 11:3 and Ephesians 5:23, and went on to criticize sharply the traditional interpretation, also Barth's, who rejected the concept of 'mutual interest' of man and woman and continued to maintain the hierarchy of God-Christ-man-woman. Her answer is: 'I believe that there is more than superiority, namely love alone. Love knows no superiority or inferiority: Christ died on the cross.'" Quoted from "Unausweichliche Fragen" (u. a. Briefwechsel mit Karl Barth 1934) in Gudrun Kaper u. a. *Eva wo bist du? Frauen in internationalen Organisation der Oekumene* (Gelnhausen-Berlin-Stein, 1981), 11-36; cited in René van Eyden, "Dietrich Bonhoeffer's Understanding of Male and Female," in Guy C. Carter, et al., eds., *Bonhoeffer's Ethics: Old Europe and New Frontiers* (Kampen: Kok, 1991), 201.

ECUMENICAL CONNECTIONS

Recovering Ecumenical Vision and Commitment in a Post-ecumenical Era

John W. de Gruchy

ost of us are probably aware that the ecumenical movement is currently going through something of a difficult period. Gone are the heady days that followed the formation of the World Council of Churches or Vatican II. Yet for many of us who were trained for the ministry during the 1950s and 1960s, whether here in Britain or in South Africa, the ecumenical movement not only caught our imagination, but also called forth a commitment to embody that vision in our own ministry.

This was particularly difficult in South Africa, where, until the ending of apartheid, ecumenism was often under direct attack from the National Party government as the servant of communism and Roman Catholicism. How it could be both at the same time was difficult to imagine, but reason was the servant of ideology in apartheid South Africa, and the media, by and large, aided its myth-makers. This negative view was reinforced by government-sponsored church groups, especially after—horror upon horrors—the launching of the Programme to Combat Racism a decade later. It became especially vicious as the South African Council of Churches and the Christian Institute, the two major ecumenical agencies, led the church attack on apartheid. Ecumenical commitment was a risky and costly business. The great pioneers of the ecumenical movement knew that, and the example of those who had paid something of the price for their commitment during the church struggle in Nazi Germany, Dietrich Bonhoeffer amongst them, inspired us. But what is this ecumenical vision and commitment we are talking about for which men and women have been prepared to act with such dedication as the pioneers and explorers of the ecumenical movement?

Ecumenical commitment and vision is not something that is derived from some international conference, though it may be discovered there and sustained through participation in such events. Ecumenical vision is not something that was thought up by a group of enthusiasts and propagated by the founders of the World Council of Churches or the Vatican Secretariat for Unity. Ecumenical commitment derives directly from the gospel; it is inspired by a vision that arises out of obedience to the gospel. It is essentially a way of seeing the world, the *oikumene*, differently— seeing it from the perspective of the creative and redemptive reign of God in Jesus Christ, and therefore acting differently in the world. Ecumenical vision and acting ecumenically belong inseparably together. This means more than a narrow focus on the church, or even on church unity and co-operation, but equally a commitment to social justice both at home and beyond our parochial and national boundaries.

We no longer live in those days when the ecumenical movement was in its first decades of flowering, when the pioneers were still with us and the vision was clear and strong, though never uncontested or unchallenged. We live in what, for want of a better term, may be described as a post-ecumenical era. Therefore the challenge to us, especially those of us who seek to remain true to the ecumenical vision, is how we are to understand and express it today. I say "understand and express it today" because implicit in what I wish to suggest is that the ecumenical vision has to be discovered and embodied afresh in every generation. Of course, it has to do with the good news of God's reconciling grace in Jesus Christ, of the unity of the body of Christ, of the mission of the Church to the world in the power of the Spirit. But how are these verities of Christian faith to be expressed at a time like ours—a time when the ecumenical vision and practice of the pioneers is no longer accepted with as much conviction as before, or when some believe that the vision has been betrayed by the actions of the contemporary custodians of the ecumenical movement?

Every movement or era labelled "post" is inevitably in continuity with what preceded, even as it takes on new character and journeys up or down untested paths. Hence it is not always possible to tell where post-modernity breaks with modernity. So the use of the term *post-ecumenical* is not intended to mean that the ecumenical movement is dead, as some would have us believe, nor does it imply that nothing of substance has been achieved by it over the past century. That would be patently untrue, and those who suggest otherwise are either ill-informed or mischievous. Ecumenical vision and action today benefit greatly from the substantial achievements of the past, many of which we now take for granted. *Post-ecumenical* refers to the fact that the first ecumenical enthusiasms of this century are past, and that there is undoubtedly something of a crisis within the ecumenical movement. This does not mean that we should opt out of the ecumenical movement, or discontinue the struggle for the unity of the church in life and mission. But it does require the renewal of ecumenical vision. The ecumenical vision we need, which is substantially no different from that of the pioneers of the movement, is one that will enable us in our time to grasp hold of what it is that God wants to give us in the next Christian millennium.

In what follows I would like to suggest four areas of reflection that might help us to focus afresh on ecumenical vision in ways that might be described as lateral. The first of these areas is the ability to see things whole, and it has to do with what might be referred to as the earthy spirituality.

AN EARTHY SPIRITUALITY, OR SEEING THINGS WHOLE

Ecumenical vision fosters and arises out of a spirituality that transcends the false dichotomies that we associate with modernity, as well as with certain forms of Christian piety on the one hand and activism on the other. Some refer to this as a spirituality of "contemplative action" or "prayerful engagement," in which the prophetic call to struggle for justice is grounded in the discernment of the mystic.

While affirming the necessary distinctions between creation and redemption, body and spirit, earth and heaven, faith and politics, prayer and action, an "earthy spirituality" refuses to allow such distinctions to become divisions, to separate what God has joined together. With the New Testament, it rejects the idea that Christian unity is only spiritual and is not meant to be expressed visibly in the fellowship of word and sacrament, worship and mission. It equally rejects the separation of creation and redemption, as though God had lost interest in the renewal of the earth and redemption were solely a matter of individual salvation. The starting premise for an earthy spirituality is an affirmation of the Incarnation, and therefore a rejection of gnosticism, that ancient yet ever-recurring enemy of Christianity and a genuinely ecumenical vision.

Models of such spirituality abound in the history of the Church, not least amongst the pioneers of the ecumenical movement and those whose lives and witness have played an influential role in generating and sustaining ecumenical vision. Let me refer to two who are well known to us all: the Catholic monk Thomas Merton and the Protestant theologian and martyr Dietrich Bonhoeffer.

As a Trappist monk, Merton devoted his life to contemplative prayer, questioning whether the actions of those Christians who engage in overt political activism have real value.[1] Yet Merton's contemplation was profoundly related to the social and political struggles of the time. As a result, he became a role model for the integration of contemplation and action. Merton the mystic became an inspiration to many Christian activists, not least that remarkable American Catholic laywoman, Dorothy Day. It was Merton who said, "We do not see first and then act; we act, and then see."

Bonhoeffer's life and theology were quite different. His was not the way of mystic contemplation within the solitude of a monastery, though he was a man of prayer and meditation on the word. His ecumenical commitment plunged him deeply into the struggles of his day, the struggle for a church that was faithful to the gospel against Nazi ideology, and eventually a more directly political struggle to rid Germany of its demented Führer. Bonhoeffer refused to think in two spheres or live in separate compartments. Towards the end of his life he summed up his conviction in words that continue to inspire Christians around the world: "Our being Christians today will be limited to two things: prayer and righteous action among people. All Christian thinking, speaking, and organising must be born anew out of this prayer and action."[2]

An earthy spirituality thus opens up another way of perceiving and acting in the world. This has many different possibilities, but at its heart it surely includes a deep concern for the earth. In the words of Eberhard Bethge in a letter to his friend Dietrich Bonhoeffer, it means nothing less than having "a good conscience about the things of the earth."[3] What did Bethge, a son of the soil turned pastor and scholar, have in mind? His comment refers to an ongoing conversation between them on the significance of the Old Testament.[4] This was sparked by Bonhoeffer's earlier statement, "It is only when one loves life and the earth so much that without them everything seems to be over that one may believe in the resurrection and a new world."[5]

Clearly, whatever Bonhoeffer himself had in mind, an earthy spirituality has a deep concern for the environment. This does not only mean being committed to the protecting of our ecological systems, but equally a concern for the environment of the towns and cities within which the vast majority of the population of modern-day countries live. An earthy spirituality is concerned about urban decay and urban renewal, about the way in which towns are planned and cities built, about the social and physical fabric within which people live their lives and discover their values. Ecumenical vision, the vision of a "new heaven and earth," is committed to the building of cities that, however inadequately, are inspired by a vision of the city of God. In a time when the earth is so ravaged by greed and life so cheapened by poverty and violence, we need to recover an ecumenical vision that loves life and loves the earth as much as God the Creator does.

THE GRACE OF HUMOR, OR SEEING THE FUNNY SIDE OF THINGS

A Congregational minister in Massachusetts once wrote to Thomas Merton and posed a question about St. John of the Cross, whose austere spirituality had both attracted and repelled him. "Did John of the Cross ever laugh?" he asked. Merton replied, "It is perhaps a good thing for us to counterbalance him with someone as human as Bonhoeffer or with the warmth of Buber's Hasidism."[6] A genuinely earthy spirituality, one that finds its roots in the Old Testament and can trace them through Celtic, African, and Hasidic tradition, will invariably value a sense of humor as an important link between earth and heaven.

Humor is not normally associated with ecumenical vision, nor is it a subject discussed by theologians, even though the Bible tells us that God has occasion to laugh! Karl Barth had a warm sense of humor, but he only refers to the humor of God once in his *Church Dogmatics*. Nonetheless, it is an illuminating reference. It comes in a section where Barth is discussing the limitations on human freedom and, in particular, the honor that God has given to us in calling us into a life of obedience. In relation to this honor, Barth writes, "What is left for man but free humor?" Referring to Sarah's famous laugh (Genesis 18:12 f.), Barth continues, "Is not the contrast between man himself and the honor done him by God really too great for man to take himself ceremoniously, and not to laugh at himself, in his quality as its bearer and possessor?" In sum, "Humor is the opposite of all self-admiration and self-praise."[7] It prevents us from thinking too highly of ourselves, from taking ourselves ceremoniously.

Jesus used humor to undermine the hypocrisy of people who saw the speck in their neighbor's eye but were unable to see the log in their own (Matthew 7:3). By extension, humor prevents us from thinking more highly than we ought of our nation, our church, our race or ethnic clan. Humor deflates the proud and undermines the idolatries of power. If an earthy spirituality is an antidote to gnosticism, whether ancient or modern, then humor, as we have defined it, is an antidote to idolatry. Hence its use by the Hebrew prophet to depict the absurdity of the worship of idols (Isaiah 44:9 ff.).

Humor can and should be means of grace. In a brief but wonderfully suggestive article, Jean Leclerq speaks of humor as a spiritual grace that "evokes a certain freshness of mind, a combination of the sense of wonder and discretion" that is deeply rooted in the Christian tradition. It celebrates the goodness of God and the world that God has created.[8] As a gift of grace, humor has its theological roots in the divine foolishness of the Incarnation, almighty God born as a wriggling baby in a manger and crucified amongst bandits on a cross, and, ludicrous as it sounds, our justification even while we were sinners. True humor is, as Leclerq puts it, "an experience of the relativity of all created things and the ability to discern what matters and what does not." This means, he continues, "stepping back from oneself, being serious but never taking oneself seriously, never considering self as being of utmost and absolute importance." This "stepping back from our own narrow outlook enables us to have a broader, worldwide and cosmic view of things, thus setting our own little ideas in the total picture and seeing history from God's point of view."[9] As such, humor not only leads to humility, but helps foster hope even in times of dark despair. It enables us to see and act differently.

Jokes, as we all know, do not usually travel well, as I have learned to my cost in lecturing in Germany. Jokes are invariably culturally formed; they easily identify the insider from the outsider. This is not necessarily a bad thing, for it is part of the way in which we express identity and enrich common experience. But, by the same token, humor can be abused.[10] It can be used to destroy others, especially those who are different from us. Hence the jokes in every nation which demean those who are the outsider, the enemy, the other. Racist jokes, sexist jokes, ethnic jokes—all are expressions of dislike, hatred, fear, and therefore a lack of love, an unwillingness to embrace the other in honest reconciliation. Such humor indicates a lack of ability to appreciate and respect difference. Instead of humor being a gift that deflates our own arrogance, we employ it to hurt and harm others. As Kierkegaard well knew, laughter can create martyrs. Instead of humor broadening our own outlook so that we can see things differently and discern what really matters, it reinforces our own stereotypes, hardens our own attitudes, and prevents us from changing. Humor, in this distorted guise, is a sign of human fallenness rather than a means of grace. "True humor," on the other hand, wrote your own Thomas Carlyle, "springs not more from the head than from the heart; it is not contempt, its essence is love." Humor at its finest, in Leclerq's words, "peeps out and winks just when everything seems to be going wrong and the situation is serious."[11] It forces us back to basics, to trust in God, to prayer, to a reliance on grace, to hope, to love.

If humor is a gift of God that helps us to get a broader picture of reality and break out of our own narrow boxes, if it helps us to see things from God's point of view, then it has everything to do with a genuinely ecumenical vision. For ecumenical vision means relocating our own sectional interests, whether ecclesiastical or political, in a much larger frame. It requires that we laugh a little at our own ethnic and denominational peculiarities and try to get them into the perspective of what really matters to God. It means respecting difference even while we seek to overcome division. Maybe if church leaders laughed together a bit more about the idiosyncracies within their own traditions, the ecumenical movement would be taken more seriously.

For true laughter does not mean that we do not take things, including our own convictions, seriously, but that we see them in perspective. "Absolute seriousness," Bonhoeffer wrote in prison, "is never without a dash of humor!"[12] Indeed, in order not to lose a sense of proportion in prison, he advocated "a cold shower of common sense and humor."[13] Good advice for old-hand and new would-be ecumenists alike. A true sense of humor is a means of grace because it means that we do not take our opinions, our foibles, and ourselves so seriously that they prevent us from seeing the truth on the other side. It means that we are called to discern that there is something more serious, more important, and more urgent than our own claims and pretensions—namely, God's reign and righteousness. But, having done so, it also leads us to a deeper dimension of ecumenical vision and action. If we can laugh at our own foibles, we can surely learn to forgive the faults and failures of others.

LEARNING TO REMEMBER RIGHTLY, OR SEEING THE PAST AS PAST

Keeping memory alive is of great importance in the life of nations and communities. We have been reminded constantly of this in South Africa during the course of the work of the Truth and Reconciliation Commission. Victims of apartheid atrocities have sought the truth from their one-time oppressors because they want to know what happened to loved ones, even to the extent of finding out where so many were hastily buried by the security forces under cover of darkness. This is all part of the process of dealing with memories of pain by knowing the truth, and reminding those who wish to hide from it. Hence, in the discussions about amnesty for the perpetrators of crimes, it has repeatedly been stated that amnesty does not mean amnesia. The stories have to be told, not just so that oppressors can be granted amnesty, but also so that the victims— and everyone else—can remember what happened. Just as in the case of the Holocaust, so in the case of apartheid, we dare not forget, both for our own sakes and for the sake of the coming generations. Erasing the memory of those who have suffered is one of the ways in which oppressors seek to destroy their victims and deny their own guilt and responsibility.

The importance of memory is therefore undeniable. But what we do with our memories is equally critical. For, while remembering the past is important, it can also be dangerous. When the Truth and Reconciliation Commission was in the process of formation, there were many people— not least on the side of the liberation movement—who were deeply worried about the possible consequences of delving into the past. They argued that the whole process could result in the further entrenchment of social and racial divisions and lead to anger rather than to healing and reconciliation. There was an even stronger plea from the former agents of the apartheid establishment to "let bygones be bygones." Fortunately, the counter-argument finally prevailed. You cannot have reconciliation without dealing with the past. The truth has to come out and be properly dealt with, and the sooner the better, no matter how painful the experience.

Afrikaner nationalism flourished after the South African War at the turn of the century, and Afrikaner nationalism eventually came to power in pursuit of its apartheid goals, largely because the British government of that time refused to face the truth of its role in the war. It showed no remorse either about the way in which it had plunged South Africa into war or about the atrocities of the concentration camps that it had established. None of that was honestly acknowledged, nor was any sense of guilt expressed either in the immediate post-war years or subsequently. On the contrary, the policy of the post-war British government was to destroy Afrikaner culture in pursuit of white reconciliation under British domination. How different the history of twentieth-century South Africa might have been if, after the South African war, there had been a genuine attempt to seek reconciliation based on dealing honestly with the past rather than pursuing expedient political goals. Tragically, the role of the English-speaking churches in all of this was entirely jingoistic—not only was there no criticism of the imperial war effort, there was total support for it.

The rise of Afrikaner nationalism and the creation of apartheid demonstrate that keeping memory alive does not heal or redeem the past. On the contrary, left to itself it invariably perpetuates hurts and hatreds and leads to a ceaseless cycle of vengeance and retribution. How often we have erected memorials in South Africa, not to heal the past, not as a symbol of forgiving the enemy, but as a constant reminder of how we were wronged. Such memorials become monuments to prejudice and hatred. They do not simply remember the suffering of the past and honor its victims, but they become means whereby we honor ourselves and legitimate our own chauvinistic, nationalistic, and ethnocentric goals. South Africa has far too many such monuments. If we are to erect memorials, they must be memorials that redeem and heal the past, not monuments that perpetuate its wrongs. This is part of the reason why Robben Island, the location of apartheid's most notorious prison, is now in the process of becoming a center for the cultural renaissance and healing of South Africa. If the past is not being healed or redeemed, then remembering it is like fanning the embers of a dying fire so that it bursts into flame again and devours us.

An astute North American observer of the Truth and Reconciliation Commission's work in South Africa summed up her observations with these words: "The most difficult task of all, the TRC tells us, is to remember and to forget. Not forget in the sense of collective amnesia but in an altogether different way—as a release from the full weight and burden of the past."[14] In his reflections on the conflict in the former Yugoslavia, the Croation theologian Miroslav Volf speaks to the point: "Only those who are willing ultimately to forget will be able to remember rightly."[15]

"To remember rightly" sets us free from the burden of the past. It is the ability to see that the past is the past, and therefore not to act as though we were living in the past rather than the present. For remembering rightly includes the healing art of forgetfulness. That is seeing things differently from the perspective of the gospel. God who alone has the right to take vengeance is precisely the God who is willing not only to forgive but also to forget. Is not the deepest insight of biblical faith the fact that, while God remembers us in our need, God blots out our transgression? "I have swept away your transgression like a cloud, and your sins like mist" (Isaiah 45:22).

To remember rightly is important for all of our nations, especially those for whom the burden of the past continually undermines peace and justice in the present. But what is true for the life of nations is also true for the life of the Church, not only in those places, but wherever divisions of the past are reinforced by memories that, as the years pass, become increasingly one-sided and perverse. For if we only remember the past in ways that are divisive and that keep enmity alive, then we actually deny the gospel of redemption.

To be true to the ecumenical vision, we have to learn how to remember the past rightly. But we also have to learn how to live in hope amidst the conflicts and tragedies of our times. History does not always work out the way we would like, even if there is a willingness to forgive enemies and work for a better future. How often those engaged in ecumenical endeavours have experienced disappointment despite the commitment and good intentions of many. How often those engaged in working for peace in the trouble spots of the world have experienced despondency as their efforts have come to naught. How many of you agonized with us over events in South Africa in the dark days of apartheid when everything was gloom and despair. Ecumenical vision and action have to cope with the tragic element in history, and yet we do so as those who live in hope.

LEARNING TO LIVE IN HOPE, OR SEEING BEYOND TRAGEDY

One of Alan Paton's finest books was a biography of Jan Hofmeyr, a scholar and politician who died at the height of his distinguished career in the 1950s. The book is in many ways a telling of the South African story as it unfolded in the first half of our century, leading, so it seemed, to the inevitability of apartheid. As you read the book, you are moved to despair, overwhelmed by the sense of impending calamity. Every hopeful moment, every hopeful movement, is somehow countered by forces that dash any such expectation. For this reason, I assume, the North American publishers changed its original title and called it *The South African Tragedy*. Honest analysis certainly suggested to those of us who lived through the darkest days of apartheid that we were participants in an unfolding tragedy of classic proportions. Prophets at home and abroad, including political and social scientists, predicted the inevitability of a racial civil war that might even engulf the world in another international conflagration. There was much evidence to support their claims even as the pillars of apartheid began to crumble. Indeed, in those heady days between the release of Nelson Mandela from prison and the elections in 1994, there were many moments of deep despair when a peaceful settlement seemed doomed. In hindsight, we now know what many then suspected, that there were sinister forces at work hell-bent on trying to prevent change, forces that seemed unstoppable.

Tragedy has to do with the fact that so often our good intentions, good plans, and courageous actions are thwarted and dashed by circumstances that seem beyond our control. In such desperate times we feel trapped, as Max Weber put it, in the "iron cage of history." But a sense of the tragic in history, at least according to the great Greek tragedians, never suggested that it was not worthwhile to resist injustice and refuse to surrender to fate. In his autobiography, *Long Walk to Freedom*, Nelson Mandela tells how in prison on Robben Island they produced Sophocles' *Antigone*. He himself was cast in the role of Creon, the despot who ruled with a rod of iron, and it was Antigone, of course, who symbolized the struggle for justice.[16] She rebelled against the decrees of both injustice and fate.

It was this spirit of rebellion against a sense of tragic inevitability that made all the difference in South Africa, not least amongst the prisoners on Robben Island, notably Mandela himself, during their long years of incarceration. As Mandela expresses it in his autobiography, "I never lost hope that this great transformation would occur. . . . Even in the grimmest times in prison, when my comrades and I were pushed to our limits, I would see a glimmer of humanity in one of the guards, perhaps just for a second, but it was enough to reassure me and keep me going."[17]

The tragic dimension of history and of life is undeniable, and it is fully recognized in our Scriptures. There is no doctrine of inevitable progress in the Bible; but there is a doctrine of human fallenness and a sobering portrayal of nature being "subject to futility" and "in bondage to decay" (Romans 8:20f.). From one perspective, Jesus is a tragic figure. Yet our whole faith revolves around the conviction that Jesus and the movement he initiated transcends and helps us to move beyond tragedy. The tragic element in history is not the controlling vision of biblical faith, and therefore it cannot be the controlling vision of true ecumenism. But those who are committed to the ecumenical vision should have no illusions.

The birth of the modern ecumenical movement at the beginning of this century arose out of a sense of Christian missionary advancement that, it was believed, would lead to the evangelization of the world within a generation. Such were the hopes of those who shared that formative vision. It was a hope dashed by tragic events as Christian nations went to war with each other twice within a generation. The recovery of the eschatological and apocalyptic framework of biblical faith within that historical context was almost predictable. But it was a recovery that had more significance than the immediate circumstances within which it occurred. Not least, it replaced the optimism of the original ecumenical vision with a theology of the cross in which hope is born amidst historical tragedy. It was this vision that guided and empowered those Christians in the Third Reich who resisted Hitler and Nazism, just as it was this vision that enabled Christians to struggle against apartheid. So, too, it is this vision that continues to challenge Christians in all parts of the world who seek to avert the inevitability of historical tragedy from determining their fate.

Apocalyptic forebodings, along with unrealistic optimism, are inevitable as the end of the second Christian millennium approaches. There is undoubtedly much cause for alarm on many fronts, and some reason for optimism, but neither is at the center of ecumenical vision. Ecumenical vision helps us to see beyond the impasse of the present and to grasp opportunities as moments of grace that can turn things round—even if, in the end, we might be defeated. I refer you again to Dietrich Bonhoeffer, who, shortly before his arrest and imprisonment by the Gestapo, criticized the pious pessimism and escapism of those for whom the present only meant catastrophe. For thereby they surrendered "responsibility for reconstruction and for future generations." "It may be," he wrote, "that the day of judgment will dawn tomorrow; in that case, we will gladly stop working for a better future. But not before."[18]

Martha Nussbaum, in the conclusion to her study of Greek tragedy, *The Fragility of Goodness*, argues that those who would find value in life must learn to take risks. It is an essential ingredient in discovering what it means to be human. The ecumenical vision, which is really about hope in action, is one that requires of us that we take risks, not just risks in the realm of the ecclesiastical, but in the wider world of public life. Nussbaum reminds us of the final scene in Euripides' *Hecuba*: "We see a group of sailors, voyaging unsafely. They consult with one another and take their bearings from that rock, which casts (under the liquid sky) its shadow on the sea." It is not for nothing that the symbol of the ecumenical movement is the ancient Christian symbol of the ship. The ecumenical movement is not a safe voyage, but we consult together, we laugh together, forgive one another, and cry together, and we take our bearings from that rock which casts its shadow over our fragile endeavours as we journey on in agonizing yet confident hope.

ENDNOTES

1. Thomas Merton, *The Hidden Ground of Love: Letters on Religious Experience and Social Concerns* (London: Collins, 1985), a letter dated 8 December 1965, 106.

2. *LPP*, 300.

3. Ibid., 181.

4. Ibid., 336 f., 374, et al.

5. Ibid., 157.

6. Merton, *The Hidden Ground of Love*, 108.

7. Karl Barth, *Church Dogmatics III/4: The Doctrine of Creation* (Edinburgh: T. and T. Clark, 1961), 665.

8. On humor in the Bible, see G. A. Herion, "Humor and Wit," in *The Anchor Bible Dictionary*, ed. D. N. Freedman (New York: Doubleday, 1997).

9. Jean Leclerq, "Humor," in the *Westminster Dictionary of Christian Spirituality*, ed. G. S. Wakefield (Philadelphia: Westminster Press, 1983), 201f.

10. A. Koestler, *The Act of Creation* (London: Hutchinson and Co, 1969).

11. Leclerq, "Humor," 202.

12. *LPP*, 376.

13. Ibid., 71.

14. Jean Bethke Elshtain, "True Confessions," *The New Republic*, vol. 217, no. 19 (10 November 1997).

15. Miroslav Volk, *Exclusion and Embrace: A Theological Exploration of Identity, Otherness, and Reconciliation* (Nashville: Abingdon, 1996), 131-32.

16. Nelson Mandela, *Long Walk to Freedom: The Autobiography of Nelson Mandela* (Johannesburg: Macdonald Purnell, 1994), 441f.

17. Ibid., 615.

18. *LPP*, 15f.

Bonhoeffer and the Great Commission: Does Bonhoeffer Have a Theology of Mission?

Richard Bliese

D oes Bonhoeffer have a theology of mission? Whereas the implications of Bonhoeffer's theology have been creatively unpacked
for years within the fields of ethics, church-state relations,
ecclesiology, liberation theology, secularity, the "death of God" movement, feminism, Christology, peace and justice issues, Holocaust studies,
debates over pacifism, and the like, Bonhoeffer's relationship to missiology
has rarely interested the theological community. Why not? Missionaries
and mission-minded Christians from around the world have gravitated to
Bonhoeffer's writings since the 1970s. But, despite this natural affinity
between Bonhoeffer and mission-oriented Christians, does Bonhoeffer
himself actually articulate a theology of mission? In other words, does
Bonhoeffer's theology have mission at its very heart?

This paper will show that, with respect to mission theology, Bonhoeffer's theology is typical of all German systematic theology of his time, that
is, it has little or no "formal" reference to mission. This very fact makes
the "informal" missional impulses emerging throughout his life and writings all the more fascinating. What is Bonhoeffer's theology of mission?
Is he an "unconscious" missiologist? How does the Great Commission
play itself out within the life and writings of this powerful martyr of the
church?

THE WIDER LUTHERAN CONTEXT: MISSIONLESS THEOLOGY

Lutheran Orthodoxy as Missionless. Using the mission question
as an acid test for judging theology is not a new technique within Lutheran

circles, nor has it been one without its share of controversy. In fact, the question was first put directly to Luther's theology at the end of the nineteenth century, with mixed results. Gustav Warneck, in his influential book in 1881, *Outline of a History of Protestant Missions from the Reformation to the Present Time*,[1] contends that Luther was *not* a man of missions.[2] Instead of accompanying his contemporary, Ferdinand Magellan, on a voyage to spread the gospel to the New World, this critic complains, Luther stayed at home. Unlike their Roman Catholic rivals (e.g., the Jesuits, who were organized to travel far and wide to spread the Christian faith), Lutherans *en masse* stayed at home because, in the age of Luther, the common theological opinion was that the Great Commission had been fulfilled. Luther said, "No one has any longer such a universal apostolic command, but each bishop or pastor has his appointed diocese or parish."[3] It is true, of course, that Luther's Reformation spread far and wide throughout Europe. Catechisms were made into posters for every home and church, and Lutheran hymnody could be heard on every street corner. Between 1520 and 1560, no fewer than five thousand students came from abroad to study theology at the University of Wittenberg and then were sent out again as missionaries of the Reformation.[4] Consequently, sixteenth-century Wurttenberg did reflect some distinctive missiological character.[5]

But the dramatic spread of the Reformation does not erase the subsequent missionless tenor of Lutheran orthodox theology, not to mention the embarrassing lack of a mission theology within the Lutheran confessional writings themselves. The subsequent development of Lutheran orthodoxy after the Reformation shows clearly that Luther's theology did little to either define mission for future generations or drive the church to mission beyond its own boundaries. In fact, there was not only an absence of mission ideas during this formative period, but an outright hostility heaped on those who dared raise their voices for mission. Since mission interests had emerged strongly among the Anabaptists and Catholics, those interested suffered from guilt by association. Mission was to be practiced at home, within the confines of Christendom. Luther's mission sphere was the paganized Christian Church. This legacy of a "home strategy" on the church's mission praxis has proven quite stifling.

As a result, there is really no great reservoir of Lutheran theology relevant to the global mission of the Church from the Reformation through Orthodoxy to Pietism. Lutheran mission theology, outside of pietistic writings, has been dominated by the goal of reforming the church, not outreach to the world.

Twentieth Century Lutheran Systematic Theology and Mission Theology: Trains Passing in the Night. The rise of mission theology in Lutheran circles begins virtually with the missionary breakthrough in

Pietism. But Pietism did not change the theology of Lutheran orthodoxy in any fundamental way. It lifted the ban on mission practice and put into motion the missionary ideas that were emerging throughout Europe. Nevertheless, the prolific missionary activity in pietistic circles from the seventeenth through the nineteenth centuries was largely a case of praxis preceding theory.[6]

Consequently, despite some promising missional lights that flickered during the nineteenth century (e.g., Friedrick Schleiermacher, Martin Kähler, Gustav Warneck, Wilhelm Löhe, Karl Graul), Lutherans have suffered from a painful divorce between their systematic theology and their mission theology. As a consequence of this bifurcation, two tendencies have emerged: (1) Lutherans have constantly flirted with other ecclesiastical traditions, especially in the United States, trying desperately to fill the obvious intellectual void within their own missional praxis (e.g., revivalism, evangelicalism, methodism), and (2) a parallel missiological tradition has emerged among Lutherans that, like Pietism, runs parallel to but rarely makes an influence upon their systematic theological tradition. In other words, Lutheran theology and mission theology have functioned, from their inception, like two trains passing in the night.

This last point is crucial, but needs some nuancing to adequately reflect Bonhoeffer's situation. German theology—through Kähler, Harnack, Troeltsch, Althaus, Barth, and Tillich—*did* have an impact on German mission theology, but not vice versa. Whereas German systematic theology greatly influenced mission theology throughout the world at the beginning of the twentieth century, mission theology throughout the world did not significantly influence German systematic theology—to the great detriment of German systematic theology.[7] This one-way street of influence describes the theological context in which Bonhoeffer did his theology at Berlin University in the 1930s. This fact, the flow of influence from theology to mission and not the other way around, is by itself significant. The nineteenth century has been called the "Great Century" of missionary outreach. There was more missiological activity within Lutheran theological circles in the nineteenth century than at any other time before or since. Ironically, the impact of this vast missionary expansion of Christianity, and the theology it elicited, was negligible on the theological faculties. Timothy Yates writes that the whole practice and thought of the church's theology and practice of mission were being appraised during the period from 1920 through 1940. Yet, despite the vitality of the reappraisal, especially within German mission circles (e.g., the mission societies), Bonhoeffer seems to take little notice of this tradition. What caused this gap in his theological education, this lacuna at Berlin? Was this gap a result of the repercussions in the mission field caused by the Treaty of Versailles? Was it the result of the missiological blind spot in the Lutheran theological heritage? Or does Bonhoeffer simply not care about the theology of mission?

Berlin University was just over one hundred years old when Bonhoeffer arrived there as a student. Although its founder, Schleiermacher, was the first to introduce the topic of mission into the theological curriculum (as a practical, not a theological, discipline), Bonhoeffer's major subject in Berlin was systematic theology, which was taught by Reinhold Seeberg. Whereas mission agencies and Pietists followed the mushrooming missiological literature, Seeberg's notion of a solid theological education did not include much reading material from this recently established field of theology.

Consequently, from the time Bonhoeffer finished his degree from Berlin until the day he was thrown into prison, he did not lay claim to any official credentials as a mission theologian, whether defined by his day's standards or our own. Bonhoeffer's knowledge of the mission data of his day appears to be minimal at best. Thus, his aim was in no way to construct a theology of mission.

BONHOEFFER'S CONTRIBUTION TO MISSION THEOLOGY: MISSIOLOGY FROM AN OUTSIDER

Despite lacking clear credentials as a mission theologian, despite lacking any detailed information as to the history and content of German missiology, and despite any ready acceptance up front of the "appropriate" agendas for writing a mission theology, it is surprising how often Bonhoeffer ends up addressing the same pertinent questions as his mission colleagues, both past and present. Bonhoeffer may not have had a theology of mission, but he was indeed a missiologist. Due to his inadequate immersion in missiology as such, Bonhoeffer does not view mission issues within an official framework or language, or from the viewpoint of any particular mission school. This might initially throw certain readers off guard when searching for missiological themes. Nevertheless, the burning questions of the day—church and culture, evangelism for individuals or a *Volk* (i.e., "nations," a people, or groups), how to view other religions, Christianity and secularity, solidarity with the poor, the world as the locus for the church's mission, a Christology focused on "the other," the "social gospel," martyrdom and witness, and suffering as central to a cross-centered understanding of discipleship—all are mentioned within Bonhoeffer's texts. It is as if Bonhoeffer is writing missiology despite himself, that is, he is doing missiology without labeling his work officially as "mission theology" in any formal manner.

The results on Bonhoeffer's "informal" missiology are sketched out below under five headings: (1) mission and the view from the *inside*, (2) mission and the view from *below*, (3) mission and the view from *outside*,

(4) mission and the view from *the world,* and (5) mission and the view from *the cruciform center.*

Mission and the View from Inside (with a Paganized Church). At a time of church renewal in 1933, when German Christians were rushing back to "the true German church" and when Lutherans after years of humiliation were once again taking pride in their church and their national roots, German theologians were enthroning culture as one of the prime loci for grasping God's activity in history. As the German nation rushed to baptize its culture, Bonhoeffer began his swim against the stream by calling the church to go back to its reformational roots. On 14 March 1934 he wrote to Bishop Bell, "The question at stake in the German Church is no longer an internal issue but is the question of the existence of Christianity in Europe."[8] Bonhoeffer called the church to return to its roots in confession. "Church stay a church! But confess, confess, confess! Christ alone is your Lord, from his grace alone. Can you live as you are? . . . The Confessing Church is the eternal church because he protects her."[9]

Part of Hitler's political strategy in 1933 was to ensure that both the Evangelical and the Roman Catholic churches in Germany would submit to the principles of his movement. In the case of Rome, he engineered conformity through the Concordat with the Papacy signed on 29 July 1933. In the case of the Evangelical churches, Hitler initially sought to achieve his ends through the German Christians. The struggle over Nazism's attempts to Aryanize the churches and co-opt pastors to Hitler's policies with the bait of a purified and united "folk church" (*Volkskirche*) galvanized Bonhoeffer's perception concerning the real issue for Christianity. The conflict, for Bonhoeffer, was between Christianity and Germanism. As he wrote in a letter in August 1933, "The conflict is really Germanism or Christianity and the sooner the conflict comes out in the open, the better."[10]

The contextual theology practiced by the German Christians, a byproduct of German mission theology of the nineteenth century and the liberal theology of the early twentieth, became that which allowed certain concepts to flourish, like "an Aryan church for Aryans" (i.e., like an independent African church for Africans, without missionary leadership and financing) and "mission to a nation (folk) not merely to an individual." As Bonhoeffer and the Confessing Church responded to this subtle misuse of contextuality and mission, German Christians responded that theology and confession should not get in the way of church and *volk.* It was thus clear to both Bonhoeffer and Barth that a *status confessionis,* the first since the Reformation, had arrived.

Bonhoeffer's action points to a first missiological principle in his life and writings: a church with a mission (e.g., German Christians) must itself be open to the church's mission of reform. If the church is always in need of reform, one of missiology's first tasks, as Bonhoeffer demonstrates, is to call the church back to the basics: "But where it (the church) is to be subjected by outside force to a law which is alien to the church it may not yield, but must bear witness in word and deed to its freedom from the alien law and its sole obedience to Jesus Christ." [11]

Mission and the View from Below (from the Underside of History). In the concluding paragraph of his essay for his co-conspirators in the resistance, "After Ten Years," Bonhoeffer writes these words: "We have for once learned to see the great events of world history from below, from the perspective of the outcast, the suspects, the maltreated, the powerless, the oppressed, the reviled—in short, from the perspective of those who suffer."[12]

Geffrey Kelly tells the story of South African theologian John de Gruchy, who invited Bonhoeffer's good friend Eberhard Bethge in 1973 to lecture in South Africa on Bonhoeffer's life and writings. Obviously impressed with what he had heard, but having heard nothing about Bonhoeffer's death, a lay person inquired after the lecture about when Bonhoeffer had visited South Africa. "He knows our situation from the inside."[13]

Bonhoeffer's phrase about doing theology from the perspective of "those who suffer" marks one of the most significant missiological insights of the twentieth century. Its impact on liberation theologies across the globe has not been lost.[14] Here is one significant chapter from liberation theology written twenty-five years before its actual introduction into Latin America. In reality, every liberation theology from Asia, Africa, and Latin America has directly drawn inspiration from Bonhoeffer's message of first grasping the mission of the church with a view from below.

Mission and the View from Outside (from the Perspective of Other Religions). The Jerusalem Conference (1928) and Tambaram Conference (1938) were significant missiological events sponsored by the International Missionary Council (IMC). These world conferences set the tone for missiology in Bonhoeffer's day.[15] One of their major themes was the relationship between Christianity and other religions.

Although there is no evidence that Bonhoeffer was conversant with these conferences in any significant way, it is fascinating to note his openness to "the other" outside the Christian world, and to the extremely "modern" missiological question of Christianity and the world religions. Jews, Hindus, and atheists all come to impact Bonhoeffer's missiology.

Jews: The brothers and sisters of Christ. While so much of Bonhoeffer's life and theology reflects a deep-seated Christocentrism and an unwavering devotion to the Christian Church, equally remarkable is his having identified so closely with the plight of those prime victims of Nazi hate, the Jews. Even Bonhoeffer's own efforts to defend Jews with the Bethel confession resulted in little progress, so that he later declared the whole church "guilty of the deaths of the weakest and most defenseless brothers of Jesus Christ."[16] No longer can the Church assert, as even Bonhoeffer did in an earlier phase of his own defense of the Jews, that the Jews were displaced by Christians in God's plan of salvation, or that Jewish persecution reflected their just, divine punishment for rejecting Jesus. Bonhoeffer insists in his "Confession of Guilt" that the Jews are the brothers and sisters of Jesus Christ. The "Jewish Question" became so central for Bonhoeffer that the church's very claim to be the church hung in the balance on whether it was opposed to the Aryan clause and prepared to stand on the side of the oppressed —meaning the Jews. Bonhoeffer wrote:

> Western history is, by God's will, indissolubly linked with the people of Israel, not only in terms of origins, but also in a genu- inely uninterrupted relationship. The Jew keeps open the ques- tion of Christ. He is the sign of God's free and merciful choice and of the repudiating wrath of God. "Behold therefore the good- ness and severity of God" (Romans 11:22). An expulsion of the Jews from the West must necessarily bring with it the expulsion of Christ, for Christ was a Jew.[17]

In response to the Nuremberg Laws in 1935, Bonhoeffer's cry rang out as more than a mere political defense of the Jews; it was theological confession as well: "Only he who shouts for the Jews has the right to sing Gregorian chants." Bonhoeffer backed up this confession with his life, for there is no doubt that his primary motivation for entering active political conspiracy was the treatment of the Jews by the Nazis regime. This was also the case for his family. But what makes Bonhoeffer's action so missiologically significant is the theology behind the Church's relation- ship to the Jews.

Hindus: "Christian" communities in the East. "If we cannot perceive the presence of Christ in our personal life, then we would like to find it at least in India."[18] Bonhoeffer was sensing already by 1934 that Christian- ity in its present form might not be so imperishable as he had once thought. In that same year, Bonhoeffer wrote to his grandmother that he was grateful for her earlier suggestion that he visit India. Should such a trip take place, he hoped to learn how to filter out all the unessential Western accouter- ments of Christianity.

> Before I settle down some place definitely, I would like to go to India. Lately I have been very concerned with the question per- taining to that place and I believe that perhaps one can learn something very important. In any case, it sometimes appears to

me as if perhaps more Christianity is found in that "heathendom" than in our entire German Church. In fact, Christianity is of oriental origin and we have so much westernized it by mere considerations of civilization that it has become lost to us so far as we now experience it.[19]

What is so amazing to remember about Bonhoeffer's comments is that he knew personally the American, Swedish, Roman, and English churches. That the German church needed internal "cleansing" was clear. But that Bonhoeffer suggested Gandhi's ashram as a resource for insights into the structure of "Christian" community *instead of these other churches* is striking. As Kelly states, "Gandhi's peaceful resistance to the tyrannical power of imperial Britain seemed to Bonhoeffer to be closer to the Sermon on the Mount than the pious piffle doled out in Germany's so called Christian churches."[20] Bonhoeffer writes to his brother, "And since I have become more convinced each day that Christianity is coming to its demise in the West, at least in its present form and interpretation, I would like to go see the East before returning to Germany."[21]

The mother church in Germany seemed to be dying the slow death of its own irrelevance. In response, Bonhoeffer wondered about the possibility of proclaiming the gospel "with entirely different words and deeds." Non-Christian India came within weeks of providing him with the resources for what would have been called a major Hindu-Christian dialogue.

Atheists: Unconscious Christians.[22] "How can Christ become the Lord of the religionless as well? Are there religionless Christians?" Bonhoeffer continues: "How do we speak of God without religion, i.e. without the temporally conditioned presuppositions of metaphysics, inwardness and so on?"[23] Bonhoeffer believed that the churches should change their harsh attitude toward the nonreligious. In his poem "Christians and Pagans" Bonhoeffer plays with a gospel that has universal implications also for the secular pagan.[24] Because Bonhoeffer's understanding of mission was not restricted to "the spiritual," he appeared to feel more and more comfortable about entering into "the world" with all its messiness, acting alongside "secular" conspirators like his brother, for example. Bonhoeffer's whole acceptance of the conspiracy represents his acceptance of God's activity in "the secular realm." In fact, the secular and sacred were never separated into two different spheres for him. This whole emphasis is reminiscent of the quotation from Luther that Bonhoeffer used the first time he sat in on Barth's lectures in Bonn: "The curses of the godless sometimes sound better in God's ear than the hallelujahs of the pious."[25]

Mission and the View from the World (Religionless Christianity in a World Come of Age). Even in prison, Bonhoeffer never gave up his appreciation for the practice of spiritual disciplines. "The secret disciplines" (arcane disciplines) was his term for prayer, worship, Bible reading, meditation, and confession. But these specifically Christian disciplines were always to be practiced in dialectical tension with "costly worldly solidarity."[26] It was, in fact, the secret disciplines that were to nurture and motivate Christians and the church to do mission, that is, to operate incognito in the world for the common good. Responsible action in a world come of age became Bonhoeffer's rallying cry for the church in mission. "Our being Christian today will be limited to two things: prayer (shorthand here for arcane discipline) and doing justice among men (shorthand for costly worldly solidarity). All Christian speaking, thinking, and organizing must be born anew out of this prayer and action."[27]

This twofold movement is critical. Mission to the world by itself would result in Christian burn-out. Spirituality by itself ends in a shallow monasticism or the construction of self-righteous ghettos. Bonhoeffer criticized the German churches, even the Confessing Church, on this very point. The churches of Nazi Germany had been fighting in these years only for their self-preservation, as though that were an end in itself, and so the church was incapable of taking the word of reconciliation and redemption to humankind and the world. Mission demands the creative dialogue between personal and corporate spirituality and responsible action in the world.

This call for a balance between spirituality and worldly action (which is more than ethics)[28] is not new in Christian theology or missiology. What makes Bonhoeffer's contribution so unique is the nature of his appreciation for "the world," especially at the end of his life. It was from this wellspring that a whole series of rich, earthy phrases sprang forth for Bonhoeffer: "the world come of age," "the non-religious interpretation of biblical concepts," "religionless Christianity," the "worldliness of the world," "living in the world as if God did not exist," and "worldly Christianity."

Recent missiology is coming, or is coming once again, to a theological appreciation of the world as a major locus for theological reflection.[29] Talk of "mission-in-reverse" is an acknowledgment of the world's mission to the church. Without any unnecessary division between church and world, Bonhoeffer discovered the richness of the world as the object of the church's mission and as a theological category in its own right. Bonhoeffer gave the world, so to speak, theological validity and christological mornings. Christ was really present *in* the world and *for* the world. It was Christ's own presence in and for the world that validated for Bonhoeffer Christian action and, therefore, Christian mission in a world come of age.

Mission and the View from the Cruciform Center. Bonhoeffer was able to affirm a vision for the church's mission in the world come of age inasmuch as this mission was informed by the theology of the cross. Responsible action, for Bonhoeffer, always amounted to a participation of the church "in the sufferings of God in the secular life." The cross is the *missio Jesu* into which Jesus' disciples are called. Bonhoeffer's letters and papers from prison reflect his struggle to discern the specific way Christ is manifest in a world torn apart by war and hatred. "What is bothering me incessantly," he wrote to Bethge, "is the question, who Christ really is for us today."[30] This is Bonhoeffer's essential missiological question. For however Christ is present in the world, he is present "for us" (*pro me* existence).

The Christ whom Bonhoeffer proclaimed as the Lord of the world must be understood from the perspective of the cross. Only the suffering Christ could disclose the true depths of God's kinship with and salvific purpose for his creatures. God was not "beyond," but through the cross he is in the very midst of life. Bonhoeffer expressed this picture of God in Christ with a new christological title, "the man for others." This distinctive title, with its emphasis on self-sacrificing service, sums up the heart of Christ's mission. In Christ, God revealed Godself as one willing to become a God who suffers.

> The God who is with us is the God who forsakes us (Mark 15:34). The God who lets us live in the world without the working hypothesis of God is the God before whom we stand continually. Before God and with God we live without God. God lets himself be pushed out of the world unto the cross. He is weak and powerless in the world, and this is precisely the way, the only way, in which he is with us and helps us.[31]

It was certainly this cruciform vision of mission that allowed Bonhoeffer throughout his writings to reflect on the issues of suffering and martyrdom. It is this great theme of missiology down through the ages about which Bonhoeffer not only reflected, but from whose cup he was to drink the dregs full dry.[32]

CONCLUSION: BONHOEFFER AS A MISSIOLOGICAL ALTERNATIVE

Christian theology must always apply itself to the double task of mission, the cleansing of the church and the spreading of the gospel.[33] Protestants have made the cleansing task a foundational principle since the sixteenth century; that is, the church always stands in need of being reformed (*ecclesia semper reformanda*). Bonhoeffer's initial missiological focus embraced the call to cleanse a Germanized church. A church primarily driven by nationality, race, culture, blood, politics, and personalities (e.g., the Führer) is a church in need of reform. To reform any church is a challenge. But to reform a church that is experiencing the giddiness of misguided renewal is a doubly difficult challenge. The contextual nature of Christian theology had run amok when faced with the tough questions of Jews and the church and church-state relations within the intense pressure cooker of Hitler's Germany. Bonhoeffer knew the problematical side of a contextualized *a priori* theology. The subsequent call for genuine confession, deeply rooted within the Reformation heritage, was Bonhoeffer's missiological call to the Church of Jesus Christ "to be the true church." Bonhoeffer's missiology of reform, i.e., the cleansing function of the church, must therefore be evaluated as one of his chief contributions to any praxis of mission.

But the cleansing function of theology occurs for the sake of the church's inherent obligation to preach the word and make disciples of all nations. This second task, the "propagating" function of the church, is a mission mandate for which theology must prepare the way in every new context. In *The Cost of Discipleship* Bonhoeffer places the church squarely under the Great Commission's mandate of "baptizing and teaching all that I have commanded you." Bonhoeffer interprets the command to "go, baptize, and teach" as a summons to obey Jesus' words contained in the Sermon on the Mount. In other words, Bonhoeffer understood that all missional proclamation involved more than just *preaching* the word and baptizing. The praxis of discipleship and confession belonged to proclamation. Any theology, consequently, that is formed outside of the actual missional praxis of the church easily degenerates into a sterile system of defending "true" doctrines, preaching bland orthodoxy, or following carelessly any missional wind that blows through the church (e.g., National Socialism).

Emil Brunner once said, "The Church exists by mission, just as fire exists by burning." Martin Kähler wrote, "Mission is the mother of theology."[34] Certainly it was Bonhoeffer's understanding and practice of discipleship within the setting of Nazi Germany which mothered his theology. Foreshadowing the teaching of liberation theologians thirty years later, the role of "orthopraxis" becomes for Bonhoeffer a critical element of "orthodoxy."

Finally, the object of God's mission, for Bonhoeffer, wasn't limited to the church. God's mission is directed to the world.[35] If Christ was the "man for others," the church was to follow Christ and be the church for others. Bonhoeffer's insights surrounding the focus of God's worldly mission—"worldliness of the world," "the world come of age," and "religionless Christianity"—played an essential role later in J. C. Hoekendijk's missiological bombshell written in 1967 attacking the German missiological notion of *Volkskirche*.[36] Bonhoeffer foresaw this elevation of the world as the object of mission in the later phase of his life. But, unlike Hoekendijk, Bonhoeffer grounded his worldly initiative within a Christology that emphasized Christ's "real presence" in the world together with Luther's theology of the cross. This christological notion of Christ crucified as the church's missiological center plays a key role in Bonhoeffer's vision for the church's future mission in post-war Germany.[37]

Having lifted up Bonhoeffer's essential missiology—the cleansing, praxis, and propagating functions of mission in the world—we can now answer more directly the question, Does Bonhoeffer have a theology of mission?

Bonhoeffer did *not* have a formal theology of mission. Because of his theological upbringing and denominational affiliation, he rarely used the word *mission*, seldom if ever read formal missiological literature, and was not associated with "the missions," aside from his pastoral work in England and Spain. Since the theology of mission in Germany was almost exclusively associated with "saving souls," world religions, and church extension abroad, the theology of mission was the science of and for the missionary and the Pietist, a practical subject.

Yet, despite his isolation from the formal discipline, Bonhoeffer's theology is inherently missiological in nature. Consequently, both the cleansing and the propagating tasks of the church's mission touch the heart of Bonhoeffer's life and writings. The views from inside, outside, and below, from the world, and from the cross are fundamental missional issues. In fact, Bonhoeffer's alternative missiology reflects in an amazingly prophetic way most of the key agendas with which missiologists struggle today.[38] Thus, Bonhoeffer can make a wonderful conversation partner for missiologists as they discuss church reform, contextual theology, the world's religions, cross-cultural hermeneutics, the church's role in the world, and a Great Commission that includes both making disciples and teaching disciples how to act responsibly "for others" in a world come of age.

Harvey Cox once remarked that the church will never move "beyond Bonhoeffer" until it "speaks with pointed specificity to its age and shapes its message and mission not for its own comfort but for the health and renewal of the world."[39] The same can be said of the church's missiology.

ENDNOTES

1. Gustav Warneck, *Outline of a History of Protestant Missions from the Reformation to the Present Time* (New York, Chicago, and Toronto: Fleming H. Revell, 1906). The original German edition was published in 1881.
2. See Albert Ostertag, *Übersichtliche Geschichte der protestantischen Missionen von der Reformation bis zur Gegenwart* (Stuttgart, 1858); Gustav Leopold Plitt,

Kurze Geschichte der lutherischen Mission (Erlangen, 1871).

3. Quoted by Warneck, *Outline of a History of Protestant Missions*, 14-15.

4. Eugene W. Bunkowske, "Was Luther a Missionary," *Concordia Theological Quarterly* 49:2.3 (April-July 1985): 170.

5. See also Werner Elert's *The Structure of Lutheranism* (St. Louis: Concordia Publishing House, 1962), Vol. 1: 385-402; and Paul Peter's "Luther's Weltweiter Missionssinn" in *Lutherischer Rundblick* 17 (1969), 162-75.

6. Carl E. Braaten, *The Flaming Center* (Philadelphia: Fortress Press, 1977), 16.

7. Henning Wrogemann, *Mission und Religion in der systematischen Theologie der Gegenwart* (Vandenhoeck & Ruprecht, 1997).

8. John W. de Gruchy, *Dietrich Bonhoeffer: Witness to Jesus Christ* (Minneapolis: Fortress, 1991), 21.

9. Ibid., 20.

10. *GS 2*, 79.

11. De Gruchy, *Dietrich Bonhoeffer*, 24.

12. *LPP*.

13. Geffrey Kelly, *Liberating Faith* (Minneapolis: Augsburg, 1984), 153.

14. Julio Santa Ana's article on "The Influence of Bonhoeffer on the Theology of Liberation" *(Ecumenical Review* 28 [2 April 1976]) was the first essay to explore this theme. See also G. Clarke Chapman, "Bonhoeffer and Liberation Theology," in *Ethical Responsibility*, ed. Godsey and Kelly (Netherlands: Kok Pharos, 1991).

15. Timothy Yates, *Christian Mission in the Twentieth Century* (Cambridge: Cambridge University Press, 1994), 57 f.

16. *E*, 114.

17. Kelly, *Liberating Faith*, 160 (quoting from *E*).

18. *GS 1*, 61.

19. *GS 2*, 182.

20. Geffrey Kelly, "'Unconscious Christianity' and the 'Anonymous Christian' in the Theology of Dietrich Bonhoeffer and Karl Rahner," *Marquette University Journal*, vol. 9, no. 1-2 (1995): 123.

21. *GS 2*, 157.

22. I thank Geffrey Kelly for this insight.

23. *LPP*, 280.

24. Ibid., 348.

25. *DB*, 132.

26. Larry Rasmussen, *Dietrich Bonhoeffer: His Significance for North Americans* (Minneapolis: Fortress, 1990), 70.

27. Ibid. Quoted from Dietrich Bonhoeffer, "Thoughts on the Day of the Baptism of Dietrich Wilhelm Rüdiger Bethge," *LPP*, 300.

28. Most commentators reduce worldly action to mere ethics. By allowing mission to substitute here for ethics, the nature of Christian action in the world is broadened.

29. David Bosch, *Transforming Mission: Paradigm Shifts in Theology of Mission* (Maryknoll: Orbis, 1991), 376 f.

30. *LPP*, 279.

31. Ibid., 360.

32. See Bonhoeffer's poem "Powers of Good," ibid., 400.

33. This formulation of the double task of mission comes directly from Friedrich Schleiermacher. See Braaten, *The Flaming Center*, 12 f.

34. Martin Kähler, *Schriften zu Christologie und Mission* (Munich: Kaiser, 1971), 190.

35. Ernst Feil, *The Theology of Dietrich Bonhoeffer* (Minneapolis: Fortress Press, 1985), 167 f.

36. J. C. Hoekendijk, *Kirche und Volk in der deutschen Missionswissenschaft* (Munich, 1967).

37. *LPP*, 300-2.

38. Compare with Bosch's list in *Transforming Mission*, 349 f.

39. Kelly, *Liberating Faith*, 153.

Healing the Wound: A Return to China with Bonhoeffer

Keith Clements

To contribute an essay in honor of such a dear friend and colleague as Burton Nelson is a sheer pleasure. Burton is one of the reasons why I am grateful to belong to the International Bonhoeffer Society. The shared times we have experienced in places as diverse as Hirschluch in the former German Democratic Republic, my alma maters of Cambridge and Oxford, his own habitat of Chicago and North Park Seminary, and the painful combination of natural beauty and human suffering on South Africa's Western Cape (not to mention a surprise encounter in a departure lounge at Heathrow Airport) have for me underlined what Dietrich Bonhoeffer wrote to Eberhard Bethge in his letter from prison of 21 August 1944: "It is certain that we are in a fellowship that sustains us." I shall always cherish two memories of Burton in particular. One was a "happy hour" for the members of the editorial board of the Bonhoeffer Translation Project meeting in Chicago in September 1989. We sat in his North Park garden in the evening light, drank wine, and let our hair down as only true friends in a shared enterprise can do. The other was when he spent a day at Bristol Baptist College, where I was then teaching. By his avuncular interest in and enthusiasm for what they were doing, he endeared himself to a group of students from the college and the University of Bristol who were working on Bonhoeffer for their term or postgraduate theses. When we sat down together as staff and students for lunch, he turned to me and said, "This really is *Life Together!*" To summarize what Burton has meant to me, I would say that it is a very rare combination of intellectual enthusiasm, deep human compassion, and—I use the words wholly positively—a beautiful piety.

As well as a shared enthusiasm for understanding the life and work of Dietrich Bonhoeffer, however, Burton Nelson and I have something else in common. We were both born in China of missionary parents. It is by reflecting on this basal factor in my own life, and in connection with certain themes in the thought of Dietrich Bonhoeffer, that I would like to shape this grateful tribute to the friendship and intellectual stimulus I have received from Burton.

THE CHINA MISSIONARY ENDEAVOR: A RETRIEVABLE PAST?

For a hundred years, from the mid-nineteenth to the mid-twentieth century, China was the scene of the greatest-ever missionary exertion by Western Christianity. My parents were part of this enterprise, serving in the China Inland Mission, the Protestant agency that was founded by the redoubtable Hudson Taylor in 1865 and became the largest mission in the whole world. My mother went to China from Australia, where her family had emigrated from England just after the First World War. My father went out to China from London in 1931. They met and married in Chungking, and served their first term together in Ichang in charge of a transit point for missionaries journeying up and down the Yangtze River. After furlough they made their way back to Chungking in 1938, circumnavigating the difficulties caused by the Japanese invasion of eastern China, and were dispatched on a perilous journey by river and on foot to Gulin, a small, remote town set amidst the mountains of southern Sichuan. There I was born, their third son, in May 1943 (I have always slightly regretted that Bonhoeffer did not write a letter from prison on the actual day of my birth, and also that Eberhard and Renate Bethge chose another date for their wedding!). In late 1944, on medical advice relating to one of my brothers, and much against their inclination, my parents decided to leave China. We had an adventurous journey into India and thence back to England. For a long time my parents hoped that this would be a temporary exit. In fact, it was for good.

I was very small when we left China. My earliest *clear* memories are of life back in England. But I always have the impression of remembering China. I was continually told stories of life in Gulin: about the colorful characters in the town and in the small congregation my parents established; about the people who came from miles around when they started a simple medical dispensary; about Lao-Ben-Yang, the cook who was a member of the household and who looked after me much of the time (learned from her, no doubt, my first spoken words were in Chinese). Fuh-In-Wan, a place up in the hills which was a center for mission among the Miao tribespeople, seemed to me a source of stories as remarkable as any in the *Arabian Nights*, as I heard of the breathtaking mountain landscape, encounters with brigands, and devastating thunderstorms. I was brought up knowing China as a place of almost magical beauty and adventure.

But I learned of it too, eventually, as a place of the past. There could be no return. By the time my brother's health problems had been resolved, it was too late to go back. Mao Tse-tung's Long March and the revolution of 1949 saw to that. From being the scene of the greatest Western missionary inflow, Protestant and Catholic, China almost overnight saw the greatest missionary exodus in history. I suppose I grew up simply accepting this. After all, life was here and now in England: cricket and soccer, comics and films. Teenage loves and school examinations were enough to occupy the adolescent soul. But to have been born in China always gave one a kind of pride. None of my peers had had that privilege. When Alan Burgess's book *The Small Woman* made famous the English missionary Gladys Aylward, and Ingrid Bergman in her starring role in the film *The Inn of the Sixth Happiness* made her more famous still, some of the kudos seemed to wash over oneself.

Later historical awareness brought problems, however. One learned about the Western imperialist and commercial inroads into nineteenth-century China, of the Opium Wars and the Treaty of Nanking, and of the ways in which the massive missionary enterprise had largely followed, benefited from, and often been protected by the gunboat. Still later, to the student of missionary history came the revelation that in the first half of this century many Chinese Christians themselves were resentful at the paternalism of the Western missionary presence, which they felt to be obstructive of the growth of a genuinely Chinese and united church. The missionary exodus that followed the Great Revolution was by no means wholly an expulsion by the wicked Communists. In many cases the departure was encouraged by the Chinese Christians, who viewed a continuing Western presence as a hindrance to their witness in the new situation. One had been told that, following the revolution, the patriotic "Three-Self" movement (for a self-supporting, self-governing, and self-propagating church) was simply a front for the Communist-dominated church, while the "true church" was underground. Now, it appeared, it was not so simple as that. The concept of a "Three-Self" church had been born much earlier, in the thinking of no less a person than the pioneer Burma missionary Adoniram Judson. Few people of the missionary generation were prepared to admit the question marks over the story of Western missions in China, a notable exception being David Paton in his angry book *Christian Missions and the Judgment of God*.[1]

All this now added up to a formidable difficulty in owning my past and my inheritance. Had I been born out of a hugely mistaken enterprise? I suppose that my problem was but one tiny, personal focusing of the whole problem of being a Westerner in the late twentieth century, faced with the guilt of generations of exploitation of Africa, Asia, and Latin America. Did I now have a past, a tradition, that I could own with any sense of respect and gratitude?

BONHOEFFER AND THE PAST

Maybe this was why, perhaps subconsciously, in my reading of Dietrich Bonhoeffer during the late 1970s and 1980s I was drawn again and again to his emphasis on the value and importance of consciously standing in a tradition. For Bonhoeffer, one vital ingredient in a fully human existence is an awareness of a historical legacy for which one can be grateful, and which supplies the theme to be taken up into one's responsibility for the future. Bonhoeffer's lifelong love for his own family tradition and for much in his German cultural legacy is well known.[2] It became especially important to him during the uncertainties of war and the perils of involvement in the resistance. On a train journey in 1942 he writes to Eberhard Bethge's younger brother:

> While I'm going through ancient cities and the summer countryside in the glorious sunshine, I keep thinking of you. . . . I have a life which is hardly like yours at all, and which must be strange to you. And yet it is in this long journey, looking at the cathedrals of Naumberg, Bamberg, Nuremberg, at the cultivated fields which are sometimes so poor, and the thought that all this has been work and joy for many, many generations, that gives me confidence that here there is still common ground, a common task, a common hope, something which overcomes the gap between the generations. When one thinks of that, one's own short personal life becomes relatively unimportant; one begins to think in terms of greater periods and tasks.[3]

From prison in May 1944, in the famous "baptismal sermon" to Eberhard and Renate Bethge's son, he writes, "To be deeply rooted in the soil of the past makes life harder, but it also makes it richer and more vigorous. There are in human life certain fundamental truths to which people will always return sooner or later."[4] Indeed, it was the prison experience which, as Ruth Zerner and others have shown,[5] gave a special psychological urgency to Bonhoeffer's "retrieval" of his own past, seen particularly in his attempts at writing fiction and poetry. It was not, however, only his immediate, familial past with which he wished to reassociate himself, but also the great intellectual tradition of Germany as witnessed to, for example, by Harnack's *History of the Prussian Academy*. To Eberhard Bethge he writes disparagingly of the current tendency to return romantically to the eighteenth century and earlier (not to mention the supposed

Teutonic Age glorified beyond belief by Nazi mythology) at the expense of the nineteenth: "Who bothers at all now about the work and achievements of our grandfathers, and how much of what they knew have we already forgotten? I believe that people will one day be quite amazed at what was achieved in that period, which is now so disregarded and so little known."[6]

The sense of *time* was central to Bonhoeffer, and therewith nothing was more perilous to responsible human existence than *forgetting*. It is a theme that emerges powerfully in his *Ethics*, above all in his depiction of the "void" that he saw in the contemporary European mind:

> In the face of the peril of the void there is no longer any meaning in the question of the historical inheritance which requires of those who receive it that they shall both develop it in the present and hand it on to the future. There is no future and there is no past. There is only the moment which has been rescued from the void, and the desire to snatch from the void the next moment as well. Already what belongs to yesterday is consigned to oblivion, and the affairs of tomorrow are still too far off to impose any obligation today. The burden of yesterday is shaken off by glorifying the misty past, and tomorrow's task is evaded by speaking rather of the coming millennium. Nothing makes a permanent impression and nothing imposes a lasting obligation. A sign of the deep forgetfulness of the present time is the film which is erased from the memory as soon as it is over.[7]

To be fully human, therefore, includes the sense of a past that can be retrieved and owned in gratitude and worked upon for the sake of the coming generation.

RETURN TO CHINA

If what Bonhoeffer said was true—and I could not help suspecting that it was—how could I deal with the fact that, not only by circumstances but also ethically, I felt excised from a vital part of my past? "Forgetting" was impossible, and endless efforts at rationalization or self-justification were proving futile. The facts were all too real. The answer came another way, not long after both my parents had died. It was not my own answer, but an answer given to me by others, by the *only* people who were in a position to offer it.

In May 1994 I returned to China as a member of a British ecumenical study team. As it happened, a good deal of our time was to be spent in Sichuan. From Hong Kong we flew to Chungking. I visited the old site of the mission house where my parents had met and the church where they had been married. The day of our arrival was in fact my birthday, which provided the local representatives of the China Christian Council with a pretext for adding even more festivity to the warmth of their welcome. The real excitement, however, came with the prospect of actually getting to Gulin itself. It was not until almost leaving Hong Kong that we had learned that our party had been granted special permission to journey to Gulin, that area having been strictly out of bounds to foreigners. As it happened, we were the first Westerners to be seen there for forty years. I need not recount my feelings on the two-day road journey, which had taken my parents many days by junk and on foot in 1938, as the scenery of mountain and river progressively unfolded, just as my father had described it in his unpublished memoirs. Gulin was still essentially as he had portrayed it, and as I too had pictured it from those early childhood stories and possibly (who knows?) my own vaguest memories: grey roofs of cylindrical tiles, crowded streets, the river slowly swishing through. Only a small community of Christians remained, but they included one very old man who could just recall our family, and the welcome was in every way a homecoming. We were taken to the place where my parents had lived, where their chapel and medical dispensary had stood—now much changed but the basic architecture still fitting their description—and where I had been born on a stifling night amid smoky oil-lamps and mosquitoes. On our return to the hotel, we found two other Christians waiting for us. Peasant farmers, tired and poorly clad, they had heard of our imminent visit and had walked thirty miles over the hills to meet us. Clearly, something remarkable was happening. That night for our evening prayers I decided that nothing was more fitting than to read T. S. Eliot:

> We shall not cease from exploration
> And the end of all our exploring
> Will be to arrive where we started
> And know the place for the first time.

But all this was as nothing compared to the next day, when we journeyed along deeply rutted roads up into the hills to Fuh-In-Wan. We had to leave our bus and walk the last mile or two down the steep, narrow path. As we approached, we heard the sound of singing. Soon we saw them: nearly two hundred Miao people who had been waiting twenty-four hours for our arrival and had prepared a feast for us. The old chapel had been commandeered by the authorities as a school, but the people still clearly regarded it as theirs. Even the local officials sent to mind us seemed to be touched, as well as highly nervous of what was going on.

We were welcome. I was welcomed back like a long-lost son. We were taken to a simple graveyard and shown the grave of the young daughter of two of my parents' older colleagues: "The loneliest grave in all the world," said one of our party. After the hours of feasting came the most emotional farewell I have ever experienced, amid the chorus "God be with you till we meet again," sung in Miao. On the long, hot trek back up to the bus, I tried to reflect on what it all meant. Yes, for all the questions about the old missionary endeavor, it was now being remembered with gratitude. It had been deeply costly in personal terms. While still in Gulin the previous night, it had begun to dawn upon me just what it must have meant to my parents: the hazardous journeyings, the sheer poverty and disease, the isolation and loneliness (they only heard of the Normandy invasion two weeks after the event). Edmond Tang, my Hong Kong Chinese colleague, said we had experienced a retrieval of the missionary history.

A few days later in Nanjing, the head of the China Christian Council, Bishop Ding, summed it all up in saying that Chinese Christians were now in a position to offer thanks to the Western churches for bringing the gospel. They still believed in a self-reliant Chinese church, but on that basis were now looking forward to a new *partnership* with their Western sisters and brothers.

We had experienced *grace* at Gulin and Fuh-In-Wan. My past had been offered back to me as a gift; and only as a gift from those people, representative of all the suffering of China, could I have retrieved it. And it had to come at the right time, the "now" to which Bishop Ding referred. Time alone does not heal, but the healing processes need time.

THE HEALING OF THE WOUND

In his *Ethics*, under the heading "Justification and the Healing of the Wound," Dietrich Bonhoeffer writes with both insight and restraint of the mystery of the overcoming of guilt in the life of the individual Christian, of the Church, and of the world of nations.[8] A complete breach with the guilty past takes place through the Church's confession of guilt and the Church's taking the form of the cross. For the nations the process is more indirect, "there is only a healing of the wound, a cicatrization of guilt, in the return to order, to justice, to peace, and to granting of free passage to the Church's proclamation of Jesus Christ." Bonhoeffer writes realistically that the wheel of history cannot be turned back: "Not all the wounds inflicted can be healed, but what matters is that there shall be no further wounds."

In the history of the Western interaction with China, it is not in fact quite so simple to separate the churches from (to reapply Bonhoeffer's words to this case) the "imperialistic conquest" which was "pursued amid contempt for law and justice and brutal mishandling of the weak." The Western churches have had to wait for their own realization of their need for confession, and for the time when their Chinese sisters and brothers felt able to accept and welcome them again. In this welcome, at the right time, comes the freedom to acknowledge also what was actually good and Christ-like in that former history: the selfless love that did motivate many missionaries, mine and Burton's parents among them, and which can *now* be disentangled from the darker side of the Western enterprise precisely because that darker side is honestly admitted. The fact that the positive thread in the history is now affirmed by our Chinese sisters and brothers, not just snatched at desperately by ourselves, gives us the grace to own it too.

Therefore I do now have an inheritance with which I can identify, and which I can cherish as of continuing value for contemporary responsibility and the future. Actually, going back to China, pondering that experience, and rereading my parents' accounts of their China days in the light of it have opened my eyes to something I had not quite seen before. Why did they wish to return to China after the war? The religiously correct missionary answer would of course be "Because they wanted to preach the gospel." I think the real reason was more basic. They had simply fallen in love with China, even with poor, remote little Gulin, and would have much preferred to live there. In his memoirs my father recalls how once in Gulin one of their Chinese friends, having referred to someone from a neighboring province as a "foreigner," and my father having asked, "Then what does that make us?" replied, "*You* are not a foreigner; you are one of us." *That* is the tradition that I am glad to have retrieved, a story of how, through friendship, strangers can learn to identify with and even re-incarnate something of themselves in other cultures. That is both a gift from my past and a hope for my world.

So I am deeply grateful to have been able to experience not only the retrieval of my own past, but the beginnings of a new relationship between the Chinese churches and the ecumenical fellowship; between, on the one hand, the generation of Burton's and my parents and, on the other hand, the new, rising, and rapidly increasing generation of Chinese Christians who are making room for themselves regardless of what the state does; between the land of our birth and the West. Let the last word be Bonhoeffer's:

> The "justification and renewal" of the West, therefore, will come only when justice, order and peace are in one way or another restored, when past guilt is thereby "forgiven," when it is no longer imagined that what has been done can be undone by means of punitive measures and reprisals, and when the Church of Jesus Christ, as the fountain-head of all forgiveness, justification and renewal, is given room to do her work among the nations.[9]

ENDNOTES

1. David Paton, *Christian Missions and the Judgment of God* (London: SCM Press, 1953).

2. Cf. Keith Clements, *A Patriotism for Today: Love of Country in Dialogue with the Witness of Dietrich Bonhoeffer* (London: Collins, 1986), chap . 5, "Accepting a Heritage."

3. Dietrich Bonhoeffer, "True Patriotism," in *LLP*, 136.

4. Ibid., 295.

5. In Dietrich Bonhoeffer, *Fiction from Prison: Gathering Up the Past*, ed. R. and E. Bethge with C. Green (Philadelphia: Fortress Press, 1981).

6. *LPP*, 227.

7. *E*, 85 f.

8. Ibid., 95-97.

9. Ibid., 97.

CONTEMPORARY ISSUES

Bonhoeffer, Democracy, and the Public Tasks of Theology[1]

Wayne Whitson Floyd Jr.

T he time of most of Dietrich Bonhoeffer's adult life, between this century's two world wars and amidst the failed experiment of the Weimar Republic, was—despite its unarguable uniqueness—a time sharing many characteristics with our own. It has been described as a time when most of the Protestant clergy were anti-Marxist, fearing Communism, a time when the rhetoric of religion was regularly employed by Christians as a means by which to condemn the dangers of secularism, the loss of nationalistic fervor, and other perceived symptoms of moral degeneracy. Few saw the dangers in the church's unholy alliance with the National Socialist Party; fewer still acted in the public sphere in light of their misgivings.

It was a time when faithfulness and idolatry often wore similar clothing—as perhaps they always do—a time when, in Bonhoeffer's later words, "evil appear[ed] in the form of light, beneficence, loyalty and renewal" of blood and soil, nationalism and strength; a time during which "every available alternative seemed equally intolerable, repugnant, and futile."[2] Yet this was a time in which Bonhoeffer had to decide, like thousands of his colleagues, what to do about being a Christian in the face of the rise of National Socialism—which promised to save Germany from all its evils and to restore a sense of national purpose, pride, and stature in the world community. It was a time in the not too distant past of great danger, which we fail to remember only at our own peril. Perhaps it was a time from which there are still important lessons to be learned for the future of democracy, as well.

Yet Dietrich Bonhoeffer's own understanding of democracy provokes in even a sympathetic reader in the 1990s a certain perplexity. On the one hand, given the new experiments in democracy being undertaken after the reunification of Germany or the dissolution of the Soviet Union, Bonhoeffer already in the early 1940s had raised some intriguing questions about "why a democracy with a Christian foundation," such as he understood the United States to be, "has never been successfully established on the European continent," or why "democracy and Christianity have always been regarded [in Europe] as in some sort of opposition, while in America democracy can be extolled as *the* form of the Christian state."[3] But on the other hand, one is quite a bit less sure of the accuracy of his claim that, in contrast to the French Revolution, "American democracy is not founded upon the emancipated [human being] but, quite on the contrary, upon the kingdom of God and the limitation of all earthly powers by the sovereignty of God."[4] Likewise, Bonhoeffer raises unresolved questions about the relationship between democratic thinking and the Christian religion given, for example, his assertion in the *Ethics* that the divine mandates of church, marriage, culture, and government do not have their authority "from below," from the people, but from above, from God.[5]

This essay, however, does not so much inquire into what this theologian, Dietrich Bonhoeffer, said *about* democracy in the midst of the collapse of Weimar Germany more than a half-century ago. Rather, my concern here is with what Bonhoeffer still has to contribute *to* our own participation in the democratic experiment and our understanding of the public tasks of theology as a potential—perhaps even a needed—voice in the forum of democracy, particularly here in the United States. The democratic revolution in Western society, both in France and in the American colonies of Great Britain, has now for two centuries proclaimed *liberté, égalité, fraternité*—liberty, equality, fraternity.[6] Yet each of these watchwords of democracy, we now are beginning to see, reveals not only something about the supposed *essence* of democracy, but also perhaps even more about democracy's *unfulfilled longings*. And each of these terms poses questions *to*—and needs to be addressed *by*—those other traditions of the West that share in a concern with freedom, justice, and authentic community, particularly the traditions of Christian theology in whose fields Burton Nelson has labored during the past generation.[7]

LIBERTÉ: FREEDOM "FROM"—FREEDOM "FOR"

Bonhoeffer was aware of the propensity of modern humanity to construe its liberty, its freedom, by means of a *via negativa*—as "freedom *from* . . ." This may be in the form of an escape from despotic, authoritarian political control, or it may come about through the disestablishment of state churches or curbing the theocratic impulse. Freedom defined in this way means a release *from* any of the various heteronomous powers that challenge human autonomy, that hold humanity back from the realization of its own maturity. Or freedom may be an escape from what Immanuel Kant called "self-incurred tutelage," that "laziness and cowardice" which rob humanity of the exercise of its freedoms and its full participation in the Age of Enlightenment, the New World Order.[8] Either way, freedom may be thought to imply a new beginning, a new Eden, a return to unconditioned possibility prior to all necessity, all determinism.

Bonhoeffer also knew about human nature's Pelagian desire to trade true freedom for mere license. On his visits to America he encountered and reflected upon our "freedoms *of* . . ."—for example, expression and religion—and our "freedoms *to*" act however we wish, so long as it does not interfere inordinately with another's right to do the same. In the sociology and politics of race in Great Depression America, Bonhoeffer, during his year at Union Seminary, glimpsed through the lens of Harlem the anxieties caused by such freedom. And he knew in his own place and time how tempting it could be to trade genuine liberty for the security of order, for a leader, a *Führer*.[9]

His own distinctive contribution to our understanding of freedom, however, was the manner in which he challenged us to rediscover, as a gift of the gospel of Christ, a *positive* view of freedom—the "freedom *for* . . ." that looks beyond our own gains from freedom and learns to ask "for the sake of what" freedom is exercised. "In the language of the Bible," Bonhoeffer wrote in *Creation and Fall*, "freedom is not something [humanity] has for [itself] but something [it] has for others."[10] He challenges us with his insight that there is no freedom that is not a bound-freedom, a freedom defined by the claim of the actual need of the concrete other—and thus a freedom drawn out precisely into the public square. "In truth," Bonhoeffer concludes, "freedom is a relationship between two persons. Being free means 'being free for the other,' because the other has bound me to [them]. Only in relationship with the other am I free. . . . The concept of freedom only exists for us as 'being free for.'"[11]

Bonhoeffer still challenges us with his assertion that any freedom that is worth its name must be exercised by the Christian as a freedom-in-responsibility[12] not just *to* or *for* but in dangerous solidarity *with* the other—a worldly, public freedom. "Responsibility and freedom are corresponding concepts," he wrote in his *Ethics*. "Responsibility presupposes freedom and freedom can consist only in responsibility"—"Responsibility is the freedom . . . which is given only in the obligation to God and to our neighbor."[13] What would such freedom look like, we in the United States might well need to ask, "now that we must conclude our long experiment of running away from . . . each other"[14] to the frontier—now that the inescapable responsibilities of an increasingly urbanized nation finally may be forcing us to define the nature of that freedom we would retain, defend, stake our very lives upon?

ÉGALITÉ: EQUALITY OF LAW—EQUALITY OF LOVE

Bonhoeffer also knew something about the difficulties human beings have with the egalitarian ideal, with equality—how quickly we turn aside from the equal application of genuine love to the unequal interests of partiality, to address which we turn to the protections of the law. He understood how willing we are to settle for the law's demand of benign tolerance of the other, rather than for justice applied with the radical equality of love. Bonhoeffer challenges us still with his bold recovery of the centrality of the command of Jesus to love not merely those to whom we are partial—family, friends, and the neighbor who is close to us—but those who are strangers. "This means that the commandment of love for our neighbor," Bonhoeffer wrote, "also does not imply a law which restricts our responsibility solely to our neighbor in terms of space, to the [person] whom I encounter socially, professionally or in my family. My neighbor may well be one who is extremely remote from me, and one who is extremely remote from me may well be my neighbor."[15] For once we commit ourselves to be "free *for*" the other, Bonhoeffer saw, we will begin to learn the public scandal of the genuine equality of love.

At the minimum, this means for the Christian an encounter with the gift of the stranger, the other human being whose sheer existence sets a limit on my egocentricity, my claim to atomistic individuality. As Bonhoeffer wrote of this encounter in *Life Together,*

> The other person is a burden to the Christian, in fact for the Christian most of all. The other person never becomes a burden at all for the pagans. They simply stay clear of every burden the other person may create for them. However, . . . only as a burden is the other really a brother or sister and not just an object to be controlled. The burden of human beings was even for God so heavy that God had to go to the cross suffering under it. . . . Therefore, the Bible can also characterize the whole life of the Christian as carrying the cross.[16]

It is the very "freedom of the other" that shocks us, that intrudes into our solipsistic solitude. "But if Christians allow God to create God's own image in others, Christians are allowing them their own freedom." And to allow the other their freedom—and thus their equality in the eyes of love—we must allow God's own freedom as well. This dual forbearance, of God's freedom and our neighbor's, is the foundation of the equality of love.[17] For what more does equality in the eyes of love mean than that others are given the very freedom to be themselves that I desire for myself? For, Bonhoeffer continues, "all that we mean by human nature, individuality, and talent is part of the other person's freedom—as are the other's weaknesses and peculiarities which so sorely try our patience, and everything that produces the plethora of clashes, differences and arguments between me and the other. Here, bearing the burden of the other means tolerating the reality of the other's creation by God, affirming it, and in bearing with it, breaking through to delight in it."[18]

To learn not merely to tolerate, but to delight in, the freedom of the other is not the maximal requirement for the Christian. It is a minimal description of our utter faith in God's ways, of our trust that all humanity is offered a gift of grace equally undeserved. It means the recognition, indeed our delight, that

> God did not make others as I would have made them. God did not give them to me so that I could dominate and control them, but so that I might find the Creator by means of them. Now other people, in the freedom with which they were created, become an occasion for me to rejoice, whereas before they were only a nuisance and trouble for me. God does not want me to mold others into the image that seems good to me, that is, into my own image. Instead, in their freedom from me God made other people in God's own image. I can never know in advance how God's image should appear in others. That image always takes on a completely new and unique form whose origin is found solely in God's free and sovereign act of creation. To me that form may seem strange, even ungodly. But God creates every person in the image of God's Son, the Crucified, and this image, likewise, certainly looked strange and ungodly to me before I grasped it.[19]

The boundaries of the hospitality of the gospel, Bonhoeffer discovered, are both wider and more scandalous the more closely we attend to the figure of Jesus—incarnate, crucified, and resurrected from the dead.

Indeed, in *The Cost of Discipleship* Bonhoeffer extends the sphere of the equality of love beyond neighbor, beyond the surprise of the stranger, to the equality of love due even our enemies. Writing of Jesus' words as told in Matthew 5:43-48, Bonhoeffer concludes: "Love is defined in uncompromising terms as the love of our enemies."[20] And lest we would attempt to restrict our love to only those least threatening among our enemies, Bonhoeffer concludes that "Christian love draws no distinction between one enemy and another, except that the more bitter our enemy's hatred, the greater [the enemy's] need of love."[21] The "supreme scandal," according to Bonhoeffer, is that this "extraordinary" demand is not just what Jesus is said to have done, with messianic extravagance. It is rather the very definition of the minimum way in which "the disciples differ from the heathen." As Bonhoeffer continues, "We can love our kith and kin, our fellow-countrymen and our friends, whether we are Christians or not, and there is no need for Jesus to teach us that. But he takes that kind of love for granted, and in contrast asserts that we must love our enemies." This is the "extraordinary," the "unusual," the distinctive and defining quality of the Christian life.[22]

Christian freedom-for is based on the radical equality of love that does not merely stretch so far as to include the enemy, but finds itself centered there. "For Jesus Christ lived in the midst of his enemies. . . . In the end all his disciples abandoned him. On the cross he was all alone, surrounded by criminals and the jeering crowds."[23] Four centuries earlier, none other than Luther himself had said, "Whoever will not suffer this does not want to be part of the rule of Christ; such a person wants to be among friends and sit among the roses and lilies, not with the bad people but the religious people. O you blasphemers and betrayers of Christ! If Christ had done what you are doing, who would ever have been saved?"[24]

FRATERNITÉ: LIKE RELATING TO LIKE— EMANCIPATORY SOLIDARITY

This is radical "fraternity," a truly revolutionary form of emancipatory solidarity, not just a "relation of like to like,"[25] "kith and kin," but a community of emancipatory solidarity with strangers and—strangest of all— even with our enemies. As Christians, we move toward such community "by seeing our enemies," Bonhoeffer preached in 1938, "as they really are"—by seeing them "as those for whom Christ died, whom Christ loves."[26] He understood, however, how easily we trade the messianic call for such community for the safety of the illusions of what Don Shriver has called "our ancient, luxurious individualism."[27] Bonhoeffer understood the fears engendered by the encounter with the other—my neighbor, stranger, or enemy—fears that the other is a threat to myself and my privileges, rather than the one who calls me to authentic freedom, the one who calls me into real community. In the public community of the visible Church, as well as the larger communities of public discourse, Bonhoeffer challenges us with the task of learning *from others in community* about who I am and the responsibilities I am called to undertake.

To break through our individualism–the religion "of inwardness and conscience"[28]—to the risk of community is nothing other than participation in the breakthrough of God becoming incarnate in the world. For "when God's Son took on flesh, he truly and bodily, out of pure grace, took on our being, our nature, ourselves. . . . Now we are in him. Wherever he is, he bears our flesh, he bears us. And, where he is, there we are too–in the incarnation, on the cross, and in his resurrection. We belong to him because we are in him. That is why the scriptures call *us* the body of Christ."[29] And conversely, this is what Bonhoeffer had meant when in *Sanctorum Communio* he called the Church "*Christ* existing as community."[30]

This breakthrough from the relation of like to like into emancipatory solidarity in community does not occur, however, only within the *Gemeinde*, the congregation of the Church. It makes possible new forms of community in society that are based not on our fears, but on our freedom—a concrete freedom to be not just *for* but *with* the other in the equality of love, to take part in that authentic community which comes only when I am bound to my neighbor.[31] It leads toward a new vision of human community based not on exclusivist privilege, but on common need—the community of those gifted by that "alien righteousness" of which Luther once spoke,[32] the community of the Crucified, which includes God's enemies and our own.

Bonhoeffer's own experiences in the Confessing Church and the European ecumenical movement made him all too cognizant, however, of the difficulties in thinking of community beyond national, ethnic, or confessional barriers. And our own ventures with ecumenism—much less with interfaith dialogue with Buddhists, Muslims, Jews, or Hindus—remind us of just how far we still have to go. Yet a part of Bonhoeffer's gift to our generation and the next is the reminder that the Christian above all must remember that to learn from others is not just to learn about the stranger, or even the enemy; it is the way we go about learning about ourselves as well. For the move to authentic community requires us to recognize that we can learn about how to be faithful Christians in our encounter with faithful Muslims and Jews, that we can learn how to be patriotic North Americans by learning from the experiences of former East as well as West Germans, from South Africans and South Americans, from the members of the former Soviet bloc. "Freedom-for," "the equality of love," and the "emancipatory solidarity" of authentically inclusive community all broaden the concerns of theology beyond the confines of the cloister, the Church, the faithful, drawing theology out into the public realm, inviting the theologian to find her or his proper function there, perhaps preeminently.

SUMMARY: BONHOEFFER AND PUBLIC THEOLOGY

Bonhoeffer challenges us with a new vision of the public role of theology—theology exercised "in correspondence to reality" both within the Church and in the broader "publics" within which ecclesial communities live.[33] Such a public theology fosters, celebrates, and yet lives beyond democracy. It knows, understands, and values democracy's virtues of freedom, equality, and participation in community. And it transforms, radicalizes, perhaps even revolutionizes these values—for their own sake, and yet in light of the gospel.

Freedom *for* the other means the freedom to act—sometimes even act out—in public. The theologian's public role is to help the Church—in the middle of the village—to see the truth of its exercise of this freedom. To act in freedom is to act in the world "in the place of other persons"; it is "the complete surrender of one's own life to the other person."[34] Bonhoeffer calls this *Stellvertretung*, intentional vicarious action on behalf of others with no question of their merit. And when freedom has *not* been exercised "for the other," it is the theologian who must call for confession. In his *Ethics* Bonhoeffer told the truth of the failed freedom of his own time—the Church's complicity in mass death and genocide, which preceded and formed the context within which we must try to understand his own involvement in the plots against Hitler:

> The Church confesses . . . its timidity, its evasiveness, its dangerous concessions. . . . It has often denied to the outcast and to the despised the compassion which it owes them. It was silent when it should have cried out because the blood of the innocent was crying aloud to heaven. . . . The Church confesses that it has taken in vain the name of Jesus Christ, for . . . it has stood by while violence and wrong were being committed under cover of this name.[35]

The public vocation of the theologian is to foster freedom for the other and to enable the confession of all failures to achieve such freedom, and thus the failure of human responsibility.

It is the public role of the theologian to interpret equality, democracy's egalitarian ideal, in light of the truth of the justice of God, who suffered the injustice of death on the cross, not for the sake of just the righteous, but for the sake of even God's enemies. Against all calls for vengeance against society's and God's enemies, it is the public responsibility of the theologian to place the Church again and again into the midst of its enemies—to demand that the Church be a church that exists for the sake of the love of its enemies, a church that remembers redemption, a church that forgoes vengefulness.

Free *for* others, free for *Stellvertretung*, human beings are freed for fraternity, participation in the emancipatory solidarity of authentic community. "The church is the church," Bonhoeffer concluded in the summer of 1944, "only when it exists for others."[36] Theology can only be true to the word it seeks to speak to and for the Church when theology remembers that God's word came to humanity in the public ministry of Jesus, the Word made flesh to free us for others—even our enemies, who can now be seen in the light of the equality of God's love—and to point us toward each other in community as the public place through which God chooses to come to us still. "The church," Bonhoeffer wrote, "must share in the secular problems of ordinary human life, not dominating, but helping and serving. It must tell [people] of every calling what it means to live in Christ, to exist for others."[37]

In the final autumn of his life, Bonhoeffer wrote a poem in which he envisioned Moses, having accompanied Israel in its escape from bondage into liberty, now looking back from the perspective of the future of his people. Facing death, and knowing that the fruits of freedom, as well as the promise of equality in community, still lay in a tomorrow beyond his own participation, Moses in Bonhoeffer's poem now says, "You let me glimpse the promise through the veil, / you let my people go, their Lord to hail. / . . . / God, who punishes and then forgives, / this people I have truly loved now lives." Dietrich Bonhoeffer died with only a glimpse of what lay ahead for the coming generation, which is now our own. He could only imagine the responsibilities of freedom, the challenges of equality, the redemptive power of authentic community that might already be approaching us out of the future. And fifty years after Bonhoeffer's death, we are those who must dare ask—from the middle of the village, with all the ambiguities of this experiment called democracy—the question Bonhoeffer asked the Church "After Ten Years" of Nazism: "Are we still of any use today?"[38] It is in lives such as those of Burton Nelson that we hear humanity's resolute reply.

ENDNOTES

1. A previous version of this essay was published as "'These People I Have Loved Now Live': Bonhoeffer, Democracy and Public Theology," in *Luther, Bonhoeffer and the Public Realm. Lutheran Theological Seminary Bulletin* 76/4 (Fall 1995): 27-39.

2. *LPP*, 3.

3. Bonhoeffer, "Protestantism without Reformation," *NRS*, 108.

4. *E*, 104.

5. Ibid., 289. On this and other questions about Bonhoeffer's conception of democracy as evidenced in the *Ethics*, see the "Nachwort der Herausgeber" of the new critical edition of the *Ethik*, edited by Ilse Tödt, Heinz Eduard Tödt, Ernst Feil, and Clifford Green (Munich: Kaiser Verlag, 1992), 432-33.

6. See *E*, 99.

7. Throughout this essay I will translate *fraternity* in terms of inclusive community and the rights of participation therein, as suggested by Wolfgang Huber and Heinz-Eduard Tödt in *Menschenrechte: Perspektiven einer menschlichen Welt* (Stuttgart, Berlin: Kreuz Verlag, 1977). The democratic revolution has not by any means been limited to "the West"–particularly Europe and the Americas; but the focus of the current essay is with the enduring challenges of this European experiment especially for North Americans.

8. Immanuel Kant, "What Is Enlightenment?" in *On History* 3, ed. Lewis White Beck (Indianapolis: Bobbs-Merrill, 1963). See Steven Schroeder, "The End of History and the New World Order," in *Theology and the Practice of Responsibility, Essays on Dietrich Bonhoeffer*, ed. Wayne Whitson Floyd Jr. and Charles Marsh (Valley Forge, Pa.: Trinity Press International, 1994), 21-38.

9. See Bonhoeffer's "The Leader and the Individual in the Younger Generation," in *NRS*, 190-204.

10. *CF*, 37.

11. Ibid.

12. See Jean Bethke Elshtain, "Freedom and Responsibility in a World Come of Age," in Floyd and Marsh, *Theology and the Practice of Responsibility*, 269-81.

13. *E*, 248.

14. Donald W. Shriver Jr., "Faith, Politics, and Secular Society: The Legacy of Bonhoeffer for Americans," in *Ethical Responsibility: Bonhoeffer's Legacy to the Churches*, ed. John D. Godsey and Geffrey B. Kelly (New York: Edwin Mellen Press, 1981), 199.

15. *E*, 259.

16. Dietrich Bonhoeffer, *Life Together*, ed. Geffrey B. Kelly, trans. Daniel W. Bloesch (Minneapolis: Fortress Press, 1996), 100-1.

17. The offense to humanity of God's freedom had been a theme of Bonhoeffer's theology at least since the 1932-33 lectures on *Creation and Fall*, where Bonhoeffer mused about God's creation "out of nothing," "in the beginning, out of freedom" (20). Bonhoeffer concludes, "If the Creator wills to create his own image, [the Creator] must create it in freedom; and only this image in freedom would full praise him and fully proclaim the honor of its Creator" (36).

18. Bonhoeffer, *Life Together*, 101.

19. Ibid., 95.

20. *CD*, 162.

21. Ibid., 164.

22. Ibid., 169.

23. Bonhoeffer, *Life Together*, 27.

24. An abridged quotation from a longer passage by Martin Luther, "Auslegung des 109. (110) Psalms" (An interpretation of Psalm 109 [110]), 1518, in WA, 1, 696-97. The quotation is taken from Karl Witte, "Nun freut euch lieben Christen gmein" (Now rejoice beloved Christians together), 226.

25. *Sanctorum Communio* (New York: Harper and Row, 1963), 24.

26. "Christ's Love and Our Enemies," in *TF*, 288.

27. Shriver, "Faith, Politics, and Secular Society," 211.

28. *LPP* (Letter of 30 April 1944), 279.

29. Bonhoeffer, *Life Together*, 33, emphasis added.

30. *Sanctorum Communio*, 203-4, emphasis added.

31. John W. de Gruchy, "The Freedom of the Church and the Liberation of Society. Bonhoeffer on the Free Church, and the 'Confessing Church' in South Africa," in *Bonhoeffer's Ethics: Old Europe and New Frontiers*, ed. Guy Carter, et al. (Kampen: Kok Pharos, 1991), 184-85.

32. Martin Luther, *Disputatio de Homine*, 14 January 1536 (WA, 39/1:82-83), where he speaks of "Christ or the justice of Christ" as "outside of us and alien to us [*extra nos et aliena nobis*]."

33. *E*, 227-35. Larry Rasmussen and Renate Bethge have argued for "The Church's Public Vocation" based upon an eschatological emphasis on "radical critique," "inclusive membership," and "relentless honesty" in *Dietrich Bonhoeffer– His Significance for North Americans* (Minneapolis: Fortress, 1990), 72-88. Closer

to the proposals of the present essay is Douglas John Hall's excellent article "Ecclesia Crucis: The Disciple Community and the Future of the Church in North America," in *Theology and the Practice of Responsibility*, 59-73.

34. *E*, 224, 225.
35. Ibid., 113.
36. *LPP*, 382.
37. Ibid., 383.
38. "After Ten Years," in *LPP*.

Bonhoeffer's Appeal for Ethical Humility

Mark Brocker

In 1939 Dietrich Bonhoeffer made his fateful decision to return to Germany from the United States. Within a year of his return, he became involved in the conspiracy against Adolf Hitler. His involvement in the conspiracy led to his imprisonment and finally to his execution by the Nazis. Today Bonhoeffer is often celebrated as an example of a modern Christian martyr, and his conspiratorial activity tends to be looked upon with favor.

It is striking, however, that Bonhoeffer deliberately sought to avoid justifying his actions. From his standpoint, any attempt to justify his involvement in the conspiracy would have been the height of ethical arrogance. In fact, according to Eberhard Bethge, Bonhoeffer "would have accepted the charge that what he had done was not a 'good response' to the challenge of the age, but, rather, a very tardy one."[1] It was one thing to give an account of his actions in the conspiracy; it was another thing to try to justify his actions. As Bethge explains, for Bonhoeffer, "the responsible attitude was not to take his justification, before, during and after what he did, into his own hands."[2] Only God could ultimately judge his actions. In the extraordinary situation Bonhoeffer found himself in, he felt compelled to act as he did, but only with a profound sense of ethical humility.

This sense of ethical humility permeates Bonhoeffer's *Ethics*,[3] which he worked on while he was engaged in the conspiracy. The purpose of this essay is to look more closely at Bonhoeffer's appeal for ethical humility, an appeal that applies not only to extraordinary situations, but also to more ordinary situations in life. This appeal is thoroughly grounded in the reality of God revealed in the life, death, and resurrection of Jesus Christ. An awareness of this grounding ought to instill in us a deep sense of ethical humility as we engage in ethical reflection and decision making.

INVALIDATING THE KNOWLEDGE OF GOOD AND EVIL

In Bonhoeffer's view, common approaches to ethics are oblivious to the revelational reality of God in Jesus Christ. Instead, the typical ethical approach embarks on a misguided attempt to secure the knowledge of good and evil.[4] For Bonhoeffer, this attempt is the height of ethical hubris. Ethical reflection tends to focus on two main tasks: an effort to identify a fundamental moral principle, and the application of that principle to various issues in life in order to determine what is good and evil, right and wrong, or moral and immoral. For example, Kant sought to identify a "categorical imperative"—that is, a universal law that would determine the way a person ought to act in any given situation. Kant's concern for universal consistency of action led him to declare that no one in any circumstances should ever utter a falsehood. As Bonhoeffer points out, Kant "carried this principle *ad absurdum* by saying that he would feel obligated to give truthful information even to a criminal looking for a friend of his [Kant's] who had concealed himself in his house."[5]

In doing Christian ethics, asserts Bonhoeffer, our first task is to divorce ourselves from these misguided attempts to determine good and evil.[6] Our desire for moral certainty leads us astray. In seeking the knowledge of good and evil, human beings fall away from their origin. Bonhoeffer affirms that, at their origin, human beings know "only one thing: God."[7] The Bible depicts this falling away in terms of the eating of the forbidden fruit. Adam and Eve ate the apple so that they might gain the knowledge of good and evil. They were not satisfied with being created in the image of God. They were not satisfied with being chosen and loved by God. They were not satisfied with knowing that God is the origin of good and evil. They wanted to know good and evil itself. They wanted to be like God. Inasmuch as ethics is the effort to gain knowledge of good and evil, it separates us from God.[8] Thus, without stating it explicitly, Bonhoeffer implies that ethics, as it is typically engaged in, is sin.[9]

THE THEOLOGICAL GROUNDING OF CHRISTIAN ETHICS

The heart of Bonhoeffer's appeal for ethical humility is his claim that ethics is grounded in the revelational reality of God in Jesus Christ. In the new German critical edition of Bonhoeffer's *Ethics*, the section on "Christ, Reality, and the Good" has been moved to the beginning.[10] This section lays out the theological grounding of Christian ethics. According to

Bonhoeffer, this theological grounding implies that we must radically alter our common approaches to the ethical problem. In particular, we need to abandon two typical forms of the ethical question: "How can I be good?" and "How can I do good?" The key ethical question is "What is the will of God?"[11] When we ask the first two questions, our focus is on the self and the world as the ultimate ethical realities. Focusing on the will of God makes clear that the reality of the self and the reality of the world are rooted in the reality of God.

Bonhoeffer identifies the starting point of Christian ethics not as the reality of the self, of the world, or of standards and values, but as the reality of God revealed in the life, death, and resurrection of Jesus Christ.[12] The reality of God revealed in Jesus Christ defines the good. Apart from this reality, there can be no human goodness or goodness of the world. Apart from this reality, all standards and values are mere abstractions. Christian ethics, therefore, has a theological foundation. The theological problem is "the truth of the revelational reality of God in Christ." The ethical problem is "the realization among God's creatures of the revelational reality of God in Christ." The question of the good "becomes the question of participation in the divine reality which is revealed in Christ."[13] Human beings participate in this divine reality both as individuals in their person and work and as members of the community of human beings and all God's creatures.[14]

ETHICS AS FORMATION

In Bonhoeffer's theologically grounded ethics, the method as well as the content reflects his concern for ethical humility. Ethics as formation is his primary methodological motif.[15] Bonhoeffer claims he is not using "formation" in the customary sense. From his perspective, formation does not focus on how we form individuals or the world by means of plans and programs. Formation is a process of being drawn into the form of Jesus Christ, of conformation with the unique form of the incarnate, crucified, and resurrected One.[16]

Bonhoeffer's key methodological insight is that we do not form ourselves or the world. We are not striving to become like Jesus. We are not simply being instructed on living a good and pious life. We ought not impose a Christian lifestyle or agenda on our neighbor or the world. God does the forming. The form of Jesus Christ is the will of God in the world. In ethics as formation, the question concerning the will of God becomes a matter of discerning how Christ is taking form in the world. The good is "action conforming to the reality of Jesus Christ; action conforming to Christ is action conforming to reality."[17]

According to Bonhoeffer, formation is both individual and corporate. Individual formation is a process of becoming a person before God.

One becomes a person before God by being conformed to the incarnate, crucified, and resurrected Jesus Christ. To be conformed to the incarnate Jesus Christ is to be free to be a real human being. To be conformed to the crucified Jesus Christ is to be a human being sentenced by God. We humbly acknowledge our own sinfulness and our dependence on God's grace. We do not present ourselves in any way as a model of goodness or the godly life. We willingly suffer for others, as Christ first suffered for us. To be conformed to the resurrected Jesus Christ is to be a new human being before God. New human beings do not elevate themselves above others, but willingly live in the midst of sin and death. Being conformed to Jesus Christ does not entail becoming like God. We are formed by God into real human beings—that is our proper form. God became a human being in Jesus Christ so that we might become real human beings.[18]

Corporate formation refers to the process of Jesus Christ taking form in the Church. As the body of Christ, the Church is the corporate form of Jesus Christ in the world. Bonhoeffer insists that the Church ought never be considered a separate form alongside of the form of Jesus Christ. The church is the "section of humanity in which Christ has really taken form."[19]

RESPONSIBLE ACTION

Bonhoeffer's concern for ethical humility pervades the central concepts he employs to develop his ethics. Responsible action is one of those central concepts. In Bonhoeffer's view, ethical humility is built into the structure of the responsible life. Responsible persons are free to live and make decisions, but that freedom is always conditioned by our obligation to God and to our neighbor.[20] Our obligation to God and neighbor is fulfilled by "responsible action"—that is, action on behalf of or in the place of others. Thus, we never engage in responsible action or make ethical decisions in isolation. The community of God is built upon the actions of responsible persons on behalf of or in the place of others.

Bonhoeffer depicts Jesus as the responsible person *par excellence.*[21] He gave himself completely on behalf of others. He demonstrates the ultimate ethical humility by taking upon himself the guilt of all human beings and dying on the cross. Those who act responsibly will not shun the guilt of other human beings. Trying to maintain our personal innocence cuts us off from Jesus Christ. Real innocence is a willingness to enter into the community of guilt.[22]

Responsible action comes in two forms: everyday and extraordinary. Bonhoeffer's involvement in the conspiracy against Hitler was an extraordinary "venture of responsibility." He had to consider the people involved, the given circumstances, the relevant questions of principle, his own motives, the chances for success, and the purpose of the action. He was responsible to weigh all these factors, to make a decision, and to act. He could not, however, as a responsible person, use any of these factors to justify his action. Such responsible action is "performed wholly within the domain of relativity, wholly in the twilight which the historical situation spreads over good and evil; it is performed in the midst of the innumerable perspectives in which every given phenomenon appears. It has not to decide simply between right and wrong and between good and evil, but between right and right and between wrong and wrong." For this reason, "responsible action is a free venture; it is not justified by any law; it is performed without any claim to a valid self-justification, and therefore also without any claim to an ultimate valid knowledge of good and evil."[23] Only God, who directs the course of history, can ultimately judge our actions.

We need to resist the temptation to turn extraordinary responsible action into the measure of all action, for not all responsible action is exercised in extraordinary situations. We do not live our whole lives as "Hercules at the crossroads."[24] God does not want us to wear ourselves out in a constant conflict of obligations and decisions. God does not intend for each moment in life to be a great crisis. Responsible action also takes a more common, ordinary form. Everyday responsible action focuses on the four mandates: marriage/family, labor, church, and government. Bonhoeffer defines a mandate as a divinely imposed task.[25] Parents, for example, are called to act on behalf of or in the place of their children. Their responsible action includes providing, caring, interceding, and suffering for them. The work of a responsible teacher is to act on behalf of his or her students. A responsible police officer acts on behalf of the citizens of a community. Everyday responsible action is also exercised in the domain of relativity. But in order to fulfill their tasks, responsible persons must be free of the constant torment of ethical conflict and decision.

In *Ethics* Bonhoeffer moves toward a concept of the Church as the responsible community, the corporate form of Jesus Christ in the world. The mandate of the Church is to proclaim the reality of God revealed in Jesus Christ.[26] This mandate includes responsible action on behalf of and in the place of others. The political responsibility of the Church entails holding government accountable to its God-given task . The Church must call sin by its rightful name and warn against sin without insisting on its own innocence.[27] As the responsible community, it willingly bears its own guilt and the world's guilt toward Jesus Christ. The Church is not called to co-opt the task of government. In exercising political responsibility, the Church must not lose sight of its main task of proclaiming Jesus Christ.

PROPHETIC BOLDNESS OR ETHICAL ARROGANCE?

The theological grounding of Christian ethics is often overlooked or neglected in ethical reflection and decision making in contemporary church circles. In my own Evangelical Lutheran tradition, this lack of theological grounding can become painfully obvious on the floor of synod assemblies, when we rush to pass resolutions on the latest controversial ethical or political issue. We are quick to pronounce ethical judgments or to baptize our personal political views as God's will. Often we do not have enough time for debate, or the resolutions are not written carefully. The most serious flaw, however, is a lack of attention to the theological basis for the position. It is not clear why the church is compelled to take a public stand on the given issue. On the one hand, we do not want to tarry too long in taking a stand. On the other hand, in our eagerness to take a stand, we need to remember that prophetic boldness can easily become ethical arrogance. We need to be careful not to neglect the daily theological and ethical homework that lays the groundwork for responsible action and decision making.

In May 1993 the Oregon Synod Assembly of the Evangelical Lutheran Church in America (ELCA) passed Resolution 6[28] reaffirming our denunciation of the political activities of the Oregon Citizens' Alliance (OCA) against gay and lesbian people. The OCA sponsored Ballot Measure 9 in the November 1992 Oregon general election. The OCA wanted to make it illegal to grant any sort of minority status to gays and lesbians or to promote homosexuality as an acceptable lifestyle. Opponents of Measure 9 viewed it as an attempt to compromise the civil rights of gays and lesbians. Measure 9 was defeated. But the narrow margin of defeat encouraged the OCA to continue its efforts to get some sort of legislation passed. In May of 1993, shortly before the Oregon Synod Assembly, a local initiative sponsored by the OCA passed by a substantial margin in a Portland suburb.

From my point of view, Oregon Synod Resolution 6 betrayed a lack of ethical humility. The tone of the resolution gave the impression that we were too sure of the goodness of our position over against the evilness of the OCA's position. Some of the rhetoric bordered on being inflammatory. It struck me that opponents of OCA measures needed to examine how our own rhetoric had thwarted fruitful dialogue and contributed to the polarization of our communities.

The lack of a clear statement of the theological basis for Resolution 6 concerned me most. The only explicit theological reference was contained in the fifth and final "WHEREAS": "the ELCA is committed to an inclusive ministry recognizing that the gospel of Jesus Christ is for all." No one in my congregation would argue that the gospel of Jesus Christ is not for all. But a number continue to struggle with the issue of whether a homosexual lifestyle is consistent with the gospel. These members are not card-carrying OCA extremists. They are faithful Christians who need "education, understanding, and compassion on issues of human sexuality."[29]

Being devoted Lutherans, they want this education, understanding, and compassion to be biblically and theologically grounded.

My contention was that we had a solid biblical and theological argument against the OCA position. According to Lon Mabon, the director of the OCA, their overall agenda was to reestablish biblically based moral absolutes in society. Ballot Measure 9 was the first step in fulfilling this agenda. This agenda lacked the very ethical humility Bonhoeffer so forcefully appeals for on biblical and theological grounds. We needed a straightforward warning to voters of the pitfalls of presuming moral certainty. My hunch was that such a warning would have carried a great deal of weight even with those inside and outside of our churches who have strong objections to homosexuality as a lifestyle. Our own lack of humility in our rhetoric may have contributed to the strength of the vote in favor of the OCA-sponsored measure. We may have upped the ante too quickly and fancied ourselves to be in an extraordinary situation, when more ordinary measures were called for to expose the folly of the OCA. The force of our rhetoric gave the OCA position more credibility than it warranted. In our eagerness to be prophetic, it appears that we fell into the trap of ethical arrogance. We seemed to lose sight of the fact that in this particular situation the way to stop the OCA was to make sure they did not win the vote. An important part of ethical humility is perceiving what is needed in a given situation.

CONCLUSION

Bonhoeffer's appeal for ethical humility is, in effect, a call for us to remove the log of ethical arrogance from our own eye so that we can see clearly the ethical pitfalls into which we and others are falling. In particular, Bonhoeffer alerts us to the danger of the quest for moral certainty and to the limitations of one-principle or one-theme ethical approaches, whether philosophical or theological. A proper understanding of the theological grounding of ethics in God's self-revelation in Jesus Christ, the responsible person par excellence, ought to instill a strong measure of ethical humility in us. The point is not to discourage us from engaging, if necessary, in bold ventures of responsibility, such as Bonhoeffer did in the conspiracy against Hitler, but to lead us to acknowledge our ethical limitations and to recognize that the ultimate judgment and fulfillment of our ethical ventures are in the hands of God. In the final analysis, Bonhoeffer's ethical courage, for which he is so admired, grew out of his profound sense of ethical humility; for he was confident that he and his co-conspirators were not acting on their own, but in the presence of the God of history, who can transform even our mistakes and shortcomings into good.

ENDNOTES

1. *DB*, 734.
2. Ibid.
3. Dietrich Bonhoeffer, *Ethics*, first Touchstone edition (New York: Simon & Schuster, 1995). The order followed in this edition is based on the sixth German edition, 1949. Work has been completed on the new German critical edition of *Ethik*, edited by Ilse Tödt, Heinz Eduard Tödt, Ernst Feil, and Clifford Green (Munich: Kaiser Verlag, 1992). Both the order and the content have been revised, and a wealth of editorial information has been added. This new edition is being translated into English as part of the *Dietrich Bonhoeffer Works* translation project. The new English edition will be published by Fortress Press.
4. Ibid., 21.
5. Ibid, 363, n. 1.
6. Ibid., 21.
7. Ibid.
8. Ibid., 22.
9. In *Church Dogmatics* II/2 (Edinburgh: T. & T. Clark, 1948), Karl Barth is more explicit. Critiquing the general conception of ethics, he writes: "Strange as it may seem, that general conception of ethics coincides exactly with the conception of sin" (518). Human beings want to be like God. They want to know, as God knows, what is good and evil. Thus, asserts Barth, "as a result and in prolongation of the fall, we have 'ethics,' or, rather, the mulitfarious ethical systems, the attempted human answers to the ethical questions" (517).
10. Bonhoeffer, *Ethik*, 31-61.
11. *E*, 186.
12. Ibid., 187-88.
13. Ibid., 188.
14. Ibid., 191.
15. Cf. Larry Rasmussen's essay on Bonhoeffer's "Method" in *Dietrich Bonhoeffer—His Significance for North Americans* (Minneapolis: Fortress Press, 1990), 89-110.
16. *E*, 81-82.
17. Bonhoeffer, *Ethik*, 228 (my translation). The first draft of "History and the Good" is not included in the current English editions of *Ethics*. Cf. *Ethik*, 218-44.
18. *E*, 84.
19. Ibid., 85.
20. Ibid., 220-21. Bonhoeffer is building on Paul's understanding of freedom in Galatians 5:13: "For you were called to freedom, brothers and sisters; only do not use your freedom as an opportunity for self-indulgence, but through love become slaves to one another" (NRSV).
21. Ibid., 222.
22. Ibid., 237-38.
23. Ibid., 245.
24. Ibid., 279.
25. Ibid., 204. For more on the mandates, see *E*, 204-10, 281-97.
26. Ibid., 294.
27. Ibid., 345.
28. The vote was as follows: Yes 216, No 77, Abstain 14.
29. This phrase comes from the text of Resolution 6. At its best, Resolution 6 tried to provide education, understanding, and compassion on issues of human

sexuality. Unfortunately, this purpose tended to get lost in the rhetoric attacking the OCA. My suspicion is that Ballot Measure 9 would have been more soundly defeated if its opponents had resisted the temptation to fight the OCA's inflammatory rhetoric with their own inflammatory retoric. It was a revelation for some members of my congregation that, even if they considered homosexuality a sin, it did not necessarily mean that they had to support OCA measures.

Bonhoeffer, Liberation Theology, and the 1990s

G. Clarke Chapman

D ietrich Bonhoeffer, his life, and his writings have had a remarkable effect in those regions of the globe that long for liberation.
Within Europe, for instance, it was above all in East Germany
where an appeal to Bonhoeffer, more than to any other modern theologian, "enabled the church to see in its oppressed situation the opportunity and promise to be the church, purified and unencumbered."[1] By
offering an alternative vision of life, his followers among German Protestants helped the church become an open space for all dissident groups
within a repressive society, and a catalyst for a wider conciliar process that
finally swept away the Communist regime. In South Africa, Allan Boesak
used Bonhoeffer's words as a motto for his dissertation, was moved by
Bethge's biography while in prison, and speaks in open admiration of
Bonhoeffer's prophetic example.[2] John de Gruchy, a tireless exponent
both there and internationally of Bonhoeffer's thought, recounts how, in
1973, when Bethge lectured on Bonhoeffer in South Africa, a layman
asked, "When did Bonhoeffer visit South Africa? He knows our situation
from the inside."[3] And as far away as South Korea, Bonhoeffer was an
inspiration for the Korean Christian Student movement in its studies on
resistance, as well as a parallel for Minjung theology in its attention to
worldly experience.[4]

But it is especially in Latin America where liberation theology has
drawn explicit encouragement from a man martyred decades earlier in
far-away Germany. This influence happened first of all among Protestant
theologians, through Richard Shaull's 1950s seminars in Brazil and later
the leadership training program of the World Student Christian Federa-

tion. From this arose the ISAL movement (Iglesia y Sociedad en América Latina), which in the 1960s explicitly used Bonhoeffer's works in reflecting on issues of secularization, proposing cooperation with ideological groups, and considering whether disciples should ever resort to violence.

The socialist revolution in Cuba was supported by some Christian student groups inspired by Bonhoeffer, and his ideas reappeared in the 1977 Confession of Faith of the Presbyterian-Reformed Church in Cuba. Bonhoeffer was highly regarded also by the Sandinistas; a Spanish translation of *Letters and Papers from Prison* was the first book published by the state press of the new Nicaragua, in 1983, and was sold widely in Central America. Other Protestants mediating Bonhoeffer's thought include Ernesto Johannes Bernhoeft (Brazil), Miguel Torres (Nicaragua), and surviving members of ISAL Rubem Alves, José Míguez Bonino, and Julio de Santa Ana.[5]

Catholics, too, in Latin America have been affected by Bonhoeffer. Gustavo Gutiérrez, in his pioneering *Teología de la Liberación* (1971), referred to him especially in grounding a liberationist threefold definition of freedom,[6] and the Peruvian's later writings continue to mention him. Jon Sobrino, although more frequently citing a theological successor to Bonhoeffer, Jürgen Moltmann, does nonetheless incorporate Bonhoeffer in his cruciform views on Christology and discipleship. Frei Betto, writing prison letters in Brazil, and Néstor Paz Zamora, Bolivian guerilla leader who was starved to death in jail, are other Catholics who were directly affected by Bonhoeffer. Less direct but striking analogies have been drawn between Bonhoeffer and the martyred Salvadoran bishop Oscar Romero.[7] In general, it is probably true that, as Paul Schoenborn remarks, the Latin American parallels are due less to explicit citations of Bonhoeffer and more to the similarities of their oppressive situation, in which a beleaguered church struggles to be faithful.[8] But his influence remains impressive.

This essay begins by examining in what respect Bonhoeffer's work and example may have contributed to liberation ethics. Next we will list several themes from his writings used by liberationists in the 1960s and 1970s, especially in Latin America, and then some fresh themes added by Third World agendas in a post-Cold War era. A few words of evaluation will conclude.

CONTRIBUTIONS TO LIBERATION ETHICS

It may seem unlikely that a person of Bonhoeffer's background and temperament could become so influential in the impoverished Third World. His family upbringing and education reflect the very privileged elites who are normally antagonistic to any social ferment. Those comfortable Berlin social circles accepted a Lutheran tradition of two-spheres thinking, dividing law/coercion/public accountability, on the one hand, from gospel/nonresistance/personal salvation, on the other hand. His own personality was conservative in temperament, even aristocratic: "The smallest offense against order shocked him."[9] Indeed, his writings often belittle Christian social programs or moralism, in stark contrast to liberationist thought, which depends, as we know, upon structural analyses of institutionalized evil. Accordingly, any form of social ethics, much less liberation thought, might seem the very antithesis of Bonhoeffer's theology.

On the other hand, however, he had an uncommon gift of friendship and empathy, an ability to learn from unlikely experiences while working alongside Berlin slum youth, Harlem blacks, and unchurched political conspirators. Life itself seemd to draw him increasingly toward a new social activism. Already in 1933 he reacted to the Nazi regime's infamous Aryan clauses with his "The Church and the Jewish Question," which marked a break with the church's customary passivity before governmental abuse of power. There he proposed a threefold course of action that in effect foreshadows liberationist thought: When a state fails its God-given mandate of order and justice, the church then (1) can point out to the state the moral consequences of its actions, (2) can aid the victims of injustice (including non-Christians), and (3) can even go so far as to "put a spoke in the wheel itself" through direct political action.[10]

In later years, Bonhoeffer's concepts of responsibility and of Christ's universal lordship continued to expand, brimming over the confines of his Lutheran heritage. No longer did personal guilt or bad conscience seem the paramount human problem; rather, it is egocentrism and domination over others.[11] By 1942 he could write, "The ultimate question for a responsible man to ask is not how he is to extricate himself heroically from the affair, but how the coming generation is to live," and that means we "must take our share of responsibility for the moulding of history in every situation."[12] These scraps of insight written near the end of his life hardly qualify Bonhoeffer as a liberation theologian, of course. But they mark beginning steps toward a theological analysis of power and mutual accountability, steps later basic to liberation thought.

Bonhoeffer's real contribution to liberationists, however, is not a social ethic, but rather his *ethos*, a meta-ethic, a theological vision preceding and undergirding moral decision making. He was ignorant of modern problems of colonialism, class warfare, and dehumanization. But the Third World still welcomes his vision of ultimate reality, a vision that undermines oppression and public befuddlement, thereby opening up possibilities for a new day.

The vision is premised on reality as both christologically defined and ethically extended.[13] The Mediator (*Mittler*) is the center (*Mitte*) of every part of existence, though his lordship be veiled in weakness. This paradigm assumes an ontology of "sociality": God is not aloof in some self-possessed, transcendent glory, but the divine freedom is a freedom "for us." God becomes present in Christ, the *Kollektivperson* of a new humanity, who himself becomes present in social form, the community (*Gemeinde*).[14] All Christian concepts thereby gain a social intention. Ethics can never be separated from theology; ethics simply deals with reality itself from a shifted perspective. Right actions come from a formation (*Gestaltung*) in accordance with reality, the form (*Gestalt*) of Christ, a penultimate approach to the ultimate.

Such ethics is no abstract ideal or programmatic consistency. Christ is the incarnate, crucified, and risen Lord, and so must be discerned here and now while coming to us in a vast polyphony of life. So our ethical response to a Christ-formed reality must be a concrete one. But this places enormous weight on the proper discernment of the present moment. Herein lies a dilemma that Bonhoeffer never quite resolved in his all-too-short life. Among his successive attempts to do so were references to "preparing the way for the word," a doctrine of mandates (four task-spheres coordinating daily life), and a fourfold "structure of the responsible life."[15] The problem remains, however, of how to recognize christocentric reality amid the polyphony of life and its competing claims.

SIX THEMES

It is the theological vision of Bonhoeffer, then, from which liberation ethics draws inspiration. There are six themes from his writings, I submit, that influenced liberation thought in its formative stages in the 1960s and 1970s. The first three have been sketched by Julio de Santa Ana, whose essay focuses on the 1960s ISAL movement. "No other western theologian," he asserts, "influenced these discussions as deeply as Bonhoeffer."[16]

Overcoming Dualism in a Secular Age. In many Third World societies, the church has long been allied with ruling elites. Such situations cry out for Bonhoeffer's critique of religion for its otherworldliness and subjectivity, its episodic and parochial character. His prison letters affirm a world come of age, which ought not be repressed by split-level supernaturalism or by law/gospel dualism. Likewise, today Segundo and Gutiérrez criticize Latin America's Christendom and its various complicities in oppression.[17] Secularization (although not "secularism") was welcomed by Bonhoeffer because we are, in Nietzsche's phrase, "loyal to the earth" and accountable for "how the coming generation is to live." Christian faith ought not seize upon the sins of weakness in persons, he wrote, and today these words would imply no collaboration with the dependence mentality so often internalized by groups under neocolonialist domination. Instead, humans should be addressed precisely in their "sins of strength"—for example, "*hubris* . . . , the breaking of the order of life . . . , fear of free responsibility."[18] Thus ethics should not be preoccupied by lust and guilt, but should focus on the domineering ego and the issue of power, its use and misuse. To this shift, later liberationists need only add a theology of history, with the socio-economic analysis and tools that Bonhoeffer himself lacked.

Ultimate, Penultimate, and the Question of Joining Coalitions. Although Bonhoeffer himself disdained the word *ideology*, his writings helped ISAL when its members were deadlocked over whether to cooperate with Marxist ideological groups. It was the old dilemma of radicalism vs. compromise.[19] But Bonhoeffer eased this dichotomy by a careful balance of the christological moments of incarnation, crucifixion, and resurrection. Together with his distinction between the ultimate and the penultimate, this framework later paved the way toward Christian-Marxist dialogue. Without fully accepting any ideology, Latin American believers found they might still enter a critical participation or "engaged criticism"[20] with a secular historical project, and might join its struggle against abusive power. One does so, relying on God's pardoning grace, to defend the penultimate values of justice. Later generations were inspired by Bonhoeffer's words, "To provide the hungry man with bread is to prepare the way for the coming of grace. . . . The coming of grace is the ultimate. But we must speak of the preparing of the way, of the penultimate"—and indeed do so for the sake of both the needy and the religious perfectionists.[21]

Discipleship and Costly Grace. Bonhoeffer's famous sentence "Only he who believes is obedient, and only he who is obedient believes"[22] is reflected in words of Míguez Bonino, "Obedience is not a consequence of our knowledge of God. . . . Obedience *is* our knowledge of God."[23] Praxis, in short, is basic to liberation theology. The ISAL group in the 1960s was torn over the question of whether to respond violently to oppression. Reading Bonhoeffer's *Nachfolge* did not settle this issue, but it did show that either armed struggle or nonviolence could be a form of "cheap grace," a triumphalist legalism. Costly grace, on the other hand, comes to those justified sinners who risk themselves in daily decisions of what to do. So the church must give up its privileges and security and take its place standing by the weak and victimized. This requires a new spirituality within turbulent societies, a new discipleship that does not know in advance what may be required. The term nowadays is *praxis*, but it echoes Bonhoeffer's call for an arcane discipline together with a life of free responsibility: "Our being Christian today will be limited to two things: prayer and righteous action among men. All Christian thinking, speaking, and organizing must be born anew out of this prayer and action."[24]

To these three themes lifted up by de Santa Ana, then, I have added three more.[25]

Freedom as Grounded in an Ontology of Sociality. Such an ontology enables liberationists to break with the static categories of Western
philosophy, which have distorted the concept of freedom. Traditionally,
freedom has been mistaken for spontaneity in contrast to principle, or
inwardness in contrast to public order—thereby detaching it from any
lasting social change. But by fusing the dimensions of act and being,
Bonhoeffer envisioned the *pro me* structure of reality itself—that is, of
God, Christ, the world, and human nature too. "In revelation it is a question less of God's freedom on the far side from us, i.e., his eternal isolation and aseity, than of his forth-proceeding . . . his having freely bound
himself to historical man, having placed himself at man's disposal. God is
not free *of* man but *for* man."[26] Transcendence is less epistemological, a
boundary experience, and more a social-ethical matter, at the very center
of life. The same is true at the human level: freedom means *für-ein-andere-
sein*, an ontology that implies an ethic of "free*ing*." Bonhoeffer's redefi-
nition has continued to undergird liberation ethics, as echoed, for instance, in Gutiérrez: "Freedom is not something man has for himself but
something he has for others. . . . It is not a possession . . . but a relationship. . . . Being free means 'being free for the other,' because the other
has bound me to him."[27]

Human Maturity, in Protest against all Dehumanization. In any
police state, whether of the Third World or the Third Reich, persons are
robbed of dignity and their power of adulthood (*Mündigkeit*). Unfortunately, the churches may be tempted to overlook this dehumanization (*Entmündigung*), because it seems to parallel the old virtues of humility and pious resignation. Even the early Bonhoeffer of the *Nachfolge*
misjudged the distinction, believing one's ego must be suppressed in favor of a commanding Christ.[28] Later, mingling with secular people in the
resistance, he appreciated more the ego skills and virtues of the Enlightenment. He came to distinguish between "power as capacity," so necessary for self-realization, and "power as dominance," a coercive subjuga-
tion over others—who may also, in their folly (*Dummheit*), willingly submit. Such a distinction between types of power removes the topic from a
simple Lutheran wastebasket of sins and allows power to be responsibly
analyzed and criticized.

Indeed, Bonhoeffer wrote, "folly can be overcome, not by instruction, but only by an act of liberation," and moreover, "in the great majority of cases inward liberation must be preceded by outward liberation."[29]
While he agreed that inward and personal liberation is the only final cure
for folly, nevertheless the outward side has a chronological priority because of the social momentum of "definite external factors." We may
recognize here the Third World's insistence later on the multifaceted dimensions of liberation. There was no further elaboration by Bonhoeffer—

except that in the *Ethics* he sketched four qualities of the structure of the responsible life. These four Eberhard Bethge has subsequently interpreted as a contrast of maturity to the life of *Entmündigung* in a police state:[30]

1. Vicarious deputyship acts on behalf of others, when the government fails in its constitutional duty to do so;

2. corresponding to reality means giving up wishful thinking, so we may analyze and work to change dehumanizing power structures;

3. acceptance of guilt means acknowledging one's complicity in past injustice, so one becomes free to risk action without lingering self-justification;

4. an act of free responsibility thereupon dares the exceptional deed, and also stands ready to accept oneself whatever the consequences may be.

Violence: Never Justifiable, but Sometimes Necessary. The very notions of violence and social disorder had long been abhorrent to Bonhoeffer. Reluctantly he moved through various stages of pacifism or selective conscientious objection and participation,[31] until he joined the conspiracy to assassinate Hitler. He came at last to recognize what systemic violence means. Latin Americans later would clarify and expand this recognition—for instance, as a "spiral of violence"[32] in three phases. Violence One is institutional injustice that violates human beings. This leads to Violence Two, revolt, and in turn to Violence Three, government repression. In Nazi Germany, Bonhoeffer certainly understood phases one and three, and his sense of reality led him ineluctably to accept the necessity of some form of Violence Two. The duty of the state is to maintain order. But in exceptional circumstances, when the state becomes a source of greater *dis*order, someone must act vicariously for others to "stop" the wheel.

Of course, Bonhoeffer had in mind the brief social surgery of tyrannicide. But would he also today support wider upheaval, even revolution? That is uncertain. "According to Holy Scripture," he wrote, "there is no right to revolution," but he immediately went on to add that every individual does retain the responsibility for his/her own calling within the *polis*.[33] Extreme circumstances may demand duties that can claim no justification, and that no one outside the situation could in principle condone. So later readers may well infer the possibility of insurrection. "It is quite true," Bethge comments, "that neither war nor revolt can be justified; rather justification belongs to God and has to be left to him. But in the same way, neither non-revolt nor non-action can be so simply justified in the context of a real totalitarian system."[34]

What circumstances, then, might necessitate taking up arms? We cannot say in advance, but can only seek the form of Christ within each situation. Perhaps, however, one may extrapolate some functional criteria. Larry Rasmussen judges that Bonhoeffer's "operational guidelines" for tyrannicide turn out to resemble the classic norms of just-war doctrine,[35] and so might also be applied to the question of a just revolution. The key is that any acts of disorder, as a last resort, must be shown with great probability to enable a wider order and justice for the future society.

CONTEMPORARY APPLICATIONS

Thus it is clear that, in the 1960s and 1970s, Bonhoeffer's writings and his personal example had an initial influence on Latin American liberation theology. But what of today? There is hardly less need, surely, for massive social change in the "Two-Thirds" world of poverty and degradation. The top fifth of our global population enjoys 83 percent of the world's income, while the bottom fifth has only 1.4 percent. Indeed, insists Otto Maduro, "the 'eighties'—and so far the 'nineties' too—were the first decade of this century when every single country south of the Rio Grande endured a sustained impoverishment and growth of its already poor majority."[36]

Clearly, the task of liberation ethics remains unfinished. Yet in many regions the challenges have shifted. With the end of the Cold War, neocolonialism has taken on more subtle forms. A number of subjugated societies, for instance in southern Africa and central Europe, have attained independence and now face new tasks of nation building. In this time of transition, the 1990s, although the legacy of Bonhoeffer endures, it has come to be applied to some different questions. Let us look at four of them.

Building a Democracy. A cursory reading of Bonhoeffer may suggest he was no friend of democracy. By nature he was reserved, even elitist. He mistrusted populism, nationalism, and individual acquisitiveness, and he blamed political liberalism (i.e., democracy) for being too bound up with all three. Democracy he understood in the light of the worst ironies of the French Revolution: "the twinning of freedom and terror; the upsurge of a terrible godlessness in human presumptions of god-likeness" and subsequent self-adoration.[37] Of course, those suspicions were colored by the failure of the Weimar Republic, Hitler's demagoguery, and the fatal divisiveness of Western democracies in the 1930s.

But, on the other hand, Bonhoeffer did affirm what we recognize as presuppositions of democracy, namely, human rights and limitation of power. His passion for justice and empathy for others clearly implied belief in human rights. Not only was he singularly outspoken when civil rights of the Jews were ravaged, but he criticized the church for evading the blatant assault on civil liberties.[38] And mistrust of unchecked human power led to his early alarm at signs of dictatorship. Undeniably, he did cherish much of what we know as democracy, even while holding that civic-mindedness needs a deeper foundation than atomistic Western liberalism can offer. "Thus exercising human freedom does not mean the same as protecting individual liberties. It is a 'founded freedom' derived from the acceptance of responsibility for others . . . [and] based on the gospel."[39]

Despite initial misgivings, then, we conclude that Bonhoeffer is, after all, a resource for building new democratic societies. John de Gruchy has written frequently of how Protestant churches, under Bonhoeffer's influence, have aided democratization in the GDR and in South Africa by being open to the world and to the victims of injustice, and by critical solidarity with others in the struggle. Now that tyranny has been dethroned in both those lands and the painful process of social reconstruction has begun, de Gruchy sketches five ways that Bonhoeffer can offer guidance:[40]

a. Since such transitional societies experience mounting crime and violence, Bonhoeffer can challenge the churches to find ways of creating peace beyond all the walls of hostility.

b. In such struggles the churches must forsake neutrality, learn critical solidarity, and side with the victims.

c. The "perspective from below" should guide church attention to the unemployed and victimized, so that chasms between rich and poor do not undermine a new democracy.

d. Genuine reconciliation is not easy; it requires a confession of guilt for past complicity in wrong, and also acts of restitution. Indeed, the original debates founding South Africa's Commission on Truth and Reconciliation referred to Bonhoeffer's distinction between cheap and costly grace.[41]

e. In a society becoming rapidly secularized, the church should neither withdraw nor yearn for restoration of its past status, but become a church for others, sustained by its secret discipline.

Coping with Modernity. Gutiérrez praises Bonhoeffer for not flinching from the challenge of *Mündigkeit*, human adulthood, calling him perhaps the first theologian really to listen to a world come of age. However, he believes Bonhoeffer fell short by lacking any economic analysis of class and the social costs of modernity. "That humanity's adulthood would be built upon a world of poverty and plunder does not come into his field of vision."[42] He ignored the bourgeois rise to power, the exploitation of the masses, years of protest movements by labor, and global colonialism.

So Bonhoeffer's image of the "modern" person remains too narrow, confined to affluent, well-educated Europeans—the very social class of his own family and co-conspirators.[43] Because of his construal of modernity mainly as science's triumph over nature so that humans at last become the agents of history, real persons, he failed to see that the same process gave rise to "non-persons," the poor and oppressed. He was so consumed by Nazism and its threat to liberal civilization that he never asked about economics and the class struggle that gives that civilization its underpinnings. In short, charges Gutiérrez, "when he speaks of a world come of age he never refers to the underside of this world."[44] Only in a few scattered sentences does Bonhoeffer mention the oppressed. This indictment concludes that, while, to his credit, "Bonhoeffer's courage led him to a mountaintop," he could from there only dimly glimpse the new paths that liberationists thereafter would have to travel.[45]

To this mixed evaluation by Gutiérrez is added a somewhat different criticism by Latin American sociologist and economist Franz Hinkelammert. For that continent, modernity is characterized less by the Enlightenment and a decline of God-language among emancipated intellectuals, and more by domination of the capitalist market system and its political agents of persecution. Historically, repression has been legitimized by appeals to an absolutist God, in contrast to the Christ who out of weakness gives life to the forsaken. So for Latin America, a pertinent critique of religion would not mean secularized rationalism, but a prophetic protest against that society's "gods of death." The example of Nazism should have warned us that a world come of age, despite its emancipation from God, creates its own gods—and then offers to them human sacrifices![46] With this twist, then, Hinkelammert nonetheless proceeds to utilize many themes from Bonhoeffer.

Such ambivalence is typical of liberationists who cite Bonhoeffer. We could term it a process of "friendly criticism" of one who could not have anticipated Third World insights. Furthermore, as Clifford Green points out, Bonhoeffer's theory of modernity was twofold and more nuanced than many critics have supposed.[47] The first of the two meanings is hardly naïve: modernity as "decay," stemming from the mixed results of the French Revolution, a liberated reason linked with nihilism. The second and better known meaning is modernity as life-affirming adulthood, climaxing humanity's childhood stages. The latter definition is not derived from Kant, as is widely supposed, but from Wilhelm Dilthey—including the very language and examples Bonhoeffer used. Unfortunately, that borrowing is encumbered with Dilthey's nineteenth-century naturalism, including a presumed psychological autonomy from social forces surrounding the individual. This latter is correctly spelled out by liberationists today. The point is, however, that Bonhoeffer himself was under no illusion that adulthood implies a doctrine of simple ethical progress, for he knew all too well the modern guises of evil—even if underestimating its economic bases. Fortunately, the abiding importance of his theology, including the proposals for nonreligious interpretation and a life of free responsibility, does not depend on his flawed concept of modernity, but rests on his Christology and its criticism of the "power God" of conventional religion.[48]

Grounding in Experience. Liberation theology appreciates the fact that, both personally and theologically, Bonhoeffer continued to grow in response to his life experiences. Not that he made personal experience an absolute, as did an earlier Protestant liberalism (thereby often confusing it with a Europeanized modernity) and as do some extremes of gender or ethnic-based theologies today. But neither did he, in reaction to liberalism, suppress the theological role of experience so as to undermine political expressions of the faith. This latter extreme, contends Werner Jeanrond,[49] was the error of Karl Barth. Germans had no adequate theological basis to withstand Nazism, Jeanrond argues, because Barth mistrusted human thinking too much, while Roman Catholicism trusted too much its own hierarchy; only Bonhoeffer succeeded in taking classical theological method and linking it with experience of the world around him. This linkage is much needed by liberation theology because, as Paulo Freire showed, the Third World masses must be able to trust their own experience of oppression. Undenied suffering becomes the soil from which liberation thought grows, and yet that same experience yields flashes of hope and inspiration. Indeed, the latter is the reason one commentator believes Third World experience must be accorded status as a legitimate theological source, in contradistinction to the type of "experience" Barth rightly rejected in his time: the sense that Europe's bleak and perverse society was at an impasse.[50]

Bonhoeffer goes further, however, than simply accepting the bipolarity of daily common experience. His theological method, as we have seen, was to seek the form of Christ amid all events, sustained by the assurance that reality is deeply christocentric. Viewed through this theological lens, daily events disclose hidden dimensions, including a dialectic of suffering and hope that might otherwise go undetected. His mature theology grew in appreciation of the material blessings of life (health, friends, food, etc.) during the very time in prison he depicted so movingly the sufferings of God. Experience is polyphonic, indeed, but it is the one Christ who meets us through it.

Confronting Nationalism. Fervent protestation of loyalty to the nation-state often cloaks repression of the poor, as liberationists well know. Indeed, the same might be said for our society.[51] Likewise, Bonhoeffer was wary of nationalism. His earliest criticism was against Hitler's idolatrous *Führerprinzip*, the capstone for a perverse blend of Germanic nostalgia and fantasies. He was also critical of the nationalism throughout Europe that blocked both Christian unity and effective action against the rise of Nazism. A path toward nihilism was begun by the French Revolution in deifying man and unleashing floods of emotion and violence.[52] With that, the religion of nationalism was born, eventuating in the bloody twentieth century.

Jean Bethke Elshtain has discussed this trend under the rubric of national sovereignty, a doctrine that centuries ago borrowed certain views of God's indivisibility and absolute right of dominion and transferred those divine attributes to the triumphalist nation-state. "When human beings begin to forget that they are not God, as Vacláv Havel put it recently, sovereign mastery was the name they gave this forgetfulness."[53] By contrast, Bonhoeffer insisted that legitimate authority takes form as "deputyship," and thus is always limited. While the state has a divine commission to preserve order and unity, it must also remain open to God's supreme ordering and should promote human maturity. Otherwise "our adoration of sovereignty makes us weak, not strong, inviting slackness of thought, incapacitation in action, acquiescence in evil. We have rendered altogether too much, and we have gotten the Caesars we deserve."[54] Bonhoeffer thus can help Third World liberationists utilize the distinction between love of country that seeks justice, and idolatrous nationalism that masks injustice.[55]

CONCLUSION

In closing, we should note briefly some shortcomings in Bonhoeffer's thought that prevent him from being accepted unreservedly by liberation theology.[56]

1. He retains enough remnants of Lutheran dualism so that, as noted above, his view of sociality is largely limited to an "I-Thou" personalism. This focus lacks the structural dimensions basic to the socio-economic analyses needed by Christians, especially in neocolonial societies.

2. Since Bonhoeffer's major contribution is to an *ethos* rather than to social ethics, his emphasis on concretion is but a first step, only a preparation for making difficult choices. Third World people must still adjudicate competing claims to God's will in specific situations. It is not easy to discern the form of Christ in particulars, least of all in a time of turmoil and transition.

3. Bonhoeffer was not able to articulate sufficiently why Christians should ally with non-Christians in working toward common goals. His passing reference to "unconscious Christianity" does not explain why secular liberationists often do exhibit conformation to Christ as a reality, even though lacking the faith to discern it. On this point, working with worldly

men in the Abwehr conspiracy, his theology had no time to catch up to his praxis.

4. Bonhoeffer's eschatology is weak, using spatial rather than temporal imagery for Christ's centrality. Together with the Lutheran premise of *finitum capax infiniti*, this imagery overemphasizes themes of Christ's incarnation and therefore the continuities of society around us. It does so at the expense of the other end of the polarity, the cross and resurrection, and its wider implications of discontinuity, which the Reformed tradition better appreciates (e.g., Moltmann). Christology becomes unbalanced, and its social extension is, as Bonhoeffer rightly foresaw, a preference for compromise over radicality.

5. Finally, Bonhoeffer's theodicy may be inadequate. Of course, his poignant words on human pain and despair being taken up by the God who suffers with us are immensely important for liberationists. But these remarks about suffering in the prison letters usually occur in the context of God's providence. Some liberationists are wary of references to providence because of the alienating function such doctrine had under colonial regimes. Even today it may stifle human efforts to overcome social evils, or underplay the radicality of human misery. Liberationists insist that evil deserves a more direct acknowledgment by the suffering masses before divine solace can be addressed

Such are some reservations Third World theologians may have towards a European who died more than fifty years ago. And in the 1990s additional issues have been placed on the liberationist agenda. It is all the more remarkable, then, that the legacy of Bonhoeffer continues to be a catalyst in our decade. His christological focus on experience offers, not so much a liberation ethics, but a liberation *ethos* that still inspires. By discrediting the "power God" of conventional religion, he undermines abuses of human power and prepares us to envision a reality in Christ taking form in this material world. Thereby a new generation may still hope and work towards liberation.

ENDNOTES

1. John A. Moses, "Bonhoeffer's Reception in East Germany, *BND*, 295. De Gruchy's writings often comment on Bonhoeffer and the former GDR; see his "Dietrich Bonhoeffer and the Transition to Democracy in the German Democratic Republic and South Africa," *Modern Theology* 12:3 (July 1996): 345-66.

2. Allan A. Boesak, "What Dietrich Bonhoeffer Has Meant to Me," in *Bonhoeffer's Ethics: Old Europe and New Frontiers*, ed. Guy Carter, et al. (Kampen, the Netherlands: Kok Pharos Publishing House, 1991), 21-29.

3. John W. de Gruchy, "Bonhoeffer, Apartheid and Beyond: The Reception of Bonhoeffer in South Africa," *BND*, 353. See the entire volume, containing papers from the Seventh International Bonhoeffer Congress, 1996, which was held

in Cape Town, focusing on Bonhoeffer's words, "Are you still of any use?"
4. Chung Hyun Kyung, "Dear Dietrich Bonhoeffer," ibid., 9-19; Wolfgang Kroger, "Erfahrung—ein Streitpunkt i Menischen Gesprach," *Okumenische Rundschau* 35 (April 1988), 185-88.

5. This paragraph relies upon Julio de Santa Ana, "The Influence of Bonhoeffer on the Theology of Liberation," *The Ecumenical Review* 28/2 (April 1976): 188-97, and Paul Gerhard Schoenborn, "Bonhoeffer in Lateinamerika: Beziehungen zwischen Dietrich Bonhoeffer und Christen und Theologie in Lateinamerika—ein Werkstattbericht," *Kirche im Spannungsfeld von Staat und gesellschaft: festschrift fur Gunther van Norden;* Hermann de Buhr, Heinrich Kuppers und Volkmar Wittmutz (Hg.); Schriftenreihe des Vereins fur Rheinische Kirchen-geschichte, Band 111 (Koln: Rheinland-Verlag GmbH, 1993): 395-446.

6. Gustavo Gutiérrez, *A Theology of Liberation* (Maryknoll, N.Y.: Orbis Books, 1973), 36-37; see 176.

7. Geffrey B. Kelly, "Bonhoeffer and Romero: Prophets of Justice for the Oppressed," in *Theology and the Practice of Responsibility: Essays on Dietrich Bonhoeffer,* ed. Wayne Whitson Floyd Jr. and Charles Marsh (Valley Forge, Pa.: Trinity Press International, 1994), 85-105. See also his "Dietrich Bonhoeffer's Theology of Liberation," *Dialog* 34 (Winter 1995).

8. Schoenborn, "Bonhoeffer in Lateinamerika," 444-45.

9. Otto Dudzus, in *I Knew Dietrich Bonhoeffer,* ed. Wolf-Dieter Zimmerman and Ronald Gregor Smith (London: Collins, 1966), 82. He illustrates this by recalling Bonhoeffer's deliberation in walking the long way around to cross some railroad tracks, instead of following his students in a short cut.

10. *NRS,* 221. Alejandro Zorzin draws the liberationist implications from this essay, observing that Latin American Christians have not given it sufficient attention; see his "Church versus State: Human Rights, the Church, and the Jewish Question" (1993), *BND,* 236-57. The metaphor of the uncontrolled wheel or vehicle that must be stopped recurs in Bonhoeffer; see Dudzus, *I Knew Dietrich Bonhoeffer,* 82, and Eberhard Bethge, *Dietrich Bonhoeffer: Theologian, Christian, Contemporary* (London: Collins, 1970), 754-55.

11. See *SCH,* 149-59, 332-36.

12. Dietrich Bonhoeffer, "After Ten Years," *LPP,* 7.

13. See G. Clarke Chapman Jr., "Bonhoeffer: Resources for Liberation Theology," *Union Seminary Quarterly Review* 36:4 (Sumnmer 1981): 225-42.

14. *SCH,* 77.

15. *E,* 135, 207-13, 286-301, 224-62.

16. De Santa Ana, "The Influence of Bonhoeffer," 189.

17. Juan Luis Segundo, *The Liberation of Theology* (Maryknoll, N.Y.: Orbis, 1976), 139-43, and Gustavo Gutiérrez, *A Theology of Liberation,* chap. 4.

18. *LPP,* 345-46, 205; see *SCH,* 323-28.

19. See *E,* 127-30.

20. José Míguez Bonino, *Doing Theology in a Revolutionary Situation* (Phildelphia: Fortress, 1975), 100; see 38. For a detailed account, see his *Christians and Marxists: The Mutual Challenge to Revolution* (Grand Rapids: Eerdmans, 1976).

21. *E,* 137.

22. *CD,* 69.

23. Míguez Bonino, *Christians and Marxists,* 40.

24. Bonhoeffer, "Thoughts on the Day of the Baptism," *LPP,* 300.

25. Chapman, "Bonhoeffer: Resource for Liberation Theology," 231-36.

26. *AB.*

27. Gutiérrez, *A Theology of Liberation*, 36, quoting Bonhoeffer's *CF*, 37; immediately therefter Gutiérrez offers his own well-known threefold integral definition of liberation. See 162, and also Míguez Bonino, *Christians and Marxists*, 105-10.

28. *SCH*, chap. 4 and 302-9, 318-32.

29. *LPP*, 9.

30. *E*, 224-62. See Eberhard Bethge, "Widerstand und Terrorismus: Am Beispel von Dietrich Bonhoeffers Schrift zue Gewalt," in *Am gegebenen Ort: Aufsatze und Reden, 1970-79* (Munchen: Kaiser Verlag, 1979), 158-74, especially 166-67.

31. See ibid. Also Larry Rasmussen, *Dietrich Bonhoeffer: Reality and Resistance* (Nashville: Abingdon, 1972), 96-116, and G. Clarke Chapman, "What Would Bonhoeffer Say Today to Christian Peacemakers?" in *Theology, Politics and Peace*, ed. Theodore Runyon (Maryknoll, N.Y.: Orbis, 1989), 167-75 (abridged version in *E*, 226-29).

32. Dom Helder Camara, *Spiral of Violence* (Denville, N.J.: Dimension Books, 1971), 29-37; see Míguez Bonino, *Doing Theology in a Revolutionary Situation*, 114-28, and Segundo, *The Liberation of Theology*, 155-64.

33. *E*, 351.

34. Bethge, "Widerstand und Terrorismus," 162. Bethge later goes on to say that confession of faith without active resistance means "complicity with the murderers," in his essay "Between Confession and Resistance: Experiences in the Old Prussian Union," in *Friendship and Resistance: Essays on Dietrich Bonhoeffer* (Grand Rapids: Eerdmans, 1995), 15-29.

35. Rasmussen, *Dietrich Bonhoeffer*, 132-46, especially 145.

36. Otto Maduro, "The Modern Nightmare: A Latin American Christian Indictment," *Theology and the Practice of Responsibility*, 78.

37. Jean Bethke Elshtain, "Caesar, Sovereignty, and Bonhoeffer," *BND*, 225. See 223-25.

38. Bonhoeffer's courage on this issue, as a model for Latin American liberationists, is underlined by Alejandro Zorzin, "Church and State," 236-57.

39. De Gruchy, "Dietrich Bonhoeffer and the Transition to Democracy," 361.

40. John W. de Gruchy, "Christian Witness in South Africa in a Time of Transition," *Theology and the Practice of Responsibility*, 283-93.

41. De Gruchy, "Dietrich Bonhoeffer and the Transition to Democracy," 366, n. 77.

42. Gustavo Gutiérrez, "The Limitations of Modern Theology: On a Letter of Dietrich Bonhoeffer," in *The Power of the Poor in History: Selected Writings* (Maryknoll, N.Y.: Orbis Books, 1983), 228-29. See the entire essay, 222-34, as well as another, 169-221.

43. As Charles West noted, "His nonreligious man in the 'world come of age' was precisely this bourgeois humanist as he knew him in his father, his relatives, his friends, and his co-conspirators in the plot to assassinate Hitler." Quoted by Clifford Green, "Bonhoeffer, Modernity, and Liberation Theology," *Theology and the Practice of Responsibility*, 131, n. 52.

44. Gustavo Gutiérrez, *The Truth Shall Make You Free: Confrontations* (Maryknoll, N.Y.: Orbis Books, 1990), 24. See Otto Maduro, "The Modern Nightmare," 80: "Our questions are not so much, for instance, if God exists or not, but, rather on whose side is God. Not so much 'how to speak of God in a world come of age,' but rather, how to speak of God in a world gone mad."

45. Gutiérrez, "The Limitations of Modern Theology," 231.

46. Franz Hinkelammert, as summarized by Schoenborn, "Bonhoeffer in Lateinamerika," 434-39. The latter commentator also agrees (444) with the broad-

ened critique of religion by liberation theology.

47. Clifford Green, "Bonhoeffer, Modernity, and Liberation Theology," 117-31.

48. Ibid., 128. See *DB*, 760.

49. Werner G. Jeanrond, "From Resistance to Liberation Theology: German Theologians and the Non-Resistance to the National Socialist Regime," in *Resistance against the Third Reich, 1933-1990*, ed. Michael Geyer and John W. Boyer (Chicago: University of Chicago Press, 1994), 295-311. Among post-war theologians surveyed who at last do offer a basis for such resistance to tyranny, Jeanrond dwells longest on Jürgen Moltmann (302-6). This is not surprising, for I believe Moltmann to be the leading modern exponent for many themes of Bonhoeffer; see G. Clarke Chapman, "Hope and the Ethics of Formation: Moltmann as an Interpreter of Bonhoeffer," *Studies in Religion/Sciences Religieuses* 12:4 (Fall 1983): 449-60.

50. Kroger, "'Erfahrung—ein Streitpunkt," 185-99.

51. Geffrey B. Kelly, "The Idolatrous Enchainment of Church and State: Bonhoeffer's Critique of Freedom in the United States," *BND*, 298-318.

52. *E*, 97-104.

53. Elshtain, "Caesar, Sovereignty, and Bonhoeffer," 228. This adulation is not limited to the far side of the Atlantic; Elshtain quotes (230) Supreme Court Justice Sutherland in the 1936 case *U.S. v. Curtiss-Wright Export Corp., 299 U.S. 304*: "Rulers come and go; governments end and forms of government change; but sovereignty survives. A political society cannot endure without a supreme will somewhere. Sovereignty is never held in suspense."

54. Ibid., 235.

55. For a discussion of Bonhoeffer's alternative, a wholesome love of country, see Keith W. Clements, *A Patriotism for Today: Dialogue with Dietrich Bonhoeffer* (Bristol, U.K.: Bristol Baptist College, 1984).

56. Further elaboration of these criticisms may be found in my earlier essay, "Bonhoeffer: Resource for Liberation Theology," 236-39.

Gospel in a Secular World: Mystery and Relationship

AN ESSAY IN HONOR OF F. BURTON NELSON, FRIEND AND COLLEAGUE

Jay C. Rochelle

The secularization of life throughout the whole world is taking radical forms and cannot be stopped. We stand in the midst of an ideological and moral evolution of our society. We must anxiously question whether our moral and spiritual forces are growing in proportion to the penetration of revolutionary changes in the world. We need powerful faith to regard the historical process without fear and to discover where we must carry on this greatest spiritual struggle.[1] JOSEPH L. HOMADKA, 1926

At the end of the fifties, Bonhoeffer was known only to a limited circle, largely through the translation efforts of John Doberstein, professor of practical theology at the Lutheran Theological Seminary in Philadelphia. Doberstein had translated *Life Together*, which was published with a succinct introduction by Harper and Brothers in 1954. *Ethics* became available in the United States through Macmillan Press in 1955. *The Cost of Discipleship*, which had been translated by Reginald H. Fuller and published in Britain in an abridged version in 1948, was published in a complete version in 1959 by SCM Press, and the book crossed the ocean into a Macmillan publication. These three books mark the beginning of the long history of Bonhoeffer publishing and spin-offs in America. The trickle became a torrent in less than a decade; by the end of the sixties, doctoral studies on Bonhoeffer were regularly finding their way into print and the bulk of his important works had been published in English, either in full or in collections like *No Rusty Swords*.

At the end of the fifties, a few other small books were available to those who had access to bookstores where SCM publications were sold:

Creation and Fall (1959), *Temptation* (1955), and a slender volume called *Letters and Papers from Prison* (1953) could all be obtained, but were usually purchased only by students in colleges and universities where one or at most two professors had heard of Bonhoeffer, delved into the English corpus, and selected books for reading in various courses. My own introduction to Bonhoeffer came in a course entitled "The Christian Witness" taught by Paul Harms at Concordia Senior College, Fort Wayne, Indiana, in the academic year 1959-60.

You have to understand the period. We college students during the Eisenhower years were the quiet ones. We did not yet protest, we volunteered. We thought rather more than we acted. We became existentialists via Sartre and Camus—who led us in turn to Kierkegaard, who had been "discovered" not long before. We listened to jazz because it was "cool" and intellectual, and we danced to rock and roll because it was for the body and the senses. We wore black berets and dreamed of going to the Hungry i in San Francisco, if we lived on the right coast, or Greenwich Village and the Blue Note, if we lived on the left coast.

The quiet consensus of postwar America was, however, beginning to break up. Nuclear protests began at the turn of the decade, and bourgeois culture was falling under scrutiny by everyone from sociologists to folk singers. "Negroes" were standing up in the growing fight for civil rights. We were losing our religion by going *On the Road* and becoming *Dharma Bums* with Jack Kerouac, by exploring *The Fire Next Time* with James Baldwin, and by entering the steamy gothic world of the South through Flannery O'Connor or Tennessee Williams or that *enfant terrible* Truman Capote in *The Grass Harp and a Tree of Night and Other Stories.* Some of us ate a *Naked Lunch* with William Burroughs, and we reveled in the poetry of Lawrence Ferlinghetti, Phillip Whalen, Gary Snyder, Denise Levertov, and Alan Ginsberg. Especially Alan Ginsberg.

As I said, we were losing our religion. Religion was becoming secondary and perhaps even less than that. The lessons of World War II had skipped the generation that experienced it and were coming to clarity and fruition in their children. Ginsberg and Kerouac and Snyder had discovered Buddhism, and they pointed us to the writings of the doctor, D. T. Suzuki, and his quirky genius accompanist, Alan Watts. The world was becoming, dare I say, *postmodern*—or at least totally secularized—because multiple options now appeared for the construction of a life.

Then my eyes fell on that page in *Letters and Papers from Prison* where Bonhoeffer says,

> The thing that keeps coming back to me is, what is Christianity, and indeed what is Christ, for us to-day? The time when men could be told everything by means of words, whether theologi-

cal or simply pious, is over, and so is the time of inwardness and conscience, which is to say the time of religion as such. We are proceeding towards a time of no religion at all: men as they are now simply cannot be religious any more.[2]

There you have it in a nutshell. "Men as they are now *simply cannot be religious* any more." Not "will not." Not "must not." Not "could not." "Simply cannot."

Bonhoeffer's words made immediate sense to me. Forty years later, they speak to me afresh. Bonhoeffer signalled the end of Christendom and, perhaps more than that, the end of piety as it was known and practiced. A century earlier, Ludwig Feuerbach had foreseen this when he identified religion with self-alienation, self-delusion, and self-intoxication. For Feuerbach, religious ideas and concepts of God are primarily tools we invent to escape from the limits of life: "seeking refuge in the realm of an ideal but unreal world of enchanting illusions."[3]

None of us Americans can understand what the interbellum period was like in Germany. *Cabaret* gets at it from one direction, Kurt Weill and Bertholt Brecht's *Threepenny Opera* from another. What is clear is the end of piety and the dawn of deep cynicism. No one could pretend about God and the comforts of religion anymore. Karl Barth had thundered forth against religion as a tool of theological liberalism, and both were dead as the dodo. The crucified Christ was becoming the center for theological thought once again. Thus far the proclamation.

Religion, of course, continued—and still does. Bonhoeffer did not see, perhaps could not have imagined, the extraordinary expansion of "spirituality" into a major publishing and technique business as we know it at century's end. Religion is big business again, most likely for all the reasons why it has sprung up again and again: the need for consolation and comfort, the yen for security, and above all the drive to disregard the word of God. For this word denies us the right to rely on our own righteousness, while it offers us an alien righteousness by which we are reconciled to God. Religion invariably replaces the community of hearers of the word who gather around the sacramental means of grace and against which the gates of hell will not prevail. Religion is that which gives us solace as individuals and which may, indeed, cocoon us in isolation one from another. Marx was correct: religion—as individualistic, isolating otherworldliness—is the opiate of the people.

The question is, what *is* this Church against which the gates of hell will not prevail? Surely not the silliness and pettiness that pass for concerns at the local level. Surely not the ongoing shelter for racism that the Church provides. Surely not the obsequious irresponsibility that is often proclaimed in the name of salvation.

The Church is the tribe of Jesus-followers. We have our rituals which, as Jonathan Z. Smith so brilliantly points out, enable us to "get the action right."[4] Our righteousness is in the portrayal of life as it is *supposed to be*, life in the light of the eschatological future of God, life in which peace and harmony and community and simplicity are the values and enactments. All this flows from being in the tribe of Jesus-followers.

There *is* a tribal factor to the Church that Bonhoeffer did not consider. In the fight of the Confessing Church against the German Christians, abstractions prevailed throughout the debates and even when the ink was dry on the Barmen Declaration. The Aryan tribe rose again and offered a powerful mythology that gave hope and purpose to the lives of many who wandered without refuge between the wars. The Jesus tribe was not able to oppose the Aryan tribe on the level of ritual and myth, which is the level where people's imaginations and hearts are engaged.

Bonhoeffer was right: "The time when men could be told everything by words . . . is over." The mythology of German Nationalism was pushed by every technological marvel at the disposal of the party. From Leni Riefenstahl, the brilliant young producer of films that propagandized the nation, to the radio programs of Joseph Goebbels, the genius of propaganda, to the mass rallies at which *der Fuehrer* spoke through the newest means of amplification, backed by the red banners of the party, a united front advanced the party's claims and ideas. That technology offered a vision words alone could not draw. The pictures overcame the preachers.

Richard Rubinstein is correct when he examines, with clear eye and surgeon's scalpel, his thesis that the Holocaust was the result of combining the most technologically advanced country in the world with the direct administration of adroit bureaucrats.[5] It was irresistible and enchanting to those mired in the hopelessness and loss of face that emerged from that railway car at Versailles.

So the task of discernment falls upon us once again at century's end. We must discern how to be Christian without necessarily being religious, how to engage the symbols, myths, and rituals of our faith without degenerating into superstitition, and how to maintain the proper humility before the word as an address to us, a humility that will eschew that humiliation of the word which has taken place in the age of visual signs.[6]

Secular Christianity at Last?

Bonhoeffer and Barth speak of "religion" in precise terms. First, the term is pejorative: both Barth and Bonhoeffer oppose the notion of religion. This seems odd to us, since we use the term to mean *cultic acts*, and we use *religion* as a neutral term. But Bonhoeffer means, by religion, those constructions which take us out of this-worldliness and plunge us into dependence upon the gods who are out of this sphere of our existence. Religion plunges us into "two-sphere thinking," which can result in the rupture between faith and ethics characteristic of the degenerate two-kingdoms theory used by the Nazi regime. Bonhoeffer seeks a way, especially in his late writings, to both discern and proclaim the presence of God in the midst of ordinary reality, which is now godless.

Bonhoeffer was not trying to turn back the clock of theology, but to tell what time it was. He rejected what he called *salto mortale* (the fatal leap) back into the Middle Ages for theological grounding. That system of scholastic theology, natural law, and natural revelation was preliminary to the modern problem of the Church. With Barth and the neo-orthodox, he rejected this system as inadequate because it created a place for theology that was easily eroded. This theological position was matched by a religion oriented toward the threefold areas of individualism, inwardness, and piety. Bonhoeffer rejected this kind of religion in his early studies about the communal nature of Christian faith. *Communio Sanctorum* and *Act and Being* treat this on a systematic level, *The Cost of Discipleship* and *Life Together* on a practical level. To some extent, one may see his Christology lectures, *Christ the Center*, as a bridge between these approaches which places the Christ proclaimed at the center of the community formed by the proclamation. In his emphasis on the communal nature of the present Christ, he overcomes the gap between system and practice. Service of Christ in the world is simultaneously our proclamation of the presence of Christ to the world, by both our words and our actions.

The world's secular coming of age moves us beyond earlier religious systems, which overcame the distance between God and world (represented by the doctrine of sin) by proposing a place where they are united. This place is occupied, philosophically, by the *analogia entis*, the "analogy of being," whereby we are in continuity with God by virtue of our being, which is shared with the Deity through the incarnation. This place is occupied, religiously, by a piety that identifies with the human figure of Jesus. In this system, God stands in continuity with the world and religion becomes adaptation to existing social conditions. Marx was correct; in this shift, religion indeed may become the opiate of the people. Bonhoeffer notes that earlier ages of faith "conceded to the world the right to determine Christ's place in the world."[7]

In the secular age, God is discontinuous from the world. For Bonhoeffer this is not loss, but gain, because it enables the Church to return to its proper task: to proclaim the inbreaking of God's kingdom into the world. There is no continuity between God and the inner person on the basis of feeling or sense (Schleiermacher)[8] that needs only to be perfected by the preaching of Christ. Bonhoeffer shifted from this position when he began to see that the proper reading of Scripture is not *for* but *over against* oneself. As Feil says, "The chief task for the theology of his generation was, in Bonhoeffer's view, to overcome religion as something which either *separates* or *identifies faith and the world*."[9] Bonhoeffer's work is, in part, an attempt to line the boundaries within which theology must work in the twentieth century. The boundary marker is the free grace of God. God's free grace reaches people in the midst of their world, and this grace must be guarded by theology, lest we lose the whole point of grace as what Barth called "God's downward action" and we end by reconstructing religion as a means whereby we either assuage or are enabled to disregard God in the world.

Bonhoeffer knows the world as the *one* sphere of the Christian's activity, whereas religion—in his view—allows for two spheres, one that is individual and inward and oriented toward private piety, the other wordly, in which one may live independent of relationship to God. Behind this is the earlier notion that God occupies a "space" that can be maintained only by separating "God" from "world."

In this secular age, God has been edged off the world. For Bonhoeffer this is not tragic, but is rather a new beginning, which enables the true nature of Christianity as the proclamation of an alien and simultaneously freeing word. When this word is proclaimed, the world is once again the "world which is loved, condemned, and reconciled in Christ,"[10] and which is "the sphere of concrete responsibility which is given to us through Jesus Christ."[11]

In his earliest period Bonhoeffer vacillated between positive and negative assessments of the world, with little recourse to Christology, and in the middle period discipleship and world are diametrically opposed.[12] In this final period he comes to a full appreciation of the world as the *one* sphere with which Christ is inseparably involved, so that Christology and secularism become merged in his thought. Christ is not only *pro nobis* in the community, but in the world *pro aliis*, "the man for others."[13] Otherwordliness has now collapsed and we are prepared to be this-wordly Christians, those who participate "in the powerlessness of God in this world."[14]

In the world come of age, we are in a godless context which is capable of either promise or despair, depending upon whether or not the word of Christ is rightly heard. Where the gospel is proclaimed, godlessness becomes the source of promise because it prepares the way for the audacious, liberating word of God's freedom from all religion and for thisworldliness in Christ. By denying a spirituality of inwardness which retreats from the world into forms of piety that supposedly relate one to God, secularism prepares the way for a renewed understanding of the gospel as the empowering of the community to lose itself in the world for Christ's sake. By denying the validity of religion as a means to construct a connection between humanity and God, Bonhoeffer's understanding of secular faith opens the doorway to genuine "autonomous" life in the world as it is, and not as we imagine it to be. This move had already been signaled in the Christology lectures,[15] but it comes clear at the end in Bonhoeffer's letters.[16]

MYSTERY

The theological term *mystery* means a revealed truth which could not be spoken had it not been revealed, and which remains mystery even when spoken. We can see that *mystery* does *not* mean a fact about natural phenomena or human relations that is discoverable and then ceases to be mysterious. A mystery, in the Bible, is the truth of God which is undiscoverable apart from revelation. To be precise, our redemption in Christ is called a mystery in Colossians, where it is "God's secret," and in Ephesians and 1 Timothy 3, which use the term *mystery:* great indeed is the mystery of our faith.[17]

Bonhoeffer distinguishes between reflection and faith, which he calls *actus reflectus* and *actus directus*.[18] Faith apprehends the mystery, reflection talks about it. God is the great mystery, but this does not mean God is unknowable: "God lives in mystery. God's being is mystery to us, mystery from eternity to eternity; mystery, because it speaks of a home (*heimat*) in which we are—not yet—at home (*daheim*)."[19] God's mystery is announced in preaching and forms the starting place for Bonhoeffer's theology. In a circular letter at Christmas 1939, he makes this point with bold clarity: "God revealed in the flesh, the God-man Jesus Christ, is the holy mystery which theology is appointed to guard. What a mistake to think that it is the task of theology to unravel God's mystery, to bring it down to the flat, ordinary human wisdom of experience and reason! It is the task of theology solely to preserve God's wonder as wonder, to understand, to defend, to glorify God's mystery as mystery!"[20] Faith is part of the mystery and cannot be wholly transformed into knowledge, which would be definable and graspable.

Theology's task is to explore how the Christian movement presents or publishes the one true mystery, namely, the revelation of God's saving will and self-emptying in Jesus Christ, which is not a *discoverable* truth, but a revealed truth. For Bonhoeffer, the presentation of this mystery occurs through preaching the word and administering the sacraments. And that requires the assembly, or *Gemeinde*.

We must not be unaware of the down side to this talk of mystery. Jacques Ellul made a case for the distinction between revelation as understood in Jewish circles and the concept of mystery. He notes that a process of sanitizing the concept takes place in Paul and Revelation, by which the notion of celebrating mystery is overcome by reference to the Incarnation as the supreme mystery of God's action in the world, which takes the concept captive. However, there was a price to pay for allowing the concept into Christian faith, which was the subsequent degeneration of mystery into its Greek idea, "a religion of escape" grounded upon the notion of communion with the god. Christians have been fighting this perception ever since.[21]

Louis Bouyer worked through the concept of mystery in his book *The Christian Mystery*.[22] He is one among many scholars who have consistently argued that Christian mysticism is informed by the Christian mystery as presented especially in the books of Colossians and Ephesians, supplemented by the Johannine corpus. Bouyer reminds us that the nineteenth century brought the rise of the study of comparative religions. This study was marked by the theory that mysticism had a common content which was covered by cultural and religious externals. Almost no one holds this theory at the end of the twentieth century. The differences are, in fact, overwhelming, and they are in the details. It makes all the difference in the world that Christian mysticism is grounded in the Christ-mystery as presented in Paul. Bouyer argues that the object of the mystical quest is of paramount importance in shaping the nature and the content of the quest itself; thus, non-Christian mysticism is really not comparable with Christian mysticism. His note about Ruysbroek's approach to the mystery is characteristic of the Western movement: "Ruysbroek is the first to make the point expressly and to explain that there can be no question of forgetting *what is essential to this Christian vision of the divine life*, first opposed to the pagan Greek one by Marius Victorinus, *that it is the vision of a God who is love, agape, movement itself, instead of a God who is One only in being a stranger to all multiplicity, all communication.*"[23] Thus the Trinity is at the heart of the Christian mystery, and all contemplation of God takes place on the basis of the self-revelation and self-embodiment of the blessed Holy Trinity. The dynamic quality of the Christian life is such that we are caught up in the Holy Trinity and brought back into life together in love. There is a personal quality to this mystery that is not at all the same as the merger with the Void which is characteristic of Eastern forms of mysticism.

Bonhoeffer uses the concept of mystery in its Christian form, such as we would find greatly expanded in the fine work of Louis Bouyer. Jacques Ellul's cautionary note, however, not only is worth remembering, but must remain a constant caveat when we refer to mystery. We do not want this to be misconstrued as yet another return of neoplatonism into Christian discourse, or else we wind up where we began: with a split between the spiritual and the material realms which Bonhoeffer is at pains to overcome.

ASSEMBLY

Protestants approach the Church as a sociological, spiritual entity called into being by the gospel of Jesus Christ. Augustana 7 is a key example of a confessional principle: the Church comes into being as "an assembly of believers among whom the gospel is preached in its purity and the sacraments are administered according to the gospel."[24] This understanding lay close to Bonhoeffer's heart as a Lutheran.

In his writing, however, he makes additional notes about the Church not always or customarily identified with Lutherans. These have endeared him to other traditions, perhaps notably Anabaptists, because he emphasizes *discipleship* and because he expands Christology to mean not only the Christ who is present in the proclamation of the word and the administration of the sacraments, but the Christ who is present among us as community.[25]

Assembly is enormously important as the place where Christ's "presence in Word and Sacrament is related to his presence in the community as reality is to figure."[26] Christ is the "community by virtue of his being *pro me.*"[27] The only form Christ takes between the ascension and second coming is the form of community (*Gemeinde* in German; contrast with *Kirche*, which can refer to an institution). Community is a living bond of faith among members of the baptized household of God; it is not the juridical term that would describe a *Landeskirche*, which occupies institutional space and has administrative organs. In the community the mystery of the Holy Trinity is enacted; the community is the place where we are brought back into community with the God who is beyond all comprehension, but who accommodates himself to us through the mode of incarnation.

Christ as community is constituted, finally and really, through the ongoing proclamation of the word and the ongoing proclamation of the sacraments. Christ as community does not, cannot, exist apart from these central *actions* of the community of faith. Bonhoeffer emphasizes that these are actions, not maxims or propositional truths, because the community is the event of God's self-revelation, not an institution.

The word, as creative action of God, constantly brings both the world and the Church into being. This community called into being by word and sacrament is the body of Christ, and no other. Thus, the faithful reception of the Body and Blood of Christ is at once the *creation* of the community as body of Christ. The community of faith is *event.*

Since this body of Christ takes up time and space, it is a *reality* in the world of humans. To call the community a *reality* is to abandon terms such as *potential* in order to claim the church as the real self-presencing of Christ in the world. The body of Christ—even as Christ himself—is at the "center of human existence, history and nature."[28]

Word, sacrament, and the present Christ are interconnected. They cannot be separated one from the other; they exist in mutual interrelatedness. The community of faith never "progresses" to a point where it no longer depends upon the proclamation of the risen Christ to constitute the community. The community of faith never "progresses" to a point where sacraments are no longer necessary. With this emphasis, Bonhoeffer denies forms of spirituality or theology that rely upon the guidance of the Holy Spirit apart from the means to which the Spirit is committed. At the same time, he denies that the means of grace are a stepping-stone to a spir-ituality that would be devoid of means entirely, in a realm of pure Spirit.

This interrelated nature of the word, the sacrament, and the presence of Christ in the community means that the self-presencing of Christ requires the act of preaching. The announcement of gospel in the congregation is at once the announcement of the presence of Christ in forgiveness of sins, life, and salvation, since "to know Christ is to know his benefits" (Melanchthon). To preach is to make clear the benefits of Christ within the assembly.

PREACHING IN THE ASSEMBLY

Bonhoeffer places more weight on the proclaimed word than upon the word enshrined in Scripture. This locates him in the Lutheran reform, since Luther's insight was that the community is a *mundhaus* and not a *schrifthaus*: a place where the word is orally proclaimed, and not solely a place for the study of Scripture. In accord with Luther's explanation of the third commandment,[29] Bonhoeffer locates true worship of God in the authentic proclamation of the word, which is the proper service of all pastors of the church, who have no authority in themselves, but only as they are servants of God's word. Where this proper authority is exercised, the body of Christ grows; where the preacher arrogates the authority, the body of Christ wanes and shrivels. In commenting on the third commandment, he says, "The consecration of the holy day occurs through the proclamation of the Word of God in worship and through the willing and respectful hearing of this Word. . . . Thus the renewal of this holy day must begin with the renewal of preaching."[30]

If we explore such renewal in Bonhoeffer's sermons,[31] a set of themes emerges. They include "insistence on human dependence on God's grace; the reminder that the Christian must not forsake the world; the concern for the Christian's relationship with others; the victory of Christ crucified; and attention to . . . the word 'religion.'"[32]

Bethge gives another list in the biography: (1) Bonhoeffer constantly reiterates the antithesis between faith and religion; (2) he emphasizes the presence of Christ in the Church as the thou that imposes restriction and commandments (the Church as place of devotional encounter, mutual intercession, and personal confession); and (3) he points to the importance of the concrete and the early so that the contemporary present is always partner to the eschatological event of God.[33] His sermons are neither political nor examples of applied morals; he strives always to render the historic, biblical Christ present through the kerygmatic act of proclamation. We note that Bonhoeffer was impressed by the nineteenth century work by Martin Kaehler on *The So-Called Historical Jesus and the Historic Biblical Christ*,[34] which deals with such matters.

PREACHING TO THE WORLD COME OF AGE

Now to return to the world come of age, Bonhoeffer says in the *Ethics* that the world can come of age only through the proclamation of this word of grace, because only preaching can bring humanity to its proper place of responsibility and "autonomy" before God. "Religion" makes us dependent upon other authorities and, ultimately, takes away our responsibility for our deeds.

This word of proclamation includes confession, so that the public and the private lives of the believer are shaped thereby. The concrete ethic, for Bonhoeffer, is made possible when we return to the office of confession, which he believed to be sacramental.[35] As he says in *Spiritual Care*,[36] confession and *seelsorge* are the personal application of the saving word to the lives of individuals, whereas in preaching one presents Christ publicly to the congregation.

He is clear about the preaching task: "What the church proclaims *is* the word of the revelation of God in Jesus Christ."[37] The preacher is thus not "the spokesman of the congregation," but the "spokesman of God before the congregation."[38] This is an extremely important point, and on it hangs the fate of the Church, insofar as our actions have impact on the fate of the Church. To fail in this task is to demit the ministry of the word. Thus, "on the basis of holy scripture, the office of preaching proclaims Christ as Lord and Savior of the world. The only legitimate proclamation of the Church is a proclamation of Christ. . . . The Church's word derives its sole right and its sole authority from the commission of Christ, and consequently any word she may utter without reference to this authority will be devoid of significance."[39]

It is important to set this in a larger context. In the *Ethics*, Bonhoeffer struggles with a set of issues in his society, chief among which is the so-called two-sphere thinking, which he terms the "colossal obstacle" to the gospel: "So long as Christ and the world are conceived as two opposing and mutually repellent spheres, man will be left in the following dilemma: he abandons reality as a whole, and places himself in one or the other of the two spheres. He seeks Christ without the world, or he seeks the world without Christ. In either case he is deceiving himself."[40] For Bonhoeffer, the world and the community that is the body of Christ are not separate spheres. The reality of Christ comprises the reality of the world within itself; the Church is thus a reality that is both sign and witness to a fuller human being in the midst of worldliness.

The comprehensiveness of this approach extends itself even to prayer. In prayer we unite with the words of Christ, our great high priest. We are enabled to pray through Christ. Prayer is the power of the human Jesus in solidarity with other humans; he lifts up the prayers of the faithful as the Christ of God.[41] In preaching as in prayer, we literally stake our lives on the faithfulness of God to the word, which invites us to pray. Bonhoeffer never loses sight of this high view of preaching, and he is disappointed when he finds in his American visits the sort of preaching that undermines such an understanding of the calling to proclaim.[42]

If the world can find its reason for being only in and through the proclamation of Christ, then it seems natural that Bonhoeffer explores, in *Letters and Papers from Prison*, the idea that the world is come of age. That the world comes of age is a function of the gospel. His other writings led us to affirm the central theme of proclaiming the mystery of God in Christ. The world can only come of age truly and authentically if and as it comes of age in Christ. Thus, the preaching of the Christian message is not in *opposition* to the maturation of the world, but rather is an antidote to all false forms of maturation which would only lead back to restrictive, irresponsible forms of faith that reject the world.

Why can humanity come of age only through the proclamation of the gospel? This is a legitimate and a crucial question. The answer is twofold. First, the proclamation of the gospel reveals to the world its godlessness; second, the gospel bears witness to that world that in Christ it can become truly and genuinely worldly. Apart from the proclamation of the gospel, the world seeks its *own* resources to answer the problem of godlessness and will eventually "set itself in the place of God."[43] The world confers upon itself a divinity that it cannot possess because of its status as creation (this includes what Bonhoeffer calls the "mandates of preservation": family, community, nation, state, church, work, marriage).[44] When the world hears, *in its very godlessness*, that it is reconciled to God in Christ, the world is then free to be what it rightfully is. At the same time, the world is freed from the burden to make itself more than it rightfully is. Those who have heard the gospel embrace the world as that fallen order which is yet redeemed in Christ, so that we expect neither too much nor too little of the institutions and social orders by which we govern ourselves. This secular faith frees us from that deifying of the orders which blocks criticism and hinders change. This is the pastoral and prophetic word that the church bears to the world. The word bears fruit in the renewal of relationships.

RELATIONSHIP

In *Ethics*, Bonhoeffer says that community (*Gemeinde*) occurs where the word of God is preached; indeed, they are "inseparably united." This means that people

> are there who accept the word concerning Christ, and who believe it and acquiesce in it, unlike others who do not accept it but reject it. . . . [People] are there who stand as deputies (*Stellvertreter*) for others, for the whole world. Certainly these are people who at the same time lead wordly lives in the family, culture and government; they do so as people whom the word of Christ has set free for life in the world, but now they also form a community, a body which is distinct and separate from worldly institutions, for they are assembled together around the word of God and they are people who are chosen and live in this word.[45]

The word creates a community that exists, on the one hand, for the effective proclamation of the gospel and, on the other hand, for the life of the world. "The congregation stands in this twofold relation of deputyship entirely in the fellowship and disciplehood of its Lord, who was Christ precisely in this, that he existed not for his own sake but wholly for the sake of the world."[46] In both cases, the community of faith lives in "deputyship" (or, better, as representative), in service *to* the gospel for the world, even as Christ is the deputy, the "man *for* others."

Mystery and relationship are connected to each other because God's grace in Christ through the power of the Spirit is at once the mystery of the Trinity. This mystery is known in relationship and through no other means. We participate in the truth of the Trinity; faith and knowledge are connected, even if they may be separated for the purpose of anaylsis. Discipleship, that radical following of Christ which Bonhoeffer proposed from his earliest days, or that spin on discipleship which he called deputyship, is the key to the connection between mystery and relationship, because discipleship involves a cleaving to Jesus Christ that draws us into the life of the blessed Holy Trinity at the same time as we are drawn into the community of faithful Christians.

We see three Christian modes and three corresponding forms of involvement in the world: In the *personal* mode, we have the *hidden discipline*.[47] A place for piety returns, but it is a piety transformed from disciplines that extract the Christian from the world into a private sphere of religion. Now our discipline prepares us *for* life in the world. In the world come of age, each person must identify and claim her own form of discipline. His way may not be yours, but we may note that the rhythm of the church year informs both his hidden discipline and his theology as well. He breathes the seasons of Advent, Christmas, Epiphany, Lent, Easter, and Pentecost as living resources for his life in the world practically and theologically. Again, intercessory prayer links us with the Christian community in part, at least, to gain strength for the pursuit of genuine worldliness. We read the Bible to identify the activity of God in that *one* world to which we are called.

The hidden discipline, in the words of Kenneth Hamilton, "is a way of witnessing to the ultimate without attempting to call attention to it or to give it structure. Both faith and church are thus utterly hidden, secret, unnoticed."[48] It may well be, as Larry Rasmussen pointed out, that the Christian has a kind of code language or shorthand that is no longer understood by the world as a whole. The hidden discipline allows us to use that language in small groups of committed Christians while we are forging a new, nonreligious language through which to communicate our faith.[49] The church and especially individual members of the community thus enter what Bethge has called "a sacrifice of silence," not because we have nothing to say, but because we are no longer willing to force our message on the world before we discover ways to interpret the faith in a new age. Meanwhile, the hidden discipline enables us, as persons and in community, to feed ourselves with the word in order that we remain an outpost of God in the secular age.

In the *interpersonal* mode, we exercise the ministries outlined in *Life Together*. Bonhoeffer speaks of the ministries of holding one's tongue, meekness, listening, helpfulness, bearing, and proclaiming authority.[50] He wants to provide ways for the community to engage in mutual support and exhortation (one of the five modes of the gospel in the *Smalcald Articles*).[51] "To speak about the brother covertly is forbidden, even under the cloak of help and good will; for it is precisely in this guise that the spirit of hatred among brothers always creeps in when it is seeking to create mischief."[52] Confession is needed for the common life, since in humility we must look to our own sinfulness in disrupting community before we accuse another. To be helpful, Bonhoeffer says, "we must be ready to allow ourselves to be interrupted by God. God will be constantly crossing our paths and canceling our plans by sending us people with claims and petitions."[53] If we pass them by, "we pass by the visible sign of the cross raised athwart our path to show us that, not our way, but God's way must be done."[54] Lastly, we take authority for this ministry only under the word. "Pastoral authority can be attained only by the servant of Jesus who seeks no power of his own, who himself is brother among brothers submitted to the authority of the Word."[55] This style is incumbent not only for pastors, but for all members of the Christian community. This relationship is formed when we focus on the Christ who comes to us in the form of our sister, and when we remember that we bear Christ's freedom and word into a sister's life. We bear the cross into interpersonal relationships not in a gloomy way, but with hilarity ("a certain kind of boldness").

These interpersonal modes of the gospel are values derived from the viewpoint of faith. We practice them only because we are aware that Christ claims us for a community unique precisely because we know his victory in the resurrection. Resurrection, in interpersonal relations, is known through forgiveness, caring, and attentiveness.

In the *societal* mode, the church engages economic and social orders to clear the pathway for the proclamation of the gospel.

> In everything which the Church has to say with regard to the institution of the world she can only prepare the way for the coming of Jesus Christ; the real coming of Jesus Christ itself lies within his own freedom and grace. It is because Jesus Christ has come and is coming again that the way must be prepared for him everywhere in the world, and it is therefore also solely for *that* reason that the Church is concerned with the secular institutions.[56]

Bonhoeffer continues:

> There are . . . certain economic or social attitudes and conditions which are a hindrance to faith in Christ and which consequently destroy the true character of man in the world. It must be asked . . . whether capitalism or socialism or collectivism are economic forms which impede faith in this way. In this respect, the conduct of the church is twofold, on the one hand, drawing negative limits, she will, by the authority of the word of God, necessarily declare those economic attitudes or forms to be wrong which obviously obstruct belief in Jesus Christ, and on the authority of the responsible advice of Christian specialists and experts, she will be able to make her contribution towards the establishment of a new order.[57]

The first task belongs to preaching, and the second is a *diakonia*.

Bonhoeffer eschews "religion" as a flight from the world. At the Incarnation, God identified with the world as it is; Christ is the ultimate truth of the world, the one in whom the world achieves true worldliness, but we Christians live in the realm of what Bonhoeffer calls "penultimate." In that realm God comes to us, calls us to faithfulness, and offers us life. The penultimates are "God's way to us,"[58] but they receive their meaning only in the light of the ultimate truth known as Christ. In Christ we are oriented away from "arbitrariness and disorder,"[59] which makes us work out our ethics in solidarity with all humanity, since we have no way to proceed from penultimates to the ultimate.[60] For Bonhoeffer the cross is the ultimate, the only ultimate which at once is God's judgment upon our penultimate work and the forgiveness and the freedom that God grants us to continue our penultimate work. For, after all, the penultimate is related to the ultimate by means of *preparation*. The penultimate represents the advent of the ultimate. When we give the cup of cold water in the name of Christ, when we feed the hungry, we prepare the way for the coming of grace.[61]

That procession toward the ultimate is the proper Christian orientation, but it is hidden like the hidden discipline which fuels individual acts of responsible freedom; it is hidden like the gospel itself, folded into the world in the human figure of Jesus of Nazareth. This orientation grounds our call to discipleship, however, which is a call into God's gracious future that can only be known by faith as "the evidence of things hoped for, the conviction of things unseen."[62]

A FAITHFUL CHURCH IN THE SECULAR WORLD

In a lengthy recitation of the confession of guilt that the Church must undergo in order to be the Church once more, Bonhoeffer speaks of confession as preparation for "the emergence of the form of Jesus Christ in the church."[63]

What is this form? It is cruciform. The theology, nature, and action of the Church must be cross-shaped in order to have a place in the secular world, for it is only through the cross that the shape of the gospel becomes apparent in our world. Disciples are called to shift their thinking and their behavior from a theology of glory to a theology of the cross. This shift is enabled by the hidden discipline of prayer, which recalls the life of Christ in liturgy and Christian year, which immerses one in the systematic reading of Scripture,[64] and which plunges us into solidarity with the poor. The hidden discipline is meant for a small community of the faithful; it is not intended as a solitary exercise, although Bonhoeffer himself was forced into such a position for much of his prison term.

Parish pastors confront the greatest difficulty when they try to implement this vision as a program for ministry for the following reasons:

First, despite the end of Christendom, which has been highly touted by all observers of the church scene at the end of the century, the surprising growth of religion and religiosity has once again taken the churches captive. "Spirituality" is alive and well in these United States, but most of it has nothing to do with the three modes and involvements we identified a few paragraphs ago in this paper. This is religion as leisure and escape, the sorts of religiosity Feuerbach identified over a hundred years ago, against which Kierkegaard railed, and the loss of which Nietzsche predicted. This is religion as filling in the blank of our aching hearts and unfulfilled lives.

Second, the supposition is that the Church is about religion, and that we are in business to provide those "intangible services" the Internal Revenue Service allows us to support and then deduct on Form 1040. This presupposition receives fuel because the culture that surrounds most of the Church's work makes the Church look like, taste like, and act like other forms of religiosity. In fact, the failure to develop viable patterns of worship predicated upon a renewed vocabulary that eschews "religious" terminology is one classic failure in which we participate at century's end.

Truth to tell, most people desire religion as that substitute reality which allows us the privilege of our illusions rather than empowers us to tear down the idols. It is more difficult to do the right thing in reality than it is to emulate or symbolize the right thing in ritual—which is the drive of ritual, according to many of its current students.[65] The secular form for the Christian faith that we seek at this time remains a project and not a reality, but Bonhoeffer's entwined thread of mystery and relationship offers us hope for constructions that will enable us to live in the narrow space between the relativistic religiosity and the complete nihilism that mark our age.

Soli Deo Gloria

ENDNOTES

1. Joseph L. Hromadka, "The World We Live In" (Prague, 1926), quoted in Jiri Otter, *The Witness of Czech Protestantism* (Prague: Kalich Press, 1970), 50.

2. *LPP*, 91.

3. Joseph L. Hromadka, *Theology between Yesterday and Tomorrow* (Philadelphia: Westminister, 1956), 82 f. The classic Feuerbach is *The Essence of Christianity*, trans. George Eliot with introduction by Karl Barth (New York: Harper Torchbook edition, 1957). See esp. 185-97 and 281-92.

4. Jonathan Z. Smith, *To Take Place* (Chicago: University of Chicago Press, 1989).

5. Richard Rubinstein, *The Cunning of History* (New York: Crossroad, 1978).

6. This is an important point on which we cannot elaborate here, but which Jacques Ellul took up in detail in one of his final books, *The Humiliation of the Word* (Grand Rapids: Eerdmans, 1984). The thesis that Ellul sustains throughout the book is this: Reality may be revealed by the visual panorama, but truth can only be given through the word. Hence, while vision is an important aspect of our sensory apparatus, the identification of what is true on the visual panorama may be made only through the word. This connects with Luther's definition of both baptism and Holy Communion, e.g., "Baptism is not simply plain water. Instead it is water used according to God's command and connected with God's Word." In

Timothy Wengert, *Luther's Small Catechism: A Contemporary Translation* (Minneapolis: Augsburg Fortress, 1994), 41. This is a deeply Protestant understanding which I think Bonhoeffer would have approved because of his central focus on the proclaimed word as the moment of God's self-presencing among us.

7. *LPP*, 327.

8. Cf. Keith W. Clements, ed., *Friedrich Schleiermacher: Pioneer of Modern Theology* (London: Collins, 1987), 66-107.

9. Ernst Feil, *The Theology of Dietrich Bonhoeffer* (Philadelphia: Fortress Press, 1985), 101, italics mine.

10. *E*, 232.

11. Ibid, 233.

12. On this, Feil, *The Theology of Dietrich Bonhoeffer*, chap. 4.

13. *LPP*, 210.

14. Ibid., 200.

15. *CC*, 43-55.

16. *LPP*, 325, 389.

17. See, e.g., Ephesians 1:9, 3:3-5, 3:9, 6:19 ("the mystery of the gospel"); Colossians 1:26f., 2:2, 4:3; 1 Timothy 3:9,16. In Ephesians the mystery is Christ in the Church; in Colossians the mystery is Christ in the faithful.

18. *AB*, 19-48.

19. *GS* 5, 516f.

20. Dietrich Bonhoeffer, *True Patriotism*, trans. E. H. Robertson and John Bowden (New York: Harper & Row, 1973), 28.

21. Jacques Ellul, *The Subversion of Christianity* (Grand Rapids: Eerdmans, 1986), 25-29.

22. Louis Bouyer, *The Christian Mystery: From Pagan Myth to Christian Mysticism*, trans. Illtyd Trethowan (Edinburgh: T. & T. Clark Ltd., 1990). Bouyer salvages mysticism from its background and locates it, renewed, in Christian context in more than one book; in this one he makes a lengthy historical study in order to show the process of transformation. Chapter 19, 260-77, covers the confusion between Christian and non-Christian forms of contemplation. In this chapter Bouyer makes a strong argument for Christian mysticism as a logical outgrowth of the theology of John and Paul.

23. Ibid., 246, italics mine.

24. Theodore Tappert, ed., *The Book of Concord* (Philadelphia: Muhlenberg Press, 1959), 32. This is a dynamic and not a static understanding of church; the thrust is on action and not systematics. The Church comes into being only where proclamation and administration are the tools to gather the assembly together. This Protestant understanding of church as dynamic organism rather than institution is found in many of the Reformation-era confessions. For a good study, see Paul D. L. Avis, *The Church in the Theology of the Reformers* (Atlanta: John Knox Press, 1981).

25. *CC*, 60.

26. Ibid., 59.

27. Ibid.

28. Ibid., 62.

29. *Small Catechism*, Wengert edition, 15.

30. *GS* 4, 611.

31. Cf. works by Clyde E. Fant, *Worldly Preaching*, rev. ed. (New York: Crossroad Publishing Co., 1991), and David Gracie, *Dietrich Bonhoeffer, Meditating on the Word* (Cambridge, Mass.: Cowley Publications, 1986).

32. Fant, *Worldly Preaching*, 8.

33. *DB*, 80 f.

34. Martin Kaehler, *The So-Called Historical Jesus and the Historic Biblical Christ*, trans. Carl E. Braaten (Philadelphia: Fortress Press, 1964). See *Christ the Center*, new edition, 70 f.

35. *E*, 259.

36. Dietrich Bonhoeffer, *Spiritual Care*, trans. Jay C. Rochelle (Philadelphia: Fortress Press, 1985), 32 ff., 60 ff.

37. *E*, 259.

38. Ibid., 260.

39. Ibid.

40. Dietrich Bonhoeffer, *Psalms: Prayer Book of the Bible*, trans. James F. Burtness (Minneapolis: Augsburg Publishing House, 1970), 9-16.

41. Cf. ibid., 63f.

42. On which cf. Fant, *Worldly Preaching*, 11-20.

43. *E*, 263.

44. Bonhoeffer discusses the mandates in *E*, 73 ff.

45. Ibid., 265.

46. Ibid., 266.

47. F. Burton Nelson has written several useful articles on the spirituality of Bonhoeffer; cf. "Food for the Soul," *The Covenant Companion*, October 1984, 16-18; "Bonhoeffer and the Spiritual Life," *Journal of Theology for Southern Africa*, 1978, 34-38.

48. "A Secular Theology for a World Come of Age," *Theology Today* 18, no. 4 (January 1992): 441.

49. Larry Rasmussen, "Worship in a World-Come-of-Age," in *A Bonhoeffer Legacy*, ed. A. J. Klassen (Grand Rapids: Eerdmans, 1981), 268-80.

50. *LT*, 90ff.

51. *The Book of Concord*, ed. Theodore Tappert (Philadelphia: Muhlenberg Press, 1959), 310.

52. *LT*, 92.

53. Ibid., 99.

54. Ibid.

55. Ibid., 109.

56. *E*, 324.

57. Ibid., 325.

58. Ibid., 141.

59. Ibid., 143.

60. The section on "The Penultimate" in *E*, 84-100.

61. Ibid., 95.

62. Hebrews 11:1, RSV.

63. *E*, 45-51; citation is on 51.

64. We need only mention Bonhoeffer's well-known devotion to the *Losungen* of the Moravian Church, that system of daily readings in Scripture with prayer and hymnody appropriate to the day. References in *LPP* to the biblical passages he is contemplating usually refer to the *Losungen*.

65. This is the message of such books as Tom Driver, *The Magic of Ritual* (New York: Crossroad, 1992).

OVERVIEW

A Periscope for Bonhoeffer's Theology[1]

Charles W. Sensel

P robably more than any other theologian, Dietrich Bonhoeffer is credited for his thinking, action, and writing in what has become known as nonreligious or worldly Christianity. This movement took specific, visible form in the "death of God" furor in the 1960s along with the "Christian self-understanding" of some social protests, even though the assumptions of the social protesters and death of God evangelists may have stretched beyond Bonhoeffer's intention.[2] Therefore, and also somewhat due to a lack of methodology, the gifts of Bonhoeffer's creativity have been forgotten in the pragmatic mixture of psychology and religion in the reactionary 1990s as I have experienced it in the local parish.

The need to dialogue in the world, with the world, and across the globe is now the cutting edge of the social processes, and therefore there is a need for methods and models. To dialogue means at least that we recognize flexible space between two or more views, and that final truth or reality is somewhere in between. Possibly Bonhoeffer will be of tremendous help in structuring dialogue in the "world come of age" today

The purpose of this paper is to build a theological frame through which we can view the concretions of life, to name these activities in a theological self-consciousness, and possibly to understand that other, non-Christian peoples may in fact be doing something quite similar to these activities.

The approach of this paper is pastoral rather than academic in the strict sense. Bonhoeffer was for me the pastoral embodiment of what he had written. Throughout his life, Bonhoeffer lived his own method of Christian mundane reality. In other words, his first writing, *Communion of Saints*, laid the theoretical groundwork for worldly Christianity, and *Ethics* was the practical application. His own life decisions to participate in the German struggle, but not to escape from prison, were concretions of this.

The following quotation indicates that our work will not be easy. Nevertheless, we must not give up the attempt to understand and communicate the depths of life in our "world come of age."

> But what does this life look like, this participation in the powerlessness of God in the world? When we speak of God in a "nonreligious" way, we must speak of him in such a way that the godlessness of the world is not in some way concealed, but rather revealed, and thus exposed to an unexpected light. . . . Forgive me for still putting it all so terribly clumsily and badly, as I really feel I am. But perhaps you will help me again to make things clearer and simpler, even if only by my being able to talk about them with you and to hear you, so to speak, keep asking and answering.[3]

The terms *nonreligious*, *worldly Christianity*, and *religionless Christianity* will be used interchangeably in this paper to point to concrete and mundane experiences of life that have theological significance. This is not to make a claim that they mean the same in every setting, but it does permit us to deal with life experiences grounded in theology without getting tied up in jargon.

METHOD FOR WORLDLY CHRISTIANITY: NONRELIGIOUS INTERPRETATION AS TRANSPARENCY —A NONPIOUS STANCE

Years ago my practical working method for attempting to use nonreligious language was at first something like reading between the lines, looking at the experience to which Scripture or theological statements pointed. Another image was that of looking through a knothole in a fence, through which you could see a whole world on the other side. These images have only one level as a point of reference, and models for doing theology require multi-levels for a means of congruence. Officially, my denomination suggests the use of four levels (Scripture, tradition, experience, and reason) for doing theology. This is practically helpful if these four are transparent screens through which we focus life through theology.[4]

The use of the term *transparent* and, later in this paper, *reflection* points to doing theology in the mundane experiences of life. In this sense, the words are used symbolically, not literally. In other words, to do theology transparently, among other things, refers to looking at ordinary human life through theological structures. This could be a radical event for the historical Church which would require changing its former self-understanding as the guardian of primordial humanness into the practice of using everyday language to reach into every religion and structure throughout the globe. The cultural revolution of the twentieth century has had an impact on the Church with its own relativity to culture, the bigotry of its myths, rites, and symbols. The question now is, Will these symbols de-absolutize our theological stance to be the servant for the people of God in every community?

Therefore, the method required for dealing with nonreligious language sees the activity of God in mundane activities of life and names this activity with some theological understanding, regardless of denomination or faith. This permits dialogue in depth and meaning without a prior value judgment of doctrine or denomination.

This method goes beyond the study of patterns of culture and comparative religions prior to World War II. It points to the ongoingness of life of every person and asks the meaning, the significance, the theological name of the mundane, regardless of the myth, rite, or symbol to which the person adheres. In such a way all religions make a contribution to experience and interpretation. The religious forms and doctrines may change, but the dynamics of human sociality will survive.

Throughout his life, Bonhoeffer was living his own method of Christian mundane reality. When he quoted Scripture, which may appear like literalism to some people, he was actually pointing to the grounded reality of that experience. He talked about Christian reality in the mundane, but not as an emotion or feeling. Furthermore, these concretions occur at the center of everyday life, not merely at the periphery of life, i.e., birth and death or other crises. Placing theology at the center of life in this one sphere of the world points to Bonhoeffer's world come of age, in which people are responsible for their decisions and actions, and not just calling upon God in a crisis.

THE PERISCOPE AS A MODEL FOR DOING THEOLOGY IN THE WORLD COME OF AGE

When my son was building a periscope some years ago, I realized that the idea of periscope mirrors spoke quite helpfully to theological reflection. The periscope model has some practical advantages. One can observe without drawing attention to oneself or threatening the participants. Unlike the microscope, which magnifies, or the telescope, which collapses distance, the periscope is used only to look and reflect on what we see. Therefore, my basic reflective model for doing theology in this world come of age has the periscope as its image.

The periscope has two mirrors, whose focus permits a view of life.

The first mirror of this model is the theological system, the second is a sociological/philosophical system. The theological mirror is composed of biblical and orthodox concepts with traditional ways of referring to the faith. The sociological mirror is composed of data from the person's way of talking about life in a secular fashion. Our total life education and experience frames these two mirrors. When an event is focused through the periscope, the first response is to name it. "What is it called? What is that which is experienced?" We try to identify it with terms that are both theologically and sociologically relevant.

In this case, the theologian may or may not be drawn into participation. It stretches the point to claim that to dialogue is to participate. In some sense, Bonhoeffer participated, at least mentally, in the life of Germany, even when in prison. But in the case of the periscope, it only permits the viewer to see activity theologically. The decision to participate is not automatic or technological. One must still observe, judge, weigh up, decide, and act.[5] This decision to participate goes beyond the method of nonreligious interpretation. It puts the model of a world come of age at the center of life. This decision is to participate in the structure of the future, the Arcane Discipline.[6]

THE PILOT PROJECT USING A METHOD OF NONRELIGIOUS LANGUAGE THROUGH THE PERISCOPE MODEL: FREE RESPONSIBILITY AS ARCANE DISCIPLINE

For me, the popular interpretation of the Holy Spirit continues to be confusing, unrelated to mundane life. For this reason, I decided to use the "Holy Spirit" as a reference to see what it might point to in a worldly view using the periscope model.

To construct the first mirror, I have chosen Bonhoeffer's paper on the visible Church, his reference to Acts 2, and particularly his reference to the Spirit. Bonhoeffer's words here are typical of his other works. The Spirit is interpreted as the experience of responsibility, which is the reversal of the tower of Babel:

> The Spirit comes in the Word, not in stuttering and stammering, but in the words that can be understood by all. That is the meaning of the miracle of tongues: It is a language understood by all. It is the unitive words. *It is a Word which makes man responsible. The Spirit says the one word that everyone understands.*[7]

There is no claim here that the final interpretation of Holy Spirit is responsibility, but these references point to it as a possible concretion of life at a deeper level than the tongues, fruits, or gifts listed in Acts, Galatians, and Corinthians.

If in this first theological mirror we see the Holy Spirit in terms of responsibility, the second mirror should focus on the experience of responsibility also. This second mirror would be sociological, as this was Bonhoeffer's way of dealing with responsibility comprehensively. To construct this mirror I will use *Ethics*, chapter 6, "History and the Good," where responsibility is written interrelatedly in some detail. The section entitled "Freedom" describes, in mundane terms, free responsibility. The responsible man offers his deed to history in obedience to what is necessary. This dynamic I have identified as Arcane Discipline. There is no proof, law, or principle on which the responsible man can be acquitted:

> The responsible man acts in the freedom of his own self, without the support of man, circumstances or principles, but with a due consideration for the given human and general conditions and for the relevant questions of principle. The proof of his freedom is the fact that nothing can answer for him, nothing can exonerate him, except his own deed and his own self. It is himself who must observe, judge, weigh up, decide and act. It is man himself who must examine the motives, the prospects, the value and the purpose of his actions. But neither the purity of the motivation, nor the opportune circumstances, nor the value, nor the significant purpose of an intended undertaking can become the governing law of his actions, a law to which he can withdraw, to which he can be exculpated and acquitted. For in that case he would not longer be truly free. *The action of the responsible man is performed in the obligation which alone gives freedom and which gives entire freedom, the obligation to God and to our neighbor as they confront us in Jesus Christ.* At the same time it is performed wholly within the domain of relativity, wholly in the twilight which the historical situation spreads over good and evil; it is performed in the midst of innumerable perspectives in which every given phenomenon appears. It has not to decide simply between right and wrong and between good and evil, but between right and right and between wrong and wrong. As Aeschylus said, " . . . right strives with right." Precisely in this respect responsible action is a free venture; it is not justified by law; it is performed without any claim to an ultimate valid knowledge of good and evil. Good, as what is responsible, is performed in ignorance of good and in the surrender to God of the deed which has become necessary and which is nevertheless, or for that very reason, free; for it is God who sees the heart, who weighs up the deed, and who directs the course of history.[8]

This is one of the most important paragraphs in twentieth-century literature because it points to both the stance and the style required for a person to be both free and obedient. The person must take responsibility for his action without any guarantees. In other paragraphs of this section, Bonhoeffer clearly lists internal and external considerations to hold irresponsibilities in check; and he also says that responsible action is the proper activity of all people, regardless of position in the socioeconomic pyramid of society. The obligation to God is the comprehensive scene in our global society; the obligation to neighbor is the particular event that impinges upon us. This obligation to God and neighbor is one obligation: the interaction of the global and the local confronting us in Jesus Christ as the possibility of the future as related to the impingement. Blueprints telling us what to do are not available. Here we are confronted with such concretions as vocation, living by faith, a cruciform style of life. Each of these categories is worthy of research and writing beyond the scope of this paper. *This paper points to the "decision" as being free responsibility, and that is the experience of the Holy Spirit.*

My personal experience is that, when I assume responsibility for my action, there is a deep sense of freedom, liberation from bondage to other people, values, or structures. Whenever I have told myself that I was appointed by the bishop, that I came to a particular church for this reason or that reason, I have felt enslaved. But when I have said that *I chose to accept* the appointment, that *I am responsible* for it and no one else, then *I am free.* Numerous examples could be made by others. The issue is whether or not we seek justification in some external structure to which we would then be obligated, and therefore not free. It is interesting to note that statements in the Nuremberg trials, in the Watergate hearings, and in other similar settings—"I am not responsible," "I was told to do it," or "I was only following orders"—do not result in a sense of free responsibility for the speaker.

Through the theological periscope, examples of Bonhoeffer's "free responsibility" point to the experience of the Holy Spirit. Wherever I observe Bonhoeffer or anyone else dramatizing the dynamics of free responsibility, I think about the liberating experiences of the Holy Spirit, regardless of religious language used or the absence of it. A thorough study of information available concerning Bonhoeffer's decision to return from the United States to Germany in July 1939 will point to this decision as free responsibility (agonizing, difficult, no guarantee—only the assurance of necessity).

CONCLUSION: WHO IS CHRIST FOR US TODAY? (DEPUTYSHIP—BEING THERE FOR OTHERS)

If we are willing to let Bonhoeffer point to the world come of age, we need to venture in that world in theological communication. All human beings experience life essentially the same way: birth, struggle, death, and the possibility of acceptance or rejection of that life. The opportunity to be responsible for our decisions is given to each person.

People of other faiths may have a different kind of periscope in structure, but we as Christians could look at the same events with them in history and in life. The question is what to call them, to name them theologically—and at that point to dialogue with each other. Possibly in Islam, when talking about the free deed of responsibility, we could compare the experience of Holy Spirit with the Pilgrimage or Submissive Obedience. I lack knowledge of their methodology, yet I am convinced that their myths, rites, and symbols have served them with meaning in the past. It seems that now, in this century, all religious myths, rites, and symbols (including those of Christianity) are collapsing, and sometimes we are wary of discussing this situation. But if the myths, rites, and symbols have permitted others to survive over against the mystery of life, surely the gifts of their stance could be valuably shared by others. For example, the submission and obedience of the Muslim and the mysticism of the Buddhist could offer much to us if we could see the reality to which they point.

There is growing space on popular bookstore shelves for books on many religions. Yet, I have been unable to find published material reporting dialogue that uses nonreligious language or methods like the periscope that permit the view of life contained in Bonhoeffer's theological understanding of worldly theology.

The World Council of Churches is engaged in dialogue with other faiths. But the mundane experience and use of everyday language are lost in their attempt to keep doctrines intact. The issue should not be and is not doctrine, but the life experience to which the doctrines point. These life experiences are had by all people of all cultures. Doing theology points to the final meaning in the center of human life. We need to develop ways of dramatically cutting across cultural and faith lines to allow every person to know and interpret life at its depths.

The position strongly defended in this paper is that building a method and model for seeing the activity of God in the concrete and mundane, and naming it with theological clarity, is one way of doing what Bonhoeffer's refers to as nonreligious interpretation. Bonhoeffer's clarity about freedom, obedience, and responsibility helps us to see and understand what true freedom is for every person, and that this is one way of seeing the activity of the Holy Spirit in everyday life and language.

While I use transparency as the method of nonreligious interpretation and the periscope as a symbolic model of a world come of age, the Church needs to be involved in life in at least two ways. First is the Arcane Discipline: doing the necessary, doing what we really believe. Here the question is, do we see the Holy Spirit as free responsibility? This is the internal form of church structure—prayer. The second form is external, the deputyship as action, doing justice among people. This missional form would look like our participation in and/or support of mundane theological dialogue with Christians and non-Christians.

With these subtitles, we continue to search for the answer to the question "Who is Christ for us today?" This question always updates the challenge of our vocation, that which God is calling us to do as the future comes. Today I think we are called to dialogue with all peoples and faiths. Tomorrow prayer and action may point to some other necessity.

ENDNOTES

1. This paper was the first of my writing projects concerning Dietrich Bonhoeffer and was presented at the Evanglische Akademie (Am Kleinen Wannsee), 2 September 1980, while attending a conference and travel seminar organized by Dr. Burton Nelson. This work is now presented in an edited format in honor of Burton's researching and teaching the Bonhoeffer legacy, and the pleasant memories of many trips with him.

2. For a stronger dissent to the "death of God," see Eberhard Bethge, *Exile and Martyr* (New York: Seabury, 1975), 24 f.

3. *LPP*, 362.

4. *Discipline of the United Methodist Church*, 1996.

5. *E*, 248.

6. Arcane Discipline is referred to as the secret discipline either historically in post-Constantine time or in terms of nonreligious language for a fresh start. I refer to it here as that which is necessary for and demanded by the future, which I think gets at Bonhoeffer's idea behind historical and hermeneutic needs.

7. Edwin H. Robertson, ed., *The Way to Freedom* (1966), 45. See also *Communion of Saints*, 115-50, 173-75, for a more detailed writing. See also Whitsuntide Letter to Parents, in *LPP*, 53. All were written before 30 April 1944, the first theological letter.

8. *E*, 248f.

BIBLIOGRAPHY

Bibliography of the Works of F. Burton Nelson

Norma S. Sutton

BOOKS

The Story of the People of God. Chicago: Covenant Press, 1971.

Bonhoeffer, Dietrich. *A Testament of Freedom: The Essential Writings of Dietrich Bonhoeffer.* Edited by Geffrey B. Kelly and F. Burton Nelson. New York: HarperCollins, 1990.

Liebholz-Bonhoeffer, Sabine. *The Bonhoeffers: Portrait of a Family.* Edited by F. Burton Nelson. Chicago: Covenant Publications, 1994.

EDITORIALS

F. Burton Nelson served as editor and wrote editorials for *The Covenant Quarterly* from volume 19, February 1961, through volume 42, August 1985, except for an occasional special issue with a guest editor.

FILM CONSULTATIONS

Dietrich Bonhoeffer: Memories and Perspectives. Produced by Bain Boehlke and Gerald Drake. Directed by Bain Boehlke. 90 min. Trinity Films, Inc., 1983. Videocassette. F. Burton Nelson was on the research staff for this film.

Hitler and the Pastor. Produced by Bea Rothenbuecher. 60 min. 2000.

Bonhoeffer. Produced by Martin Doblmeier. 120 min. 2000.

ARTICLES

"30 Years after Auschwitz." *The Covenant Companion* 65 (1 April 1976): 3-5.

"1934: Pivotal Year of the Church Struggle." In *Remembering for the Future: Working Papers and Addenda*. Vol. 3, *The Impact of the Holocaust and Genocide on Jews and Christians*. Edited by Yehuda Bauer, Alice Eckardt, Franklin H. Littell, Elisabeth Maxwell, Robert Maxwell, and David Patterson, 2986-2999. Oxford: Pergamon Press, 1989. Reprinted in *Holocaust and Genocide Studies* 4 (1989): 283-97.

"Accent on Citizenship." *The Covenant Companion* 53 (23 October 1964): 4-6.

"Augustin Cardinal Bea: An Appreciation." *The Covenant Companion* 58 (1 January 1969): 26.

"Barmen 1934: A Lesson in Christian Faithfulness." *The Covenant Companion* 73 (May 1984): 10-12.

"Biblische Ethik in einen Neuen Zeitalter." In *Aufbruch der Evangelikalen*. Edited by Fritz Laubach, 106-14. Wuppertal: R. Brockhaus, 1972.

"Bonhoeffer and the Spiritual Life: Some Reflections." *The Covenant Companion* 67 (1 June 1978): 3-5. Reprinted in the *Journal of Theology for Southern Africa* 30 (March 1980): 34-38.

"Bonhoeffer at Sigtuna 1942: A Case Study in the Ecumenical Church Struggle." In *Ethical Responsibility: Bonhoeffer's Legacy to the Churches*. Edited by John D. Godsey and Geffrey B. Kelly, 131-42. Toronto Studies in Theology, 6. New York: The Edwin Mellen Press, 1981.

"A Bonhoeffer Pilgrimage in Europe." *North Parker* 45 (December 1979): 2-4.

"A Bonhoeffer Sermon [on a Psalm of Vengeance (Psalm 58)]." Translated by Daniel Bloesch and edited by F. Burton Nelson. *Theology Today* 38 (January 1982): 465-71.

"Bonhoeffer's Troubadour." *The Covenant Companion* 85 (February 1996): 8-10.

Nelson, F. Burton, and Ronald L. Magnuson. "A Bookshelf on Christian Citizenship." *The Covenant Quarterly* 23 (February 1965): 33-39.

"A Bookshelf on Christian Worship." *The Covenant Quarterly* 21 (August 1963): 34-43.

"A Call to Church Unity." In *The Orthodox Evangelicals: Who They Are and What They Are Saying*. Edited by Robert E. Webber and Donald Bloesch, 190-210. Nashville: Thomas Nelson, 1978.

"Christian Concern for Health Care." *The Covenant Companion* 78 (November 1989): 40-41.

"Christian Concern for Peace: The Kirchentag's Challenge to the Churches." *The Covenant Quarterly* 25 (August 1967): 32-42.

"Christian Faith and Public Policy: The View from Below." *The Covenant Quarterly* 40 (May 1982): 31-41.

"Christianity and Communism." *The Covenant Companion* 52 (22 March 1963): 6-7.

"The Church Center for the UN." *The Covenant Companion* 54 (22 October 1965): 12-13.

"The Church for Others." *The Covenant Companion* 61 (1 November 1972): 6-7. Reprinted in *The Post-American* 2 (March-April 1973): 11.

"Church History in the Church." *The Covenant Quarterly* 19 (February 1961): 22-30.

"The Church of South India: A Report." *The Covenant Quarterly* 22 (August 1964): 31-39.

"The Church's Encounter with Communism: The Communist Faith." *The Covenant Companion* 50 (21 July 1961): 2-4, 10.

"The Church's Encounter with Communism: The Right Wing of Anti-Communism." *The Covenant Companion* 50 (28 July 1961): 6-7, 12.

"The Church's Encounter with Communism: Sharpening Our Sensitivity." *The Covenant Companion* 50 (4 August 1961): 2-3.

"Come Along to the Fair." *The Covenant Companion* 54 (27 August 1965): 8-9.

"*The Cost of Discipleship* Revisited." *Fides et Historia* (Fall 1997).

"Dietrich Bonhoeffer: Man of Vision, Man of Courage." *The Covenant Companion* 59 (1 August 1970): 8-9, 20.

"Dietrich Bonhoeffer and the Jews: An Agenda for Exploration and Contemporary Dialogue." In *The Holocaust Forty Years After*. Edited by Marcia Littell, Richard Libowitz, and Evelyn Bodek Rosen, 87-93. Symposium Studies, 22. Lewiston: The Edwin Mellen Press, 1989.

Nelson, F. Burton, and Carl G. Lugn. "An Ecumenical Bookshelf." *The Covenant Quarterly* 19 (November 1961): 37-42.

Nelson, F. Burton, and Arthur A. R. Nelson. "An Ecumenical Bookshelf." *The Covenant Quarterly* 26 (August 1968): 41-48.

"An Evangelical Approach to Biblical Authority." *The Covenant Quarterly* 41 (August 1983): 94-95.

"An Evening with the Twin Sister of Dietrich Bonhoeffer." *The Covenant Companion* 76 (August 1987): 20-21.

"Faith Active in Love—Politically." *The Covenant Companion* 70 (15 March 1981): 8-11.

"The Faithful Guide." *The Covenant Companion* 48 (15 May 1959): 3-4.

"Family, Friends and Co-conspirators: Significant People in Dietrich Bonhoeffer's Life." *Christian History* 10 (1991): 18-21.

"Fear, Love, and Trust God above All Things." *The Covenant Quarterly* 41 (November 1983): 3-5.

"A Final Word to American Christians from Jean Lasserre: An Interview by F. Burton Nelson." *Radix* 16 (November/December 1984): 27-29, 24.

"Food for the Soul." *The Covenant Companion* 73 (October 1984): 16-18.

"Friends He Met in America: Three Colleagues from Union Theological Seminary Who Deeply Influenced Bonhoeffer." *Christian History* 10 (1991): 36-37.

"Give Them Something to Eat!" *The Covenant Companion* 53 (20 November 1964): 8-9.

"Go to School Where You Are." *The Covenant Companion* 60 (1 November 1971): 14-15.

"A God for All Seasons." *The Covenant Companion* 72 (1 March 1983): 16, 27.

"God's Guest on Earth: A Model for Sojourning Discipleship." *Sojourners* 13 (May 1984): 27.

"The Gospel and the Ten Commandments." *The Covenant Companion* 49 (23 September 1960): 4-5.

"The Gospel and the Ten Commandments." *The Covenant Companion* 49 (30 September 1960): 6-7, 18.

"The Gospel and the Ten Commandments." *The Covenant Companion* 49 (14 October 1960): 4-5.

"The Gospel and the Ten Commandments." *The Covenant Companion* 49 (28 October 1960): 6-7.

"The Gospel and the Ten Commandments." *The Covenant Companion* 49 (4 November 1960): 8-9.

"The Gospel and the Ten Commandments." *The Covenant Companion* 49 (18 November 1960): 8-9.

"The Gospel and the Ten Commandments." *The Covenant Companion* 49 (2 December 1960): 8-9.

"The Gospel and the Ten Commandments." *The Covenant Companion* 49 (9 December 1960): 8-9.

"The Gospel and the Ten Commandments." *The Covenant Companion* 49 (16 December 1960): 8-9.

"Healing an Ancient Rupture." *The Covenant Companion* 52 (1 February 1963): 3-5.

"Holocaust and the American Churches." In *Dictionary of Christianity in America*. Edited by Daniel G. Reid, 547-48. Downers Grove, Ill.: InterVarsity Press, 1990.

"The Holocaust and the American Future." *Radix* 12 (January-February 1981): 5-9.

"The Holocaust and the Oikoumene: An Episode for Remembrance." In *Faith and Freedom: A Tribute to Franklin H. Littell*. Edited by Richard

Libowitz, 71-81. Supplement to Holocaust Genocide Studies. Oxford: Pergamon Press, 1987.

"The Holocaust and the State of Israel." *Christian Life* (November 1987): 54-56.

"How Important Is a Pastor?" *The Covenant Companion* 62 (1 January 1973): 6-7.

"Kristet Lärjungaskap—ett ekumeniskt tema inför 2000-talet." In *Levande: om församling, teologi och samhälle.* Edited by Lennart Molin. Stockhom: Verbum, 1996.

"The Life and Martyrdom of Dietrich Bonhoeffer: A Modern Chapter in the Acts of the Apostles." In *The Cambridge Companion to Dietrich Bonhoeffer.* Edited by John W. de Gruchy. Cambridge Companions to Religion. Cambridge: Cambridge University Press, 1999.

"The Lordship of Christ over Our Daily Work." *The Covenant Quarterly* 21 (February 1963): 17-27.

"A Martyr's Poetry: Dietrich Bonhoeffer's Poems from a Nazi Prison Cell." *Christianity and the Arts* 3 (Spring 1996): 4-6.

"Ministerium Discusses Baptism." *The Covenant Companion* 53 (3 July 1964): 8-9.

"New Frontiers in African Theology." *Evangelical Review of Theology* 14 (July 1990): 209-24.

"A News Report: Kirchentag." *The Covenant Companion* 64 (September 1975): 16.

"Pastor Bonhoeffer." *Christian History* 10 (1991): 38-39.

"The Pietist Heritage and Social Concerns." *The Covenant Quarterly* 28 (1970): 99-105.

"The Population Explosion: Cause for Concern." *The Covenant Companion* 49 (29 April 1960): 10-11.

"The Reformation and the Word of God." *The Covenant Quarterly* 25 (November 1967): 3-14.

"The Relationship of Jean Lasserre to Dietrich Bonhoeffer's Peace Concerns in the Struggle of Church and Culture." *Union Seminary Quarterly Review* 40, nos. 1 and 2 (1985): 71-84.

"A Sabbatical Pilgrimage." *The North Parker* 42 (May 1976): [8-10].

"Significant Landmarks of the Modern Ecumenical Movement." *The Covenant Quarterly* 19 (November 1961): 28-36.

"Special Studies: A Report." *The Covenant Companion* 65 (15 October 1976): 16.

"The Summer at Covenant Harbor." *The Covenant Companion,* Central Conference Edition 60 (15 November 1971): 1.

Nelson, F. Burton, and Donald W. Dayton. "The Theological Seminary and the City." In *The Urban Mission.* Edited by Craig W. Ellison,

114-21. Grand Rapids: Eerdmans, 1974.

"This Is the Church: The First Fifteen Hundred Years." *The Covenant Companion* 50 (13 October 1961): 6-8, 20.

"This Is the Church: The Lutherans." *The Covenant Companion* 50 (20 October 1961): 4-5.

"This Is the Church: The Presbyterians." *The Covenant Companion* 50 (27 October 1961): 8-9.

"This Is the Church: The Episcopalians." *The Covenant Companion* 50 (3 November 1961): 8-9.

"This Is the Church: The Methodists." *The Covenant Companion* 50 (10 November 1961): 8-9.

"This Is the Church: The United Church of Christ." *The Covenant Companion* 50 (17 November 1961): 8-9.

"This Is the Church: The Baptists." *The Covenant Companion* 50 (24 November 1961): 10-11.

"This Is the Church: The Disciples of Christ." *The Covenant Companion* 50 (1 December 1961): 8-9.

"This Is the Church: New Frontiers in Mergers." *The Covenant Companion* 50 (8 December 1961): 8-9.

"We Live in a Broken World." *The Covenant Companion* 51 (27 July 1962): 6-7. Reprinted in the *Gospel Messenger* 111 (27 October 1962): 4-5, 11.

"The Week That Changed the World." *The Covenant Companion* 60 (1 April 1971): 3-5.

"What Churches Can Do." *Christianity Today* 34 (10 September 1990): 36-38.

"What Did Uppsala Say to the Churches?" *The Covenant Quarterly* 26 (August 1968): 18-29.

"What Do We Mean When We Say a Person Is an Evangelical?" *The Covenant Companion* 48 (23 October 1959): 10-11.

"What Do We Mean When We Say a Person Is a Fundamentalist?" *The Covenant Companion* 48 (16 October 1959): 4-6.

"What Do We Mean When We Say a Person Is a Liberal?" *The Covenant Companion* 48 (30 October 1959): 8-9.

"What Do We Mean When We Say a Person Is Neo-Orthodox?" *The Covenant Companion* 48 (6 November 1959): 10-11, 20.

"William Stringfellow: Prophet to Our Time." *The Covenant Companion* 54 (1 January 1965): 8-10.

"Wittenberg '75: Still Intact." *The Covenant Companion* 64 (1 November 1975): 16.

"Wittenberg's Agony and Ecstasy." *The Covenant Companion* 56 (1 December 1967): 17-19.

"Zionism and American Christianity." In *Dictionary of Christianity in America*. Edited by Daniel G. Reid, 1303-1304. Downers Grove, Ill.: InterVarsity, 1990.

Bonhoeffer, Dietrich. "Come, O Rescuer." Translated by Daniel Bloesch. Introduction by F. Burton Nelson. *Sojourners* 12 (December 1983): 26-27.

Bonhoeffer, Dietrich. "Confident Hope: Sermon on Totensonntag." Translated by Daniel Bloesch. Introduction by F. Burton Nelson. *The Christian Ministry* 14 (November 1983): 20-22.

BOOK REVIEWS

Review of *Bench Marks*, by Jozsef Farkas. *The Covenant Quarterly* 29 (May 1971): 48.

Review of *Biblical Ethics and Social Change*, by Stephen C. Mott. *Theological Students Fellowship Bulletin* 7 (November-December 1983): 24.

Review of *The Big Change: The Challenge to Radical Change in the Church*, by Rex R. Dolan. *The Covenant Quarterly* 27 (February 1969): 46-47.

Review of *The Big Change: The Challenge to Radical Change in the Church*, 2d ed., by Rex R. Dolan. *The Covenant Quarterly* 27 (August 1969): 48.

Review of *Bonhoeffer for a New Day: Theology in a Time of Transition*, by John W. de Gruchy. *The Covenant Quarterly* 56 (February 1998): 34-35.

Review of *Christ and Crisis*, by Charles Malik. *The Covenant Quarterly* 21 (May 1963): 43-44.

Review of *The Christian New Morality*, by O. Sydney Barr. *The Covenant Quarterly* 29 (August 1971): 42-43.

Review of *Christ's Suburban Body*, by Wilfred M. Bailey and William K. McElvaney. *The Covenant Quarterly* 29 (February 1971): 34.

Review of *The Church as a Prophetic Community*, by E. Clinton Gardner. *The Covenant Quarterly* 27 (May 1969): 44-45.

Review of *Church Unity and Church Mission*, by Martin E. Marty. *The Covenant Quarterly* 22 (May 1964): 42-43.

Review of *Communism and Christian Faith*, by Lester DeKoster. *The Covenant Quarterly* 20 (May 1962): 44.

Review of *Confessions of a Workaholic*, by Wayne E. Oates. *The Covenant Quarterly* 31 (May 1973): 45-46.

Review of *Conflict and Social Change*, by Marcus Borg; *Celebrate the Earth*, by Donald Imsland; and *Breaking Bread with the Hungry*, by Arthur Simon. *The Covenant Quarterly* 29 (November 1971): 46-47.

Review of *Cries from the Hurting Edges of the World*, by Oscar J. Rumpf. *The Covenant Quarterly* 29 (February 1971): 34-35.

Review of *Criterion for the Church*, by J. Robert Nelson. *The Covenant Quarterly* 22 (August 1964): 42.

Review of *Decisions! Decisions!* by George A. Chauncey; *Foreign Policy Is Your Business*, by Theodore R. Weber; *Rich Man Poor Man*, by Donald W. Shriver; and *Leader's Guide to Christian Ethics for Modern Man*, by Richard F. Perkins. *The Covenant Quarterly* 31 (May 1973): 44-45.

Review of *Dietrich Bonhoeffer: Reality and Resistance*, by Larry Rasmussen. *The Covenant Quarterly* 30 (May 1972): 46-47.

Review of *Documents of the Christian Church*, ed. Henry Bettenson. *The Covenant Quarterly* 22 (February 1964): 41-42.

Review of *The Ecumenical Movement: An Anthology of Key Texts and Voices*, ed. Michael Kinnamon and Brian E. Cope. *The Covenant Quarterly* 55 (November 1997): 43-44.

Review of *Education for Renewal*, by David J. Ernsberger; *God's Frozen People*, by Mark Gibbs and T. Ralph Morton; and *The Church Inside Out*, by J. C. Hoekendijk. *The Covenant Quarterly* 24 (August 1966): 44-46.

Review of *Eerdmans' Handbook to the History of Christianity*, ed. Tim Dowley. *The Covenant Quarterly* 36 (November): 44-45.

Review of *Extremism Left and Right*, ed. Elmer West Jr. *The Covenant Quarterly* 31 (May): 43-44.

Review of *For the Nations: Public and Evangelical*, by John Howard Yoder. *The Covenant Quarterly* 56 (November 1998): 45-46.

Review of *Freedom and Grace*, by J. R. Lucas. *The New Review of Books and Religion* 1 (March 1977): 11. Reprinted in *The Covenant Quarterly* 35 (May 1977): 55-57.

Review of *The Freedom Revolution and the Churches*, by Robert W. Spike; *Mandate for White Christians*, by Kyle Haselden; *The Church in the Racially Changing Community*, by Robert L. Wilson and James H. Davis; and *The Edge of the Ghetto*, by John Fish, Gordon Nelson, Walter Stuhy, and Lawrence Witmer. *The Covenant Quarterly* 24 (November 1966): 34-37.

Review of *God's Lively People*, by Mark Gibbs. *The Covenant Quarterly* 30 (February 1972): 36-37.

Review of *Good News to the Poor: The Challenge of the Poor in the History of the Church*, by Julio de Santa Ana; *Religious Life and the Poor: Liberation Theology Perspectives*, by Alejandro Cussianovich; and *The Eucharist and Human Liberation*, by Tissa Balasuriya. *The New Review of Books and Religion* 4 (February 1980): 23-24. Reprinted in *The Covenant Quarterly* 38 (May 1980): 44-47.

Review of *Handbook of Denominations in the United States*, ed. Frank S. Mead. *The Covenant Quarterly* 19 (August 1961): 45.

Review of *Hope in Time of Abandonment*, by Jacques Ellul. *The Covenant Quarterly* 32 (August 1974): 45-47.

Review of *Hunter and Hunted: Human History of the Holocaust*, by Gerd Korman. *The Covenant Quarterly* 32 (August 1974): 47.

Review of *I Am Adolf Hitler*, by Werner and Lottie Pelz; *Messengers from the Dead: Literature of the Holocaust*, by Irving Halperin; and *Here I Am: A Jew in Today's Germany*, by Irving Halperin. *The Covenant Quarterly* 29 (November 1971): 44-46.

Review of *The Impact of the Future*, by Lyle E. Schaller. *The Covenant Quarterly* 29 (February 1971): 36-37.

Review of *In Place of Folly*, by Norman Cousins. *The Covenant Quarterly* 20 (February 1962): 46.

Review of *An Introduction to the Great Creeds of the Church*, by Paul T. Fuhrmann. *The Covenant Quarterly* 20 (May 1962): 45.

Review of *Jesus and the Holocaust: Reflections on Suffering and Hope*, by Joel Marcus.*Christianity and the Arts* 4 (August-October 1997): 55-56.

Review of *Last Letters of Resistance: Farewells from the Bonhoeffer Family*, ed. Eberhard and Renate Bethge; *Spiritual Care*, by Dietrich Bonhoeffer; and *Exile in the Fatherland: Martin Niemoller's Letters from Moabit Prison*, ed. Hubert G. Locke. *The Covenant Quarterly* 46 (February 1988): 41-43.

Review of *Liberating Our White Ghetto*, by Joseph Barndt; *Black Power and the American Myth*, by C. T. Vivian; *Your God Is Too White*, by Columbus Salley and Ronald Behm; *Black Jargon in White America*, by David Claerbaut; *Locked-Out Americans*, by John R. Fry; *The Spirituals and the Blues*, by James Cone; and *Break Down the Walls: A Christian Cry for Racial Justice*, by Johannes Verkuyl. *The Covenant Quarterly* 29 (February 1971): 37-39.

Review of *Life in One's Stride: A Short Study in Dietrich Bonhoeffer*, by Kenneth Hamilton. *The Covenant Quarterly* 27 (August 1969): 47-48.

Review of *Life Together and Prayerbook of the Bible: An Introduction to the Psalms*, by Dietrich Bonhoeffer, ed. Geffrey B. Kelly and Daniel W. Bloesch. *Christianity and the Arts* 4 (August-October 1997): 55.

Review of *Luther*, by Franz Lau. *The Covenant Quarterly* 21 (May 1963): 42-43.

Review of *Luther: Lectures on Romans*, ed. Wilhelm Pauck; and *Spiritual and Anabaptist Writers*, ed. George H. Williams and Angel M. Mergal. *The Covenant Quarterly* 36 (November 1978): 44.

Review of *Man's Faith and Freedom: The Theological Influence of Jacobus Arminius*, ed. Gerald O. McCulloch. *The Covenant Quarterly* 22 (May 1964): 43-44.

Review of *Minister's Service Book for Pulpit and Parish*, by Jesse Jai McNeil. *The Covenant Quarterly* 19 (August 1961): 45.

Review of *My Friend the Enemy*, by William E. Pannell. *The Covenant Quarterly* 29 (February 1971): 46-47.

Review of *On Moral Medicine: Theological Perspectives in Medical Ethics*, ed. Stephen E. Lammers and Allen Verhey. *The Covenant Quarterly* 56 (November 1998): 48.

Review of *The Passion for Life*, by Jurgen Moltmann. *Foundations* 22 (April-June 1979): 184-85.

Review of *Patterns of Reformation*, by E. Gordon Rupp. *The Covenant Quarterly* 29 (February 1971): 35-36.

Review of *The Politics of Hope*, by Bernard P. Dauenhauer. *Journal of Religion* 68 (July 1988): 479.

Review of *Politics, Poker, and Piety: Perspective on Cultural Religion in America*, by Wallace E. Fisher. *The Covenant Quarterly* 31 (February 1973): 46.

Review of *The Predicament of the Prosperous*, by Bruce Birch and Larry Rasmussen. *The Covenant Quarterly* 38 (February 1980): 47-48.

Review of *A Private and Public Faith*, by William Stringfellow. *The Covenant Quarterly* 21 (November 1963): 42-43.

Review of *The Promise of Protest*, by George C. Reese; *A Choice of Loyalties*, by Eleanor Haney; and *Family Planning on a Crowded Planet*, by Wilson Yates. *The Covenant Quarterly* 30 (February 1972): 37-38.

Review of *Recording Angel: Poems by Fred W. Moeckel*, ed. Will Vance. *The Covenant Quarterly* 27 (August 1969): 42-43.

Review of *Reflections of a Post-Auschwitz Christian*, by Harry J. Cargas. *Holocaust and Genocide Studies* 6 (1991): 91-92.

Review of *Rich Christians in an Age of Hunger: A Biblical Study*, by Ronald J. Sider. *The Covenant Quarterly* 36 (August 1977): 45-46.

Review of *The Secular Relevance of the Church*, by Gayraud S. Wilmore. *The Covenant Quarterly* 21 (November 1963): 41-42.

Review of *Situation Ethics*, by Joseph Fletcher. *The Covenant Companion* 55 (6 May 1966): 4-5, 20.

Review of *Social Ministry*, by Dieter T. Hessel. *The Covenant Quarterly* 41 (May 1983): 45.

Review of *The Spirit of the Reformed Tradition*, by M. Eugene Osterhaven. *The Covenant Quarterly* 29 (August 1971): 43-44.

Review of *Theology and the Practice of Responsibility: Essays on Dietrich Bonhoeffer*, by Wayne Floyd Whitson. *Critical Review of Books in Religion* 8 (1995): 477-80. Reprinted in *Pro Ecclesia* 6 (Winter 1997): 110-12.

Review of *The Theology of Dietrich Bonhoeffer,* by Ernst Feil, trans. Martin Rumscheidt. *Word & World* 8 (Winter 1988): 89, 92.

Review of *Vocabulary of Communism,* by Lester DeKoster. *The Covenant Quarterly* 22 (February 1964): 37-38.

Review of *War: A Call to the Inner Land,* by Eberhard Arnold. *Journal of Religion* 68 (April 1988): 356.

Review of *War and Conscience in America,* by Edward LeRoy Long; *Peace! Peace!* by Foy Valentine; *War and Moral Discourse,* by Ralph B. Potter; and *The Christian and Revolution,* by Melvin Gingerich. *The Covenant Quarterly* 27 (August 1969): 43-46.

Review of *Wars and Rumors of War,* by Roger L. Shinn. *The Covenant Quarterly* 31(February 1973): 45.

Review of *The Way to Freedom,* by Dietrich Bonhoeffer; *I Knew Dietrich Bonhoeffer: Reminiscences by His Friends,* ed. Wolf-Dieter Zimmermann and Ronald Gregor Smith; and *Letters and Papers from Prison,* by Dietrich Bonhoeffer. *The Covenant Quarterly* 25 (November 1967): 44-46.

Review of *What Freedom: The Persistent Challenge of Dietrich Bonhoeffer,* by Keith W. Clements. *Journal of Church and State* 33 (Autumn 1991): 818.

Review of *Who Trusts in God: Musings on the Meaning of Providence,* by Albert C. Outler. *The Covenant Quarterly* 26 (November 1968): 43-44.

Review of *Zinzendorf, the Ecumenical Pioneer,* by A. J. Lewis. *The Covenant Quarterly* 22 (May 1964): 42.